Human Nature

To Karen and David,
In appreciation for all your help.

Dich Minnuly

Human Nature

Rethinking Psychology and Astrology

Dick Minnerly

Copyright © 2008 by Dick Minnerly.

Library of Congress Control Number   2009901527
ISBN: Hardcover   978-1-4363-7378-4
             Softcover   978-1-4363-7377-7

All rights reserved. No part of this book may be reproduced or transmitted in any form or by any means, electronic or mechanical, including photocopying, recording, or by any information storage and retrieval system, without permission in writing from the copyright owner.

This book was printed in the United States of America.

To order additional copies of this book, contact:
Xlibris Corporation
1-888-795-4274
www.Xlibris.com
Orders@Xlibris.com
51931

Table of Contents

Preface.   *i*

Chapter 1. Introduction
Where We Are Today   1
A Basic Traditionalist Error   7
Our Reasoning Perspectives   17
Arealistic Reasoning   24

Chapter 2. Reasoning
The First Question   27
The Consideration Cycle   28
    1. Essence and Universals   34
    2. Existence and One   38
    3. The Relational Paradox   43
Intellectual Systems   50
Reasoning Biases   52
The Priority Controversy   58
    Rationalism   59
    Empiricism   61
    Formalism   63
    Realism   71
Natural versus Explicated Reasoning   72

Chapter 3. Reality
Metaphysics   74
1. The Principle of Occurrence   77
    The Epistemic Refutation of Theism   85
2. The Principle of Abstraction   86
3. The Principle of Dimensionality   88
    Traditional Confusions   90
    Extra Dimensions   93
    Measurement   94
    Time   97

4. The Principle of Displacement	103
5. The Principle of Correspondence	105
The Six Forms of Helical Motion	107

Chapter 4. The Science of Human Nature

Metaphysics and Psychology	109
The New Science	110
Human Nature	113
The Dilemma of Uniqueness	114
Character vs. Personality	117
Other Issues	119
Our Need for Astrology	121
The Theory of Humanology	125
The Principle of Unique Character	125
Conception vs. Birth	126
Destiny	127
Forecasting	128
Free Will	128
The Principle of Spatial Interference	129
The Principle of Event Relation	130
The Study of Human Nature	131

Chapter 5. Our Psychologic Process

General Issues	136
The Whole Cycle	136
Impulses	138
Systems and Phases	139
Consciousness and Subconsciousness	141
Our Five Conscious Systems	143
The Impulse Pattern	144
The Standard Impulse Pattern	148
Applying the Standard	150
Speed	151
Congenital Pathology	153
Psychologic Strength and Weakness	155
Political Attitudes	155
Memory	156

Other Implications	161
Education	161
Overpopulation	162

Chapter 6. Our Five Psychologic Systems

Discussing the Five Systems	166
Will	168
(B) The Planner	171
(+) The Creator	172
(-) The Follower	173
(R) The Denier	177
Thought	184
(B) The Reasoner	185
(+) The Speaker	186
(-) The Listener	188
(R) The Skeptic	190
Feeling	193
(B) The Harmonist	196
(+) The Emotionalist	196
(-) The Sybarite	198
(R) The Spectator	199
Judgment	203
(B) The Moralist	209
(+) The Egoist	210
(-) The Altruist	211
(R) The Nihilist	216
Our Four Judgment Terms	219
Power	221
(B) The Progressive	224
(+) The Radical	226
(-) The Liberal	231
(R) The Conservative	240

Chapter 7. Judgment and Power

The Hypothetical Judgment-Power System	255
The Generational Clash	260
Conclusions for the New Era	267

Chapter 8. The Natal Chart

Realistic Astrology ... 269
The Basic Problems ... 270
    The Zodiac ... 270
    Dividing the Zodiac ... 272
    The Quadruplicity ... 274
    The Triplicity ... 274
    The Beginning of the Zodiac ... 276
    Untimed Charts ... 278
The Houses ... 279
    The Body Parts ... 314
Planetary Rulership ... 315
Planetary Aspects ... 320
Planetary Distribution ... 324
Chart Interpretation ... 326
    The Aspect Path ... 327

Afterword ... 330

Appendix A

Calculating the Impulse Pattern ... A1

Appendix B

List of Tables 1-16 ... B1
Understanding the Tables ... B1
Comments on the Tables ... B11
Tables of Individuals ... B22

Appendix C

The Psychologic Eras ... C1

To my wife, Irene O'Connor, the sunlight of my soul.

Preface

This book is unusual in our time. The principal reasons why it differs from the academic, journalistic, and pragmatic works that have long dominated the nonfiction market in publishing are these. First, it reasserts the importance of philosophy, which intellectuals have hardly mentioned in the past half century or so. Second, it proposes new theories and methods rather than just reciting old flawed ones. Third, it is comprehensive, and hence directed to a broad audience with varying interests, occupations, and levels of knowledge.

A comprehensive work can be invaluable because it tries to give the whole picture of its subject, but invariably some of its readers will complain that it is not sufficiently directed to their particular purposes, specialty, preferences, or needs. With this work, there are three classes of such readers whose concerns I feel I must address in a preface.

Some readers, knowing only contemporary works that ignore philosophy and the theory of their subjects, may not see the need for my second and third chapters, which discuss reasoning and reality, or epistemology and metaphysics. I can only advise them that those chapters go to the heart of the matter, that we cannot develop or use a science of human nature without some such theory, and that our practice in any science will be arbitrary and random if we don't take pains to explicate the theoretical assumptions that we are making and must make.

Another group of readers may belong to that sizeable minority of people in Western cultures who are skeptics as to astrology. Their doubts are unsound, but their illogic on this is caused by our traditional system of thought and belief. Realistic traditionalists find it hard to see why some astrological methods are valid, but this is so only because they have adopted that flawed and essentially ancient system, especially its false notions of space and time. So I must ask these readers to suspend their doubts temporarily while they consider my new theories and my proofs of the validity and value of some astrological methods. I can assure them that what I propose throughout, philosophically and practically, is not mysticism but realism.

Finally, I expect that most of my readers have never studied astrology and have no intention of using it professionally. Since they want only to understand themselves, the specific people who affect their lives, and human nature in general, they may be wondering how much astrology they must learn to use the valuable new psychologic method I propose here. Well, while they can benefit from a greater knowledge of astrology, to use that method they need only this book and the natal charts they want to study, which can be made with an inexpensive computer program or bought from a charting service. Though my last chapter, *The Natal Chart*, is written for those who have a basic knowledge of traditional astrology and who I hope to convert to realistic astrology, readers with only a general interest might appreciate it anyway. It will acquaint them with some disputed issues in astrology, and its section on the houses of a chart, which applies my psychologic theory to another context, adds things to my earlier explanation of it.

But no matter what your interest in this work is and no matter how much you have studied the subjects it considers, I can promise you this: that when you finish it, you will know far more about yourself and others than you do now. At home, at work, and in politics, you will finally understand, as the traditionalists about you cannot, what truly causes people to say what they say and to do what they do.

Chapter 1. Introduction

WHERE WE ARE TODAY

Like most realists, my judgment of human development to date is not positive. On balance, we are still beasts and self-defeating fools, hardly advanced from our tribal days in the wilderness. Though we have progressed technologically, our psychologic progress has been undetectable, at least since the Greeks invented the alphabet nearly three millennia ago. A few centuries after that event, or about a hundred generations ago, our basic beliefs on reality and human nature reached an explicated form that differs little from their present form. So, though we can split the atom, we are still functioning from a profound ignorance of what we are as individuals and societies.

The major cause of this self-ignorance is a set of intellectual errors that compose our traditional system of thought and belief, some of the worst of which are corrected in this work.

I see our historical development in terms of psychologic *epochs* and *eras*. By *psychologic epoch* I mean any period in which we humans are not physically altered enough (by any cause) to significantly change our specieal logic and psychologic functioning. Reasonable speculations and historical evidence support the claim that our present epoch began slightly less than three millennia ago. Even so, the intellectuals of that time in Greece, India, China, and elsewhere based much of their work on the traditions of earlier societies. For instance, the basic premises of our major religions today were not conceived during our epoch, but in the more-primitive prior epoch, and yet those fictional assumptions are still with us today, still preventing progress in our reasoning and causing great injustices across the world.

We of the *modern era* might wonder how our ignorance could last through such long epochs, since we were taught that everything progresses continually. Well, it does not. Our psychologic development is not the straight-line advance that our traditionalists assume it to be; rather, it is cyclical, so that in each cycle we mature and then regress, making a little progress in some intellectual and practical areas, and none at all in other areas. And the history of our present epoch can be clarified in the context of this psychologic cycle, the conception of which is not based on my opinion, but rather on a natural event that has been empirically proven to affect our psychologic functioning *en masse*, whatever our individual differences. This is the cycle of the planet Pluto; its period is about a quarter of a millennium (247.7 years), which is about twelve human generations, and this cycle is what I mean by a *psychologic era*.[1]

The table in *Appendix C* shows the dates of these psychologic eras and their subdivisions from about 600 BCE, which is as far back as the software I have can calculate the Pluto cycle. This table gives us an objective tool for historical analysis. That is, this cycle can tell us where we are today psychologically and where we are headed—provided that our solar system is not basically altered, that we can validly assume a psychologic correspondence in these eras, and that we have a sound (valid and true) hypothesis on human reasoning. And indeed our history in these eras confirms on a social scale my psychologic proposal here that all human reasoning is cyclic and has a necessary sequence, or universal logic. Specifically, each era begins with a burst of intellectual progress,

---

[1] In August 2006, The International Astronomical Union changed its definition of the term 'planet' so that Pluto is now called a 'dwarf planet' instead of a 'planet'. This change in what astronomers mean by 'planet' has no effect on astrology. That word, which literally means 'wanderer', has had two meanings since astronomy was separated from astrology: (1) an *astronomical planet*, or the heliocentric meaning of astronomers, and (2) an *astrological planet*, or the geocentric meaning of astrologists. During the seven decades that astronomers said there were nine heliocentric planets (Mercury to Pluto), astrologists claimed that there were ten geocentric planets: the eight astronomical planets besides the earth, plus the sun and the moon, which are also 'wanderers' around the earth. Some practitioners also track the larger asteroids as astrological planets. The zeal of astronomers to discredit astrology is irrational; since their science doesn't study how celestial events affect living things, they have no grounds for objecting to one that does.

because people then are more realistic, willful, objective, and creative than they are later in that era, and it ends with regression, because people then are more pragmatic, narrow-minded, and restricted by old reasoning than they were earlier. This regression then provokes progress in the next era, which provokes regression again, and so on. But not everything progresses, as we see plainly from the inhuman history of our governments and our business and religious corporations.

I number these eras from the first one that the software I use can calculate, though I suspect that our present psychologic epoch may have begun about an era or so before then. In this work I use temporary descriptive names for six of the eras to which I refer: Era 2 is *the sophist era* (449-204 BCE); Era 4 is *the Christian era* (42-287); Era 9 is *the scholastic era* (1270-1516); Era 10 is *the classic era* (1516-1762); Era 11 is *the modern era* (1762-2008); and Era 12 is *the new era* (2008-2254). The new era began on January 25, 2008. So while we who live today are of the modern era, since it is when we were born and educated, our work belongs to the new era.

If my psychologic theory is correct, our first criterion for defining and classifying any intellectual or practical work is the period of the psychologic era in which it was created. The major divisions of an era are its *quadrants*, which are not equal in years because they are dimensionally defined parts of a natural cycle that is elliptical, not circular. These quadrants identify the psychologic context in which people of a given time live and work, and their work reflects its quadrant. In the fourth quadrant of the modern era (1971-2008), for instance, we experienced the extremes of human greed, cruelty, political rightism, religionism, and other forms of intellectual and political regression, even as new thinking was in progress in several areas that will change the public's perspective in the new era.

In other words, the creative first quadrant (2008-2066) of the new era will yield a general surge of intellectual *realism* and of psychologic and political *leftism* (terms I define later) that will establish the premises of, or the underlying tone and agenda for, all human activity until 2254. If this new quadrant's influence is felt beyond that, it will only be in a form that is redefined for the next era.

Our traditional education makes it hard to accept this new cyclic way of seeing our history and our psychologic functioning, especially since it uses an astrological premise that many Western academics denigrate. But we must correct that miseducation here if we want to understand our social situation. Perhaps traditionalists can offer another explanation for the fact that, though these beliefs are with us at all times, *leftism* and *rightism* and *realism* and *arealism* achieve social dominance alternately in cyclic waves, but I have not heard it.[2]

The modern era, the history of which we know best, shows the psychologic regression that occurs in any era. For instance, the political thinking in its first quadrant (1762-1822) was far more fundamental and logical than any of the confused political thinking that followed it. And no argument can convince us that the twentieth century, or more precisely the last two quadrants of the modern era (1912-1971 and 1971-2008), was not a period of sharp psychologic and political regression from that excellent eighteenth-century beginning.

Indeed, testifying perhaps to an even broader historical regression, the twentieth century was the most barbaric and inhumane century in all recorded history. This is so whether we judge it by the millions of needlessly slaughtered, starved, tortured, poisoned, or diseased people; by our incredible destruction of our own ecosystem, including tens of thousands of living species and vast regions of indispensable wilderness; by the overt inhumanity of our mindless and heartless commercial, academic, and religious corporations; by our political systems and their police and military forces, whose first purpose is to satisfy the greed of those elitist corporations; or by

---

[2] I coin the term *arealism*, meaning 'without realism', to refer to all constructs that are not realistic, or philosophic, in origin. Today these include most scientific ideologies and all mystical ideologies, including *theism*, which term I use generically to mean all views that propose one or more deities. *Arealism* is like *atheism*, coined in the sixteenth-century, in that realists and theists assume a single standard of belief—reality or divinity, respectively—by virtue of which all contrary views are deemed fallacious. And since the first principle of *realism* is that reality is the only natural and proper standard of all human reasoning, it is the true opposite of *theism*. So a realist is not a theist, but is also not an *atheist*, since we need this old term now to distinguish arealistic from realistic nontheists.

the life-stifling overpopulation of our own stupid (self-betraying) species. And judging from that entire history, rather than from the few neatly excised pieces of it that our rulers and their lackeys tell us to consider instead, we have every reason to expect, barring revolutionary thinking that changes our old ways dramatically, to see far worse than that in the new era ahead.

Any pride we humans take in what we have accomplished to date is a false pride. Though our most sane and moral people are few and far from typical of our species, it is they who give us our sense of the human potential. And compared to that great potential, our so-called 'progress' is too trivial to mention, let alone boast about. On the whole we are beasts, we are stupid in all senses, we are indifferent to the suffering of other people and living things, and we ignore the dire situation in which we now exist and in which our progeny may exist, after a fashion. It is plain, then, that unless we change our traditional ways and think 'out of the box' that our ancestors have put us in, our species is doomed, and is not worth the saving in any case.

There is no other way. To correct a prevalent modern-era misassumption, there is no guarantee that our species will progress physically or psychologically. There is certainly no deity to ensure it. Nor is there any mystical scientific force, biological or otherwise, that ensures our endless incremental progress, as was newly proposed in the first quadrant of the modern era and then echoed by all the positivists and Darwinists of the nineteenth and twentieth centuries.[3]

---

[3]   Godwin's *An Enquiry Concerning Political Justice, and Its Influence on General Virtue and Happiness* (1793) and Condorcet's *Sketch for a Historical Picture of the Progress of the Human Mind* (1795) were two of the several works of the first quadrant that led nineteenth-century intellectuals to embrace the unrealistic doctrine of our continual incremental progress, which was then proposed in some form in biology and all our human sciences—including modern psychology and our social, economic, and political sciences. No intellectual notion is more characteristic of the modern era than this unproven linear conception of both specieal development and progress in general. And yet many of our academics still claim that the unoriginal and incomplete thinking on evolution by Darwin and Wallace in the modern era's second quadrant (1822-1912) was the greatest intellectual achievement of our time.

The truth is that some cataclysm of natural or human origin might end it all for us at any time, or might, in but a few generations, make us all even more stupid than we are today. On the other hand, it could make us brighter in some way, which seems to have happened nearly three millennia ago, after the great natural cataclysms proposed by one historian.[4]

Though we have little reason today to respect our species, we must do what we can for it anyway, on the chance that it will make a difference. Natural cataclysms aside, we are negatively altering our species with each generation and we will cause its extinction, unless we can quickly learn to reason more realistically than we have in the past. But this is not likely,

---

[4] See Immanuel Velikovsky, *Worlds in Collision* (New York: Doubleday & Company, Inc., 1950). His academic critics disparaged his views, but they never disproved them. He tried to explain, through reasonable hypotheses supported by facts, the extraordinary terrestrial and celestial events reported by ancient cultures on all continents, most explicitly in Homer's Iliad and the Hebrew's Old Testament. So he proposed celestial cataclysms early in the first millennium BCE involving Mars, the earth, and a large comet (originally a piece of Jupiter) that became the planet Venus. He then showed the errors in Lyell's widely accepted geological hypothesis and in the views of other historians on the dates of ancient events. And he alone predicted from his hypothesis, long before space explorations proved these claims, both the remnant magnetism of the moon and the great heat of the planet Venus.

But though he was a psychologist also, he didn't dispute the Darwinists in biology, psychology, and the other human sciences, which he might have done had he noticed that within a few generations of the last cataclysm he proposed, and certainly by the late seventh century BCE, human intellectual powers progressed dramatically. The evident psychologic changes in our species that followed the dates of his proposed cataclysms intrigued me, for I was already a critic of the hypothesis of evolution by gradual adaptation. That is, I agree with the Darwinists that our species changes incrementally over time, but these gradual changes are always subject to nature's cycles, and they may not last through the next natural cataclysm or human-caused environmental disaster. Moreover, speci333l evolution occurs between such events not only by the passive adaptation that they propose, but also by the active exercise of individual will, more or less as proposed by Bergson (1859-1941).

for new thinking is difficult. To be original in thought, one must soundly criticize all the opposed thinkers of the past and then confront the certain opposition of all traditionalists, even those who agree that new thinking is needed. But few of us will do that, for it is far easier to think as we were taught to do by the traditionalists who rule us and control our academic institutions and major media.

Nevertheless, that is the choice we each face, and given our grave situation today, only a fool will choose the traditional way. The rest of us will see that we must escape from that old psychologic box, or mental prison, into which we are all born and in which we are all educated, and that to do this, we must find the causes of that massive wall of opposition to new thinking. For instance, we need to know why some intellectuals propose humane utopias while others work only to rationalize the greed and other evils of the worst people among us, our rulers. And we need to know why we differ, if we do, from those selfish rulers, who will continue to impose on our bodies and minds and steal everything we own, in private or in common, until enough of us learn to see through their false explanations of our natural, social, and political situations.

But this requires us to understand reality and human nature first, and that we have never done. It is the height of folly to believe that we humans can continue to be as ignorant of the causes of human nature as we always have been and still be personally happy or have sane societies. Our species is marching rapidly to its death, and, fools that we are, we won't take the pains to understand why this is happening to us.

A Basic Traditionalist Error

My chief criticism of traditionalist thinkers is that they are virtually all *descriptive reasoners* and not *definitive reasoners*. But before we consider this common error in general terms, let us consider two famous instances of it that pertain to the subject of human nature: the psychologic hypothesis of Plato (c.427-347 BCE) and the variation of it by Freud (1856-1939).

Some believe that Plato based his political reasoning on a theory of human nature, but he never presented such a theory. What he did say, in his *Republic*—a work that both Thomas Jefferson and John Adams rightly dismissed as ridiculous—was that its purpose was to show his view of human nature better by writing it large, in the terms of society rather than the individual. But this was just a rationalization for his backward reasoning, which proceeded from the artificial society rather than from its real individuals. His goal in that work was not to propose a theory of human nature; it was to defend his antidemocratic politics, and its few psychologic comments were vague and unrelated to his political opinions, none of which was implied by any explicit understanding of people.

Plato knew, as we all do through our common logic, that we must understand people before we can understand their politics and how best to organize them socially. But the psychologic hypothesis he offered was so incomplete that no one could derive a sensible political theory from it. And indeed no intellectual today takes that hypothesis seriously, except perhaps in its imitative Freudian form. It was clearly borrowed from Pythagoras, the renowned academic and mystic of the prior psychologic era who described society as consisting of Three Classes: the lovers of *Wealth*, of *Honor*, and of *Wisdom*. A Pythagorean in many beliefs, including mysticism and numerology, Plato merely restated this old description of society in equivalent psychologic terms. That is, he proclaimed what he called 'the Three Parts of the Soul', which he labeled respectively our *Appetite* (wealth), *Spirit* (honor), and *Reason* (wisdom). Then in his political system, using this arbitrary triadic description as if it was a universal Law of human nature, he proposed a parallel social structure consisting of (if we ignore the slave class that he wished to retain) three social classes. Again changing the words into equivalent terms, he called these classes the *Workers*, the *Soldiers*, and the elitist *Guardians*, or rulers.

So his purpose in the *Republic* was not what he claimed it was, a literary analogy by which he could better explain his psychologic hypothesis. On the contrary, his weak psychologic hypothesis was derived backwards from his old view on social classes, Pythagoras' description of society. And even if we all did have these 'Three Parts' of our 'Soul', and only those, it doesn't follow that our society must have that same threefold division. In fact, it would then have only one social class, because all individuals, even women and slaves, would have those three parts, which he proposed as universal human attributes. A universal attribute of human nature is true of all individuals, so all that can be inferred politically from his narrow hypothesis on human nature is that we are all workers, all soldiers, and all guardians. But to propose that is to propose democracy, which was just what he detested in Athens and meant not to propose.

Plato's triadic conception of human nature was neither deep nor original, and Aristotle (384-322 BCE), his student and successor at the Academy in Athens, had little interest in improving it. At root it is meaningless because it is *merely descriptive*, by which I mean that it lacks any true definition, or causative explanation, of our nature. Why are there exactly three parts of the soul? Why not eight or seventy-seven? And just what, *in reality*, is this thing that he called a 'soul'? The entire notion is arbitrary, for it doesn't follow by virtue of any objective fact of our external or internal reality. Worse yet, he proposed it even though he reported Socrates' observation that we cannot reason correctly if we don't consider the underlying causes of the superficial effects we observe. That was the whole point of the famous 'parable of the cave' in his *Republic*, which advises us not to be fooled by mere shadows, or as I put it, to be definitive rather than descriptive reasoners. But since he routinely ignored that lesson in his work, we must conclude, as his story implies, that he did indeed hear this tale from Socrates.

The Platonic model of human nature stood unchallenged for millennia, not because it was widely accepted, but rather because later intellectuals, who until the eighteenth century were virtually all theists, adopted the disdain of their religion for the subject of human nature. Religions ignore our nature because they don't need to know the true causes of anything so long as they can receive their tithes and control the practical world through the pretense of divine edicts. And theistic intellectuals aren't bothered by the problems of human nature so long as they consider their god or gods to be ultimately responsible for our nature and our fate.

Plato's absurd view of human nature even survived into the modern era. Indirectly, it lies behind the descriptive class-based view of society proposed by the rightist Marx (1818-83), who put Plato's worker class first and proposed the broader form of communism that Plato favored later in life.[5] But it appears more directly in modern psychology, for the rightist Freud offered what was basically Plato's hypothesis as his own final explanation of human nature.

The rightists Plato, Marx, and Freud never developed a sound intellectual system, and much of their work just expanded on original notions proposed by leftists before them. They were traditionalists and borrowers of others' thoughts, an academic reasoning style that is typical of psychologic rightists, a class I define later. Most of Freud's premises were taken from his contemporaries or our ancient literature. His chief premise on human development was the notion of *psychic determinism*, the flaws of which I list later. But his two other core notions came from Plato. One is the so-called *'pain-pleasure principle'*, which was clearly though not originally stated by Plato and then later by Epicurus (341-270 BCE), and the other was just the old Pythagorean-Platonic triadic scheme disguised in Freud's own set of equivalent terms.

That is, Freud proposed the human *psyche*, a vague Greek term that only differs from the vague Platonic *soul* in that it has no theistic meaning, and then he claimed that this undefined thing in us consists of three innate and universal parts, to which he gave Greek-based names: our *id*, *ego*, and *superego*. But plainly this descriptive scheme of his simply used equivalent terms to echo Plato's division of the human 'soul' into our innate appetite (id), spirit (ego), and reason (superego), which itself echoed Pythagoras' division of our social nature into the seekers of wealth, honor, or wisdom. Obviously there is no *theory* of human nature in any of these ex post facto, merely descriptive triadic schemes. They are more accurately described as incomplete and unproven *hypotheses* about people that say nothing real or important about us.

---

[5] In my psychologically based political theory, *leftism* means individualism and *rightism* means collectivism. Therefore, contrary to the prevailing view, any form of collectivism, whether it is socialistic or capitalistic, is a rightist and not a leftist political ideology.

My chief criticism of the psychologic hypotheses of Plato and Freud, and of traditionalist constructs in general, is methodological; it is that they are yielded by merely descriptive reasoning, not definitive reasoning. We will consider the psychologic causes of our different reasoning modes later; here I wish only to show the limitations of the descriptive reasoning that composes the bulk of our traditional intellectual system.

The definitive method tries to explain a thing's causes, at least its proximate cause, because that determines its nature, or defines it. But the descriptive method uses the opposite kind of explanation: ex post facto statements about an existent thing's observed or inferred attributes, or parts. For example, to describe a book's parts without identifying and describing its author, its proximate cause, tells us something about that book, but does not define it. Or, to say that the hypothetical thing called our 'soul' or 'psyche' has three parts does not tell us either what the thing is or what event caused it to exist in us, and with exactly three parts. Only definitive reasoning, which is *analytic* and hence fundamental, refers to a thing's causes, and if it is sound, it will give us objective and certain knowledge. But descriptive reasoning is *synthetic* and hence superficial; that is, it is arbitrary and hypothetical, or contingent on relative circumstances, including the intelligence, logic, and psychologic state of the describer.

Using the descriptive method, one arbitrarily selects one or some of the observed effects, or parts, of some perceived whole event and then synthesizes class notions for those selected parts, which are then nouned. Thus armed with a set of hypothetical *class* terms, which are the direct opposite of true *universal* terms, the descriptive reasoner goes back to reconsider the initial whole context, and this time he or she creates an incomplete dissective scheme for it. This classificatory scheme is then used as the pseudotheory that guides that thinker in all further consideration of that context. The triadic division of human nature by Plato and Freud is just such a pseudotheory. Three mere effects (appetite-spirit-reason or id-ego-superego) are observed, generalized, nouned, and assumed to be causes, and then, reasoning backwards, it is said that the initial whole event, a person, consists of only those three parts, which are invalidly universalized and then proposed as composing the complete nature of any real person.

Subsequent reasoning from such a partialized dissective scheme is unsound because it ignores realness, wholeness, and process, or the whole event that was first considered. It assumes that its classifications are the whole of the matter when they are not, and that they are objective facts rather than a construct built on incomplete, biased, and arbitrary observations and selections. But in spite of this illogic, the descriptive method is our traditional way of thinking about any complex subject, and every renowned intellectual work in history either is based entirely on it or is marred by fundamental instances of it. This is why anyone who seeks the root answers to a problem by traditional means can find nothing but different mere descriptions of it.

The definitive method, on the other hand, is always logically valid, even when its factual assumptions are not the case. Here one first notes that, by definition, every observed effect has at least one underlying cause, and that therefore we must distinguish between a definition, which is a causative proposition, and a mere description, which is a proposition that makes no reference to any cause. In a statement a mere description can be a definiens, but it is not a definition because it does not propose a cause of the definiendum, the object of reference; it refers to it, but does not explain it. We can only define a distinct whole thing by identifying its cause *as an event*, after which we can validly describe the parts that compose it. But it is invalid to start from mere descriptions of some discretely observed parts and then claim that these descriptions explain the whole event to which those parts belong.

Mere descriptions can work for us in practice, but only because every description we utter presupposes a prior definition, or cause, that we do or don't know explicitly. And when we don't know that cause explicitly, the mere description is ersatz knowledge posing as real knowledge. Thus, the descriptive method is the language of ignorance; it is easier, and it permits subjective thinking that is ambiguous, vague, or deceiving. Accordingly, it is widely used by intellectuals and nonintellectuals alike. But it is only valid in the narrowest of reasoning tasks, in superficial taxonomy; that is, only when the cause of the parts referred to is irrelevant to their classification, as it is in many practical or scientific applications. Otherwise, when the cause is relevant, we get two opposed kinds of classifications: the hypothetical and arbitrary ones yielded by the descriptive method, and the fundamental and real ones yielded by the definitive method. The latter are fundamental because they are based on the cause rather than some of its effects, and they are real because any cause is an event, or an actual external or internal process.

In our human sciences, such as psychology, politics, sociology, economics, linguistics, and jurisprudence, the defining causes are human *motives*, and since the descriptive method cannot define those inner motives, it cannot be validly used in those sciences. When it is used there anyway, it imposes two blanketing presuppositions on us: that descriptive classes matter while individuals don't, and that we humans should be seen as functioning in life with no motives; that is, without the proximate cause of all of our actions, our psychologic process. Thus, besides being unable to define their terms, our mere describers classify us humans in such artificial collectivistic ways that we are seen as having no personal will, logic, mind, passions, needs, compassion, conscience, morals, and so on. But surely these are also parts of our 'soul' or 'psyche'. If descriptive reasoners even mention such psychologic attributes, they are tacked on as afterthoughts that have no connection to their classifying scheme or to anything in reality.

Descriptive reasoners are also prone to another error of explicated reasoning, the frequent failure to notice a shift of context in their references. As you know—excluding only Reality, or the Whole of Everything—we can consider any divisible thing either as a part subsumed by some whole thing or as a distinct whole event itself, with its own parts. Well, traditionalists routinely confuse these two references. If we consider X as a part of some subsuming whole event, then its proper explanation is a mere description, but if we consider X as a whole event itself, then its proper explanation is a definition, or a proposition as to the cause of that unique whole event. But those who speak of X without noticing this shift in their context will assume that their mere description of it when they consider it as a part is also its definition when they consider it as a whole, whereupon they illogically infer the general semantic rule that there is no essential difference between a definition and a description, and that therefore it is valid to use arbitrary mere descriptions to 'define' any term or thing.

Note that throughout this work I use the definitive method before I describe things. For instance, I don't describe Marx and Freud as 'rightists' in a conventional descriptive way, such as on the basis of some dictionary, of 'rightists' I know, or of my personal judgment of their views or biographies. Rather, I say this on the basis of what my psychologic theory proposes to be the natural and objective cause of rightist political reasoning in any human. This label for them therefore does not mean what the traditional word means, because I first defined the category 'rightist' theoretically, or objectively and universally in anyone, as a psychologic event. And this is the prior work that our mere describers try desperately to avoid.

We can see this clearly in the biographies they write. They try to explain their subject first by selecting many confirmed objective facts, and for the rest they just assemble a set of arbitrary descriptive terms and opinions by themselves or others that (from their own experiences, biases, training, and subjective judgment) seem to fit that person ex post facto, or that in any case make a more compelling story for sale. Traditional biography is thus partly a science but mostly a fictional art, or the epitome of mere description. And yet this descriptive method is our traditionalists' sole conception of how to understand people or anything else—as if, like simple-minded empirics, we have no power to reason about any subject except through such ex post facto biographies or specific 'case histories'.

Most descriptive reasoners understand naturally that only a causative explanation can yield a valid definition, but they refuse to accept this logical law as binding on them. They will accept a nonhuman hypothesis like 'gravity', but not the invariable universal law that, wherever they may be in the cosmos, they can never reason validly by mere description. They assume that to do so or not is their choice, so they observe this principle only when it suits their motives. This is why the descriptive method is the chief reasoning tool not only of ignorant empirics and misguided intellectuals, but also of willfully ignorant opportunists who seek to profit from proposing subjective moral, legal, theistic, or political premises as universal law.

But definitive reasoners, who are realists, base their reasoning on real and whole events, not on their effects, so they reject any explanation of a thing that does not propose its cause. They also know that when the cause of an effect cannot be known for certain, they must still posit one speculatively, and they do so fully aware that their consequent reasoning in that context is contingent upon that speculative cause being so.

For each of us, then, the question of proper method reduces to this: Is it better to reason descriptively, even though this is invalid, or should we insist that our reasoning be valid from the start, which it can only be if we propose a cause, known or not? With the descriptive method, we can't build a sound system for any context, and since we began by ignoring the whole, even the true statements we make cannot be validly related to each other. But with the definitive method, our systemic reasoning is always valid, and we can test our proposed cause for objective truth later. If it fails that test, we must propose another cause and repeat the process, but if it passes it, we have learned something new, something that descriptive reasoners could never uncover.

We can see plainly that the definitive method is not the traditional way in our dictionaries, where many of the word 'definitions' are just word descriptions. There are some factual definitions there—as when a name for a color is defined by its measured light wavelength and, by implication, its effect on us—but not many. And there are some speculative definitions there; for example, the noun 'greed' is vaguely defined by reference to a desire, which is a psychologic cause. But otherwise our lexicographers merely describe most of our words. This is acceptable in explaining a word's form and history, where psychologic cause is not an issue, but not in explaining its meaning, for we must know a word's psychologic referents, which are its causes, before we can state its true definition. But since we have never had a complete explanation of human reasoning, our lexicographers cannot know the causes of our words, so they pretend to explain the meaning of most of our words with circular references to other undefined words. For instance, they say that 'existence' means 'being' and that 'being' means 'existence', as if there were no psychologic reason why we humans coined and use those two words distinctly. But these words can be distinctly defined, as we will see in the next chapter.

Guided by their academic conventions, descriptive reasoners ignore these facts: that any symbol is a product of our psychologic functioning, that it can only be defined by identifying its three reality referents (explained in Chapter 2), and that, even when we are referring to external events, those referents are events in our internal reality; that is, impressions (cognitions, ideas) in our psychologic process that cause us to coin a given term. But these causes are mysteries to traditionalists, even though they are the sole means by which all humans who know our language will comprehend the meaning we intend in coining a new term. That and the ability to translate a language into another would be impossible if there was no common psychologic process, or universal natural logic, underlying all of our meanings and language systems. And though this truth is obvious, it has never moved our traditionalists to explain that process, our common logic.

So it is often wise to ignore the dictionaries that our traditionalists regard as sacred and inviolable texts. These works don't have the term definitions that we need most, both to see what is real and to record that reality in our language constructs, and they have no conception of semantic completeness, which can only be revealed by a sound standard of human reasoning. But in this work the missing definitions that apply to our various contexts are provided as the need arises because, having seen that the essential issue was human reasoning, I first developed a universal standard of our psychologic functioning that shows the underlying causes, or intended meanings, of all our symbols.

I trust that the foregoing shows why we must reject this old familiar way of trying to solve our problems: the descriptive method that is born in our *explicated reasoning* and thus denies our *natural reasoning*, or common logic. We can't understand any subject if we can't judge the soundness of our reasoning about it. And this is not just an academic issue, for our lives and welfare depend on our achieving the power to see what is truly intended by anyone who tries to persuade us to a specific political conclusion, course of action, manner of thinking, or way of life.

Of course, the issues of human logic and proper reasoning go far beyond this single issue of whether one employs the definitive or the descriptive method in constructing an intellectual system. I discussed this error first only because I think it is one of the simplest ways for us to see whether an intellectual is dealing realistically with our problems or is wasting our time. I could list hundreds of examples of pretentious academic or intellectual works that depend entirely on mere descriptions and arbitrary classifications based on them, many of which were famous in their time. But I think it's better to criticize in general terms with a few examples and let people find other instances of it for themselves.

As you know, academics and intellectuals continuously impose upon us to make us believe what they believe, and if pressed they will defend their mistakes or lies, as the case may be, by insisting that we humans reason in a way we don't use. Knowing this, and that most of them are hired by political and economic interests that mean us no good, we need to know in self-defense how to identify the illogical reasoners in our midst. In our time—when lying is the official way to speak in all our social and political institutions—it is so important for us all to have this skill that I will summarize these differences now before we consider them more formally later. I do this also, of course, to explain in this introduction why I believe that my approach is correct and all the contrary ones are not.

Our Reasoning Perspectives

Our practical reasoning is integrative reasoning; it is the reasoning that we do to integrate all the known facts of our selected context and all of our prior reasoning about that context into a final unitary understanding. It is shaped by what we are, where we are, when we are, and how we reasoned to get to the final understanding that immediately precedes any decision to act. The common view that our practical reasoning causes our actions is thus correct, but it is incorrect to assume, as 'practical people' do, that this reasoning is not itself caused by prior fundamental reasoning and all the external factors that affect how we reason to a decision. It does not come into existence on its own; we reach all our decisions through a process, a train of reasoning, and our reasoning *perspective* is just a question of which part of that train we prefer to jump onto.

By innate impulse or conscious choice, we each decide our current habit of perspective, which is the level of causation (or implication) in the entire chain of our reasoning that we select as the beginning point of our conscious reasoning towards a practical understanding, decision, and action. Most people use the same conscious beginning point for most contexts (events, subjects) they consider, while others differentiate these points by context, but we all choose our perspective for each case, and the possibilities range in degree from the least to the most analytic.

The least analytic perspective is that of our empirics, who do no focused reasoning, except to invoke their practical reasoning immediately before a decision must be made. The most analytic perspective is that of our philosophers, who delve into the causes of their practical reasoning until they believe they have found, in Reality itself, the ultimate cause of all things. Most people take an intermediate perspective, with the mean being very close to the empiric extreme, where the inertia of shallow and rushed reasoning dominates their choices and then shapes their personalities, beliefs, and consequently our societies. This vast class of empirics and near-empirics consists of the slothful, those who hate mental effort, the dull-witted, and all, even hard-working and highly intelligent people, who see life in superficial material terms only. These are the practical or spontaneous "men of action" who Dostoyevsky insisted are "stupid and limited."

> ...I repeat, and repeat emphatically: all spontaneous people, men of action, are active *because* they are stupid and limited. How is this to be explained? Like this: in consequence of their limitations they take immediate, but secondary, causes for primary ones, and thus they are more quickly and easily convinced than other people that they have found indisputable

grounds for their action, and they are easy in their minds; and this, you know, is the main thing. After all, in order to act, one must be absolutely sure of oneself, no doubts must remain anywhere. But how am I, for example, to be sure of myself? Where are the primary causes upon which I can take my stand, where are my foundations? ...I practice thinking, and consequently each of my primary causes pulls along another, even more primary, in its wake, and so on *ad infinitum*. That is really the essence of all thinking and self-awareness. Perhaps this, once again, is a law of nature. And what, finally, is the result? The same thing over again....[6]

Our pure empirics have no notion of the prior reasoning that causes their understandings, decisions, and actions. We see this clearly in children, who start reasoning as pure empirics, after which, by their nature and their experiences, they mature to some degree in some areas. Indeed, physiologists have recently shown that a teenager's brain is not yet fully grown. Children aside, our world has masses of adult empirics or near-empirics, including many intelligent and highly educated 'men and women of action', who remain like children in their intellectual habits and development until they die. This mental blindness is caused by both congenital and experiential factors, but most academics, human scientists, and educators today address this problem of mass ignorance, if they consider it at all, as solely an experiential or social problem.

We will not make that mistake here. Instead, we will look for the objective causes of the fact that a large majority of all individuals are born with psychologic impairments, meaning congenital reasoning flaws that cause lifelong illogic in individuals, regardless of their education or other postnatal experiences. Most people, across history and all societies, are

---

[6] Fyodor Dostoyevsky, *Notes from Underground*, 1864, translated by Jesse Coulson in *Notes from Underground/The Double* (Harmondsworth: Penguin Books, Ltd., 1972), p.26-27. Though mere description is the chief method of all literature, great literature like his employs definitive reasoning also. Here Dostoyevsky validly and insightfully proposed a psychologic cause for people's mindless acts.

empirics or near-empirics by birth. We know this from our observations, and we call them 'practical people' or 'practitioners'. But these terms don't distinguish nonintellectuals from intellectuals, who also engage in practice, so here let us distinguish all *empirics*, meaning pure empirics and near-empirics, from all *intellectuals*, who range in type from the many pragmatists who just miss being empirics to the successively fewer intellectuals who reason on deeper levels, ending with our rare, if not nonexistent, genuine philosophers.

The conventional view on this is that our intellectual level is determined by our education and profession, and before that by our innate 'intelligence', a vague descriptive term that no one has actually defined because at root its cause is a complex physiological issue. But it is more precise to define an *intellectual* as one who inquires on any level, with whatever intellect and education he or she may have, about the causes that imply any or all practical reasoning.

The only sound way to distinguish our types of intellectuals is to start from the whole, and that whole is the universal process of human reasoning, my hypothesis on which is presented over the next five chapters. But the relevant point now is that it is conceived as a cycle, which I have named *the Consideration Cycle*, with four quadrants that naturally define four sequential levels, or modes, of human reasoning. Thus, the 'train' of our reasoning, or our psychologic functioning, has only four 'cars' for us to jump onto in our explicated reasoning, though each car has distinct compartments. As I explain later, these quadrants of the Cycle, its modes, are in reality the four different *spatial directions* in which we reason.

To indicate their logical sequence in our whole psychologic process, we must name these four modes with ordinal terms, so in the epistemic context I refer to them as our *primary*, *secondary*, *tertiary*, and *quaternary* reasoning. In other contexts, other names are more appropriate, but these will be *equivalent terms* with this same sequential (logical) meaning. For example, our terms 'metaphysical reasoning' and 'psychological reasoning' refer respectively to instances of primary and tertiary reasoning, so now we will understand these old terms as having an ordinal, or logical, meaning also. What I call 'equivalent' or 'corresponding' terms are related semantically by identicality in one reality referent; they are thus distinct from synonyms, which loosely speaking are terms that are identical in two of their reality referents, and strictly speaking in all three.

It follows that this dynamic distinction in our reasoning is the only realistic way to classify our intellectuals and their work. We will therefore discard the traditional way of classifying them, which is by the ex post facto descriptive criteria of their professions or preferred academic subjects, and instead use these ordinal terms that correspond to the four reasoning modes: (1) *theorists*, (2) *analysts*, (3) *hypothesists*, and (4) *pragmatists*. These general terms apply in the psychologic context, but in the more-fundamental epistemic context, discussed in the next chapter, we will use these equivalent ordinal terms instead: (1) *realists*, (2) *rationalists*, (3) *empiricists*, and (4) *formalists*. And now that we are defining our intellectuals ordinally, or by where in the cycle of their natural reasoning they prefer to begin their explicated reasoning, all our terms for them or their work have a logical significance that they lacked before. That is, the reasoning of each intellectual type precedes and implies that of any subsequent type or types.

For instance, our hypothesists (empiricists) are tertiary reasoners who cannot be theorists (realists) or analysts (rationalists), but who may also be pragmatists (formalists) and practitioners because these subsequent roles are implied by their tertiary work. Only theorists, or primary reasoners, can work on all four intellectual levels, though they might choose to ignore any of the three later levels. But since these terms are based on the division of our whole reasoning cycle, they are partialized terms, and so they are all opposed to the wholistic term *philosopher*. If this term is to have any distinct meaning to us, it can only mean *a complete reasoner*, or one who creates theories pertaining to all four of the quadrantal modes of human reasoning. The first two theories must be analytic, a theory of reality and a theory of human reasoning (logic, knowledge), but there may be more than one theory in the two synthetic modes, the tertiary and quaternary modes. And of course the entire philosophy must be internally consistent.

Contrary to the claim of those who denigrate philosophy to disguise the incompleteness of their own reasoning, our psychologically based definition shows that our need for philosophers is fundamental and continual, since every practical construct we build needs a sound and realistic theoretic foundation. This is so even though every prior effort to create a sound philosophy has failed. That historical failure does not mean, as many pragmatists (formalists) in the past century and a half have claimed, that philosophy is useless; it only means that intellectuals must discard the fallacious assumptions and methods of the past and try harder than before. If it ever seems to us that we don't need a philosophy, this only means that we are in fact using some old one.

Traditionalist academics don't share this wholistic view of philosophy because they have no standard of human reasoning to tell them explicitly what a whole intellectual system is and how its parts are logically related. This is why they can only describe the word 'philosophy', as they do when they say that it originally meant 'a *love* of *wisdom*', two vague descriptive words that do nothing to define it. If they had such a standard, they would see that a philosophy must start from a *metaphysical theory*, which implies an *epistemic theory*, which implies (at least) a *psychologic theory* and a *moral theory*, which in turn imply all our reasoning in every area of practice or science, each of which has its own *pragmatic theory*.[7]

Historically, these four kinds of theories were never seen as a whole, or as composing a complete philosophy. Traditionalists could only see them as independent and unconnected theories, to which they assigned distinct and logically unrelated terms. Thus they studied *metaphysics*, *epistemology*, *psychology*, or *ethics* as detached academic subjects, and often confused these with pseudotheories such as 'ontology', 'formal logic',

---

[7] Except that any pragmatic theory is in fact an hypothesis that was derived in its subsuming context. Because traditionalists seldom track whole contexts of reference, people usually use the term *theory* when what they mean is *hypothesis*. A theory of Reality, or the Whole Event, is not a pragmatic theory; it is the ultimate and only true theory. When anything else is called a 'theory', this merely refers to what is an hypothesis in its causatively prior context. For instance, we can speak of a psychologic *theory* as a whole system, but actually it is born as a partialized *hypothesis* in a subsuming theory of Reality, which traditionalists don't explicate when they propose a psychologic hypothesis.

and 'theology'. And they gave each of their many pragmatic theories a distinct name without distinguishing its level in our whole reasoning process from the three more fundamental levels that logically implied it.[8]

If our definition of philosophy here is strictly interpreted, it leads to the perhaps surprising conclusion that in all recorded history we have not had even one genuine philosopher or philosophy. This may violate every reference to deeper thinking in our traditional literature, but it is correct. Only a few intellectuals approached this standard; the rest never came close. And even those whose systems were most complete (Plato, Aristotle, Kant, and Hegel) don't fit our standard here because they were idealists and not realists; that is, not theorists. As you know, the intellectuals who are farthest from the theoretical level, those pragmatists who teach the thinking of others, use their academic distinctions to call their own kind 'philosophers', but our definition denies that label to any professor of philosophy who is not a realist and who does not create a conceptually complete intellectual system.

Another old misconception that is refuted by this wholistic view of our reasoning is the assumption that deeper reasoning is more complex than shallow reasoning. But the deepest reasoning we can do is our primary reasoning, which is our simplest and most instinctive level of reasoning. This is so because it is closest to the reality of a matter, or to the real and whole *event* from which all shallower technical and practical reasoning is derived through three subsequent levels of increasing complication. This fact limits me in choosing a name for my philosophic system. It can only be *realism*, because this is the only proper name for any genuine philosophy, which must begin from our primitive monistic perception of Reality itself.

---

[8] I reject the old definition of an *epistemology* as a theory of *knowledge*, and say instead that it is a theory of *reasoning*. Knowledge is static, but reasoning is a process, and the process is what we must explain. This change makes the rarely used adjective *epistemic* useful to us now, since we never had a good adjective for the noun 'reasoning'; that is, the adjective 'reasoned' is often inappropriate, and the adjectival form of 'knowledge' is the same as that of the noun and is equally ambiguous. Moreover, *epistemic* lets us refer to a more fundamental level of human reasoning than the adjectives *psychological* and *logical* do; namely, to our secondary reasoning rather than to the tertiary or quaternary reasoning that is derived from it.

No other term would distinguish my intellectual system clearly from the three arealistic kinds of systems (discussed next) that compose our entire intellectual tradition to date.

It follows that metaphysics is not really the subject of dispute that traditionalists claim that it is, because if 'metaphysics' is properly defined, it pertains solely to the one undivided Reality, or the Whole Event, which we all know and presuppose in every thought we have and every act we perform. It seems to be controversial only because all secondary, tertiary, and quaternary reasoners deny it. But there is no such thing as a fundamental dispute between metaphysicians, because any intellectuals who are not monists as to Reality must begin their reasoning by denying the Whole Event they initially perceive, so all their talk thereafter has nothing to do with metaphysics, or *the* Reality. The only real disputes in our intellectual history are those among analysts, hypothesists, and pragmatists (rationalists, empiricists, and formalists) on their derivative levels, and for millennia traditionalists have misdescribed these as disagreements among 'philosophers'. The most common pseudometaphysical dispute is the one provoked by monotheists or other idealists who claim to be discussing Reality when in fact, as hypothesists (empiricists), they begin by denying primary *metaphysical* issues so that they can consider tertiary *mystical* issues without the restrictions that Reality imposes on our reasoning.

The squabbles among our arealists result from their failure to explicate their primary reasoning, the source of our common view of Reality, and from their failure to use this realism as their standard in judging their subsequent reasoning—all of which is based on the dualisms of their secondary reasoning, where they dissect our whole Reality into two parts, only one of which is real. Italicizing the fictional term in each pair (as I do throughout), examples are the traditional divisions of Reality called '*heaven*-earth', '*mind*-body', '*spirit*-substance', and '*time*-space'.

Arealistic reasoning

This opposition between realists and arealists is the most fundamental intellectual dispute because at root it is the clash between truth and ignorance. We can see this by the substitution of terms, for the basic sense of 'true' (or truth) is equivalent to what we mean by 'real' (or reality), and 'ignorance' means that something is lacking. And that is what the terms *partialism, idealism,* and *pragmatism* mean. They are arealistic views because respectively they divide, deny, or ignore reality, and all traditional reasoning is fallacious in one of these three ways.

The identity of reality with wholeness and process is a cognitive fact, for we must perceive a thing as a whole and as a process to perceive its reality. So the dispute between truth and ignorance is settled simply by noting (1) that partialists cannot be realists because the parts are not the whole and only a whole event is real, (2) that idealists cannot be realists because any form of idealism, whether mystical or scientific, is predicated on a prior denial of a reality, some realities, or the one Reality, and (3) that pragmatists cannot be realists because they consider only superficial issues and ignore the reality that underlies all appearances.

We should consider the term *idealist* now, because we have intellectual and political reasons to avoid its conventional ambiguity. In one sense, it means someone who pursues a future perfection, or a speculative hypothesis that is commonly called an 'ideal'. This is the natural and often-laudable process of trying to improve something according to a fabricated paradigm. But if this is what we mean, we should use 'perfectionist' or its variants instead. The other sense of 'idealist' is its logical or philosophic sense, which refers to the fallacy of detached tertiary reasoning, and this opprobrious meaning is the only sense for which we need the term.

The universal standard of reasoning proposed in this work shows us the two greatest errors possible in an intellectual system, and all three types of arealists make them both. The first is the failure to reason explicitly from primary reasoning, the true beginning of our reasoning process. It is the denial of all the reasoning that logically precedes and implies one's favorite mode of reasoning. Thus, *partialism* is fallacious secondary reasoning that denies primary reasoning, *idealism* is fallacious tertiary reasoning that denies primary and secondary reasoning, and *pragmatism* is fallacious quaternary reasoning that denies primary, secondary, and tertiary reasoning. The second major error follows from this. It is to adopt as a premise of one's own reasoning an unsound conclusion from a prior level of reasoning that one did not personally consider, which is what people do when they adopt erroneous traditional assumptions.

Individually and collectively, our prior knowledge systems are our foremost problems today, and so I condemn them as a class. I express this blanket criticism by speaking of our 'traditional intellectual system', or our 'traditional system of thought and belief'. This rhetorical device overgeneralizes, of course, but it simplifies our discussions by allowing me to avoid academic digressions into what intellectuals of the past said about each issue we discuss. We can leave the history of our intellectual systems to our estimable professors of philosophy, for that is properly their work. A philosopher's task is to present a new and complete intellectual system, which is necessarily offered as against the class of all prior intellectual systems. No one would bother creating a new philosophy unless he or she thought that every prior intellectual system is flawed in its fundamental assumptions about reality and human nature.

In sum, we can only reach a true understanding of any science or other practical subject though philosophy. And this means that only a philosopher can be *truly* practical. Far from being the antithesis of our practical reasoning, philosophy is the very essence of it.

Now that we know the only valid way to achieve a sound understanding of human nature, let us proceed to the initial elements of our new philosophy; namely, the epistemic, metaphysical, and psychologic theories that imply both the new methods that I propose here to understand people and the new moral and political theories that I will propose in my next work.

Chapter 2. Reasoning

THE FIRST QUESTION

Reality is the first thing we know, but it is not our first subject of inquiry. Our first question must be about our knowledge of reality; it is the epistemic question, How do we humans perceive any real thing in the first place? So before we can explicate our reasoning about any real subject, we must consider how we reason. If we don't, we will confuse our explicated reasoning with our natural reasoning, or what we say with what we mean. The former is how we reason through our symbols and languages, while the latter is how we reason through our common human logic, and the clash between the two has created some of our greatest dilemmas. For one thing, it is the difference between our 'primitive' and 'civilized' societies, since all that we mean by 'a *civilized* society' is a highly explicative society, and such societies are historically infamous for routinely denying both our natural reasoning and our humanness.

Traditionalist intellectuals have seen this distinction, but they haven't bridged the gap it causes because they ignored the issue of our common logic, or universal standard of reasoning. If we don't know the common elements of our reasoning, we cannot know what our terms mean or understand the logic that rules and relates our language constructs. Though words and other symbols are the building blocks of our explicated reasoning, the mortar that holds them together is our common logic, or our natural reasoning. To understand ourselves better and build more natural societies, then, we must first construct a more natural verbal language than we have now, and for this we need that missing standard.

Most of us agree that our words and other symbols refer to our psychologic impressions; indeed, they cannot refer directly to anything else, since our psychologic process lies between all realities (external or internal) and our explanations of them with symbols or languages. My view on *term reference* is this. Each word or other symbol we form results from our cognition of some real external or internal event. And because, as I argue in the next chapter, Reality has only three dimensions, every term has three reality referents, which correspond to those three dimensions. A term's first dimension is its *context-referent*, meaning its reference to the perception of a whole event that provokes an act of consideration in us. Its second dimension is its *idea-referent*, meaning its reference to a specific idea that is cognized at some point in that cycle of consideration. And its third dimension is its *tense-referent*, meaning its reference to where the context-referent and the idea-referent stand with respect to the past, present, or future.

Our other goals won't allow us to pursue all of the issues related to our common logic here, but we can at least consider its framework as a cycle and agree on our basic terms for its dynamic structure as a moving process. This will show us what is logically required of our theory of reality, from which we can then derive our psychologic, moral, and various pragmatic theories.

The Consideration Cycle

My epistemic theory differs from traditional epistemologies mainly because it focuses on *knowing* rather than on *knowledge*, or on our reasoning process rather than on detached static notions. This focus led me to sketch diagrams of the dynamic structure of a single entire act of human knowing, or consideration, and after many unsuccessful attempts I felt that I finally had the framework of the universal standard of human reasoning that we need. I refer to that standard as *the process of human consideration* or *the Consideration Cycle*.

In the next chapter, my metaphysics proposes that all events are three-dimensional, and from this it follows that there is no structural distinction between an external and an internal event, or between 'body' and 'mind'. The Consideration Cycle is thus conceived as the spatial structure of any complete act of consideration, and its three-dimensional form is proposed as the natural structure of all human logic, or psychologic functioning. It thus purports to define all of the unit cognitions that we can have along its path and all of the natural relations that can exist among any of those psychologic impressions.

Note that I say 'cognition' rather than 'idea'. Our conventional term *idea* has been ambiguous since the classic era, when Plato's original sense of this term (meaning one of his ideal Forms) was replaced with our present sense of the term, which means a psychologic impression. But this sense is ambiguous because it can mean a unit psychologic impression, a combination of simple impressions, or generically both. Locke (1632-1704) dealt with this ambiguity by distinguishing between simple and complex ideas, as we must also. So I use *idea* only in its indefinite generic sense; otherwise I use *epistemic idea* or *cognition* to mean a unit psychologic impression, and *notion* or *conception* to mean a compound impression. The Cycle is similarly ambiguous, for in its universal form we consider its unit impressions as epistemic ideas, but when we relativize it by selecting a particular event as our context, those impressions are compound notions that occur in us in the same logical sequence as our epistemic ideas.

We will ignore the Cycle's third dimension in this work as not relevant to our subjects here, and we will add other psychologic features to it later in this work. All that we need now is a general understanding of the Cycle's major elements as shown in *Figure 1*: its cyclic path, two of its three dimensional axes, the four points on its path defined by those two axes, and the four reasoning directions between those points, which are the reasoning modes mentioned earlier.

The Cycle is a process, and its path represents the directed course of our reasoning in a single act of consideration, starting from that act's context of reference. This process can be interrupted at any point, voluntarily or involuntarily. Each distinguishable point on its path is an *epistemic idea* in an act of original consideration or a *compound notion* in any reconsideration of the same context. These cognitions vary in the intensity of their impression on us, and we may either cognize them or skip over them as we rush ahead in the Cycle, a choice that more often depends on our congenital character than on any conscious selection we make.

Some people distinguish these unit points better than others do. For instance, all things being equal, our tertiary intellectuals (hypothesists, empiricists) will cognize the third-quadrant points better than other intellectuals do, because of their natural preference for that reasoning mode and hence their greater experience in it. Our old descriptive term 'intelligence' no doubt refers in part to this ability to distinguish the unit epistemic ideas of the Cycle finely and to see their logical relations easily. But no one can cognize every possible point.

However, every normal person can at least distinguish the four numbered points in *Figure 1*, which are the directional extremes of the moving process, the absolute limits and spatial turning points of the reasoning modes, the Cycle's quadrantal directions. These are the sharpest of all our unit cognitions, and I refer to them as our *cardinal ideas*. This term is apt since these cognitions are dynamically equivalent in their nature and relations to the four extremes of spatial direction, the cardinal points of a compass. And the fact that the Cycle proposes four cardinal ideas rather than the conventional two (a percept and a concept) is a fundamental difference between our new theory of human reasoning and all prior epistemologies.

Let us consider the elements of the Cycle first, before we consider the significance of each in the whole dynamic. *Figure 1* shows these basic elements: the Cycle's counterclockwise motion (explained later), its assumed reference plane (the page), the two directional axes on that plane, and the four points on the path defined by those axes.

The vertical axis is the *axis of particularity*, or *specificity*. Its polar points on the Cycle's path are two cardinal ideas that I refer to as *percepts*, by which I mean *cognitions of particularity*. The Cycle, and our primary reasoning, begins at the top of this axis, and this first cardinal idea is our direct perception of a real and whole *event*, which cognition is *the context of reference* for all the reasoning that follows in that one act of consideration. I have named it *the complete percept* because it is our only totally particular cognition, which makes it our most important epistemic idea. Midway through the Cycle, after analyzing that whole event, we cognize the opposite percept on this vertical axis, which I have named *the partial percept*. It differs from the complete percept in being our cognition of a part rather than of its subsuming whole. It is also a particular idea, but an imperfect

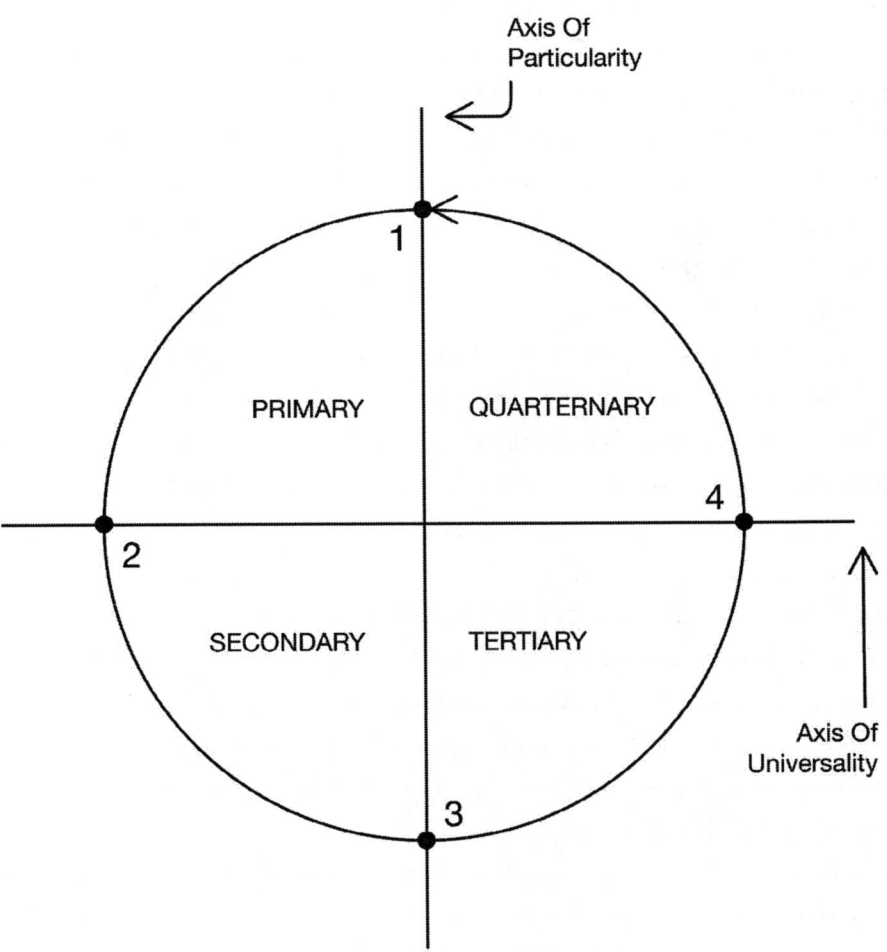

Figure 1. The Four Reasoning Modes

1 = Complete Percept; 2 = Abstract Concept; 3 = Partial Percept; 4 = Concrete Concept

one because it is not a direct perception; that is, we derive this cognition of a part by reasoning through intervening general ideas.

The horizontal axis is the *axis of universality*, or *generality*. Its polar points on the Cycle's path are the two epistemic ideas that I refer to as *concepts*, by which I mean *cognitions of universality*. As with the two percepts, the first concept, named *the abstract concept*, is universal to the entire context, but the opposite concept, named *the concrete concept*, is not. The abstract concept is the most general idea we can have because it is derived, with no intervening cardinal idea, directly from the initially perceived whole event; it is the universal cognition that ends our primary reasoning mode. The opposed concrete concept is also 'universal', but not completely so, for it is not derived directly from either the complete percept (the whole event) or the abstract concept (the essence of that event); rather, its antecedent cardinal idea is the partial percept.

Since it is derived from our additive tertiary reasoning, the concrete concept is our 'sum-of-all-parts' cognition, and it has two basic forms that depend on what we sum to achieve it. In our secondary reasoning we dissect a whole thing (event), completely or not, into some perceived parts (attributes, properties), and in our tertiary reasoning we sum those parts to reach the concrete concept. Its first form is when we hypothetically sum *all* or *some* of those parts of the whole thing; here our concrete conception is of a particular *set* of parts, so in different cases it is our conception of a thing's *form*, *substance*, or *being*. Its second form is when we hypothetically sum all the possible instances of any *one* of those parts. For example, if we see multiple objects on a table, one of which is a pen, the first form is our cognition of *all the objects on this table*, and the second form is our cognition of all possible things like this one, or of *all pens*. Both are class ideas, both are hypothetical summations since they are not an actual count of all the particular instances, and both are static and timeless conceptions when first cognized.

Of course, we can assign a time to them later in an act of reconsideration, but to do that we must first *perceive* our hypothetic summation (a mere concept) as if it was a real and whole event, which it is not. This is where things get complicated in traditional epistemology, because the initial event (context) that we are analyzing in an act of reconsideration can be either a real external or internal event, a genuine percept, or an imaginary event, a false percept. And if it is imaginary, we cognized it not with the complete percept, our only cognition of realness and wholeness, but with the concrete concept, in the tertiary reasoning of a prior act of consideration that produced a class idea. Every class idea is a hypothetical and static, or timeless, *ideal*. But when we imagine that ideal (form, substance, being) as if it was a real perception of an event, it still starts the Cycle's analytic half, diagrammed in *Figure 2a*, which concludes with our deduction of the imaginary parts of that ideal—such as the 'things' that might compose, say, a utopia, pure justice or beauty, a heaven, a god, or a perfect person, square, or action.

So all the terms that we use to refer to our cognition of the concrete concept in either form are hypothetical. They are our artificial *class terms* that refer to form, substance, or a state of being, or to any kind of ideal, total, or perfect conception. We can also refer to them as *concrete terms* when we wish to note their opposition to the two kinds of *abstract terms*.[1] The concrete concept is not universal to the whole context; it is only 'universal' to some relative class within that context. For example, our abstract-concept terms 'existence' and 'space' refer to a universal attribute shared by every event whatsoever, but concrete-concept terms such as 'red', 'species', 'large', 'beautiful', and 'just' refer to relative attributes that are shared only by some events.

Figure 1 shows that the axes of particularity and universality divide the Cycle into quadrants, and the path of our reasoning in each quadrant is plainly a different *spatial direction*. These quadrants are fundamental to cycles of any kind, physical or psychologic. In this work they are the basis in nature for our distinctions in the quadrants of a psychologic era, in our four reasoning modes, and in our four basic types of intellectuals.

---

[1] Let us not confuse these two newly defined terms with our linguists' terms *abstract* or *concrete words* (or nouns). Their distinction, unlike ours, is merely descriptive because it is based on how our words are used rather than on their psychologic referents.

All epistemic ideas other than the four cardinal ideas are *intermediate ideas*. These are the cognitions that occur on the Cycle's path within each quadrant, and they are of four basic kinds, as defined by their quadrant.[2] Each intermediate idea is either a percept in the process of becoming a concept or a concept in the process of becoming a percept, and we can give these intermediate ideas class names according to the quadrant in which we cognize them; that is, *primary ideas, secondary ideas*, and so on. But these class terms don't apply to our four cardinal ideas, each of which is a border that ends one reasoning mode and simultaneously initiates the next mode. We can also distinguish our intermediate ideas quantitatively, by their degree of particularity or generality. But for the four middle (50%) ones, this ratio relates any intermediate idea directly to one in the opposite quadrant and inversely to one in each adjacent quadrant.

This explains only the basic elements of the Consideration Cycle as diagrammed in *Figure 1*, but we don't need more than these elements to show the power of the Cycle to solve some unsolved ancient dilemmas. The three old puzzles that follow should suffice both to show the fundamental importance of the Cycle's dynamic framework and to explain the key distinctions it makes that we should all observe hereafter in our reasoning and speech.

1. *Essence and Universals.* As you may know, the term 'essence' has been much considered by intellectuals since the sophist era. Their discussions of its meaning have centered on the issue of 'universals', a term that has remained undefined and ambiguous because traditionalists failed to distinguish either between our two concepts or between those concepts and the terms that refer to them. To avoid the latter confusion, we must always distinguish between a *term* and its epistemic *referents*, and so refer

---

[2] If we consider the third dimension also, which we are not doing in this work, we would say instead that there are *six* cardinal ideas, and that each intermediate idea occurs between *three* cardinal ideas, and so is one of *eight* kinds, as in the octants of a sphere that result when it is thrice divided into halves.

Figure 2. The Cycle's Halves

2a. Qualitative Reasoning

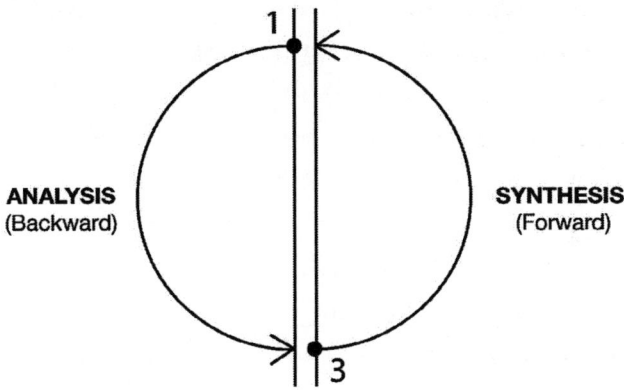

2b. Quantitative Reasoning

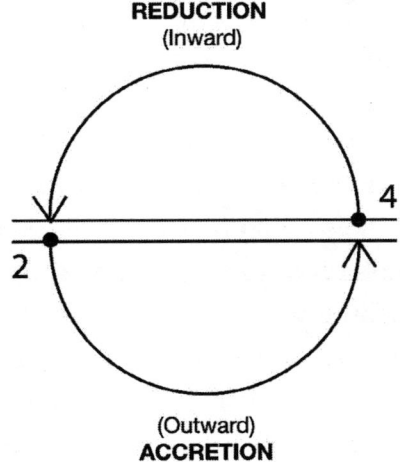

1 = Complete Percept; 2 = Abstract Concept; 3 = Partial Percept; 4 = Concrete Concept

to our concept terms not as 'concepts' or 'universals', as if a term could be an idea, but rather as 'abstract terms' or 'concrete terms'.

My proposal that we have two concepts and not just one is a new conception, and it explains why Aristotle and Locke offered contradictory explanations of how we reason to cognize 'a universal', meaning their traditional notion of 'a concept', or generalized idea. Aristotle described the accretive tertiary reasoning that I say we use only to cognize the concrete concept, and he specified the second form of it, where we pluralize one part (property, attribute) to reach the hypothetical notion of the class of all such parts ever. He called that part the 'essence' of the class term, meaning the one thing that all possible members of that nouned class have in common. But Locke, to explain that same concept, described the opposite process, the primary reductive reasoning that I say we use only to cognize the abstract concept. He held that we achieve 'a concept' by reduction, not accretion, or by imaginatively stripping away the attributes of a whole event until we cognize the least possible thing about it. And since this least thing is common to any event and all its parts, it is a universal idea and the 'essence' of that whole.

But in his criticism of Aristotle's explanation, Locke failed to see that he was defining a different cognition, so he failed to see that we humans cognize two *quadrantally opposite* (90°) 'essences' and two *directly opposite* (180°) concepts, or 'universals'. The only traditionalist I know who came close to seeing this conceptual duality was Vygotsky (1896-1934).[3] At one point in reading the work cited, I thought that he was about to propose the two-concept solution I had reached. But as a research psychologist he was not trying to map the entire process of human consideration as I was, and so, though his study implied it, he (like Locke) stopped short of concluding this notion that violates all traditional views on the subject; namely, that we have two concepts, not one, and that we cognize them by opposite reasoning modes, or directions.

---

[3] See L. S. Vygotsky, *Thought and Language* (Cambridge, MA: The M.I.T. Press, 1962), specifically Chapter 5, *An Experimental Study of Concept Formation*.

As a result of this error, traditionalist intellectuals since Locke have been confused over what an 'essence' is. The abstract concept *is* an essence, for it is our reductive cognition of something that is universal to every particular context (event) and hence to all possible parts of any context, but the concrete concept *is not* an essence, it is a hypothetical summation. What Aristotle meant by an 'essence' is the partial percept that we synthesize to form a hypothetical class. That percept is the cardinal source of any class idea—the one element that is, or set of elements that are, common to all members of the class. So we have quadrantally opposite senses of the term 'essence': the major sense that refers to the abstract *concept* and the minor sense that refers to the partial *percept*. Locke described how we reach the former, the abstract concept that is the *defining essence* of a whole event, but he didn't distinguish it from Aristotle's *descriptive essence*, the partial percept that is universal to only one class among all the classes that can be formed from different parts (properties, attributes) of that same whole event.

Consider the partial percept named *red*. In one sense, this is the 'essence' of the class of all red things, but that is not the sense we mean when we say that the 'essence' of a perceived event is its *existence* or *space*, which are universal to every distinct event. Traditionalists confuse these quadrantally opposed meanings of 'essence' and the directly opposed meanings of 'universal'—universal to every part of a whole or universal only within one class, form, or ideal synthesized from one or more of its parts. To avoid these ambiguities, we must use *universal term* to mean only a term whose idea-referent is the abstract concept, and we must not use *essence* without specifying whether we mean a *defining* (universal) or a *descriptive* (partial) essence.

Three cardinal ideas are involved in these two confusions: the abstract concept (#2) by which we cognize a defining essence, the partial percept (#3) by which we cognize a descriptive essence, and the concrete concept (#4) by which we cognize a hypothetical summation, or a class notion that applies only to a part of the whole context. And, unlike the complete percept (#1) but like all intermediate ideas, those derived cardinal ideas cannot refer to anything external to us; they refer solely to internal psychologic events and are only real in that sense.

2. Existence and One. These are universal terms. They are equivalent because the idea-referent of both is the abstract concept (#2), but they are not synonyms because they differ in their context-referents. I call the source context of the term *existence* 'the processual context', and the contexts of the two main senses of the term *one* are the mathematical context and what I call 'the relational context', discussed next. With these terms we see that the Cycle yields precise psychologic definitions of terms that previously could not be defined. Modern-era existentialists claimed that *existence* cannot be objectively defined, but the Cycle defines it by not ignoring the primary reasoning that causes the abstract concept to which it refers. Similarly, mathematicians could not define the foundational mathematical terms *one* and *zero*, so they merely described these universal terms with class terms that are ultimately circular.

We reach the abstract concept by reducing a whole event to its defining essence, but oddly enough this first concept has two forms, depending upon whether our analytic reduction is ultimate or penultimate. That is, just before we cognize this second cardinal idea, we have a choice to make. If we reduce our whole context ultimately, then nothing is left of our initial event to which we can refer, and so any further consideration of that context is aborted at that point by denial. This ultimate (total) reduction is the idea-referent of our terms of complete negation, such as 'nonexistence', 'nothing', or 'zero'. But an ultimate reduction is not a universal cognition, nor are any terms that refer to it, since they end all further consideration of a context by denying its existence, and hence its universality. They have no universal meaning because there is no such thing as *something* that is universal to *nothingness*. But while our negative terms cannot be universal terms, they can be class terms, since class negations deny only a part of the whole context being considered. For example, we can deny that a thing is red without denying that it exists, and we can even speak of the class of all 'not red' things.

Existence and *one* refer to a universal idea because every distinct thing in Reality exists and is a unique one. These equivalent terms mean *the penultimate analytic reduction of an event, or thing*. But the terms *nonexistence* and *zero* do not refer to universality, for it is absurd to say that every distinct thing does not exist or is not a unique one.

Here, then, is another important distinction in how we reason. Primary reasoning (and hence realism) is based on affirmation alone, because we have not yet reduced the whole to reach our second cardinal idea, the cognition at which we either affirm or deny a whole context. With the abstract concept (#2), dualistic reasoning enters into our considerations for the first time, for here we must choose either to affirm or to deny our initial whole context. This is why theorists (realists, primary reasoners) are positive in outlook, while analysts, hypothesists, and pragmatists are 'either-or' in outlook; that is, positive or negative and hence always subject to doubts.

We can only see this fact, that in our analytic reasoning we must choose between a penultimate or ultimate reduction of the whole we are considering, by thinking processually rather than statically. Subject to our congenital nature and barring interruptions, we are free to choose whether to affirm or deny any context, or event, even our life, and we do this by deciding whether to cognize the dualistic abstract concept (#2) with a penultimate or an ultimate reduction. We choose the former, the affirmation, when we want our current act of consideration to proceed into our secondary reasoning, and we choose the latter, the denial, when we wish to abort all further consideration of that context (event).

But when we stop just short of nothingness, and thus affirm our context's defining essence, that essence is a universal cognition; that is, it is common to everything that is subsumed by that whole context, and to all things whatsoever if that context is metaphysics, or the event of Reality itself. So we must take pains to speak unambiguously here. Only those nouns that we assign to the abstract concept in its penultimate form are *universal terms*; the nouns that we assign to the abstract concept in its ultimate form are *denial terms*. And these are our only two kinds of *abstract terms*.[4]

---

[4] We can't call denial terms 'negating terms' because we must distinguish between the complete negations of analytic reasoning and the partial negations of synthetic reasoning. Our traditional terms of negation are vague and ambiguous, since we never had a universal standard by which to distinguish them. They permit us to say indiscriminately that we 'deny' or 'negate' either a whole or a part, but now we must observe this semantic distinction: that we *deny* whole contexts only and *negate* their parts only.

The old question now arises whether our abstract terms refer to anything that is objectively real, and the answer is 'yes and no'. For instance, if we ask, Does *existence* exist?, the answer is 'yes' in the sense that the cognition to which this term refers is a real psychologic event, and 'no' in the sense that the referent of this universal term is nothing more than an internal cognition we humans have. Every cognition refers to a real event within us, but only the complete percept (#1) can refer to either real external events or to real internal events, including imaginary ones.

To see this ambiguity is also to expose a fallacy in the old existential arguments that a god (or anything else) exists. To prove that something *exists* is not to prove that it is a real and whole event; it merely proves that someone has affirmed that there was such an event. And since people affirm both external events that they have perceived and internal events that they imagine are external events, no one can dispute that the *cognition* called 'god' exists; the only issue is whether or not there is such an external thing in Reality. In fact, this is what arealistic people are: those who fail to distinguish between external and internal reality, and who then fallaciously assume that there must be a counterpart in external reality for their psychologic cognitions, which they are more likely to do if some other people also affirm these same internal cognitions.

What remains after a penultimate reduction is the last point to which we can reduce a thing and still have something left to refer to and name, and that is the defining essence of our context and hence a perfectly universal cognition within it. It is this abstract conception, for instance, that permits us to count a variety of different things, for what we really mean when we count 'one, two, three' is 'one existence, two existences, three existences'. We don't count whole things; we ignore everything else about them and count only their universal essences, their mere existence. This is why we can count how many apples are on the table or how many books are there or how many apples and books are there. Everything that exists, whether externally or only internally, can be counted, but nothingness cannot be.

Thus, our term *one* is correctly defined as *the affirmation of an existence*, and our term *zero* is correctly defined as *the denial of an existence*. And since both terms refer to the same epistemic idea, the abstract concept, they are not opposites, or contradictories. Zero denies one, but it is not its contradictory. Contradictories must exist at the same time, but deniances and their corresponding existents cannot coexist.[5]

It follows that the ancient 'law of contradiction' is only properly named if it is stated as our logicians do, as an artificial law of explication, "No statement can be both true and false." But that name is not appropriate for the existential statement, "Nothing can both be and not be at the same time," because this speaks of *denial* (complete negation) and not of *contradiction* (partial negation). Either we cognize the complete percept or we do not, and if we do, then we derive either an existence or a deniance. So we must now give this latter 'law of thought' two *epistemic* names: as the *law of perception* it is, "We either perceive an event or we do not," and as the subordinate *law of conception* it is, "We either affirm or deny any event we have perceived."

Our term 'existence' refers to our penultimate reduction of any context, so *everything exists* and every event, or thing, can be reduced to this next-to-nothing state and given a unique name. Applying this fact personally, in various contexts we refer to our own defining essence as our *self*, our *uniqueness*, our *dignity*, our *name*, our *character*, and so on. 'Existence' is thus our paradigmatic universal term, and since it is not relative, or descriptive, it cannot be biased or refer to any contingent class idea. Every universal term refers to a universal cognition that allows no discrimination or comparison between things subsumed by the whole context. So everyone is unique and has an individual dignity, and from this

---

[5] Since this basic distinction must be reflected in our speech, we should use *denial* to mean complete (analytic) negation and *contradiction* to mean partial (synthetic) negation. For example, in the *square of opposition* of traditional logic (where S is any subject and P any predicate), 'All S is P' and 'Some S is not P' are contradictory propositions, as are 'No S is P' and 'Some S is P'. But that propositional logic presupposes that every statement exists, so the relations it calls 'contradictions' are not complete denials. In that logic, the terms 'no' or 'not' compare existents but do not deny an existent, as 'nothing' does. So a *contradictory* of 'All S is P' is 'Some S is not P', but its *denial* is no statement at all.

it follows, in the political context, that every individual has equal natural, universal, and inalienable *rights*.

Denial terms like 'nothingness' or 'nonexistence' are not the opposite of 'existence' because opposition is a logical relation between existents only. It therefore must be that we have some conventional term to refer to the direct opposite of our term *existence*, and we do. That term is *being*, the idea-referent of which is the hypothetical and static concrete concept (class idea, ideal, substance, form). This gives us two opposite generalized cognitions of a particular whole thing: (1) the affirmation of its universal essence and (2) the hypothetical summation of its constituent elements, both those that we know and those that we don't cognize individually but that we drag into our concrete concept by our act of hypothetical summation. So, in what I call 'the processual context'—because now that we have defined the terms 'existence' and 'being', we must deny the old subject called 'ontology'—the universal term *existence* and the concrete term *being* are direct opposites on the axis of universality, and their quadrantal opposites on the axis of particularity are the complete-percept term *cause* and the partial-percept term *effect*.

When we begin our primary reasoning, we know *that* we have perceived an event, but we don't yet know *what* we perceived. If we are certain that we perceived something real and whole, we consider it proven by our personal *affirmation*, the first of the four kinds of proof that the Cycle requires of us. (The others, in quadrantal order, are *verification*, *substantiation*, and *justification*.) Since the abstract concept is dualistic, we must either affirm the whole event to which it refers or conclude the nonexistence of that event. With the denial, we decide either that the context was an illusion or that it was a real event that we have no personal reason to consider further. In the case of the illusion, we might abort further consideration of that context or we might continue considering it anyway, perhaps because it is fun to do so or because we see a practical use for a fiction or lie we can construct from it. But our secondary reasoning proceeds in either case. Thus, the mere fact that something *exists* and can then be considered in our secondary, tertiary, or quaternary reasoning does not prove that it is an externally real thing.

Terms of denial are as important in our explicated reasoning as affirming terms. Indeed, after we cognize a whole event and reduce it to its defining essence, we can say that all of our subsequent reasoning is based on this inherent dualism of the abstract concept. Without the binary logic of this *either-or* and its equivalents *real-unreal*, *true-false*, and *one-zero*, we would have no language constructs, all of which are based on the laws of perception and conception. For instance, formal logic is based on the universal affirmation term *true* and the denial term *false*, and mathematics is based on the universal affirmation term *one* and the denial term *zero*. And, remarkably, this is so even though these terms refer only to internal psychologic events.

Thus the Cycle explains yet another ancient paradox: why our logical and mathematical systems refer to *infallible universal truths*, or Laws of Reality, even though their basic terms do not refer to anything that is externally real. And the fact that these artificial linguistic constructs have this power substantiates my claims about our common logic; namely, (1) that it is real, (2) that it follows the objective Laws of Reality, and (3) that it can reveal those absolute Laws to us.

3. The Relational Paradox. It is not probable today, but you may have heard of the ancient dilemma called 'the paradox of the Whole and the Parts and the One and the All'. If so, you will appreciate that the Cycle's structure yields its solution. In spite of the importance of solving this dilemma, few scholars today even mention it. They ignore it not because they don't know it or think it trivial, but only because it is beyond solution with their old epistemic premises.[6]

This paradox is relevant for us now because, with four very common terms—*whole*, *part*, *one*, and *all*—it illustrates and clarifies our cardinal

---

[6] I last saw it mentioned in print decades ago, in Russell Coleburt's *An Introduction to Western Philosophy* (New York: Sheed & Ward, 1957). But in spite of its fundamentality, it is not even an entry in the philosophic encyclopedias I have seen. It was also mentioned years ago on television, on *The Dick Cavett Show*, by Paul Weiss, a professor of philosophy who cited it as one of the three major dilemmas of philosophy. (One of his others was to find the missing standard of all human reasoning.)

ideas and how they relate to each other, as well as the general nature of all logical or terminological oppositions. I call it 'the relational paradox' because its dilemma is one of idea relation. For some reason that traditionalists couldn't explain, these terms seem especially important, and yet each has a perplexing relation to the other three; that is, they are in one sense opposites and in another sense nearly synonymous. As traditionalists, we don't know why we do so, but we erroneously equate a Whole to a One, a One to a Part, Parts to an All (a class), and an All to a Whole. And yet we know that *whole* means the opposite of *part* and that neither is quite what we mean by *one* or *all*, and that *one* means the opposite of *all* and that neither is quite what we mean by *part* or *whole*.

Traditionalists saw this relational peculiarity as unique to these four terms—in spite of more obvious instances of it, such as the cardinal directions of a compass—because their epistemic hypotheses never proposed *four* cardinal ideas. Most of them believed that there are only *two* kinds of unit epistemic ideas, which they called 'sense percepts' and 'concepts'. They saw that these two epistemic ideas are opposites, but they couldn't see how any epistemic idea could have three opposites, as the idea-referent of each of the terms in this paradox does. And yet their formal logicians had just such a notion in Aristotle's *square of opposition*. But because their incomplete epistemologies could only explain the relational terms Parts and All, they confused Parts with One and All with Whole. We could say that a third elemental idea was proposed by the rationalists, if we assume that their mystical hypothesis of 'innate ideas' adds One to the empiricists' Parts and All, but we must deny this case for the reasons given below.

One has solved this ancient paradox only if one can explain all the apparent similarities and oppositions of the four terms, such that no ambiguity or contradiction remains to plague our reasoning. And this the Consideration Cycle does with a simple picture. *Figure 3* shows us the solution to this old puzzle. The Cycle proposes that every epistemic idea, whether cardinal or intermediate, and hence every term that refers to it,

Figure 3. Solution of the Relational Paradox

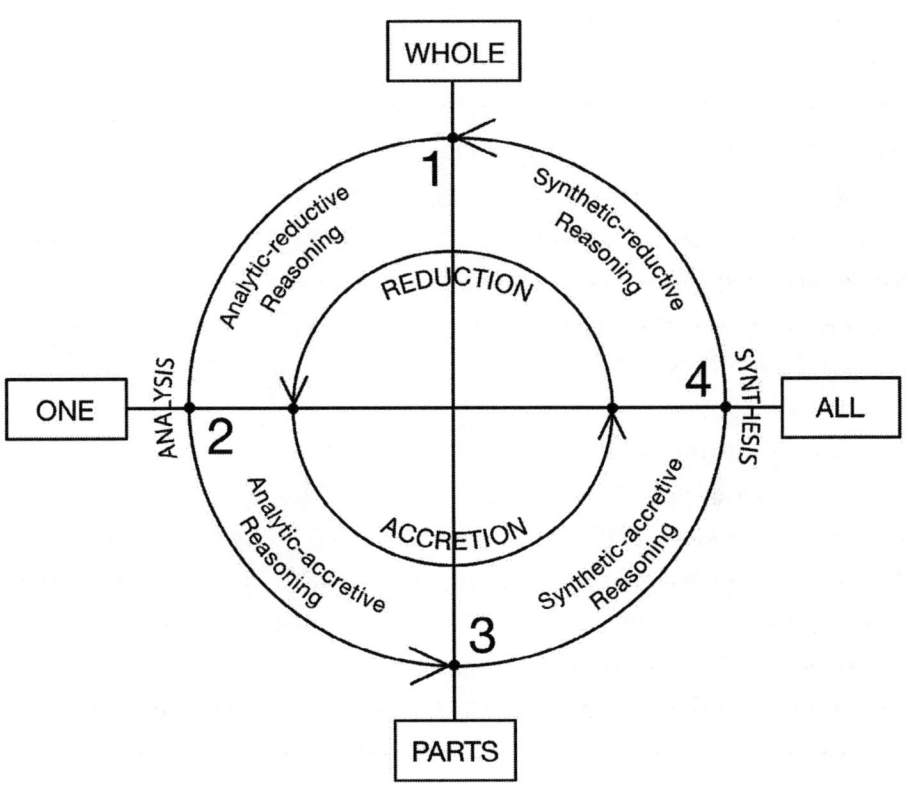

1 = Complete Percept; 2 = Abstract Concept; 3 = Partial Percept; 4 = Concrete Concept

has a *direct opposite* and two *quadrantal opposites*, an antecedent and a consequent opposite.[7]

Thus, each term we create has four cardinal senses, whether our symbols for them differ or are the same but for an article or other term that makes this distinction—such as *this X, any X, an X*, and *all Xs*. Also, there are as many equivalent sets of four terms that refer to those four cardinal cognitions as there are possible contexts of reference. In the epistemic context, these four terms are *the complete percept, the abstract concept, the partial percept, and the concrete concept*; in the processual context, they are *cause, existence, effects, and being*; in the directional context, they are *north, east, south, and west*; and in the relational context, they are *whole, one, parts, and all*. Some other sets are listed in *Table A*.

In every such set of cardinal terms, the first and third term (say, Whole and Parts or Cause and Effects) are *qualitative* terms because their idea-referents are our two percepts, and the second and fourth terms (say, One and All or Existence and Being) are *quantitative* terms because they refer to our two concepts.

Now let us return to the Cycle's dynamics. *Figure 2a* shows that the qualitative axis of particularity (perception) divides our considerational act into the semiprocesses of analysis and synthesis. The initial semiprocess of analysis begins from our *context* (#1), or our perception of a specific whole event, and leads us to the dualistic abstract concept (#2) that begins our analytic dissection of that whole into parts, from which we then perceive and select one or some of the parts revealed to us by our analysis. That partialized selection is then the *subcontext* (#3) that begins the semiprocess of synthesis, which leads us to a tertiary hypothesis, or

---

[7] Our logicians should compare this new relational conception to their own square of opposition, in either its Aristotelian or its Boolean form. But we won't bother doing this here, since the dynamic notion of ideational opposition presented by the Consideration Cycle supersedes those old static notions, which were limited conceptions when conceived because they were not psychologically defined.

Table A. Some Cardinal Terms and Quadrant Functions

Context	I	II	III	IV
REALITY				
State	Event	Essence	Response	Form
Processual Mode	Cause	Existence	Effect	Being
Causal Mode	Initial Cause	Analytic Cause	Synthetic Cause	Formal Cause
Relational Mode	Whole	One	Parts	All
Sources	Beginning	Conception	Formation	Birth
Systemic Direction	Inward	Backward	Outward	Forward
Graphic Direction	North/Up	East/Left	South/Down	West/Right
KNOWLEDGE				
Cardinal Idea	Complete Percept	Abstract Concept	Partial Percept	Concrete Concept
Systems Built	Theories/Plans	Structures/Symbols	Hypotheses/Fictions	Languages/Institutns.
Knowledge Form	Philosophy/Planning	Dissective Schemes	Science/Art/Theology	Education/Services
Education Form	Sources	Conventions	Subjects	Styles
Parts of Speech	Proper Nouns/Verbs	Nouns/Adjectives	Adverbs	Nouns/Gerunds
Knowledge Mode	Purpose	Method	Means	Ends
Knowl. Products	Essences/Principles	Dissections/Facts	Beliefs/Speculations	Forms/Decisions
Form of Proof	Affirmation	Verification	Substantiation	Justification
Arithmetic Mode	Subtraction	Division	Addition	Multiplication
REASONING				
Epistemic Premise	Realism	Rationalism	Empiricism	Formalism
Logical Type	Primary	Secondary	Tertiary	Quaternary
Reasoning Mode	Fundamental	Explicative	Evaluative	Formal
Vertical Function	Analysis	Analysis	Synthesis	Synthesis
Horizontal Func-	Reduction	Accretion	Accretion	Reduction
Reasoning Type	Analytic-Reductive	Analytic-Accretive	Synthetic-Accretive	Synthetic-Reductive
	Wholistic-Categorical	Wholistic-Symbolic	Partialistic-Symbolic	Partialistic-Categorical
Reasoning Purpose	Structure	Communication	Explanation	Execution
PSYCHOLOGIC				
Reality Orientation	Objective to Subjective	Subjective to Objective	Subjective to Objective	Objective to Subjective
Cognition Mode	Instinct	Insight	Intuition	Idealization
Conscious System	Will	Thought, Feeling	Feeling, Judgment	Power
Motive	Meaning	Organization	Efficiency	Style
Impressions	Realities	Abstractions	Illusions	Concretizations
Creative Products	Systems, Wholes	Symbols, Dissections	Needs, Classes	Forms, Methods
Focus	Wishes, Possibilities	Statements, Kinds	Desires, Hopes	Classes, Decisions
Drives	Survival, Control	Self, Pleasures	Passions, Morals	Status, Power
Avoids	Chaos, Old Ways	Order, Silence	Purpose, Theory	Analysis, Meaning
Pref'd Social Image	Dignified, Intense	Intelligent, Objective	Creative, Just	Conforming, Elite

the concrete concept (#4), from which we enter our quaternary reasoning and finally perceive a new but lesser whole event of our own construction (#1). Thus, *analysis* is reasoning from a specific whole to a specifically perceived part or set of parts, and *synthesis* is reasoning from there to a specific whole, one that is contingent on but different from the whole that yielded its part or parts.

As the synthetic semiprocess nears its conclusion, we reach the quaternary cognition that is best called an 'understanding'. This term is conventionally used to distinguish between the two main senses of the term 'knowledge'. One sense means a bit of data, a distinct fact or inference, and the other means our integration of all such bits into 'an understanding' of our subject, which is the broad sense Plato meant when he spoke of 'knowledge'. This understanding then provokes a *decision* that ends that turn of the Cycle.

Here is where we decide how to act relative to our selected context and selected subcontext, if we choose to act. If we do, that action is a new event that we may or may not consider further, in a new turn of the Cycle. We must have this personal understanding, such as it is, before we can decide on any act. We can act on our decision then or retain it for some time: that is, we can use it now or store it in memory as a personal power, which is our potential to perform an act in accordance with that understanding. We thus have two kinds of psychologic power: power in action and power in reserve, which can be likened to kinetic and potential energy.

In *Figure 2b* we see that the second axis, the quantitative axis of universality, divides our act of consideration into the semiprocesses of accretion and reduction. *Accretion* is the antecedent semiprocess by which we extend our abstract conception of a One to a hypothetical conception of an All relative to that One. *Reduction* is the consequent semiprocess by which we reduce that conception of an All until we again cognize a One. Each semiprocess is divided by a distinct perception of particularity, either the complete percept (#1) or the partial percept (#3).

These four semiprocesses are integrated as shown above in *Figure 3*, where they give us our technical terms for the four reasoning modes, or quadrants. Primary reasoning is *analytic-reductive* reasoning, secondary reasoning is *analytic-accretive* reasoning, tertiary reasoning is *synthetic-accretive* reasoning, and quaternary reasoning is *synthetic-reductive* reasoning.

This skeletal structure of the Cycle is plainly not all that we need in order to understand ourselves, but it suffices for our purposes in this and the next chapter. One of our goals in this chapter is to correctly analyze and classify, for the first time, all of our intellectual views and formal constructs. This is a large task, but it is manageable in a small space if we don't pursue it into the details of synthetic (scientific) reasoning. The new things we must know to objectively define and classify our reasoning biases and the ideologies we construct from them are the dynamics of the Cycle just discussed and one additional fact. This is that intellectuals always assume, with the concurrence of all who share their bias, that the cardinal idea that begins their most-preferred quadrant is the first and most fundamental cognition in all human reasoning.

The Consideration Cycle gives us two major new powers: the ability to see and judge the logical validity of an entire intellectual system, and the ability to compare two or more entire systems fundamentally. Traditionalists don't have these powers; they are limited to judging the truth and validity of the propositions that compose a system, which leads to the error of not seeing the forest for the trees. But with this new wholistic standard of human reasoning to guide us, we are not restricted to propositional logic as they are, and so no expressed ideology is beyond our ability to judge as a formal construct. Previously, we had to study an intellectual's entire system to find its flawed propositions one by one, but now we can tell whether that whole system is soundly conceived or not just by noting where its reasoning begins in the Cycle, which is usually clear from an author's introduction or stated scope. If the proposed system doesn't begin from primary reasoning, either the author's or someone else's, then it is not a realistic system and it is invalid regardless of its stated facts, internal coherence, or literary brilliance.

INTELLECTUAL SYSTEMS

Just as the term 'knowledge' means either mere data or an integrated understanding, so we must distinguish between a *knowledge system*, which is any combination of two or more related ideas in the same context, and an *intellectual system*, which yields whatever total understanding of a selected context we have. An intellectual system is an explicit and structured consideration of the real and whole event that is its context, and if it is valid it will reflect the entire logical process defined by the Consideration Cycle—not because the Cycle is beyond dispute, but because it is the only standard of logical completeness yet proposed.

An intellectual system can have only one analytic theory, but it can have as many synthetic constructs as it has perceivable and classifiable parts, or subcontexts. A *theory* is our explication of the first half of our natural reasoning cycle, the analytic half that refers back to the complete percept, or the selected context, and a *construct* is our explication of the second half of that cycle, the synthetic half that refers back to the partial percept, or the selected subcontext. A theory and a construct are opposite kinds of systems because a context and a subcontext derived from it are opposite kinds of references. An intellectual system consists of one theory plus multiple constructs, but it is not a philosophy, which must consist of at least four intellectual systems.

We use the term *theory* ambiguously, because after we develop a synthetic construct we can make it our narrowed context for a new act of consideration, where we analyze it and derive a set of principles that are universal solely to its narrower realm. We then call those derived principles a 'theory' even though they pertain to what was initially a construct. A theory is any set of principles that we have ordered logically in our secondary thought system, even if our context was born in our synthetic reasoning as a speculative tertiary notion, which is the case with any mystical or scientific 'theory'.

The unit conception of a theory is a *principle*, meaning an analytic proposition in universal terms that applies to the entire context and that will hold true in every synthetic construct within the initial context. The unit conception of a construct, and the direct opposite of a principle, is an *hypothesis*, which is a synthetic proposition in class terms that applies to a subcontext. Thus no hypothesis has any theoretical (universal-to-the-whole) significance. The assumption that it does is a common error of synthetic reasoning committed by both the tertiary hypothesists who create class terms (ideals) and the quaternary pragmatists who build formal constructs from those terms.

The validity of any reasoning we do therefore depends on our always knowing clearly which perceived real and whole event is our current context of reference, for otherwise we cannot keep track of the perceived parts and our plurality of hypotheses and constructs regarding them. This logical rule may seem too elemental to state, but it is routinely ignored by traditionalists, and that error causes what I call 'the fallacy of context shifting', which is to refer to more than one context (thing, event, object, subject) in the same line of reasoning. A common case of this is when in context X we speak of one of its subcontexts as such and also as the whole context Y that we can later make it in a reconsideration. But that is to shift to another context, or to abort our initial consideration and begin another one, one in which our initial logic no longer applies.

But we can freely shift from one subcontext to another in the same context, for choosing a different part of the same whole for synthetic reasoning doesn't violate our intellectual system's dynamic logic. Our theory of that context still applies. In the metaphysical context, every other subject is a subcontext, so if we have a metaphysical theory and remember throughout that our context is the Reality, then we can shift freely in considering all other subjects. This freedom to shift between subcontexts is why mathematics can be used in all scientific constructs, even though it has no function in the all-subsuming theory of metaphysics, which implies it and every other synthetic science, or language. But shifting our contexts, which is what we do also when we imagine a second kind of 'reality', violates our logic because it breaks our train of thought, or the sequence of the cyclic reasoning that is our logic.[8]

The only way we can resolve this kind of illogic, the contradictions between two or more synthetic constructs, is to shift our perspective to a higher level, to another whole event (context) that subsumes them all. This technique works because it raises the level of logic, so that we can see those conflicting constructs as sibling subcontexts rather than as the discrete whole contexts they were to us before. This is why the ultimate context, Reality, is the source of our universal logic. And of course we must reject the claim of our pluralists that there is no such ultimate standard because this denies that there is such an ultimate subsuming whole, or the Reality.

REASONING BIASES

We previously distinguished our intellectuals by their quadrantal preferences; that is, as theorists, analysts, hypothesists, and pragmatists. But this classification is sometimes imprecise because many people prefer two or even three reasoning modes about equally. To correct this

---

[8] It follows that when Gödel (1906-78) proposed his incompleteness theorems, which held basically that a *knowledge system* always has propositions that cannot be proved by its own axioms, this was not the universal condemnation of all systems that he and other formalists took it be. The dilemma his theorems posed is a synthetic dilemma pertaining only to artificial language constructs (like mathematics) derived from subcontexts, not to *intellectual systems* derived from whole contexts. Since his theorems denied the theories (from metaphysics to psychology) that implied his own science, he ignored the distinction between natural and explicated reasoning, and the fact that all of our language constructs are related by a natural theory that subsumes them and dictates their common logic. No metaphysical principle, such as one proposing that all systems whatsoever are unprovable, can be validly proposed through mathematics, because mathematics is a quaternary language system derived from metaphysics and its abstract terms.

we must ask not which *quadrant* is preferred, but which *cardinal idea* is the preferred beginning point of one's entire explicit reasoning. So, if two or three quadrants are preferred, then the dominating cardinal idea is the one that begins the first of those quadrants in their numerical order. This distinguishes our intellectuals not by their favored mode, but rather by their favored premise on epistemic priority, or on which cardinal idea comes first in our psychologic process. And this means that we have four fundamental perspectives on epistemic priority, not just the two epistemologies that are traditionally recognized: rationalism and empiricism.

Whichever bias one has, it is the most forceful psychologic impression for a hypothetical fourth of us, and the other three-fourths oppose that view of epistemic priority. But in spite of this broad disagreement, we each feel that our preferred way to begin our explicated reasoning cannot be doubted, and that the cardinal idea that we favor most is more fundamental than the other three. Subjective reasoners will then universalize this bias and insist that where they prefer to begin reasoning is where all humans begin it, and that any ideology or social construct that is not based on that priority premise must be rejected.

The two axes of the Cycle's reference plane define the broadest distinction possible in human reasoners: a *perceptualist* prefers to begin explicit reasoning at either pole of the qualitative axis of particularity, and a *conceptualist* prefers either pole of the quantitative axis of universality. The perceptualists divide into *wholists* who favor the complete percept and *partialists* who favor the partial percept, and the conceptualists divide into *dualists* who favor the abstract concept and *pluralists* who favor the concrete concept. In the epistemic context, the wholists are *realists*, the dualists are *rationalists*, the partialists are *empiricists*, and the pluralists are *formalists*. Our earlier distinctions among intellectuals (theorist, analyst, hypothesist, and pragmatist) remain useful, but they don't specify an epistemic perspective, which is the most fundamental aspect of any intellectual system or construct.

Since the Cycle defines all of those italicized words, their new meanings don't correspond exactly to their dictionary descriptions. For instance, traditionalists don't use 'formalism' in the epistemic context because they assume that pragmatism is not a position on epistemic priority. But it is, for if we habitually start our explicit reasoning at some point late in the Cycle, then that point is our position on epistemic priority whether we declare it to be such or not. So the term 'formalist' means a quaternary reasoner, or pragmatist, who assumes, usually without saying it, that our reasoning always begins from the concrete concept, or from the hypothetical class terms, ideals, language constructs, and rule systems that we form from it.

Our formal language constructs include those of speech, music, mathematics, logic, and moral or legal codes. In fact, *formalism* is the name Hilbert (1862-1943) gave to one of his mathematical constructs, and one academic rightly called that formalism "cousin" to the older view known as *nominalism*.[9] And we call our ancient propositional logic 'formal logic' because, like mathematics, it too is a cousin of nominalism, or a quaternary logic that pretends to be universal even though it is only a piece of our entire logic. Few logicians or mathematicians would propose that formal logic or mathematics is the beginning of all human reasoning, but they don't object when a nominalist makes that same claim for our language constructs in general.

But our definition of *realism* here differs even more from the traditional descriptions. Most traditionalists associate realism with empiricism or some form of conceptualism, but this is not so. Various academics have labeled as realism such views as Plato's rationalism, Aristotle's empirico-rationalism, the neoplatonism of Plotinus, Augustine, or Scotus, or some later form of rationalism or formalism. Some even speak of 'conceptual realism', which is a self-contradictory term because our conceptualists ignore reality. A *realist* is a monistic perceptualist who asserts the epistemic priority of the complete percept, our sole means of perceiving a distinct whole event, and so realists are quadrantally opposed to all conceptualists, both the rationalists who put abstract terms before reality and the formalists who put concrete terms before reality.

---

[9] This comment was by Steven T. Kuhn in his brief entry on formalism for *The Cambridge Dictionary of Philosophy* (Cambridge, Eng.: Cambridge University Press, 1995).

Having an idea is a real event, of course, but our concepts are not our only epistemic ideas, and if we begin our reasoning from either concept or from the nouns (abstract terms or class terms) that refer to it, we are denying our whole context, which we can only cognize through the complete percept. Our conceptualists therefore cannot be realists, and the quaternary formalists are even more unrealistic than the secondary rationalists, given where they start their explicit reasoning. *Figure 4* shows these relations as they occur in the Consideration Cycle.

These four opposing views on epistemic priority cause sharp conflicts in a society. Perceptualists and conceptualists function as if in different worlds, or dimensions, but the two kinds of each type, though directly opposed, have axially similar views. That is, realists and empiricists share the perceptualist's bias for natural and qualitative reasoning, and rationalists and formalists share the conceptualist's bias for explicated and quantitative reasoning.

But the 90° relation between any perceptualist and any conceptualist causes hostilities that are not equally severe on both sides. A general rule here, which holds in three of the four cases, is that we are more hostile to our antecedent opposites than to our consequent opposites. This is so because if the epistemic priority premise of our antecedent opposites is correct, then ours is flatly refuted, but if ours is correct, then that of our consequent opposites is not entirely objectionable to us because it follows logically from ours.

For instance, realists oppose their consequent opposites, the rationalists, for arguing that all human reasoning begins from the terms, or innate 'ideas', that refer to the abstract concept, but they tolerate this error because, by reasoning from the complete percept, they can define the abstract terms that rationalists (and hence empiricists and formalists) cannot define. But realists strongly oppose their antecedent opposites, the formalists, who argue that all meaningful human reasoning begins from the quaternary formal constructs that are built by academics, such as linguists, mathematicians, formal logicians, jurists, religionists, and scientists. They consider this priority premise absurd because it argues that our last cardinal idea comes first, and because it implies that the traditional language constructs previously created by humans cannot now be improved by humans—or, more broadly, that creativity itself is unnecessary and meaningless.

Similarly, rationalists tolerate empiricists but not realists, and empiricists tolerate formalists but not rationalists. This explains why the historical debates between empiricists and rationalists were more heatedly argued by the empiricists than by the rationalists.

The formalists are the exception to this rule, since they are sharply divided from their consequent opposites, the realists, by the complete percept, which ends one act of consideration and begins another. So formalists are not tolerant of any other kind of intellectual, which is why they are collectivistic and form into tight cliques related to their profession or academic specialty. They oppose their antecedent opposites, the empiricists, because if the partial percept comes first, then so do subjective passions, needs, and moral judgments, which are the antithesis of their supposedly objective class terms, language constructs, and rule systems. But they clash even more with their consequent opposites, the realists, because they arrogantly believe that their own total understanding in a context precludes any further consideration of it. And yet realists won't accept their constructs as dogma, or as 'final' understandings, since these are offered on no better authority than the arbitrary opinion of some formalist clique in, say, government, religion, science, academia, commerce, the military, or the media.

In other words, realists (primary reasoners) are naturally inclined to start a new reasoning cycle with every event that they see as important enough to consider. They instinctively say, "I must think this out for myself," and if the event is the proposal of a formalist's construct, their reasoning about that 'final' understanding is a critical reevaluation of it, starting from its first premises. And this valid approach usually results in the denial of the proposed construct, for if formalists devised it, it cannot be a conceptually complete system. Needless to say, this critical reaction by realists, this refusal to presume what all the 'experts' presume, frustrates our formalists—just because, as Dostoyevsky observed, they are easy in their minds and are absolutely sure of themselves, in spite of the limitations of their arbitrarily truncated reasoning.

Figure 4. Natural Reasoning

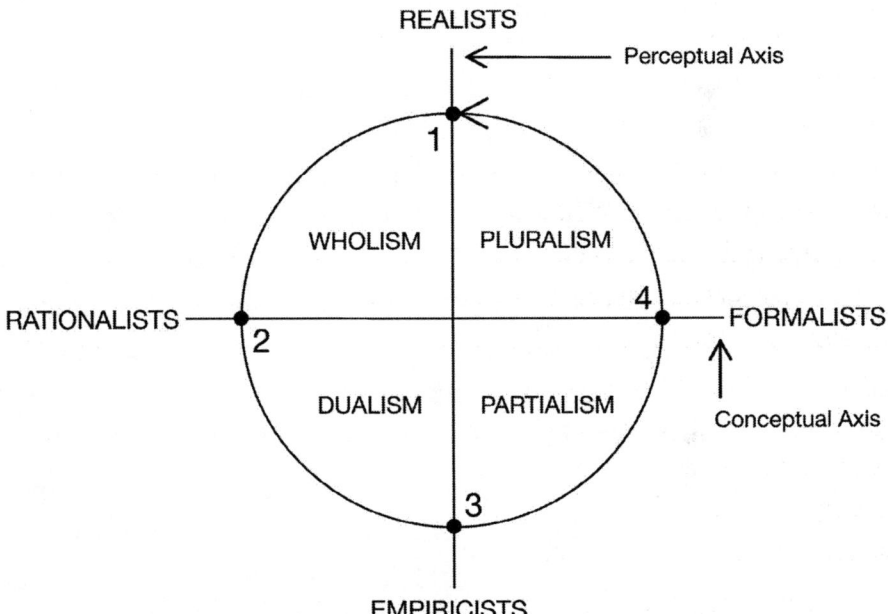

1 = Complete Percept; 2 = Abstract Concept; 3 = Partial Percept; 4 = Concrete Concept

This epistemic fact, that our consideration begins anew each time we cognize the complete percept, has the important social consequence that the clash between realists and formalists (or theorists and pragmatists) is the sharpest of all conflicts, intellectually or otherwise. It is the conflict of primary with quaternary reasoning, of creative generation with conformity (if not plagiarism), of revolution with tradition, and of progressivism with conservatism.

The Priority Controversy

People rarely realize that their nonmaterial arguments are at root arguments over epistemic priority. This is unfortunate, for if they saw this and agreed on the correct view, their ideologic disputes could be resolved naturally and logically, without hatred or wars. Some intellectuals have argued the wholistic position of realism before, but not in a way that could win out over empiricism and the two forms of conceptualism, which are characteristic of academic reasoning. So traditional epistemologists ignored realism, the natural solution to the problem of epistemic priority, just as they had overlooked two of our four cardinal ideas.

We can liken the disputants on epistemic priority to four men standing on a different corner of a square, each considering his corner to be the most important one, since from his angle it comes first in the process. But the Cycle changes this, for now the disputants must admit that there are four corners, or four cardinal points at which the very direction of our reasoning in space—forwards, backwards, inward, or outward—is changed. Now they must account for all four views, show the logical relation of each one to the others, and prove that their favored cardinal idea does come first in our reasoning process. But then they will find it difficult to disprove the epistemic position of realism, which is that perception comes before conception, and that we must perceive a particular whole before we can perceive any of its particular parts.

There is little need to pursue the historical debate on epistemic priority here, because it pertains almost entirely to rationalism and empiricism, neither of which is defended by sensible intellectuals today. For decades now, intellectuals have refused to argue for the priority premise of either view, because modern-era intellectuals from Hume (1711-1776) to the mid-twentieth century exposed whatever rationalistic or empiristic absurdities had not already been exposed in the classic era. But formalism escaped this fatal criticism because traditionalists didn't see that it was a position on epistemic priority. So, in the late nineteenth century, formalism (pragmatism) became the last bulwark of traditional epistemic error, the final wall that all traditionalists who wished to maintain their arealism, even the defeated rationalists and empiricists, had to defend.

But while rationalism and empiricism are dead in the intellectual arena, they are still alive in the public's mind as old rationalizations for illogical reasoning, so let me explain their errors briefly before we consider the fatal flaws of formalism and the truths of realism.

Rationalism. Epistemic rationalism was discredited by the end of the classic era (1516-1762), and consequently the errors of empiricism characterized the modern era. Many views arose in the modern era that were called 'rationalism' or 'rationalistic', but only because they opposed empiricism, not because they defended rationalism's priority premise, which is the claim that our reasoning process begins from certain 'concepts' that we all have in us at birth.

The classic-era rationalists saw that the empiricists' priority premise was wrong; that is, they knew that sense data cannot be the beginning of our reasoning process because, unless these come to us in some context, they will be nothing but meaningless 'static' to us. So they tried to explain how we get that whole context first, and the best they could do in their time was their weak notion of innate ideas, which has three main errors.

First, their proposal that our reasoning begins with a set of 'concepts' that are somehow known to us *a priori* (meaning innately, or without experience) contradictorily proposes that we can have a psychologic *cognition* (idea) that is not derived from our psychologic functioning, or mental experiences. This claim may seem reasonable to theists, who can accept the mystical tertiary notion of a god-being that puts these prêt-àporter 'cognitions' into us before birth, but nontheists can't accept it because it proposes a nonpsychologic state in us all—in effect a mystical realm where undefinitions dwell—that denies any need to causatively define these 'ideas'. The rationalists thus sidestepped the epistemic issue of how we humans reason to achieve our cognitions of universality or nothingness. And they did so because their primary reasoning, which causes all of our abstract terms, impressed them with little conscious force, while the abstract concept it yields was strongly impressed on their consciousness. "I think, therefore I am," the rationalist and dualist Descartes proclaimed, a statement that merely affirms that he started his own explicit reasoning at the abstract concept (#2), which begins our psychologic *thought* system and to which our universal term *existence* refers.

Second, they illustrated these innate 'ideas' with arbitrary shortlists of concept terms. But they never defined those terms; nor did they give us an objective explanation of why each term on their varying lists belongs there of necessity, of how we cognize the epistemic ideas to which those terms refer, or of how (other than being innate) these universal terms differ from the synthetic class terms that refer to the concrete concept.

Third, they spoke of innate epistemic 'ideas' that are 'universals' or 'concepts'. Their error here, common in speech even today, was to confuse our many abstract *terms* with the one epistemic *idea* to which all such terms refer, *the* abstract concept. Their notion of innate *ideas* thus makes no reference to a cognition, since no epistemic idea can compose a plurality.

Rationalists are conceptualists, so their epistemic proposals are all about our symbols, or terms, and not about objective realities or the psychologic referents of our terms. Every shortlist of innate 'concepts' that they offered is only a list of terms that refer to a concept, usually the abstract concept but sometimes the concrete concept. So rationalism is not an epistemology at all, since it doesn't explain our reasoning, it explains how we don't reason, for it holds that there is a mystical realm within us where some key 'concepts' exist with no reasoning process to cause them. But even if we grant that what they mean by a word on their list is its idea-referent, the epistemic problem is not how to describe that kind of idea with a list of words, it is how to explain its psychologic cause as a cognition. Conceptualists (rationalists and formalists) are biased in favor of explicated reasoning, so they can't propose an epistemology, because epistemic issues don't pertain to our symbols or languages; they pertain to our natural reasoning, or to the psychologic functioning that causes all of our ideas and defines all of our terms.

Empiricism. Tertiary empiricists rejected the secondary rationalist's notion of innate ideas by proposing the priority of sense 'perceptions'. The *Random House Dictionary of the English Language*, Second Edition, Unabridged (New York: Random House Inc., 1987) describes a *perception* as "1. the act or faculty of apprehending by means of the senses or of the mind; cognition; understanding. 2. immediate or intuitive recognition or appreciation..."

This description attempts definition by proposing the causes of a perception, such as the senses, 'the mind', or our 'intuition'. But the empiricists propose instead that our five sense faculties are our only faculties of perception, or particular cognition, while the mind produces only conceptions; specifically, the synthetic class concept. A realist, however, holds that our five sense faculties cannot function unless some non-sensual faculties function first, and that these faculties include our ability to *perceive* (not *conceive*) wholeness, or events.

We can say that the cause of a percept or concept is either the physiological faculties that provoke that cognition in us or the reasoning process with which we deduce or induce it. But while the issue of which physical faculties provoke our cognitions is medically important, at present it can tell us nothing about the epistemic issues of what those cognitions are and how we process them in our reasoning. Our sense faculties play a role in provoking some cognitions, mainly our intermediate ideas, which are partly general and partly specific ideas. But other than leading us to our cardinal ideas, they do not cause any of these. Our two concepts are caused by what we vaguely describe as our non-sensual 'mental' faculties, and our two percepts are caused by some other mental faculties, such as the 'intuitive' faculties that physiologists have not yet identified but that in any case are not sensual.

Empiricists are correct to oppose conceptualism, but they make these incorrect assumptions: (1) that our percepts are caused solely by our sense faculties, (2) that all of our reasoning begins from our perception of the parts of a whole, and (3) that our generalized cognitions are achieved solely by the accretive synthesis of parts, and never by the reductive analysis of wholes. Empiricists seldom state the second assumption, but it is implied by the fact that our senses cannot inform us of wholeness. Locke disagreed with Aristotle on the third assumption, but his commitment to the first two prevented him from proposing that we have a second concept.

The Consideration Cycle, on the other hand, holds that our reasoning begins from our perception of a whole event, or our awareness that *something has happened*, though at the first instant we don't know *what* has happened, and that we begin to know this 'what' not through the synthesis of discrete sense perceptions, but rather through the analysis of that whole event.

The empiricists prevailed over the rationalists early in the modern era mainly because the best intellectuals of that time rejected mystical theism, which led them to reject the mystical notion of innate 'ideas' that were not caused by earthly reasoning and to accept the empiricists' simplistic notion that our reasoning process begins from tangible sense data. But the empiricists' could not explain how sense data, which can only inform us of the parts of a whole, can also inform us of *wholeness*, a particular cognition that is indispensable to our reasoning. Sense data have no such power, and indeed many tests have proven that our senses can and often do deceive us as to our real and whole situation. We can't imagine an instance where, with no involvement of our 'mental' or 'intuitive' faculties, sense data can inform us of wholeness, so it is reasonable to assume that the most our senses can do to inform us of real and whole events is, in some cases, to trigger the nonsensual faculties that perform this function. In all other cases, meaning the imagined events that are either (a) fictional or (b) real but beyond the range of our senses, the faculties by which we perceive whole events function with no direct sense stimulations.

The empiricists overlooked both the abstract concept (#2) and the complete percept (#1). And yet this first cognition of particularity is our most important epistemic idea, for we use it to select a specific whole context, which is the object of reference of all the analysis and synthesis that we do later in that context. Also, every living thing must share at least this one cardinal cognition with us; that is, since all living things must respond to changes in their outer and inner environments, they must be able to perceive events, or the fact that something has happened. But our sense faculties by themselves can't perceive events, and the same may be so of our so-called 'mental' faculties also. The main function of the senses in our psychologic process is the secondary function of telling us something about the parts of a whole event—after we perceive that whole through the complete percept, conceive its defining essence through the abstract concept, and are ready to divide it into its parts, which is the true role of our senses.

Finally, note that empiricists argue in two ways. Some call themselves 'empiricists' and defend the empiristic premises, but most of them don't mention those discredited premises. Instead, they propose them indirectly, with some new class name that means 'empiricism' but doesn't say it; a name that often includes the term 'realism'. These reluctant empiricists say only that our reasoning begins 'from experience', but their arguments show that what that they mean by this is the experience of the senses in giving us knowledge of the parts of a whole event.

Experience is an extraordinarily vague term to use in an epistemic discussion, because every cognition we have is an experience. Their motto, 'experience comes first', thus avoids every epistemic issue except their intention to deny the proposal of innate ideas by the rationalists. It doesn't explain why our first perceptual experience must be of waves of sense data pertaining to the parts of a whole event rather than our direct perception of that whole itself, and it does not establish empiricism positively, since it doesn't distinguish an empiricist from a conceptualist, let alone from a realist who puts our perception of a whole before our perception of its parts.

Formalism. With rationalism dead, empiricism was belatedly laid to rest late in the modern era's second quadrant (1822-1912) when some intellectuals, impressed by the great strides made then in mathematics, physics, logic, and other sciences, concluded that philosophy was dead, that it had never given us a valid epistemology, or theory of reasoning, and that in any case we didn't need one. From this negativism, most intellectuals then embraced formalism, or pragmatism, which basically holds that it is a waste of time to look beneath the surface of things as philosophers do, and that we should instead just focus on our existing linguistic constructs. We must understand this error fully, for it is the worst one an intellectual can make and we are all suffering greatly from its dominance in the world today.

As conceptualists, formalists make much of our words and other symbols, but only as these are formed into language constructs. They therefore try to explain everything through the ex post facto study of speech, mathematics, logic, scientific languages, moral codes, legal systems, and other formal knowledge systems. But this is to put the cart before the horse, which in this case is the psychologic process that gives all of our symbols and languages their meaning. And to defend this inverted view of our reasoning, formalists must use convoluted technical arguments that make the other three epistemic positions seem simplistic by comparison.

For one thing, they propose all forms of *scientism*, meaning ideologies that see science not as the derivative reasoning that it is, but rather as our prior and highest form of knowledge. A good example is *phenomenology*, the construct of Husserl (1859-1938), who began as a logician and mathematician. Husserl's rationalization for ignoring the root epistemic dilemmas, basically by 'bracketing' them and focusing on pragmatic issues instead, produced an epistemic pluralism that was then used by gestalt psychologists to explain our global perceptions through twisted quaternary reasoning rather than direct primary reasoning.[10]

---

[10] This was illustrated by the gestalt psychologist Wolfgang Köhler in his *The Place of Value in a World of Facts* (New York: Liveright Publishing Company, 1938). Reflecting any formalist's need to refute empiricism, he offered an excellent criticism of 'the empirical method' in his first chapter, *The Case Against Science*. But then he tried, unsuccessfully, to defend our primary wholistic reasoning, the essence of gestalt psychology, through the evasive quaternary arguments of phenomenology.

Realism holds that the source of all our reasoning is our perception of wholeness, but the other epistemic views assume that we only know wholeness as allness. Rationalists may equivocate on this empiristic view, but formalists embrace it because it lets them propose that our language constructs, which begin from the concrete concept (the All) and its class terms, are the source of all human reasoning.

A tight chain of formalistic error that spanned three psychologic eras was forged by four famous nominalists: Occam (c.1285-1349), Luther (1483-1546), Hobbes (1588-1679), and Wittgenstein (1889-1951). Each, in the academic fashion of his time, opposed realism, rationalism, and empiricism. This is not easy to do through quaternary reasoning, for to defend their conceptualist view on epistemic priority, formalists must argue that our natural reasoning is irrelevant, and that no reasoning is 'meaningful' until it has been formally explicated. One must first deny our natural reasoning before one can argue that all human reasoning begins with our explicated reasoning, or existing formal constructs, and not with our psychologic cognitions.

This formalist premise was indirectly advanced by the American pragmatists, headed by Peirce (1839-1914), James (1842-1910), and Dewey (1859-1952), who soon had prominent supporters in Britain and elsewhere. It has been argued, and can hardly be refuted today, that Dewey's pragmatism effectively destroyed public education in America. Anyway, the first principle of their pragmatism is the common practical view that no reasoning or conception is important unless it is useful; that is, unless it has what the academic psychologist James called a "cash value," meaning a practical function. Not surprisingly, most twentieth-century academics enthusiastically accepted this claim, even though it proposes no objective way, other than by a consensus of academics, to know what is or is not intellectually meaningful.

This claim that only our quaternary (pragmatic) reasoning has 'cash value' is in one sense true and in another sense absurd. It is true to say that our practical goals are proximately furthered by our explicated constructs, for that is their purpose. But it is absurd for formalists to claim, as they do, that the psychologic causes of our languages are meaningless, for this means that our language constructs are meaningless too. We don't suddenly have a construct and then acquire a practical goal with it. We determine that goal before we build any formal construct, in the prior reasoning that yields our primary will intentions, secondary thoughts, and tertiary desires and beliefs. We are not so imbecilic that we would build any tangible construct, of wood or words, with no motive for doing so, and every old construct has motives and duties that we of our time played no part in deciding. What else can a proposition's practical 'cash value' be but the goal that one intends to achieve by proposing it? But a language construct is not an intention, though as a means to a specific goal it synthesizes prior intentions. So, whence its integrated intentions, why do they vary among us, and which are unacceptable because they are unrealistic, illogical, or immoral? These are the real issues that pragmatists never address.

Nothing can have any kind of value to us, not even a cash value, unless we have already *evaluated* it in the preformal psychologic functioning that our formalists deny. Our values are products of our subjective tertiary reasoning; they don't arise out of nothing in our objective quaternary reasoning. So, if 'cash value' is important, then the psychologic process by which we determine that value is even more important, and therefore formalists, who deny that prior process of evaluation, are not reasoning validly. In our politics, this denial of the first three-fourths of our natural reasoning makes the 'cash value' perspective of our formalists excessively bureaucratic, opportunistic, traditionalistic, narrow-minded, collectivistic, and conservative.

To argue their case, formalists must shift the discussion away from the primary issues of reality and theory, the secondary issue of how we reason, and the tertiary issue of how we give our class terms intention and value (or meaning), to the quaternary issue of our languages as preexisting traditions. That done, they then collectively assume that the meaningfulness of any practical reasoning can be established or disproven simply by showing that most members of their own academic or practical clique agree with their subjective opinion on this valuation.

In different contexts, our formalists' concrete-conceptualism is described as nominalistic, pragmatic, academic, linguistic, religious, bureaucratic, pluralistic, or collectivistic reasoning. But it is always derived from the tertiary reasoners who create its source rationalizations, or its nouned ideals. A good historical example is Luther, the German Augustinian monk, theologian, and religionist. When the scholastic era's fourth quadrant (1479-1516) ended, along with the period described as the 'Renaissance', there was no German language as such; there were only disparate German dialects. Luther, an elitist conservative by my system, is credited with integrating these dialects into the modern German language, but in the process he also endowed it with his own prejudices, idealism, religionism, elitism, and maleficent political goals—which were directed broadly against the common people and particularly against papists, Jews, and other 'infidels'.

Seeing Luther as their common linguistic source helps explain the long chain of confused German-speaking idealists and formalists of the classic and modern eras, including the German Marx and the Austrian Hitler, who were both rightists and political formalists. It is relevant that Luther, like the Austrian Wittgenstein of the twentieth century who also put language before human reasoning, admired the work of Occam, the English Franciscan theologian who after his excommunication fled to Munich and worked there for years until his death in 1349.

The work of theological formalists such as Augustine, Aquinas, Luther, and Calvin shows us that quaternary religious corporations are widely accepted by the public mainly because the fundamental illogic of theism can be so easily disguised by a religionist's language constructs. This gives us another, a truer, meaning to the New Testament's claim (John 1:1), "In the beginning was the Word...and the Word was God." Any religion is an instance of formalism and its characteristic denial of complete reasoning. This is why a religion is all words and other symbols, an elaborate construct of formal language and ritual with only one real meaning: its political goal, or 'cash value'. As realists see it, and as impartial historical works confirm with innumerable examples, a religious corporation does nothing for humanity but bring it destructive illusions and wars, while it enriches itself at the people's expense in the hope of doing this to them forever. For instance, the entire history of the papacy shows only a struggle among petty politicians who, in their specialist language, were only bickering for more wealth and power.

The Cycle distinguishes between tertiary *additive* reasoning and quaternary *reductive* (or integrative) reasoning, and accordingly our quaternary formalists are much concerned with issues of economy, which to their disgust our additive rationalists and empiricists ignore. To support their call for linguistic economy they often cite *Occam's razor*, a maxim that was not original to him and that all professional editors observe anyway. It holds that we should not unnecessarily increase the number of things needed to explain something. This sounds good since superfluity hinders understanding, but in fact they use it to rationalize their claims that some cases of necessary reasoning are unnecessary. This 'razor' is like the sword that the pragmatist Alexander (356-323 BCE) used to chop the Gordian knot in half. Such blades, real or symbolic, are dear to the heart of all pragmatists, who say we must use them to economize in our reasoning, but who use them instead to chop off all of the prior fundamental reasoning that they prefer not to do and to rationalize their denial of others' judgments and needs.

But the Cycle shows that realists (primary reasoners) are even more economy minded than formalists, since they oppose all waste, including that which formalists accept without qualms—such as irrational traditions, needlessly convoluted intellectual and bureaucratic constructs, and the destruction of the earth and its living inhabitants.

The integrative process of our quaternary reasoning produces a final understanding that, when explicated as a construct, is what we mean by 'an ideology'. It is a structured set of hypotheses that supports a pragmatic purpose, or 'cash value', that is always a political (power) end. So, by *ideology* we always mean a political construct, but this can be any construct from a formalist's knowledge system that has no foundation in prior reasoning to a realist's intellectual system that does. An ideology is the power part, the political part, of any intellectual system, whether it is a complete system by a realist (theorist) or an incomplete system by a formalist.

If we apply our pragmatists' notion of 'cash value' to their proposals, we must look for the motive behind their truncated ideologies, and we find one or both of these 'bottom-line' motives in every case: (1) the political or material goal of denying the needs of others, and (2) the moral or intellectual goal of denying the judgments of others, meaning classes of people other than their own class. Class prejudices are inherent to the ideologies of all pragmatists, because in denying the three reasoning modes that precede their quaternary mode, they also deny what makes people unique as individuals. As we see plainly in the cases of Luther, Marx, and Hitler, this is the psychologic cause of all class prejudices. Formalists simply don't see individuals, because their quaternary reasoning begins from tertiary class terms, and their compulsion to economize then leads them to deny the needs of entire classes of people and to turn a deaf ear to any judgments (evaluations) proposed by others in support of those class needs.

People in a rush, which includes pragmatists, always deny others' needs and judgments. Our formalists deny not only the deeper intellectual dilemmas that they refuse to confront, but also any moral judgments by themselves or others that obstruct achievement of their 'bottom line', which is always political control. One must deny all moral reasoning somehow before one can dare to say to another person, "I can take anything that I want to take from you," or "In these circumstances, the needs of your class are irrelevant, but the needs of my class are not."

Formalists are men or women of action, in Dostoyevsky's sense, and they are linguistically rather than realistically oriented. A *formalist* is any intellectual who denies the three prior modes of reasoning that yield our languages, and a *nominalist* is any formalist who studies language itself and then universalizes that quaternary study into a rationalization for those denials. So formalists are not necessarily nominalists, but they are when they make the epistemic claim that all of our reasoning is based on language or on language constructs such as any sacred text, bible, or constitution. Nominalists deny that we need to interpose the 'superfluous' notion of a psychologic process to define our terms, and positively they claim that we can just skip (bracket) that middle stage of reference and jump right to our terms' final referents in external reality.

But the flaw in this argument is evident. Our linguistic process has three main stages: our words (symbols) refer back to our psychologic process (or internal reality) which can refer back to external reality. Nominalists truncate this to remove the middle step, our psychologic process, thereby denying the internal reality of all individuals, including their needs and judgments. As they see it, by a process they have never explained, our words only refer back to external reality. This is why their constructs are nonhuman—or materialistic, bureaucratic, conservative, and cold—and why they only reason about people in intentionally unsympathetic class terms.

By the end of the classic era, most intellectuals were empiricists. Then, as the modern era advanced, they came to realize, belatedly, that the criticisms of empiricism by Hume could not be overcome, so they raced to embrace conceptualistic formalism and its pluralism. This gave us many negativistic constructs, such as the various forms of 'positivism' and pseudorealism, variants of Kantian or Hegelian idealism, nihilism, scientism, pragmatism, phenomenology, and existentialism, all of which led finally, in the mid-twentieth century, to the resuscitation of Occam's nominalism by Wittgenstein. As our academic formalists saw it, this was the *coup de grace* that allowed them to declare philosophy dead, which in turn prepared the way for the modern era's highly pragmatic, or theoryless, fourth quadrant (1971-2008).

This is why our intellectual world today consists almost entirely of the work of uncreative academic formalists, which in turn is why, as we say, we are going to hell in a hand basket. Our formalistic academics claim that we should not even try to understand our natural reasoning, but should instead rely blindly on our past failures, or the traditional languages and explanations that they consider 'good enough for all practical purposes'. They tell us not to reason deeply, but to trust naïvely in the plurality of our disconnected linguistic, mathematical, logical, scientific, academic, theistic, artistic, legal, economic, commercial, governmental, and other language constructs, constructs in which even simple-minded people can become experts by mere memorization and literal application, which is the first purpose of formal education today.

So their advice to us all is to become formalists like them. We too should see people in class terms only and forget about reality, human nature, and the common needs of all humans. We too should use the fallacious traditional constructs as our guides in the supposedly disparate things in our lives, without questioning how these enslave us. We too should have no hope for a much-improved world in the future. And we too should ignore the fact that their reasoning perspective has caused the ersatz politics that is being suffered by every living thing in the world today. It is formalists who rationalize political theft and oppression, and they do this with 'sacred' texts or truncated ideologies that are supported only by a broad academic consensus or conspiracy.

Realism. The only natural position on epistemic priority is realism. It has already been defined here as an epistemic perspective, and in the chapters that follow we will see its meaning in its metaphysical, psychologic, and political senses. But this is a good point to make two comparative observations about it, the first ideologic and the other psychologic.

An ideology is not distinguished by the 'ism' suffix on its name, but only by the fact that it is a quaternary language construct, which necessarily has a political motive and is based on class terms and relative hypotheses. And since every ideology is a political program, the term 'political ideology' is redundant. Epistemically, an explicated ideology corresponds to the penultimate cognition in the Cycle, which is the integrated understanding, or potential power, that precedes a concluding decision and that is only sound if its construction began in primary reasoning. It follows that only a realist's ideology merits consideration, and that this wholistic ideology will be a form of *progressivism*, the opposite of formalistic *conservatism*.

The Cycle shows us what motivates our realists psychologically. Since they begin their explicit reasoning from real and whole events, they are our explorers and analysts of natural, social, political, intellectual, or psychologic events. If they have the requisite intellectual inclination and abilities, they will concern themselves with the ideologies of others in which they were educated. But then they will begin a reductive analysis of those old constructs, and will deny any traditional ideology that conflicts with what they personally will to be so in life.

Being primary reasoners, realists are more consciously aware than other people are of their own *will*, which I propose later as the first of the Cycle's five psychologic systems, so they understand that their purpose as theorists is to affirm or deny events according to what they will to be so, on the whole. If they see elemental flaws in any ideology, and they are best at seeing these, they will deny that construct and the reasoning that led to it. Much of their intellectual effort is therefore spent trying to determine which of the formal constructs they encountered in their schooling are the most fundamental and which should be affirmed or denied, on the whole. If they find that they must deny a major traditional system, they may make it their goal in life to construct their own such system, one that overcomes the old system's failures. And that is why we have both philosophic realism and political progressivism.

Natural versus Explicated Reasoning

Our symbols and language constructs benefit us in many ways, but our failure to understand their psychologic origin has harmed us greatly. As we humans developed, those symbolic constructs came to be seen, excessively so by those with much formal education, as more important than our natural reasoning, and as a result human society became increasingly less realistic and humanistic than it was in times that were more primitive, or less explicative.

Indeed, the main reason why every 'civilized' social construct becomes a totalitarian construct is psychologic, and basically it is that when we reason through symbols or a language construct, we must detach our reasoning from reality and our own nature. Any form of explicated reasoning—such as social codes, literature, mathematics, music, graphics, sculpting, science, technology, and so on—is artificial, not in spite of its tangible form, but because of it. So if we wish to be realists, we must keep this distinction between our natural and explicated reasoning in our minds, and never let our preoccupation with the former, our languages, lead us to denigrate the latter, our common logic.

For instance, our states will never be humanistic or sane until their only absolute ruler is our natural human logic, to which even their constitutions must be subordinated. But so long as the final authorities of our institutions are nothing but sets of empty (undefined) words—as are our present constitutions, legal codes, linguistic references, encyclopedias, bibles, and other sacred texts—we may be sure that our rulers will be quaternary reasoners who are more robotic than human, and so won't hesitate to commit or accept any imaginable terror.

Chapter 3. Reality

METAPHYSICS

The first of all external subjects is Reality, and *a metaphysics* is a theory of Reality. One reference says that metaphysics is "the philosophical study whose object is to determine the real nature of things" and that, "although it has been subjected to many criticisms, it is presented by metaphysicians as the most fundamental and most comprehensive of inquiries, inasmuch as it is concerned with reality as a whole."[1]

By the ancient description of the term—the study of first causes—any mystic or pluralist could propose a metaphysics, but our definition lacks that vagueness because we have defined a theory and have observed that there is only one Reality that subsumes all subevents. The Consideration Cycle tells us that a theory of that Whole must be analytic-reductive reasoning, by which we reduce it to its fundamental universal principles, the set of which is our metaphysics.

Traditionalists confuse metaphysics with either mysticism, mainly theism, or with science, mainly cosmology or physics. Logically, this is to confuse primary (analytic-reductive) reasoning with its opposite, tertiary (synthetic-accretive) reasoning. But theism is not about Reality, if by this we mean an external event; its sole concern is a narrow set of internal psychologic events, or fictions. And the sciences of cosmology and physics are each concerned with a narrowed set of external realities, so the 'principles' of those sciences pertain not to all events whatsoever, but only to observable external events.

As realists, then, we will reject tertiary mysticism and won't confuse a primary metaphysical proposition with a tertiary proposition on cosmology

---

[1] "Metaphysics," Encyclopædia Britannica, from the *Encyclopædia Britannica Ultimate Reference Suite 2004 DVD.* Copyright © 1994-2003 Encyclopædia Britannica, Inc. May 30, 2003.

or physics. Metaphysical principles are not scientific hypotheses derived from our microcosmic or macrocosmic observations; they are logical propositions derived from our reasoning about Reality, before we make any external observations. All scientists do some universal primary reasoning before observing anything, but they don't explicate it, and that omission is what a metaphysics corrects.

Except on epistemic priority, primary and tertiary reasoners are not in competition, because their opposite kinds of propositions—analytic principles and synthetic hypotheses—complement each other in our reasoning process. We can say that a scientific hypothesis is flawed when it doesn't follow from sound universal principles, and that a metaphysical principle is flawed when it fails to imply scientifically verified hypotheses. And since sound metaphysical principles imply all language constructs, including mathematics, the only true tests of a metaphysics are that it denies all arealistic reasoning and implies all substantiated hypotheses. But it is never proposed as a substitute for the tertiary or quaternary work of scientists.

A metaphysics is wholistic, but a science is partialistic, which is why scientific languages are logically disconnected. This poses a communication problem for us here, since traditionalist readers, whether specialists or not, will take the key terms of our metaphysics to mean only what they are said to mean by the academics who claim responsibility for the sciences involved. But a theory of Reality cannot be expressed in their partialistic terms, so I say again that to understand Reality and its parts in spite of academic fields, we need a generic natural language, one that has priority over all synthetic terminologies.

So here our goal is not to develop competence in any of our specialists' languages, but rather to surpass the incompleteness of their class-based, tertiary reasoning. What we wish to express is an all-subsuming theory of Reality that, while it is not incompatible with any proven scientific facts, yields our first structurally complete explanation of human reasoning. Though the standard of reasoning that results is derived from our metaphysics, it is a tertiary hypothesis limited to the class of all humans, or in its elemental dynamics to the class of all living things on earth. Still, any standard so derived will define the one logic that rules all of our synthetic constructs, including our sciences, political structures, and languages.

A metaphysics is not disproven merely because contemporary scientists disagree with it, and those who try to judge it by their standards are seeing that theory as being just another partialized scientific construct, which it is not. A theory's first test is its internal consistency as a set of principles; after that, the only true test of a metaphysical theory is a plurality of tests—namely, whether it implies every sound hypothesis and practical construct we know. In the contexts of this work, that second test will be whether or not our metaphysics correctly explains how all humans reason, and hence how our various psychologic perspectives and dispositions differ. But then others must also test it by how well it implies the synthetic constructs that I know little about or don't consider here. But if some scientists then think that one of these metaphysical principles conflicts with the latest findings of their specialty, they should first ask if this is just a linguistic problem, for it may be that it could be restated in narrower terms to fit their specialty's more limited theory. For instance, restating our fifth metaphysical principle in the narrower class terms of physics can yield Einstein's proposition (which he mistakenly called an 'axiom') that "the laws of physics are the same in any inertial frame of reference."

Reality defines the natural Law of all subcontexts, so it defines their common logic before we give each subcontext its own relative (contingent, internal) logic with our descriptive terms and language rules. But to understand Reality, we must first conceive and state its universal principles, which will compose the theory that is the foundation of our common logic and the still largely undeveloped generic language that results from it. And the Cycle tells us that we need only five universal principles as the fundamental divisions of any complete theory, though each has deducible corollaries, most of which are not relevant for our purposes here.

As an overview before we consider them in turn, here are my five metaphysical principles, in the sequence that the Cycle dictates as their natural and necessary (logical) relation. I have given each a generic name to guide others in creating a complete theory for any narrower context.

As we discuss each principle, you will see that it follows with more certainty than the one before it, which implies it. But this does not mean, as traditionalists might assume, that the first principle is an unproven axiom. On the contrary, it is proven by the fact that we humans cannot do or say anything except through this common perception of the Whole of Everything. And no matter how one may express a denial of that perception, it is presupposed in that proposition anyway.

Occurrence: Reality is the whole event.

Abstraction: Any subevent of Reality is a motion system.

Dimensionality: Any motion system consists of particles in helical motion.

Displacement: Any motion system shall be displaced.

Correspondence: Motion systems correspond in their dimensionality.

1. The Principle of Occurrence

Our first metaphysical principle is the simple boundary (spatial) proposition that *Reality is the whole event*. We can assert this with confidence, first because we are introspectively aware that no reasoning arises within us without a context (a source assumption of wholeness and reality, or event occurrence), and because we all deduce from this that there is one real event that subsumes every other real event. So, by the event 'Reality' we mean the Whole of Everything, of which nothing further can be said. *It is what it is*, the ultimate tautology on which all possible human reasoning, logic, and activity is based. But everything else is by definition a lesser event internal to Reality, a subevent, and every subevent differs from the Whole in that *it is more than what it is in itself*. We cannot say of any subevent that it is what it is, because it exists in some *relation* to all the other subevents in Reality.

The failure to define this relation through a sound theory led some idealists, such as Berkeley (1685-1753) with his 'idea in the mind of

God' and Hegel (1770-1831) with his 'Absolute Idea', to conclude that everything is only an idea. But however it is expressed, this idealistic notion psychologizes (personifies) Reality, which is the device by which mystics instantly transform primary reasoning into tertiary reasoning, and then argue that what they don't know, Reality, is like what they do know, people. Anyway, though we can perceive any subevent of Reality as if it was a whole, our perception of it, as a whole or a part, doesn't tell us how it relates to all other subevents and their parts, which we must know to reason validly about it.

Since Reality is the cause of all that was, is, or will be, it is the limit of fundamentality in our reasoning. At this ultimate level, we encounter no dilemma, because what is, is, and we must accept it. If we even think that we could go farther than this, that there lies 'beyond' it a cause of Everything, or a creator, then we are committing a logical blunder, violating our context and universal Law. As the ultimate cause of everything, Reality itself had no cause.

The traditional debate over this first principle is between *absolutists* and *relativists*, equivalent terms for our two kinds of perceptualists: the realists who perceive a monistic absolute and the empiricists who deny that whole and perceive only its parts. Dualisms arise in our secondary reasoning and are given tangible forms in our quaternary reasoning, so rationalists and formalists join empiricists in dividing Reality into parts, but it is the empiricists who offer the arguments for relativism. So the chief tertiary views that oppose our first principle are those of monotheists and those of relativistic scientists.

I defined *idealism* earlier as a fallacy of tertiary reasoning resulting from the prior denial of Reality or other whole contexts, and this denial is the essence of relativism in any form. Our tertiary reasoners begin reasoning from their arbitrary selection of certain parts, which they then generalize to yield ideals, or Alls, which are named with class terms. Any such All is conceived as a static state of being, which they may then offer in opposition to a whole event proposed by realists. Both they and the formalists who build on their reasoning then use this ersatz whole as if it was a real and whole event. This is all that any ideal is: a static ersatz reality, or fiction, that arealists need in their synthetic reasoning to appear to be reasoning as realists do.

For instance, monotheists believe in one god, but they believe in two realities. They are plainly not considering the Reality when they hypothesize a second kind of 'reality' that is the home of a fictional deity that created the lesser world they call 'the universe'. And neither do our physicists and cosmologists consider Reality when they hypothesize about the nature or form of what they too call 'the universe'. The term 'the universe' appears to be a proper noun, like the complete-percept terms 'the Reality' or 'the Whole Event', but it is born as a class term, so it is an All posing as a Whole. Realists and idealists are not referring to the same epistemic idea with these different proper nouns. What monotheists and physicists mean by their proper noun 'the universe' is a class notion derived from a prior division of the one Whole Event into parts.

Monotheists divide the Whole Event by juxtaposing the Reality that we all perceive, which they call 'the universe', and an idealized realm, which they call 'heaven', the *place* (which can only mean the space) where their idealized Supreme Being 'resides'. They thus propose two realities with distinct sets of laws, natural Laws and divine 'laws', and they use 'the universe' to avoid saying 'the Reality', because this term doesn't permit either the multiplication of realities or the possibility of a temporal 'whole' that can be created or destroyed.

Scientists also use 'the universe' to divide Reality into parts. What physicists mean by it is some All that doesn't include psychologic events, though these are as real as any external event, and obviously those who speak of 'parallel universes' are not using 'universe' to mean the Whole of Everything. Also, given their traditional misunderstanding of time, which I explain below, they often imagine their 'universe' as existing in the present only, with its past gone and its future not yet here. But in reality, the past, present, and future are just different spaces of the Whole Event as seen from different relative (or moving) reference points. Nevertheless, many physicists contradict this fact by assuming that their 'universe' had a beginning in time.

We must beware the idealistic zeal that inclines tertiary reasoners to universalize their partialized perceptions and arbitrary selections of parts. They say 'the universe' as if they meant 'the Reality', but they didn't derive it through primary reasoning; if they had, then their proper noun would mean what ours means. Theirs is derived not from their initial perception of the Whole Event, but from the perception and hypothetical synthesis of selected parts that defines a science or a mystical area of study. This pluralistic source allows theists to propose multiple realities and supreme beings, just as it allows scientists to propose a relative and temporal 'whole' that doesn't account for all real events.

"Time is relative," our relativistic physicists say, following philosophic intellectuals from ancient times to Hume and Kant in the first quadrant of the modern era, and we must agree with them on this. But if time is relative, then it cannot be predicated of Reality itself, and this means that the Absolute Whole cannot be said to have a beginning or an end, or a 'time' of its own. The tertiary scientists who hypothesize an absolute beginning of 'the universe' are thus committing the same logical error as our tertiary monotheists, who attribute a time to 'the universe' so that they can say that it has an omnipotent Creator and potential Destroyer.

In this connection, consider the claim of most cosmologists today, which the Vatican found acceptable, that there was a 'Big Bang' that began 'Everything'. They see that all the cosmic parts they can perceive by technological means are moving away from each other. But this evidence for expansion can be veridic without being complete; that is, it may pertain only to a small *universe*, which is a class term, and not to *the Reality*. To support their claim they must also show that those expanding pieces actually do compose the Whole Event, but since they can't prove this, some of them make the absurd claim that everything was created from nothing.

Maybe Reality was once just the size of a pearl, as cosmologists who wish to avoid the absurdity of 'something from nothing' say, but even then it was still the Whole of Everything, still eternal (timeless), and still a three-dimensional continuum. Size has nothing to do with metaphysics, because measurement is a tertiary reasoning process, not a primary one. If the

Reality was once that small, it may have been larger before it reduced itself to that size, so there is no necessary reason why that size was its *beginning*. It is more logical to propose a pulsating Reality than to attribute relative time to the Absolute Whole and then claim that something was created from nothing. If the 'Big Bang' hypothesis is proposed as a beginning of Everything, it is absurd. Otherwise, it is just a relative comment on size and motion from our own perspective which can be useful to scientists as that, and as such it has no metaphysical meaning at all.

This wholistic view, that Reality always was and always will be, is not a new proposition; if it was, I couldn't claim that it was a natural perception of all humans. Several pre-Platonic intellectuals, disputing the idealists (relativists) of their day, proposed the timelessness of the absolute Whole, saying explicitly that it was not created and will never end. In fact, this was the general assumption in ancient Greece, and it explains why its theists were polytheists rather than monotheists. The most basic distinction among the forms of theism, therefore, is whether a theist says that *time* is absolute or relative. Thus, theism is properly classified into two main branches: *external theism*, which falsely holds that time is absolute and so applies to the Reality; and *internal theism*, which truly holds that time is relative and so cannot apply to the Reality.

External theism, which we must reject for that error on time, is monotheistic, but only because external theists can not easily defend the claim that a Committee of Divine Creators agreed to make our Reality exactly what it is. That is, their personification of Reality would logically require conflicts among those Creators. Monotheism was first proposed in ancient Egypt and later in turn by Judaism, Christianity, and Islam, none of which have benefited humanity. But internal theism, or *pantheism*, proposes no external cause, so we cannot reject it for an erroneous conception of time. It can be either monotheistic or polytheistic, depending on whether it proposes one or more natural Laws. Spinoza (1632-77), for instance, opposed Descartes' dualisms by proposing only one such Law, or one deified substance within the Whole.

It is surprising, and to a degree conspiratorial, that virtually everyone today accepts the claim of relativistic physicists that Newtonian physics was in error for assuming that time is absolute, while so few people reject monotheism for making that same error.

Augustine (354-430) dealt with the dilemma of time by holding that the issue is, so to speak, academic. He said that time could not even have existed before his God created 'the universe', which merely states the relativity of time in different words. So he understood that time is relative, as earlier thinkers known to him did, but he ignored the fact that therefore there could not have been a creative act that *began* Everything in time. A creative act is always an event in time, so the term *creation*, like *time*, has no absolute sense; everything that can be created is relative, or a subevent of the Whole Event. To be consistent, which he often was not, what he should have concluded from the relativity of time is not an external Creator, but internal theism, such as the polytheism of ancient Greece or the pantheism that Spinoza found in the religions of India. Since Reality could not have been created, the only valid conception of a deity is as something that pervades that Whole internally and universally. But this notion is redundant, for anything it could mean is already implied by our nontheistic notion of universal principles, or the Laws of Reality, and no proof can be offered for it that is not also a proof of those spatial Laws.

Kant held that this issue, whether Everything was created or is eternal, is an 'antinomy', meaning that both of its contradictory sides can be validly argued. Though others have shown that the arguments he offered on each side are flawed, his view of it as an antinomy correctly suggests the psychologic nature of this dispute. To put it in our terms: realists will not reason from the parts first, and arealists will not reason from the whole first.

These views on time by Augustine and Kant are discussed by the cosmologist Stephen W. Hawking (b.1942) in his interesting book *A Brief History of Time: From the Big Bang to Black Holes* (New York: Bantam Books, 1988). He explains there why he reverted to the ancient view that makes both a divine act of Creation and a Big Bang singularity impossible. (Nevertheless, he too speaks of 'the beginning of the universe'.)

> It is perhaps ironic that, having changed my mind, I am now trying to convince other physicists that there was in fact no singularity at the beginning of the universe...it can disappear once quantum effects are taken into account.

Reality is singular and its Laws are plural, so we must be primary monists before we dissect Reality to see its natural Laws, deduce its parts, and reason about some of those parts as tertiary relativists. Only absurd conclusions follow from the claim that Reality is pluralistic and temporal rather than monistic and timeless. But tertiary reasoners make that claim because they can only see the Whole as an All that is the sum of some parts, or what is absolute as relative instead.

I refer to this tertiary claim as *absolute relativism*. This is a self-contradictory term, but it follows from the absolute and contradictory skepticism of Hume, who perhaps did more than any other intellectual to define the modern era (1762-2008). Hume proclaimed, to the applause of all doubters, that we humans delude ourselves if we think that we can know anything for certain. We think only what it arbitrarily pleases us to think, he said, and no more than that. And therefore, since nothing is absolutely certain, *everything is relative*. This is the motto of all skeptics, including our relativistic physicists, some of whom (Einstein, for one) admitted their debt to Hume. But if *everything* is relative, then this statement, which is an absolute proposition, is itself false, and this means that an intellectual's task is not to deny absoluteness, it is to find out just what is absolute. We must doubt the soundness of any science that starts from the absurd contention that everything is relative, or that if something is absolute then we scientists have no idea what it is. Actually, all scientists do have a veridic epistemic idea of the Whole of Everything, for otherwise they could not reason or speak intelligibly.

Relativistic physicists of the modern era criticized Newtonian physics for assuming that time and space are absolutes. Then, guided by philosophic intellectuals before them, they showed us once again, this time in their specialist language, that time is relative. But they erred by saying that this evidence also proved what it does not prove: that space is relative too. More precisely, they failed to point out that while generic 'time' has only a relative sense, resulting from the plurality and motion of Reality's parts, generic 'space' is an ambiguous term with both a relative and an absolute sense. Time is linear, so we can only extend or reduce it quantitatively in its one dimension, but space is three-dimensional, so whenever we extend or reduce our view of it, we perceive an hierarchy of subsumed spaces. Their error was in failing to distinguish *a space* from *the Space*. Obviously any space other than the ultimate subsuming Space is relative, but this does not mean that there is no absolute Space. Their proof that *a space* is relative was as plain to everyone as their proof that *a time* is relative, but it is irrelevant to the issue of generic space, because relative spaces cannot exist unless there is an absolute Space that subsumes them all.

The proper nouns 'the Space' and 'the Reality' are equivalent terms; their context-referents differ but they have the same idea-referent, the complete percept. But there is no equivalent proper noun, 'the Time', because *time* is an abstract-concept term, or defining essence, not a complete-percept term. And if we later derive a complete-percept term from any concept term, be it abstract or concrete, we are then speaking of an ersatz whole, a fiction that only exists in our explicated reasoning. 'The Space' refers to a real event, but 'the Time' does not. Our term 'time' presupposes both a subevent (or lesser space) and its relativity to all other subevents (or spaces), but this is not so with our generic term 'space', the use of which requires us to know just which space we mean. And if we mean the all-subsuming Space, then that is certainly absolute.

Also, if the Space was not absolute, physicists could not validly propose any absolute constant, such as the speed of light or the Planck constant. An absolute constant must be a quantity that refers to something about the absolute Space and its Laws. If nothing is absolute, then there cannot be an absolute constant, though there could be a *universal* constant, if we use this term to mean only a part of the Whole. Since it is contradictory for absolute relativists to claim that there is any absolute constant, they speak ambiguously of 'universal' constants instead.

Those who claim that 'everything is relative' or that 'theory is irrelevant' are apparently trying to claim that there are no absolute Laws that bind them. Only realists consistently deny absolute relativism and respect the logical boundary of the Reality we all know. And the purpose of our first metaphysical principle, *Reality is the whole event*, is to state this absolute boundary to our reasoning at the start, since everything else, including our common logic, depends on it. Realists respect this primary boundary, first by denying that there is anything beyond it and then by denying any mystical or scientific universalization of any of its parts. In fact, it is the paradigm for all their other reasoning, since it tells them to begin reasoning in all lesser cases only from the real and whole event that they have selected as their context of reference.

The Epistemic Refutation of Theism. What I have said so far in proposing realism also represents the first *epistemic* refutation of theism and other forms of mysticism. Historically, with only empiricism or rationalism to guide us, we didn't know our epistemic process well enough to know for certain that any form of mysticism is illogical. But we now know that *we cannot derive any notion of a deity or a nonspatial 'reality' in our primary reasoning*, and yet this is the only part of our psychologic process in which we can consider what is real or whole. This means that theists and other mystics never propose a metaphysics, or primary theory of Reality; they only propose tertiary hypotheses derived from the bifurcation of Reality. That is, in their secondary reasoning they divide the whole Reality that they, like the rest of us, perceived in their primary reasoning, and then in their tertiary reasoning they universalize a fictional part of it—one that also seems real to others, such as *time, mind, heaven, consciousness, idea,* or *spirit*.

Though mystics ultimately deny our one Reality, initially they must affirm it, because they cannot otherwise dissect it into parts. To say that there are two kinds reality is to deny that there is only one reality, but we can't say that there are two things of any kind without first having affirmed that there is one whole that subsumes them both. Since we can only derive the number *two* from the number *one*, the claim that the Whole of Everything consists of both a 'heaven' and the spatial world we all know presupposes that one Reality. The question then is how theists can *know* that this 'heaven' is real, since the only reality that they know for certain is the spatial world that causes everything, including their passions, faith, and fictional hypotheses.

A theist may object to this argument from the Whole of Everything by saying, "I do start with one reality, and it is god; *then* I divide his (or her) reality into two worlds: heaven and our spatial reality." The problem with this defense, though, is that 'god' is not a cognition of wholeness, for no one can perceive the Whole except as 'all the space there is'. A theist's god is not direct epistemic knowledge; it is explicated learning. Every theist perceives the spatial Whole as an infant, but they all learn of 'god' only later, from the words and stories of their elders. So they could not have known of a single whole called 'god' first; it's an add-on.

Initially, our tertiary mystics know just as we all do that there is only one Reality and that it is spatial, but they deny this later when they return to their primary reasoning to *reconsider* their fiction as if it was a real and whole event, and that fiction, like any fiction, *can only be formed in their tertiary reasoning*. Then they falsely claim that we can propose multiple kinds of reality if we wish, since our 'metaphysical' reasoning lets us assert any number of different 'realities'.

Mystical reasoning is born with people's tertiary *passions*, which always pertain to parts and not to wholes. Theists *choose* to love certain fictions (like life after death) and to hate the Reality that denies these, and each such passionate choice leads them to synthesize some fictional All, or hypothetical state of beingness, that they then claim is the real 'Whole'. And this psychologic error is the source of every theistic, mystical, or pseudometaphysical hypothesis.

2. The Principle of Abstraction

All that we can predicate of Reality itself is that it is a particular Whole, that it is what it is, and that it always was and always will be. And we perceive its wholeness and its timelessness even though we cannot cognize these remote attributes with any of our five senses. To reason further than that, then, our second metaphysical principle must be one that pertains, not to that Whole, but rather to everything contained within it, or to every temporal space, or subevent.

Reality is not the first context we consciously consider in our life, so we don't reflect on this primary context as if in a primitive state in which we have no prior knowledge of other contexts. In fact, we use our entire psychologic process when we consider any event completely. We cognize space as a percept, either the complete percept or the partial percept, and time as a concept, either *one* specific time (now) or *all* such times (forever), and we mix these cardinal ideas in our intermediate ideas. This is also to say that we cannot perceive a whole without subsequently perceiving its parts, that we cannot conceive a particular time without subsequently conceiving all time, and that the combination of space and time gives us our cognition of motion.

So the next logical step in our analytic reasoning about the Whole Event is to assert that there are many spaces within the absolute Space. But we can only distinguish these lesser spaces from the Whole because they consist of particles, all of which are in motion, and so I refer to these subevents as 'motion systems'. This gives us our second metaphysical principle, the principle of abstraction, which asserts that *Any subevent of Reality is a motion system.*

This second principle is simply stated, but it implies these fundamental proposals: that there are events subsumed by Reality, that they must all observe the Laws of that timeless Reality, and that the most fundamental of these Laws for subevents can only be the dynamic Laws of motion, or of process rather than of static beingness.

Note that our first two principles resolve the old dispute of *Change versus Permanence*, simply by uniting those notions logically (sequentially) in the same theory. Scholars say that this issue was argued in ancient Greece by Heraclitus (c.540-c.470 BCE) and Parmenides (born c.515 BCE), but their full positions on the issue are unknown. In any case, this old dispute only arises in our reasoning because of the whole-part ambiguity between *the* Space and *a* space. All things within Reality are in flux, and this continual change is the reality referent of our equivalent terms *motion* and *process*. But if we reason back more deeply, we see that nevertheless the

Whole Event is permanent, timeless, and changeless. It is therefore not an 'event' in the same sense that a subevent is. The Whole is only an 'event' in what we might call the 'psychologic' sense, meaning that it is a whole with internal moving parts. But any relative motion system, such as our self, is an event in both the external and the internal senses, since it has moving internal parts and it moves as a whole in its subsuming space.[2]

3. The Principle of Dimensionality

At this point we can only advance our metaphysical reasoning by predicating something of motion itself. That is, we concluded that all of the subevents of the Whole Event are moving, but now we need to know how they move, or what the essential elements of any motion system are. In other words, we are now considering the universal term 'space' not as *the* Space but as *any* space, and we realize that any space is limited in its expanse, and that its extension is uniquely defined only by the things that move within it. But what are those things?

If the context of our metaphysical reasoning is a timeless, immovable, and indestructible Whole, and if it has moving parts, then the smallest of those parts must also be eternal and indestructible. It follows that every relative, temporal, and destructible part of the Whole must consist of timeless ultimate particles in motion, which I will call 'ultiparticles' for short. As its historical persistence testifies, this notion of indivisible ultiparticles is a product of our natural reasoning, or common logic, and all who consider metaphysics derive this conclusion, however they may then describe these ultiparticles. But I make no claim here as to how many kinds of ultimate particles there are, for that is not an analytic matter of our reason; it is a synthetic matter of observation, and hence something that only physicists can determine. Our reason only tells us that ultiparticles must be

---

[2] This second principle seems to resolve the multiplicity of conservation laws in physics, for if motion itself is the second principle of Reality, then all other conservation laws are derived from the conservation of motion, or of angular momentum.

indestructible and must exist throughout the Space—though not uniformly so, for then we couldn't perceive discrete subevents of Reality or their motion.

We have thus defined the two limits of our metaphysical reasoning. Reality is a timeless immovable Whole that contains timeless ultiparticles in perpetual motion. We know that both these extremes exist and that only they are permanent, so now we must explain all the real motion systems that can be created and destroyed and that lie hierarchically between these two absolute limits, the Space and its ultiparticles. And those motion systems can only be complexes of ultiparticles and the spaces they define. We must also propose the universal structure of motion in any space, the essence of which is its dimensionality. Hence our third metaphysical principle: *Any motion system consists of particles in helical motion.*

To be a principle, a proposition must be universal to every part of the whole context. We know that all events on earth, in our solar system, and in our galaxy move helically, or in a three-dimensional spiral direction, so we have good reason to propose this kind of motion as universal, at least until we encounter a contrary case. But if that happens, we would then have to propose some other universal structure for motion systems, for our subsequent reasoning about particular events cannot be logical if we do not have a dimensionality principle.

Figure 5 diagrams helical motion in general. It is defined by two spinning motions, which are in turn defined by three analytic points. Let us distinguish these points as a *particle*, a *center*, and an *origin*. So to see a helical motion system analytically—but not geometrically, since quaternary mathematics plays no part in primary metaphysics—we must identify its three reference points. There is the object particle P that spins about a center C, which spins about that system's final reference point, an origin O that we imagine as stationary. If we considered only P's motion around C, then it would be circular, not helical, and we deny that possibility here because we know of no case of apparent circular motion that is not actually helical. In a three-dimensional continuum, two-dimensional motion is impossible.

For the purpose of analysis, we must imagine the origin of this relative motion system as stationary, for otherwise our reasoning would shift from the whole event that we selected as our context and we would be considering the motion system that subsumes it instead, where the static origin O is now its moving center C, and so on. That is, we pretend that a motion system is a whole, or an inertial frame of reference, in imitation of the absolute Whole that cannot move because there is no space beyond it.

This defines helical motion generically. Any motion system's final reference point is the origin O, and its reference plane (which is not flat, but twisted in three dimensions) is the one determined by the revolving axis that connects P and C. By graphic convention, our diagram ignores P's motion in the third dimension. An actual motion system that corresponds to *Figure 5* is your own system, in which P is you, the object of the system, C is the center of the earth about which you rotate, and O is the origin of the system, the center of the sun about which you spiral continuously. This systemic structure applies to everything on earth, so we will refer to it as the *terrestrial system*. Its proximate subsuming system, also shared by everything on earth, is the *earth-sun system*, where the object P is the earth's center and the reference plane is the *ecliptic plane*, defined by the revolution of the earth's center P about the center of the sun C. This higher system's final reference point O is the galactic center, about which the sun revolves.

Traditional Confusions. In order to understand the full import of this third principle we must first correct some errors in our traditional view of dimensionality. A proposition on the structure of *any* motion system is a dimensionality principle because it must be based on our definition of a dimension and on our claim as to how many dimensions that universal structure has. By a *dimension* we mean an imaginary and exclusive directional axis in space that passes through a specified reference point. And we say 'exclusive' because we realize that only three of the innumerable axes that we could imagine as passing through any point are mutually exclusive, or unique, in their spatial direction.

We can therefore propose, as a corollary of our third metaphysical principle, the common-sense view that *any motion system is three-dimensional*. This places yet another border (limit) on human reasoning, for it requires us to deny that any event, whether external or internal to us,

Figure 5. Elements of Helical Motion

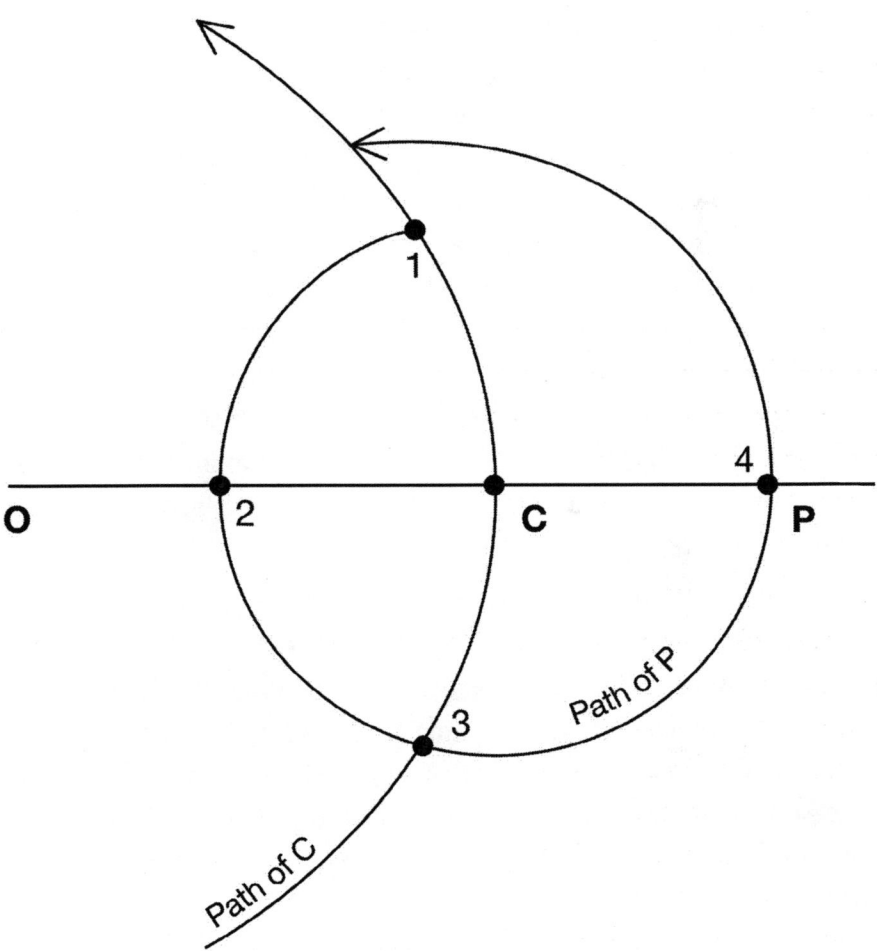

1 = Complete Percept; 2 = Abstract Concept; 3 = Partial Percept; Concrete Concept

can have either less than or more than three dimensions. And since no one seriously proposes less than three dimensions—except perhaps modern psychologists who speak of internal events as linear, or moving through time only—what this corollary denies is both the ancient assumption that time is a fourth dimension and the view of contemporary superstring physicists who claim that there are ten or even more 'dimensions'.[3]

Most of us are ignorant of our physicists' area of synthetic specialization, but since all humans reason with the same dynamic logic, we can all judge any fundamental reasoning, even in technical specialties and especially when the issue involves analytic reasoning, or theory. Of course, we must accept our specialists' views on strictly synthetic issues, so here we accept our physicists' claim that they need more than three measurements in their microcosmic explorations. This is no surprise to us, for we all know from experience that we need a fourth measurement to relate two three-dimensional motion systems or to analyze one such system at two hypothetically static positions in its path of motion. But this fact, that physicists need more than three measurements to *relate* a motion system they encounter in their microcosmic studies to the higher level of our terrestrial system, does not mean that these additional *measurements* are *dimensions*. In other words, that act of relating does nothing to define the motion system itself.

We have been deeply confused about this issue of dimensionality since ancient times, so let us consider the three old errors that cause this confusion that limits our understanding of many other subjects. The first is the confusion of a measurement with a dimension, the second is the illusion that time is something distinct from space, and together these yield the third error: the universalization that there are more than three dimensions in reality.

---

[3] To consider the perspective of a superstring physicist on this issue, I recommend the clearly written popular work *Hyperspace*, by the physicist Michio Kaku (New York: Oxford University Press, 1994). Hawking, in the 1988 work cited above, expresses objections to the superstring view, but that is a debate for physicists. We can only object, on the grounds of our common logic, to its erroneous claim that there are more than three dimensions in reality.

Extra Dimensions. Let us start with the third error, the composite error of assuming four or more dimensions. Imagine that our physicists could sit in the ultimate microcosmic space where ultiparticles move and make all their measurements of that space from there. They would find, as they do in our terrestrial motion system, that three measurements suffice to define the event (space, motion system) in which they are partaking. They wouldn't need a fourth measurement there until they wanted to *relate* their tiniest motion system to another one, either a sibling system or the parent spatial system that subsumes all systems on their level. But then they would also need a fifth measurement to relate their tiny system to the one that subsumes the one that subsumes theirs, and then a sixth, and so on, until their measurements from their tiniest level reach the terrestrial and earth-sun levels that yield our common time standards (days and years), or even beyond these if they wish, to yield who-knows-how-many measurements.

Now perhaps all these measurements up to our mundane level do yield ten or more numbers, but this has nothing to do with the *dimensionality* of any specific motion system. This synthetic measuring exercise across different levels of reference tells us that there is a Whole Event with a vast hierarchic chain of moving subevents, but we already knew that from the primary reasoning of our common logic. The only new knowledge that such tertiary measurements give us pertains to *our perception* of realities from our own relative and changing position within the Space. Since any subevent of Reality is more than what it is in itself, we cannot define it unless we explain its relations to the Whole Event and all of its subevents. But to *relate* a plurality of motion systems is not to define the dimensional structure of any one of them. That structure is inherent to *any space per se*, and our relational reasoning is a subsequent cognitive issue that presupposes such universal spaces and their hierarchic structure as motion systems. In any form, such relating (and relativism in general) is only about our perception of two or more *particular* events; it is not about the universal attributes of *any* space, such as its dimensionality.

Our analytic consideration of *any* space shows us that it is a three-dimensional continuum, and that this is also the case with *a* particular space, *all* particular spaces, and *the* Space, or the Whole Event. And no observational complexities that we encounter in our technical efforts to relate (measure and compare) selected motions systems can change this dimensional fact. But now let us consider the two separate errors that make this composite error seem valid.

Measurement. The first of these errors in the traditional denial of a three-dimensional continuum is the confusion of a measurement with a dimension. We measure things only to meet our practical needs, so it was our hypothesists and pragmatists who shaped our understanding of the various forms of *measurement*, equivalent terms for which are *judgment*, *evaluation*, *relation*, and *comparison*. Some ancient measurements were sophisticated. For instance, suggesting that talk of 'the Copernican revolution' is parochial, we know from the Great Pyramid of Khufu (c.2680 BCE) that the Egyptians had correctly calculated the circumference of the earth and its distance from the sun, and this knowledge was apparently available to the ancient Greeks in Alexandria. Today most of us are familiar with the Cartesian coordinate system of the classic era, which has the mutually perpendicular x, y, and z axes used in geometry. But Descartes' coordinate system isn't the cause of the confusion; it is caused by intellectuals who erroneously employ this synthetic measurement system in their analytic theorizing, where dimensions are all-important and measurements are irrelevant.

When we reason analytically (universally) about *any* space, we know that it may be larger or smaller than any other space, but it has no specific measurements then. Measurements arise only in our tertiary reasoning, when we consider and evaluate *a* particular space, as a selected part of our whole context. But 'dimension' is a universal term, born at the juncture of our primary and secondary reasoning. It is our abstract-concept term for our analytic reduction of any space to its defining essence, its dimensionality, which we know consists of three such dimensional axes, or six exclusive directions from any point in that space.

But we reach this universal conception without measurements. In our analytic reasoning, we don't think about *coordinates* for our measurements, but only about *directions in space*, either exclusive or combined, and we call the exclusive axes 'dimensions'. So, in speaking generically (analytically) of the *dimensions* of any space, we don't mean the axes of an artificial coordinate system that we use synthetically to measure particular spaces. The Cartesian coordinate system is useful in tertiary reasoning because it imitates dimensionality, or *describes* it hypothetically, but this doesn't mean that it can be validly used to *define* dimensionality. *Dimensionality* is an abstract term and *measurement* is a concrete term, and we have already seen that no consequent cognition in the Consideration Cycle can be validly used to define an antecedent cognition.

In our natural reasoning, the term 'dimensions' does not refer to the x, y, and z axes of our explicated reasoning, or the Cartesian coordinate system, for there are no straight lines in Reality. It refers to the three perpendicular, mutually-exclusive *curved* axes though any reference point.

Contrary to our dictionaries, the root sense of our universal term 'dimension' is its theoretical sense, not its derivative mathematical sense. It is not a mathematical term, for it doesn't mean a measurement, it means *what* is being measured; that is, what is real about any space that permits those later quantitative evaluations of its extension. The idea-referent of the term 'dimension' is the defining essence of the Space that makes possible six and only six exclusive (uncombined) directional extensions from any point in any space. All other senses and uses of the term 'dimension' are imitative and relative, and hence potentially confusing.[4]

---

[4] My Random House Dictionary says of 'dimension' that *in mathematics* it means a property of space, which falsely implies that space results not from nature, but from the quaternary explications of mathematicians. It then expounds solely on the senses that equate the term to measurement, or evaluation. My Oxford English Dictionary (Glasgow: Oxford University Press, 1971) proposes measurement as its first meaning, and then gives its 'second', supposedly derivative, meaning as "Measurable or spatial extension of any kind." These academic works show some awareness of the term's real idea-referent, but in both it is overpowered by our long history of confusing it with measurement, and hence with mathematics, which cannot be validly used to define 'dimension' or any other abstract term.

To eliminate the ambiguity and confusion here, we must use 'dimension' solely to mean the three naturally curved lines that define the six exclusive directions in any space from its moving object of reference, P. Otherwise, since any straight line is an artificiality, only the term 'axis' is correct. Of course, we can also use these curved coordinates of a real motion system for practical measurements, as we have done for millennia in our celestial measurements from earth.

The broader distinction here is that our analytic reasoning is always universal and never relative, while our synthetic reasoning is always relative and never universal. In fact, relativism is measurement, or the comparative evaluation of some relation. Measurements are useful in practice, but they are artificial, or just instances of explicated reasoning in mathematics or another language construct. They are specific or vague quantifications used to compare (relate) the spaces of different motion systems perceived as subcontexts, so they presuppose a space's dimensions, or the *what* that is being measured. The terms *dimension* and *measurement* (or *axis*) have directly opposite idea-referents; the former is an abstract term, and the latter a concrete term, and we err if we confuse these opposite cognitions.

Since our conception of measurement is synthetic and arbitrary, we apply it to many cases other than spatial dimensions. We measure all real phenomena; not only objective things like distance, direction, temperature, mass, energy, velocity, and so on, but also psychologic events. We can refer to a measurement (evaluation) in mathematical terms or in vague terms of degree, such as 'she is *very* angry', 'he is *mildly* amused', or any such use of our stock of tertiary adverbs. Psychologically, as I explain later, all such evaluations in the tertiary phase of our reasoning are made in what I call our 'judgment system', where we do the relational reasoning that yields our relative standards, such as our ideals, morals, and values. And since traditionalists are trained to see measurements mathematically rather than psychologically, they see the measurement of all properties other than distance or direction as being essentially nonspatial. *But no measurement is nonspatial.* Our metaphysics tells us that Reality is Space, so we realists expect that all measurements, even the evaluations of our psychologic functioning, are ultimately reducible to purely spatial terms.

The dimensionality of any space does not involve mathematics, not even geometry. Our analytic (primary and secondary) reasoning yields the universal Laws that imply all mathematics, but the converse is not so. Mathematics makes no reference to Reality, or to the Space; its measurements only compare relative spaces as parts. While mathematicians confine themselves to their quaternary specialty, they are not concerned with Reality. Like theologians and other mystics, they are intellectually detached from it, and nothing they conclude through their specialty speaks directly to that primary subject. We know that our language constructs, notably mathematics and formal logic, can reflect absolute necessity and hence universal truths. But these are nature's truths, not ours, and we know them from the analytic half of our common logic. Our specialists merely explicate these truths in their different language constructs.

Time. The second ancient error that leads traditionalists to deny a three-dimensional continuum is the illusion of 'time'. We must reject this old notion that time is something distinct from space. We don't know for sure when this distinction first arose, but it appears to have been clearly expressed first by Greek intellectuals before the sophist era. Some generations after they devised the alphabet, we find references to the dualistic notion that reality consists of two inherently different kinds of stuff, called 'time' and 'space'. And from this schism several other fallacious dualisms of ancient Greek thought were proposed and became entrenched in Western traditions. They are in Eastern traditions too, but some differ in form, and we have no need to pursue the similarities or differences here.

These ancient dualisms imitate the natural polarizations in our psychologic process, which I will identify later, except for the fact that one term refers to an objective external reality and the other to a subjective mystical hypothesis. Italicizing the mystical half again, examples are *time*-space and the derivative cases of *god*-man, *heaven*-earth, *spirit*-substance, and *mind*-body. This secondary illusion, that time is a different kind of stuff from space, is what encourages tertiary mystics to claim, with as much reasonableness as our scientists exhibit when they speak of 'time' as a fourth dimension, that other kinds of undefinable phenomena are also objective realities—nonspatial things such as 'god', 'heaven', 'spirit', and 'mind'.

In physics, near the close of the modern era's second quadrant, Lorentz (1853-1928) and Einstein put these ancient misunderstandings of time and dimensionality into new scientific terms. In his popular writings, following Lorentz' formula, Einstein said that we need four numbers (measurements) to define any event, and he illustrated this with a hypothetical particle on a line of motion. He then applied the artificial Cartesian coordinate system to this motion by placing its origin at two different points on its path, *Origin 1* and *Origin 2*, and then taking the difference between the three axial measurements (x, y, and z) from each origin. Then he said that to define this event (or motion) we also need a fourth number, in order to reflect the difference in the 'time' of the event at each origin point. And this difference he and Lorentz imagined to be a 'dimension', though it was only an additional measurement taken along a hypothetical t axis—a time axis that no one can sensibly conceive of or diagram except as a spatial axis.

However, that fourth number serves only one purpose in that example: to record the fact that these physicists moved their artificial coordinate system from *Origin 1* to *Origin 2*. Thus, their t 'axis' is not objectively real, it is just an imagined axis, or an explication that they need to record the *spatial* change that results when they move their entire Cartesian coordinate system from one point to the other. But *their* perceptual position on their hypothetical t axis has nothing to do with the reality of the event they are describing, or measuring. Their 'fourth dimension', or 'time', is just another spatial measurement added to the first three. Its only purpose is to *relate* one motion system to another one or, in this case, to the same one as seen from a different spatial position, and that position is still a *where*, not a *when*.

So in reality this fourth number does not measure some mystical stuff called 'time'; it only measures a spatial distance in the next higher three-dimensional continuum, the motion system that subsumes the particle's motion from *Origin 1* to *Origin 2*. But, logically speaking, these physicists have committed a fallacious shift in their context of reference. When they placed their artificial coordinate system at *Origin 1*, they selected one motion system as their context, but when they put another coordinate system at *Origin 2*, they shifted their context of reference to the space of the next higher motion system, the one that subsumes both those origin points. And their failure to explicate this shift to a higher context is what deludes them into thinking that there is a separate kind of stuff called 'time'. If they had instead specified that higher motion system as their context from the start and used its three natural dimensions to measure that motion, then they could have described that event with only three spatial measurements.

Now compare their artificial four-term method of measurement to the realistic method we all use in measuring an actual motion system, such as the rotating or revolving earth, which is the human level of reality. Here we don't need a fictional coordinate system, since we know this system's three reference points (*P*, *C*, and *O*) and their directional extensions objectively, apart from our own position or imaginings, and we can measure everything in that system with respect to them. The relative *time* of the terrestrial motion system is thus a *spatial* measurement along any of its three dimensions, or naturally defined curved axes. In that system, everything on earth, let us say *you*, defines a unique motion system with three distinct 'times'. One of these 'times' measures the spatial distance you rotate around the center of the earth, or through our common *day*. Another measures the spatial distance you move with the earth's revolution around the sun, or through our common *year*. And the third measures the spatial distance moved by you and the entire earth-sun (ecliptic) plane in the third dimension, for which we have no common 'time' name because we ordinarily ignore this larger motion of the solar system in our galaxy.

But these so-called 'times' in our terrestrial system are all spatial measurements, and we have no need for a fourth number if we are referring only to movements in the terrestrial motion system. All that we need are our *spatial* clocks and calendars, which tell us our relative position in the space of our own motion system, or where we are located now in the subsuming day or year or in any arithmetic extension of those spatial distances. Our scientists would never claim that a *year* means anything but the spatial distance traveled by the earth in one revolution about the sun, and yet, in seeming contradiction, they call that spatial distance a 'time'. A real, or natural, coordinate system with three axes suffices to measure our motion in our terrestrial system because we are not then comparing it to another motion system. So each real motion system has its own unique time, but this is the same as saying that it has its own unique space.

We can call the three spatial coordinates of a motion system its 'time axes' if we wish, but this is redundant. And since we now know explicitly that the stuff that we have been calling 'time' is only space, we can define it correctly, as another corollary of our third metaphysical principle: *time is space specified*. More fully, our generic term 'time' is a universal term that we use in our explicated reasoning as a substitute for the universal generic term 'space'. These two old terms are equivalent terms because their idea-referent is the same, the abstract concept, even though their context-referent differs. The context-referent of 'any space' is *the Space*, and the context-referent of 'any time' is *this particular space* within the Space.

The Cycle shows how we reason here. From our complete-percept term *the Space*, we derive our universal term *any space* and then our partial-percept term *a space* and our class term *all spaces*, after which we cognize a new and lesser whole: *this particular space*. So we derive this second complete-percept cognition from a part of the initial whole, a space, but to analyze it in a new consideration, we pretend that this former part is a whole instead. This former subevent is now our 'whole' context in an act of reconsideration, or explicated reasoning. It too would be natural reasoning, except that we assigned terms to our cognitions in our initial consideration of *the Space*. And now in analyzing (analytically reducing) this lesser context, we realize that it would be nonsensical to say that the defining essence of *this particular space* is *any space*, so we say instead that it is its *time*. Thus, our generic term *time* was created to mean *any space*.

To put this another way: for any subcontext that we later treat as a whole context, we need derived universal terms for that context that also convey that it is a relative context and not an absolute one. This may seem contradictory but it is not. The defining cause of an act of reasoning is our context of reference, but it can be the Whole Event or any subevent. So in any lesser context, we must transform the *absolute universal* terms that we coin in our metaphysics into *relative universal* terms. And to meet this logical need in our explicated reasoning for a relativized universal term, we must either use the absolute universal term ambiguously or coin a new term. In this case, since we must avoid the absurdity of saying that the universal defining essence of *this particular space* is its *space*, we say instead that its abstract essence is its *time*. In our metaphysical reasoning, 'time' means space, so we just say 'space'. But the context-referent of our relative term 'time' is always a subevent of the Whole Event, so that term means that we are specifying a particular space. Hence our definition, that *time is space specified*. And from this it follows—not from physics, but by analytic definition—that time is necessarily relative.

The Lorentz formula requires four rather than three calculated differences only because it doesn't specify the motion system that subsumes both *Origin 1* and *Origin 2*. Its hypothetical t variable is needed to compensate for its failure to mention its shift of context to the higher motion system that subsumes both origins, and this is all that its fourth measurement, which is not a dimension of any real motion system, means in reality. In our natural reasoning we don't need this fiction, this separate stuff called 'time', but in our explicated reasoning it simplifies our numbers and references—thus, like so many of our explications, it is a fiction, but a useful one.

You can test this yourself, as practice in your new perspective as a realist. Whenever you hear any reference to 'time', think 'space' instead, and as you become more familiar with this realistic spatial conception of time, you will see that they are equivalent terms and that all of our common temporal expressions could as well be spatial expressions. For example, the phrase 'I am X years old' could also be 'I am Y miles old'. To give the age of anything on earth, it is arithmetically easier to speak of *days* or *years* than to calculate the *miles* that it and the earth has traveled in its spiraling course, but these are equivalents terms nonetheless. Or the cliché 'at this point in time' could as well be 'at this point in space', which is also disposable, for we can now say more economically 'at this point', which can only mean a point in space. And we can now use the term *farther*, a spatial reference, in a temporal reference where convention dictates *further*. Or, instead of asking *when* Socrates died, we could ask *where* Athens and the earth were as he died.

Also, the old notion of time as used in our physicists' definitions of velocity and acceleration is not essential; it is just a mathematical convenience. Physicists define *velocity* as distance divided by time, or v=d/t, but it can also be defined as a ratio of two spatial distances, as one distance divided by another distance, or $v=d_1/d_2$. And they define *acceleration* as a change in either velocity or direction. But this is redundant, for once we see that velocity is only a spatial proportion, it suffices to define acceleration solely as a change of direction.[5]

In our explicated reasoning, we need to substitute the term 'time' for the term 'space' for two main reasons: for arithmetic simplicity and, when it applies, to communicate that we mean a relative subevent and not the Whole Event. So now that we know what the word means, we can continue to use the term 'time' for these purposes, but we should not use redundant terms like 'space and time' or 'space-time', which falsely imply that time is not space.

This false view of time as a mystical nonspatial stuff, or a magical 'fourth dimension', is one of the most significant errors in our traditional

---

[5] For example, if you travel by car, the numerator of your velocity is the miles you travel on the earth's surface and the denominator is the spatial distance in miles of the earth's rotation during that trip. And since each spatial 15° that the earth turns is an *hour*, the phrase 'miles per hour' means the ratio 'surface distance traveled per 15° of distance of earth rotation'. Your path in our terrestrial system's space is thus a vector determined by those two motions (actually three, but physicists ignore the third dimension in defining velocity). As for acceleration, if you double or halve your velocity, you are said to be 'accelerating' or 'decelerating' your car, but actually you are only changing your vector, the spatial direction and length of your composite path of motion. If two racers on the same track don't arrive at the finish line at the same time, it is because the faster one took a shorter route in three-dimensional space.

intellectual system. It is the source of the deceiving dualisms of traditional explicated reasoning, which idealists rationalize by pointing to this mystical 'dimension' used in our sciences. If physicists can falsely claim that a nonspatial stuff called 'time' is real, then theists can falsely claim that a nonspatial stuff called 'god' is real, mystics can falsely claim that nonspatial 'spirits' are real, and psychologists can falsely claim that our 'mind' is governed by nonspatial laws. So, as in the past, our arealistic scientists are still giving essential support to those who promote these mystical delusions in our world.

4. The Principle of Displacement

At this point, from our new understanding of time and our observations of many events, we know that no motion system is permanent. Change at each instant is inherent to its motion, and sooner or later the entire system is terminated. Hence our fourth metaphysical principle: *Any motion system shall be displaced.*

This proposes that decay in or interference with the motion of every subevent occurs continuously, and that ultimately this structural (dimensional) displacement must be fatal to that motion system as a unique event. The greatest and smallest limits of Reality are absolutes and are forever preserved, but all subevents between those two limits are relative and temporary. And just as we must accept our certain knowledge of the one Whole Event, so we must accept as certain the limited duration of any subevent's unique space. What is born will die, and what is not born, which is only the absolute Whole and its spinning ultiparticles, will never die.

If we wonder why every motion system must be displaced, we are engaging in synthetic cosmological speculation on why all things within the Space are moving and where they are headed. Some cosmologists speculate that their universe is pulsating, and others that all motion systems are moving toward the same ultimate destination, perhaps the 'boundaries' of the Whole, only to be hurled back to its 'center' to move away from it again. These are sensible guesses since the eternal regenerative cycle they propose does not deny the relativity of time, but we don't know anything about this for certain. What we do know, from our common logic, is that no synthetic hypothesizing can determine a metaphysical principle, and that we can propose this displacement principle with confidence because no exception to it has yet been observed.

Our third principle told us that any motion system is unique because of its spatial relativity (formerly its 'space-time relativity'). This is all that something's uniqueness is, the where of it (formerly the 'where and when' of it). But to propose the uniqueness of each system is not to deny that motion systems can be subsumed by other motion systems or that their spaces can overlap partially, for even in these cases a motion system is defined by its own unique space (formerly 'space-time'). Though no two motion systems can share exactly the same space (formerly 'the same space at the same time'), they can share some space.

To say that a three-dimensional system dies, or is totally displaced, is only to say that it has lost its unique identity as a motion system, and when this happens, one or more new motion systems are born from that displacement. Displacement is the cause of creation. Our third principle tells us that there are ultiparticles that will be preserved in their helical motion forever, so all that happens when a motion system is displaced is that its object particle P (or if that particle disintegrated, its constituent particles) joins another unique motion system, and then continues moving in response to either the same center C or a new C. The death of a unique event is just the disruption of its dimensionality, which can also be described as its sudden or gradual disintegration into energy. What is destroyed is not its ultiparticles, but its dimensionality, and hence its identity as a unique motion system.

Since our fourth principle holds that this interference shall occur, it proposes that chaos is a consequence of the universal order proposed by the first three principles. We see this in our daily life; order it as we may, sooner or later it will be disrupted, and chaos ensues. A political implication of this Law is that if we try to impose too much social order in a collective, meaning more than the least that is essential, we will increase the social chaos that is certain to follow—because of that imposed order, not in spite of it. Since both order and chaos are real, any theory must account for both. No theorist or hypothesist can validly propose a state of reality or a political state that is all order or all chaos. Disintegration is a consequence of integration, but chaos then creates a new order, which in turn leads to new chaos, and so on infinitely.

Every event within the Whole Event encounters continual interference from other events that are either lesser or greater than itself in spatial expanse, and sooner or later this barrage of spatial displacements will terminate it as a unique motion system. This imposition may be a direct invasion of one motion system by another, meaning a collision of either their particles or of their spatial fields only, or it may be the spatial distortion (formerly 'gravity') caused by near or remote motion systems, which results in some deterioration of the particle orbits of all motion systems within the affected field. In any case, every distinct event, our self included, will be continuously altered and then terminated by this Law of Reality, displacement, which is to say by some combination of impacting motion systems within or beyond its unique space.

5. THE PRINCIPLE OF CORRESPONDENCE

The final principle in our theory of Reality is our correspondence principle, our analytic principle of the universal relation of every motion system. But first we must correct our conventional ambiguity in what we mean by *relation*, which we use to refer to both an analytic and a synthetic cognition. Analytically, relations exist because all events correspond by universal internal criteria, which ultimately is their dimensionality and structure as motions systems. Synthetically, relations exist because some specific parts of a whole event are somehow externally tied to each other, as by sharing some space or by a causal or logical connection. Epistemically, *relations* arise only in our secondary reasoning, from our analytic division of a whole context into pieces, and they exist among all the dissected parts of a subject whole, but *relativity* or a *relationship* arise only in our tertiary reasoning, after we have selected some specific parts for comparison. So we can speak of the universal relation of cause and effect or of the class relation of sisterhood, but only specified parts can be relatives or have a relationship.

It is therefore better to use a term other than *relation* when we mean its analytic sense, or 'universal relation by internal criteria', and for this I use *correspondence*. And since metaphysics is our most inclusive subject, the broadest possible relation of parts is their dimensional correspondence. Hence our fifth principle: *Motion systems correspond in their dimensionality*.

In other words, any two motion systems are related by their dimensional structure and helical motion. Any subevent is unique in its space, but in its three-dimensional structure as a motion system it corresponds to every other subevent, subject to the six permutations of helical motion described below. What this principle means in practice is that if we can identify the respective reference points P, C, and O of two or more motion systems, then we can align their cycles and consider them as equivalent in all essential respects, much as geometricians apply their narrower correspondence principles of congruence or similarity. This is also to say that any two subevents of the Whole correspond *in their defining essence*, wholly or partially depending on their type of helical motion. And just as all measurements are ultimately only spatial measurements, so all synthetic laws for any tertiary subcontext are derived from the Laws of Space, or motion.

Moreover, since our metaphysics does not otherwise distinguish among events, it is a fundamental premise of realism that psychologic events are also real three-dimensional events, which means that all human standards and rules are similarly reducible to metaphysics, or to the spatial Laws of Reality that define our universal logic, which is our species' defining essence.

Our metaphysics, and proximately its fifth principle of correspondence, is thus our only foundation in reality for any synthetic standard of judgment that we may later hypothesize and apply in practice. In fact, we considered metaphysics here mainly to see this conclusion clearly. And in this we differ from all traditionalists, who have carelessly hypothesized idealistically and preached pragmatically with no foundation in reality, except for what was unwittingly embedded in the logic of their language constructs. If we have no explicit theory of Reality to guide us, we cannot know for certain if a synthetic construct is real or fictional.

The Six Forms of Helical Motion. We considered helical motion generically in our first four principles, but now with the fifth we must consider the permutations of it, meaning the distinct patterns of motion taken by everything within the Whole Event. These patterns reflect the elemental structure of every tangible form that we hypothesize in our synthetic reasoning. And since there are only six possible forms of helical motion, there are six and only six elemental forms of anything that is conventionally called 'matter' or 'substance'. If this is not so, then either helical motion is not universal or the following analysis of it into six kinds is flawed.

Our generic description of helical motion said that P spins about C and C about O, but it did not specify the direction of their spin, clockwise (CW) or counterclockwise (CCW). The first permutation, shown earlier in *Figure* 5, applies to the terrestrial system. This is our personal motion system, so I propose it as the three-dimensional structure of our psychologic functioning, so long as our terrestrial system is not displaced or we do not travel to a different kind of motion system. This is the CCW-CCW case: the reference object P on earth moves counterclockwise about C, the earth's center, which moves counterclockwise about the static origin O, the sun's center. The second permutation is the CCW-CW case, an instance of which is the earth-sun system. Here P is the earth's center revolving counterclockwise around C, the sun's center, which revolves clockwise about O, the galactic center. The third and fourth permutations, of course, are the CW-CCW and the CW-CW cases.

These first four permutations differ in P and C's direction of spin, which is a basic aspect of space, but they are alike by virtue of a second essential criterion; namely, that in all four cases the distance between P and C is *less than* that between C and O—for example, you are closer to the earth's center than it is to the sun's center. We must ignore any case where distance PC is *greater than* CO, because then there is no helical motion, which violates our third metaphysical principle. We are thus left with only two other permutations, those in which the distances *PC* and *CO* are *equal*. In these two cases, *P* and *C* spiral together as siblings rather than as parent and child, and their motion system is a double helix. To form a double helix, *P* and *C* must have the same direction of spin (CW or CCW); they can't spin in opposite directions because that would dissolve their systemic relation and they could not travel together.

So there are only two kinds of double-helical motion, each with an opposite direction of spin and an opposite direction in the third dimension from a given reference point, and adding these two double-helical forms to the four simple cases gives us six and only six kinds of motion system. It follows that every subevent in Reality can be causatively explained and fundamentally compared through the dynamics of one of these six kinds of helical motion.

Chapter 4. The Science of Human Nature

METAPHYSICS AND PSYCHOLOGY

Our doctrinal dispute with traditional thought is the dispute between realism and idealism, which can mean scientific pluralism as well as mysticism. I have proposed that there is only one Reality and that its indestructible ultiparticles are the only material things in it, but our traditional sciences reject this wholistic materialism. Though few scientists today believe in nonsensical dualisms like '*heaven*-earth', '*god*-man', and '*spirit*-substance', most of them still rely on the equivalent dualisms of '*time*-space' and '*mind*-body', and that makes them idealists, for to be a realist one must reject all fundamental dualisms.

Our metaphysics holds that all is space; that all events within the Space are processes, or three-dimensional motion systems; that each event, whether external or internal to us, is dynamically equivalent to every other event in its essential dimensional structure; and that any two events may be compared through that structure. So we can compare, say, 'the event of the life of a plant' with 'the event of a lunar cycle', and we can compare the dynamic structure of any such external event with the structure of any internal act of consideration, such as the event of a political decision or of any life choice. In our new metaphysics, the old mind-body dualism—which some scientists criticize even as they use it daily in their reasoning—is at last dead, and we must not resurrect it. All events are related as events, and this means that our sciences' pluralistic materialism is the pseudomaterialism of the past.

So our metaphysics is the first realistic proposal of a bridge between the traditionally detached realms of physical and mental events. If no such bridge existed, we couldn't illustrate our reasoning graphically and we couldn't even say that a psychologic event 'takes time' to be completed. But there is such a bridge, and this means that we must change our notion of what kind of science we should call 'psychology'.

The modern-era science of that name is based on the classic-era dualism of Descartes that reaffirmed the *mind*-body dualism of ancient intellectuals. Some scholars say that modern psychologists are beholden to Spinoza's work, but not enough, it seems, to make them join him in denying Cartesian dualism and looking for a monistic solution instead. For instance, the modern psychologists Freud (1856-1939) and Jung (1875-1961) both described our mental functioning in the old dualistic terms that deny the Laws of Space, and hence of our common logic. They believed, as Jung said specifically, that our psychologic processes follow different laws altogether, *nonspatial laws* that they couldn't define or describe realistically. But our metaphysics unites all of our physical and human sciences under one set of spatial Laws.

So all of our traditional academic subjects, even physics and psychology, must now be seen as essentially related to each other. How could it be otherwise, since all things are related as parts of the same Whole? And as Socrates said long ago, we can only see this relation if we look beneath the surface of what we perceive to uncover its causes. We have done this here, and we have found that their essential causes are their dimensional structure as motion systems, and that this is the universal relation that is shared by everything in Reality.

Our problem historically was that our intellectuals could not explain this universal relation. But now our correspondence principle lets us validly compare any two events, external or internal, on the most fundamental level, and this lets us derive a new logic and a new science of human functioning. There is no logical or psychologic process that is not determined by the universal Laws of Reality, all of which pertain to space, so any claim that there are *nonspatial laws* is absurd. That term is self-contradictory, and it will remain so until some idealist proves, for the first time, that there is indeed something in Reality that is not spatial. And since time is space, this can no longer be said of our 'temporal' mental processes.

THE NEW SCIENCE

We move now from analytic to synthetic reasoning, and our first subcontext is what we call 'human nature', a term that conventionally refers only to our psychologic functioning and consequent behavior.[1] This usage reflects the fact that traditional views of human nature are based on *mind*-body dualism, which is the main reason why our two old psychologic sciences, astrology and modern psychology, could never adequately explain our nature.

We needn't trace the history of our psychologic reasoning here, but generally it parallels the development of our philosophic and theistic thought. However, I disagree with those who see ancient Greek thought as its source; the Greeks are largely responsible for our traditional intellectual system, but not for psychology. The first psychologist in history appears to have been Gautama, called 'the Buddha'. Contrary to the popular misconceptions about this creative intellectual from India, he was not a philosopher, idealist, mystic, or theist. Rather, like our modern psychologists, he was a pragmatist (formalist) with no interest in theory.[2]

Almost all of the major intellectuals since the sixth century BCE contemplated our reasoning process in some respects, so they were our earliest psychologists. And the first science of human nature was a branch of astrology known as *genethlialogy*. Today, in the West at least, 'astrology' means *horoscopic astrology*, developed in Hellenistic Egypt late in the 2nd or early 1st century BCE. This science differed from the previous efforts,

---

[1] The word *psychologic* is conventionally used only as an adjective, but I will now use it also as a noun, to replace the phrase 'psychologic functioning'. This avoids the ambiguity in the term 'psychology', which means both that functioning in us and an academic field of study or professional practice. Literally it means 'the study of the mind', which fits the academic sense only, and since 'mind' has only been vaguely described to date, I suggest that we use *psychology* to mean the study of the process of consideration in any organism, and *the psychologic* as our generic name for that process itself.

[2] Gautama was born as Prince Siddhartha, and, unlike Jesus or Moses, he was a real person and not a myth. Scholars agree that he lived for eighty years, but they put his birth year anywhere from 623 to 560 BCE. It says something of his time that he was a contemporary of several famous seers, including Thales of Miletus (630?-546? BCE), who many scholars regard as the first philosopher.

initially in Babylonia, to interpret isolated celestial events as omens. Its zodiac's *signs* were not constellations of stars, but rather twelve 30° divisions of *the ecliptic*, the plane that passes through the centers of the sun and the earth. *Genethlialogy*, often called '*natal astrology*', uses the *natal chart* (an astrological chart cast for the time and place of an individual's birth) mainly to determine the native's congenital nature. But then this chart is used for *continuous horoscopy*, meaning other charts relative to it that seek to predict future psychologic, physical, or external events in the native's life, and to thereby say something about the native's developed nature as well.

By the time of the neoplatonists Plotinus (205-70) and Porphyry (c.232-c.305) in Rome, horoscopic astrology had produced a well-developed science of genethlialogy. So we must disagree with those who hold that modern psychology was the first psychologic science or that its practitioners are the only ones who are properly called 'psychologists'. This may be a legal requirement in some places, but it is not a logical one. I define a *psychologist* as anyone who studies the process of consideration, in general or of any species, and this describes many intellectuals before the modern era.

Modern psychology was conceived in the first quadrant of the modern era (1762-1822), a time when many intellectuals began to doubt theism and its religions, and it was formalized later in the second quadrant (1822-1912). It originally promised to explain 'the psyche', which means our defining essence, or innate nature, but which under academic control soon came to mean only 'the mind'. From the people's perspective, its greatest failures have been that it never explained the psychologic impairments of our immoral political, religious, and business leaders, and that it never was what we need most: a theoretically supported science of human nature that is dedicated to the public welfare rather than to governmental or corporate interests.

So here again we must think outside the traditionalist box. We need a dedicated science of human nature for the new era (2008-2254), and because neither astrology nor modern psychology concerns itself primarily with that subject, I am proposing one now. This new science, let us call it *humanology*, will use any valid methods developed in those old sciences, but it will surpass them in the study of human nature. We can refer to psychologists and astrologists who accept the premises of humanology as *realistic psychologists* or *realistic astrologists* respectively, and of course *humanologists* will have to study the relevant parts of both of those old sciences. In any case, the main purposes of humanology can be clearly stated. These are to achieve a sound understanding of human nature and human reasoning, to promote the logic and sanity that is now lacking in our social and political institutions, and to help all individual humans understand and improve themselves.

Human Nature. The term 'human nature' has a range of meanings. It can mean how all humans are alike, how each of us is unique within that specieal framework, or any of the relative and collective aspects of our nature that are shared only by some people. But in all these senses we must remember that the individual is the only reality here, while the species and all of its subordinate classes are conceptual, or artificial hypotheses. Thus the only logical position on human nature is that of individualists—not extreme individualists, but only those who understand that our relations to others and otherness are also a real and important part of our nature.

We saw earlier that our formalists, being pragmatists who deny the prior reasoning that defines what is real, are necessarily collectivists. As such, they reason in class terms and then try to convince us that our collectives, from our family and culture to our state and the corporations it sanctions, are more real and important than our individual lives, which they then expect us to subordinate to, or even sacrifice for, those fictional collectives. Not surprisingly, then, the formalists of modern psychology have made so much of our collectivistic (class, social) attributes that these are well known to us now, if only superficially. But we don't understand our individuality anywhere near as well, and this is due mainly to the failure of our traditionalists to solve two basic problems about us: how we reason and why we are each unique.

I have offered my solution to the first problem, the standard of all human reasoning, so now we must consider our uniqueness, since we must solve this old problem in order to apply the Consideration Cycle to individuals as well as to our species.

The Dilemma of Uniqueness.   We all know through our common logic that we are each unique as individuals. No one else is you. So it is surprising that our intellectuals never explained what makes us unique. Modern psychologists never did, and our geneticists have only explained a few of our relative, or shared, attributes. Genethlialogic astrologers have always known implicitly what makes us unique, since it is the basis of their spatial analysis of a person's congenital nature, but even they haven't answered this question explicitly.

Some ancient Greeks dealt with this dilemma obliquely by positing the *psyche*, which literally means 'to breathe' and which is equivalent to mystical terms such as 'soul' or 'spirit'. They believed that we are each unique because we innately possess this defining essence, which was god-given or forever unknowable. It was then long assumed by most people that this single internal thing about us caused our uniqueness, and that no other cause needed to be found. Astrologers adopted this mystical view of uniqueness without analysis, and then came modern psychology, which soon divided into three conflicting schools of opinion on our uniqueness.

The *mystics* propose a fiction to account for it. This school includes the Freudians and Jungians, who accept the ancient assumption that we each have a unique 'psyche', 'soul', 'spirit', or 'mind' that somehow doesn't observe the Laws of Space. But to have their views accepted in the modern-era, they had to propose substitute causal 'laws'—such as psychic determinism, Freud's hypothesis of 'the unconscious', his division of the psyche into 'the id, ego, and superego', and Jung's proposal of 'the collective unconscious', none of which were ever proven to refer to anything real about us that could explain our uniqueness.

The *negativists*, who are mostly behaviorists, deny our uniqueness outright. They do so because they can't accept the old or the new mystical explanations and because, as pragmatists, they don't want to consider the theoretical dilemma of uniqueness anyway. In fact, *behaviorism* means the denial of the cause of our uniqueness and of nearly all reasoning we do that precedes our actions.

The *positivists* reject any form of psychologic mysticism, but they differ from the negativists because their common logic tells them that we are each unique and that they cannot build a valid psychologic construct without explaining this. Unfortunately, their consensus solution fails, but since it is the only nonmystical explanation of our uniqueness by modern psychologists, we should understand its illogic. They began by denying all of the old claims by mystics that there is *only one* thing about us that causes our uniqueness, but then they universalized this denial by claiming that there is *no* single attribute that causes our uniqueness. This is a logical error, but it suited their formalism because let them deny theory and build their constructs with hypothetical class terms only. Here is their 'solution'.

From their premise that the cause of our uniqueness was not any one thing about us, they concluded that it must be a set of things about us, all of which are descriptive attributes with concrete (class) names. But then they saw that no limited set of descriptive attributes could confer uniqueness upon us, because it is conceivable, even if less probable, that any partial set of attributes could be duplicated in another person. So they corrected this to reach their final hypothesis on uniqueness, which is that duplication is impossible if the set to which they refer is the set of *all possible* attributes of a person.

But they failed to see that this is a truism, since such a total summation will refer to our uniqueness whether their premise is true or false. If it is false, if there is only one cause of our uniqueness, then it will be one of the innumerable attributes that they never identified but that is included in their hypothetical sum of all possible attributes. Thus, they never explained our uniqueness, they just presupposed it. And since this was the only nonmystical explanation of uniqueness in their science, they agreed as a body that they would refer to this class conception of our uniqueness as a human's *personality*, an ambiguous term with many conflicting senses. You can see this ambiguity clearly in the now-classic text, *Theories of Personality*, by Calvin S. Hall and Gardner Lindzey

(New York: John Wiley & Sons, Inc., second edition 1970), where modern psychology's hypotheses on 'personality', starting with Freud and ending with 'existential psychology', are summarized. Of course, the authors never defined 'personality'; they were content to just describe how others in the field have used that term.

My Random House Dictionary shows one of the ambiguities in modern psychology's technical use of 'personality': "3. *Psychol.* **a.** the sum total of the physical, mental, emotional, and social characteristics of an individual. **b.** the organized pattern of behavioral characteristics of an individual." Two descriptions (a. and b.) are needed here to reflect the positivist-negativist disagreement on our uniqueness, but since "the sum total of" and "the organized pattern of" are equivalent phrases, 'personality' is a hypothetical class term either way. As such, it can explain how a person appears to a describer, but not what that person actually is.

The positivists' illogic here is the same fallacy that arises in logical terms in *Russell's paradox*, which, expressed in its verbal form, is this: Does not *the class of all classes*, since it too is a class, contain itself as well? No it doesn't, for the Cycle shows us that any set of related classes cannot be subsumed by another class, but only by a whole event; that is, by whatever context relates them all as siblings. And no class can subsume *all classes whatsoever*, for that absolute collection is only subsumed by Reality, or the Whole Event, and our perception of *the Reality* is plainly not a class cognition.

By the same logic, the class term 'personality' cannot mean the sum of all descriptive class terms *and* all universal terms that pertain to a whole person, for only a whole event can subsume all of its parts. The positivists' explanation of uniqueness begs the question, because any tertiary cognition presupposes our primary cognition of the uniqueness of the whole event that we selected as our initial context of reference. We can only describe a thing if we have first distinguished it as a unique context, and by that initial act, by pointing to *this* thing rather than some other thing, we affirm its uniqueness before we consider or sum any of its parts.

Here's another way to see their illogic. They claim that a person is unique only by virtue of being a certain *unique collection* of descriptive class attributes, but if no single attribute causes our uniqueness, as they say, then no sum or product of such attributes, none of which is unique, can magically introduce uniqueness into their total. Uniqueness is in their total, but it gets there another way. By their very act of hypothetical summation, they drag in through the back door, unannounced, the one attribute that causes anything to be unique. And since they never explicitly identified that attribute, they could not see why the genethlaic methods of astrology were indispensable to a sound understanding of human nature.

The solution to this dilemma is so well known to us all in our natural reasoning that I was surprised to find that no intellectual had stated it to explain our uniqueness. The ancient Greeks were correct in saying that only one attribute makes a person unique, but it is not the mystical psyche or soul, or any of the equivalent terms coined by later intellectuals. The concrete term 'personality' refers to a set of descriptive essences, but the abstract term 'uniqueness' refers to only one thing, a person's defining essence. People are not unique because of, say, the color of their eyes, their race, their gender, or any summation of such shared attributes. They are unique only because each person is a distinct event, a motion system that occupies a unique *position in space*, which is the one attribute that makes anything unique.

Nothing is unique to us until we identify its position in space. Because no two things can occupy the same space (formerly, the same space at the same time), *our space is our defining essence*, and it is necessarily unique. We share some spaces with other things, true, but not *our space*, which is defined by the spatial point (formerly, time) at which we leave our mother's womb. Every other property of anything in Reality is relative, or shared with some other things, and yet, amazingly, a plurality of these relative things is all that any formalist in our human sciences can propose as constituting our nature, either as a species or as individuals.

Character vs. Personality. The Cycle shows that we have two concepts, one reached by reduction and the other by accretion. Our new science therefore needs an abstract term for our essence, or congenital nature, and a concrete term for the sum of all our attributes at any later position, or 'time'. The terms *character* and *personality* are appropriate for this distinction, even though modern psychologists use these terms ambiguously and interchangeably.

Since 'personality' is a class term, it cannot be used to mean our unique congenital nature, which is a universal notion that applies to all people. But we can assign that universal meaning to 'character', which literally means a distinctive mark (with permanence implied, as in an engraving). So we must reject the use of 'character' in modern psychology as a concrete term that can be confused with 'personality'.

Our remaining problem is that 'personality' is ambiguous. Traditionally, as in the dictionary's sense 3 above, it is confused with uniqueness. It is also confused with 'character', for sense 5 in that same dictionary says that *personality* means "the essential character of a person." But the most common sense of the term is sense 4 in that dictionary: "the quality of being a person; existence as a self-conscious human being." But to use 'personality' in this sense—to mean a whole, unique, and existent person—is to use it as a complete-percept term, and not as the concrete-concept term that it is in sense 3 or as the abstract-concept term that it is in sense 5. In sense 4, its common-sense sense, it means a person's *complete nature*, or wholeness and realness as an event, and this means a person's uniqueness and character plus all of his or her private or shared experiences from birth to some later time of reference.

Obviously we must avoid this confused picture of human nature that modern psychologists entertain. We will therefore use 'character' to mean someone's innate, or congenital, nature, and will use 'personality' in only one of its many senses. That is, we will reject all of modern psychology's technical senses (such as 3a. and 3b. above and the other senses in the textbook cited) because these don't include our congenital character. If some modern psychologists wish to refer to some set of parts, or descriptive attributes, that they have arbitrarily selected for summation, then they should give that hypothesis its own class term. All that we need is the common-sense sense of 'personality', meaning the complete-percept sense. This is a reductive term, of course, since it doesn't mean the whole *person* that we first perceive, but only the whole of that person's *complete nature* as we now perceive it. For example, we first perceived *John*, but now in an act of reconsideration we are nonsensually perceiving (not conceiving) *John's personality*, just as we perceive any other lesser but real whole.

Other Issues. *First*, to maintain our distinction between our character and our personality, we must also distinguish our congenital *characteristics* from the postnatal *traits* we acquire after birth. By ignoring this distinction, modern psychologists can pretend that they are dealing with our essential nature when they are not, for their class term 'personality' not only drags our uniqueness into its summation, but also our other innate characteristics. A congenital characteristic can be described ex post facto just as any postnatal trait can be, so descriptive reasoners can't distinguish the one from the other or determine the cause of either.

For example, later I will define a certain congenital disposition in politics with the class term 'conservative', and traditionally one who believes the dogma based on the fiction of Jesus is described with the class term 'Christian'. We can even combine these terms to coin the narrower class term 'Christian conservative'. But those who don't know that conservatism is a congenital disposition will erroneously assume that we call people 'conservatives' by the same logic that we describe them as Christians, and then that, just as we can indoctrinate a Jew to make a Christian or vice versa, so we can indoctrinate a conservative to make a progressive. But that will never happen; the best we can do is to explain the innate psychologic impairment of conservatism and hope that some conservatives will work to mitigate its illogic in their decisions.

Second, since modern psychologists can't distinguish our innate dispositions from the ones we acquire later in life, they must assume that everything about us as individuals is collectivistic and subject to alteration by experience—either by our will or by socially imposed indoctrination, rules, discipline, punishments, rewards, or other manipulations. So two common premises in their science are that all people are manipulable, and that children and adults who disobey a society's rules should be controlled by manipulation. But our psychologic theory tells us that only some people are manipulable, and only in some respects that not all people share.

Third, we must avoid both the assumption in astrology that our innate characteristics are caused solely by spatial factors and the assumption in modern psychology that they are caused solely by genetics, conceived as if space didn't even exist.

To elaborate on this last point, there is no such thing as an hereditary factor that does not occur in space and is not affected by spatial displacements, so it is invalid to speak of 'the influence of heredity' on an organism if we mean by this a hereditary process that functions apart from the spatial Laws of Reality. We know that spatial displacements, in our solar system for instance, affect people and their traits after birth, so it is reasonable to assume that their effects are even greater on a more-sensitive embryo or fetus. So, just as it is illogical to study spatial displacements as if there was no hereditary process being affected by them, it is illogical to study the *hereditary* process, which is more than just the *genetic* process, without considering spatial displacements. But heredity is not our subject here, so let us just say that by 'character' we mean what *space and heredity together* have made of us by the time of our birth.

Fourth, our two old sciences of human nature, astrology and modern psychology, are empiristic (synthetic, nontheoretical) disciplines that observe and describe some parts, speculate on them, and then test these hypotheses in practice. But astrology also uses analytic (definitive) methods to study character, which modern psychology ignores, except for the few bits of knowledge offered by geneticists. I don't advocate either science as against the other, of course; instead, I hold that we need a new science because neither of these can meet our urgent need to understand human nature. Humanology won't replace them, it will just supersede them by proposing the fundamental theories they lack and by assuming responsibility for intellectual progress in its two main contexts: the psychologic in general and human nature in particular.

Nevertheless, since some people don't accept the validity of any astrological premise or method, I must defend those specific assumptions and methods of genethlaic astrology that my metaphysics defines as realistic and sound.

OUR NEED FOR ASTROLOGY

In 1975, an obscure academic magazine printed articles attacking astrology, clearly with the foreknowledge that *The New York Times* would join this conspiracy against free thought in science and report those opinions as a first-page 'news' event that, as usual, would be repeated by most other media corporations. This effort was unusual because academics rarely offer explicit arguments against astrology, since this reveals their own biases and illogic, and though this was a poor attempt to prove their case, I know of no better one to mention in their behalf. (See *The Humanist*, September/October 1975, published by the American Humanist Association and the American Ethical Union; editor, Paul Kurtz.)

The first article, *Objections to Astrology*, was just a short statement by 186 "leading scientists," mostly astronomers, denying astrology's validity. This was followed by a critical article entitled *A Critical Look at Astrology* written by an astronomer, Bart J. Bok, whose science qualifies no one in the epistemic and psychologic issues that alone tell us how to define a science and judge the validity of its reasoning. He began with the naïve argument from substance:

> The foundations of astrology began to crumble when we came to realize how vanishingly small are the forces exerted by the celestial objects on things and people on earth—and how very small are the amounts of radiation associated with them received on earth.

Beyond this, he offered a straw-man argument against mystical astrologers only; that is, he ignored the fact that every science has both mystical and realistic practitioners, and the fact that a science must be judged by its best practitioners, not its worst ones. He then appended to his article an irrelevant opinion by a modern psychologist who railed against this "magical practice," without mentioning that many modern psychologists were already using astrology then.

The next article, *Astrology: Magic or Science?*, was written by Lawrence E. Jerome, a freelance writer who offered a narrowed history of the science to buttress his claim that the roots of astrology lie in primitive magic. His basic argument was this: magic uses "the principle of correspondences" and so does astrology; therefore, astrology is like magic, and since we all know that magic is inane, it follows that astrology is also inane. The illogic here is plain, for one could similarly show that the historical source of any modern science was just such primitive reasoning, or 'magic'. From his reasoning it follows that our geometricians, psychologists, physicists, and other scientists are also practicing magic, since they all use a form of the real principle of correspondence (similarity, equivalence, congruence) daily in their work. If they didn't, they would be like empirics, who can't apply what they learn in one case to any other case or cases.

This conspiracy didn't work because it is not true that all astrological practice is mystical and illogical, and because many intelligent people know this by their common logic or their study of astrology. They also know that none of astrology's root assumptions have ever been refuted by any science. Moreover, no science today has the metaphysical and epistemic foundation that is needed to make it competent to judge the validity of any science or theory.

The old arguments for or against astrology are made irrelevant by what we have considered here, but let me state the new and conclusive argument that follows from our theories.

Our metaphysics holds that the defining essence of any event is its spatial field, and that every motion system shall be disrupted and ultimately destroyed by the influence of other motion systems within it or around it. But it defines this influence as solely spatial, which means that motion systems have collided merely if their spaces overlap, even if their defining particles (substance) never touch each other. Therefore, any interference in the *space* of an event is a displacement of that whole event, which is also to say that any overlapping of the spaces of two or more motion systems must cause mutual alterations in those systems.

Reality's extremes, the greatest and the least possible space, mark the limits of our displacement principle. Reality has no space beyond it in which to move, so it cannot be displaced, and though we can split an atom, we cannot divide or internally alter the smallest possible space; it can only be altered externally, in its direction of motion, as when light waves bend. So our metaphysics accepts Heisenberg's (1901-76) interference hypothesis, so long as it is not applied to the two spatial limits of Reality.[3]

So our premise here is a corollary of our displacement principle, one that was confirmed by quantum physics: *Any interference in the space of a motion system alters that system.* But if this is so, then astrology is a fundamental science, because its method is to define the *spaces* of major objects moving around us and to study those external spaces as the causes of displacements that alter all motion systems in their range, including our internal processes before, at, and after birth.

Most of astrology's truths result from its analysis of the terrestrial and the earth-sun motion systems, two spatial fields that are continually altered by their own motion and by that of major bodies of or intruders in our solar system. I know of no astrologer who has ever made the absurd claim that celestial bodies emanate particles (or "radiation") that affect us on earth; that is merely what ignorant scientists from other fields assume that astrologers believe. As their methods prove unequivocally, astrologers have always known that the *only* effects celestial bodies have on us result from *changes in their spatial position*. And, much as physicists hold that gravity is a warping of space rather than a 'force' of radiating particles, those effects on us occur solely because our personal spatial field is being *continually displaced* by the movements of bodies in the space that surrounds us.

Astrology doesn't study substances, it studies spaces, or dimensionality, and this requires the analytic reasoning that alienates synthetic reasoners such as astronomers. We can understand our astronomers' antagonism towards astrology this way: originally there was one science, astrology, but

---

[3] Like Einstein's correspondence (relativity) 'axiom', Heisenberg's hypothesis is a 'principle' only in the narrowed context of physics. And like our fourth principle, it applies only to motion systems between the two limits of Reality, neither of which is uncertain or indeterminate. It is better named the *interference* principle of physics, since 'uncertainty' and 'indeterminacy' refer only to internal states of mind, while 'interference' and 'displacement' can refer to either internal or external conditions.

it split into two because the astrologers who began astronomy as a distinct science were formalists who disliked primary, secondary, and tertiary reasoning. Far from "crumbling" in the modern era, astrology's foundation as a science has been confirmed by modern physics: first when it restated the ancient metaphysical views that time is relative and that our common notion of substance is an illusion, and then by its proof of its interference principle.

But astrology is also unique among all our sciences for another reason: because it tries to relate the apparently discrete realms of internal and external events. The critics of astrology would have us believe that we humans must never try to relate these realms, both of which consist of real events. But they can only deny that there is a bridge between these two kinds of events with arguments based on the mystical dualisms of *time*-space and *mind*-body, which are the truly inane notions in this debate. And since those dualisms also deceived traditional astrologers, they could not properly defend their science against these dogmatic attacks.

Astrologers tried for millennia to bridge our psychologic and nonpsychologic worlds, but this cannot be done through our traditional intellectual system. So the most serious criticism of traditional astrology possible is that its practitioners can't explain why the spatial displacements they study have the psychologic meanings they ascribe to them. Of course, modern psychologists also cannot substantiate their speculations about human nature. We see this same flaw in theology, which proposes a supernatural external reality without explaining how it could possibly be linked to our internal realities.

Without such a bridge, the psychologic premises of theology, modern psychology, and astrology are just fictions or unproven suppositions. But our new science changes this. With its correspondence principle and standard of human reasoning, we can now assign true meanings to the earlier efforts by astrologers to relate external spatial displacements to internal events.

The main reason why some astrological methods work in practice is that they analyze and compare certain distinct spaces of Reality and their displacements, or mutual alterations. With this understood, we can now end the old confusions about astrology's psychologic premises by stating its actual theory, which has not been explicated before. But we can only do this in the context of humanology. Traditional astrology cannot be our science of human nature because it also deals with nonpsychologic subjects and because, like modern psychology, it has no theory, no standard of human reasoning, and doesn't include all the disciplines and methods that are needed in a science of human nature.

THE THEORY OF HUMANOLOGY

As with our metaphysics, the theory of any science begins with the principles of occurrence and abstraction, or the propositions that '*Context X* is the whole event' and that 'Any subevent of *Context X* is a motion system'. So in expressing the theory of a science, we don't need to state these two primary principles each time, but when we reach the abstract concept, which begins our secondary reasoning, we have distinctions to make, so we must always state the last three principles, expressed in the terms of the science that we selected earlier as a subcontext.

For example, modern physicists might propose the following three principles as the distinct theory of their science. *Third*, as its dimensionality principle, their belief (if they can state it) that any physical motion system has four or more dimensions, with a companion proposition on how its parts move. *Fourth*, as its displacement principle, a broader statement of Heisenberg's interference principle. And *fifth*, as its correspondence principle, Einstein's statement that the laws of physics are the same in any motion system, or inertial frame of reference.

The theory of humanology is similarly analytic, and since its distinction between congenital character and developed personality is equivalent to the epistemic distinction between the abstract and concrete concepts, it will seem more like the assumptions of astrology, which studies the former, than those of modern psychology, which studies the latter.

3. The Principle of Unique Character. This is our metaphysic's dimensionality principle stated in characterological terms: *Any thing is* *uniquely defined by its spatial position.* From this it follows that a diagram of the major overlapping spatial fields at the birth of any event, living or nonliving, is a dynamic illustration of that event's character, or spatial relativity.

Every event is stamped at its birth with the character of its space (formerly space-time). Nonliving events also have this character, and a psychologic science must consider such events to the extent that they affect living things. Astrologers have always studied the character of nonliving events, especially human creations (such as a state or constitution) that directly affect human affairs, and our new science must do this also. When an event begins, it starts to acquire its personality, but this doesn't alter what it was at first: a distinct spatial event with a limited life and range of motion. Some old confusions are clarified by this third principle, mainly these four.

Conception versus Birth. Critics of astrology have argued that the true beginning of an event is its conception and not its birth, but this is not the case. Since the uniqueness of an event is its spatial position, any reference to the process that produced it refers to a different spatial event, and it is fallacious to mix two contexts of reference in an argument. If we don't hold consistently that the point of birth is the true beginning and distinct identity of any creation, such as a new organism or a new notion, then either we are proposing an infinite regression of causes or we are arbitrarily selecting as its direct cause one event in the chain of prior events.

Our metaphysics keeps our thinking straight on this, for it tells us that a whole event is only defined by its spatial relativity. Nothing is a distinct event or a valid context of reference until it has been born and exists separately. To refer to an unformed notion in your mind or fetus in your womb, therefore, is not to refer to the unique event of that future notion or child. Until it is born into its own space and path, it is not a distinct event; it is just an internal part of its carrier's space and path. The confusion here results from speaking of two events, the birthing process and the process of the thing's later life, as if they were one and the same process. But by definition an event's *conception* is internal to its parent motion system, so while we can speak hypothetically of a notion or person being formed *as if* it had been born, it is not yet a separate event in reality.

An internal event that has not yet been externalized has no life (character, space) of its own.

Therefore any human science, including jurisprudence, must begin its reasoning about a person from the point of his or her birth in space and independence from the mother's space, for otherwise it is not reasoning logically. Until there is a time of birth, no real person, legal person (corporation), or fictional character exists.[4]

Destiny. It is an ancient belief that the birth, or character, of an event determines its *destiny*, meaning the future end that is a consequence of its beginning in space. This is an enticing notion, but it cannot be justified. It is based on the observation that we cannot alter the broader path of motion on which we were dispatched at birth. True enough, but we do have a limited power of locomotion, or a power to accelerate (change our direction), so within certain limits our future path can be changed by our will or external forces. Some events occur to us as a result of our inalterable congenital characteristics, and in this sense we can say (redundantly) that

---

[4] Hence the US Supreme Court's confusion in its abortion decisions. Rather than settling the issue directly by granting legal protection against murder only to a person, it granted it to a nonperson. And its failure to distinguish the birthing process from the life process also led it (in *Roe v. Wade*) to the fictional notions of a pregnancy's 'trimesters' and (in *Planned Parenthood v. Casey*) of the 'viability' of a fetus. True to its character as a rightist creation, it again introduced contradictions into our legal system; this time by clouding the previous legal definition of a real person, as recorded by a birth certificate. And it did this *solely* to allow the old irrational religions to which it members were biased to use the power of the state to subordinate women to men (who have no such issue) and to intrude on the natural right of a female to control her private space and internal processes. Thus does the Republican Party use religion and party loyalty to dupe many women into supporting their gender's social and political inequality. As even the father must recognize, a woman's womb is not a public matter, no more so than is her mind. A just state will always have an *overriding social justification* for denying the natural rights of an individual, which include the sanctity of his or her mind, body, or womb. As for a womb, this objective justification does exist in our insanely overpopulated world, but for preventing births, not for requiring them.

they are 'destined' to be, but most events are either beyond our control or are a consequence of postnatal changes or decisions that are not destined in that sense.

Forecasting. Destiny aside, a methodological issue in our new science is how best to predict future changes in a personality. Psychologists seldom try to do this, and when they do, they have no objective method for it. Astrologers attempt it with various kinds of postnatal charts, some of which are and some of which aren't scientifically acceptable. But no astrological chart in itself, apart from the intuition of its interpreter, can predict changes that are caused by external interferences or our will, because any forecast assumes either that a current trend will continue uninterrupted or that an expected disruption of that trend will probably occur.

For instance, an astrological chart for a future date assumes that our solar system will be basically unchanged then, but nothing precludes a celestial cataclysm that will change it. Similarly, our learning experiences include many interferences that cause us to accelerate (change our direction) voluntarily. Forecasting changes in personality is thus largely a matter of making educated guesses, or synthetic speculations, about future events and their psychologic effects on us. And the character-personality opposition tells us that in some psychologic areas astrologers will make the better guesses and in others modern psychologists will.

Essentially, all forecasters track only changes of direction (acceleration). But astrologers differ in this because, rather than only tracking changes in ex post facto measurements or statistics (such as population shifts, market indexes, public-opinion surveys, and so on), they first track events like the seasons and planetary motions—broad spatial trends that have been proven to affect the human psychologic and all human affairs, including our politics, markets, and social relations. These celestial trends are also altered by interferences, but far less often than human affairs, which are manipulated daily by proactive human conspirators.

Free Will. Our metaphysics tells us that any organism is *free* only to the extent that it has the power of locomotion and acceleration; that is, the ability to change the direction of its present path in space, physically or psychologically. We know, for instance, that some people stay in one community all their lives and travel only passively, as the spinning earth or other people dictate, and that some, in the same passive way, never voluntarily alter the direction of their reasoning. Both kinds of change give us an altered perspective and a new personality, but everything that lies beyond our personal power of acceleration is determined for us, either ultimately by Reality or relatively by other motion systems (including people) that dictate our motion or otherwise interfere with it. As for absolute determinism, or fatalism, there is an element of truth in this, but only in the ways that we are subject to the inalterable Laws of Reality that rule every subevent, such as our spatial relativity and our termination as a unique event.

Anything else that affects us is relative, so it is subject to interference and alteration. Nothing relative is fixed forever, so our path in life, like the direction of a market or of our politics, is merely our current trend. We can alter it voluntarily in some respects, but not in others, and it is a task of our science to distinguish those cases.

4. *The Principle of Spatial Interference.* The fourth principle of humanology's theory has been implied by astrological practice since its inception: *Any interference with the space of a motion system alters that system and its environment.*

Astrologers use the same coordinate systems and mathematical methods used in astronomy. By these objective methods, they track the motion systems in our field of experience and then, with the hypothetical reasoning used in every science, they study the effects of these motions on us. They study a person's motion on earth, the motions to which the earth subjects us in its rotation and revolution, and the motion of all significant bodies within the solar system. Some also look for effects on us caused by more-distant spatial events such as constellations, fixed stars, black holes, supernova, and so on.

No one knows for certain how far beyond the earth the spatial displacements that affect us extend. But in an organic science it is invalid to speak of *environmental* influences on an organism when what we mean by this is arbitrarily restricted, as it is in modern psychology and biology, both of which study only an organism's social and proximate natural environment. There is no good reason why one arbitrarily selected piece of the earth or even the whole earth should be considered the upper limit of environmental influences on terrestrial organisms. Those who use such a narrowed limit have the burden of proving that it actually is the upper limit of effects. But they have never done that, and they have unwisely ignored all the empirical evidence offered by astrologists which proves that the limit of spatial displacements that affect us lies far beyond the earth. And until we know that limit for certain, any science is unsound if it narrows this distance merely to make the work of its practitioners easier.

5. The Principle of Event Relation. Humanology's correspondence principle is: *Every event is related to every other event in its dynamics as a motion system.*

Both astrology and modern psychology observe this principle, but they don't express it. It is plainly used in astrology, which tracks motion systems and uses this principle to relate various motions systems to their different psychologic effects on people. Its use in modern psychology is less obvious, but just as a physicist cannot study events in the Andromeda galaxy without assuming that the universal laws of physics (its theory) that hold here in our galaxy will also hold there, so a psychologist cannot study humans without assuming that the universal laws of psychology (its theory) will hold for all of them. We can't avoid using this relational principle because to do so we would have to reason without our concepts, our universal and class ideas.

Here again humanology disputes modern psychology and biology on limits, for our theory holds that any organism's relations extend even beyond the limits of its species or genus. Since every subevent of Reality is subject to the Laws of Reality, each has a dynamic relation to every other subevent, or process in space. As individuals, we are each related in different ways to all other humans, all living things, and all nonliving processes in Reality. If we think that we are not related to nonliving things, it is only because we have chosen to ignore the patterns of motion that do relate us to them.

The Study of Human Nature

Following the theory just described, humanologists will reason about human nature from these premises: (1) Individuals are unique and are the only reality in any collective, so we must understand them before we speculate about their artificial collectives. (2) To understand our uniqueness as individuals we must consider the spatial factors that cause it, and then distinguish its opposite conceptual senses, character and personality. (3) Our character is caused by all the prenatal factors of *heredity and space* (environment) that shape it, and it is complete only at the instant of our birth as an independent motion system. (4) Every postnatal factor that affects our developed personality does so through our congenital character.

Our first methodological question is how to determine an individual's character. When we learn that genetic factors cause our gender, the color of our eyes or hair, our propensity to certain illnesses, and so on, we learn something about human nature, but very little, and nothing at all about our psychologic, or how we reason. The belief that genetic factors alone will someday tell us what we need to know about our character is wishful thinking, since those factors are the substance of the matter, not the dynamics of it. To understand an individual, we must consider genetic and other prenatal factors only in the subsuming context of the spatial displacements in the environment, and this requires astrological methods or something much like them.

Our work as humanologists would be easier if we could assume that a natal chart shows only the inalterable characteristics of a person, but this is not so. It diagrams the major spatial fields at birth, but these record both inalterable factors of character and alterable factors of personality that start changing immediately after birth. Astrologers therefore supplement the natal chart with other spatial diagrams based on it, such as *progressed*, *relocation*, and *return* charts for later times. Those natal factors that are alterable with aging or relocation introduce most of the complications and disputes in astrology, but these will not concern us in this work.

The four intellectual dispositions that we considered earlier are determined by some natal factors that are inalterable and by some that can be changed by relocation. But the four dispositions in any of our five psychologic systems (which are defined later), such as our moral and political attitudes, are inalterable characteristics—not in the sense that their effects cannot be modified by experiences and decisions after birth, but rather in the sense that their directional impulses are always a part of our psychologic. Each such impulse is like a tide against which we must swim or to which we must surrender. And to determine these fundamental dispositions of character, humanology uses an entirely new astrological method that I derived initially from the Consideration Cycle, a method that employs only a subject's natal chart.

Besides the new methods introduced here, our science must also use the valid methods of genetics and astrology that reveal factors of character and those of modern psychology and other human sciences that reveal the factors of personality. But our geneticists have never considered the effects of spatial displacements on the processes they study, and they may not do so for some time, so until they correct this error, we must proceed with the study of human character without them, or with astrological methods only. We must also break our bad traditional habit of trying to explain people partialistically, or in congenital or postnatal terms only. Our new science helps us here, for its methods tell us objectively how we differ or are alike in our congenital impulses and psychologic dispositions, and why throughout our life we make the same errors or positive contributions regardless of our education, ideologies, cultures, religions, families, political parties, or other postnatal experiences.

Humanology also frees us of the illogical conception in modern psychology known as *psychic determinism*. This methodological hypothesis, which Freud borrowed from others and put in his own terms, holds that traumatic experiences in early life shape our later choices and personality. Of course they do, for that is what we mean by 'a traumatic experience'. But what caused that experience in the first place? To what extent was it caused by a subject's congenital character or by postnatal spatial displacements or by other people? Though this old assumption about us is circular, vague, and plainly wrong, it is deeply imbedded in all modern thought about human nature. Indeed, there is hardly a novel, play, or movie of the past century that has not used it, and only it, to give its audience a simplistic and unrealistic explanation of the 'causes' of its characters' situation or behavior.

There are several logical errors in this basic assumption of psychoanalysis, and hence in every news article, academic study, court decision, biography, or work of art that relies on it. The first is the circularity, or question begging, just noted. There are always earlier events in our life that have influenced our present personality, but identifying them doesn't tell us their cause or their relative importance in our nature. The second is its causal assumption, for the claim that an earlier experience caused a later effect must be proven in each case, and not just assumed from an unsubstantiated general hypothesis on psychologic causation. The third is that an analyst cannot know whether the two events, the traumatic one and the later one said to be caused by it, were not both the effects of some earlier cause that he or she is ignoring, such as a congenital characteristic. The fourth is that, at all of the times involved, it ignores spatial displacements. The fifth is that it applies determinism to relative life events, which is to universalize a synthetic hypothesis in order to use it invalidly as an absolute analytic principle. And the sixth is its failure to acknowledge congenital character. In a world where inherent character, or uniqueness, is not understood, an analyst has no basis for concluding that a certain kind of early 'traumatic' event will cause the same kind of psychologic problem (or any problem, for that matter) in everyone.

Determinism applies only to our universal attributes, not our relative ones, which are alterable and subject to interferences. For instance, as subevents of Reality our death is predetermined, but how, when, and where we die is not. And if we were affected by a major event earlier in life, we may no longer be; we may have suppressed it, but we may also have surpassed it. Psychoanalysts propose both psychic determinism and the power of their therapy to overcome its harmful effects, which is to admit that those effects are not unavoidable. This we all know anyway from the healthy people around us who have overcome such early-life traumas without their help, and the astrological method presented in this work tells us objectively just which people are most or least likely to do that.

The chief error of psychic determinism—and of historical, economic, biological, environmental, and political determinism as well—is its denial of our free will. It denies our power to accelerate, to change our direction psychologically or physically, as well as the power of others to force or entice us to do so against our will.

Psychic determinism is also cynical, for it universalizes the fact that almost all of us have had some unpleasant experiences in childhood in order to conclude the universal 'principle' that we are all sick. Freud, a conservative, expressed this absolute cynicism in his 'Oedipus complex'. Here he borrowed from ancient Greek literature again, and this time from a work that expresses the strict view of justice (or criminal liability) that no sane society would ever impose on its people. This fictional 'complex' of his is just a nontheistic form of the fallacious religious doctrine of original sin, which suggests that psychoanalysis, like behaviorism, has the social intention of serving rightist political ends.

If a psychoanalyst is not reasoning from a person's character and later spatial displacements, it is question-begging and arbitrary to search for early-life experiences that may have influenced later events, and then to imply that genetics plus one or a few of these traumatic experiences suffice to define a human's personality. Modern psychologists who use this illogical and unscientific method prejudge the individual at the first interview, so they know the kind of early events they are searching for, hence the question begging, and they must select those events from an incomplete list of events in a subject's memory, hence the arbitrariness. Any composite picture of a person that they reach in this way is thus subjective and seriously incomplete.

In seeking the causes of someone's personality, it is invalid to stop wherever one chooses in the backward chain of causation; such a search must go back at least to that person's birth. Modern psychology tells us nothing of our innate character; at best it can only give us a small piece of the picture of our present personality. And any conclusions that jurists, politicians, or social scientists reach from its arbitrary snapshots are similarly fallacious, and hence unjust.

Astrology and modern psychology are both theoryless practices, and consequently they are often unrealistic. It has been suggested that we should merge these sciences, but two wrongs cannot make a right, as misguided attempts to do this have proven. Each has different goals, methods, and patrons, and neither is dedicated to understanding psychologic processes in general and human nature in particular. Their lack of theory and logic blocked their progress in many areas, so they contributed to the failures of the other human sciences, which in a vicious circle then blocked further progress in them.

The larger problems we face in understanding human nature can only be solved by establishing a new science such as I am proposing here. It may be a while before humanology is accepted and coopted by our academic institutions, but we can establish it now in our minds, work, and intellectual networks without academia. Only such a science will ever be able to explain our nature as humans and individuals, and if we structure it soundly, it will then be hard for any state, religion, science, communication medium, or other corporation or social institution to manipulate us. They do this, remember, in two time-tested ways, the sole purpose of which is to make us all irrational. Their blunt way is to promote fears in us, through words or terrorist acts; their other way, which is even more effective, is to teach and continually repeat false notions about our individual, social, or specieal nature.

Chapter 5. Our Psychologic Process

General Issues

We have considered the Consideration Cycle analytically to explain its structure, cardinal ideas, and quadrantal modes, but now we must consider it synthetically, or psychologically, in order to add to that analytic framework the intermediate ideas that we cognize within the quadrants. People vary in how many intermediate ideas they can cognize, as I said, but since we must keep our standard universal to our species, we will differentiate only those intermediate ideas that, barring abnormal physical damage, are cognized by us all.

The Cycle's structural elements and cardinal ideas are defined by our terrestrial motion system, but our intermediate ideas are defined by the spatial displacements caused by the ten astrological planets, which have long affected every organism on earth. My tertiary hypothesis here, for which I provide empirical evidence later, is that, as a result of our distinct cognition of each of those spatial displacements, the Consideration Cycle has ten major divisions, or epistemic ideas, with which we perform our most important psychologic functions. Though other factors will be considered later, these ten cognitions and the five psychologic systems they cause in us, which are shown in their logical order in *Figure 6*, are the heart of my psychologic theory. We will consider each system in turn in the next chapter; in this chapter our task is to understand the general psychologic issues that apply to them all.

The Whole Cycle. The Consideration Cycle moves from our initial perception of a real and whole event to a final internal or external act. The entire process is basically this.

Our consideration begins with our perception of an event, and if we consider that event further, we next cognize what I call a 'wish response' relative to that event. In the rest of that reasoning cycle we transform this

Figure 6. The Consideration Cycle

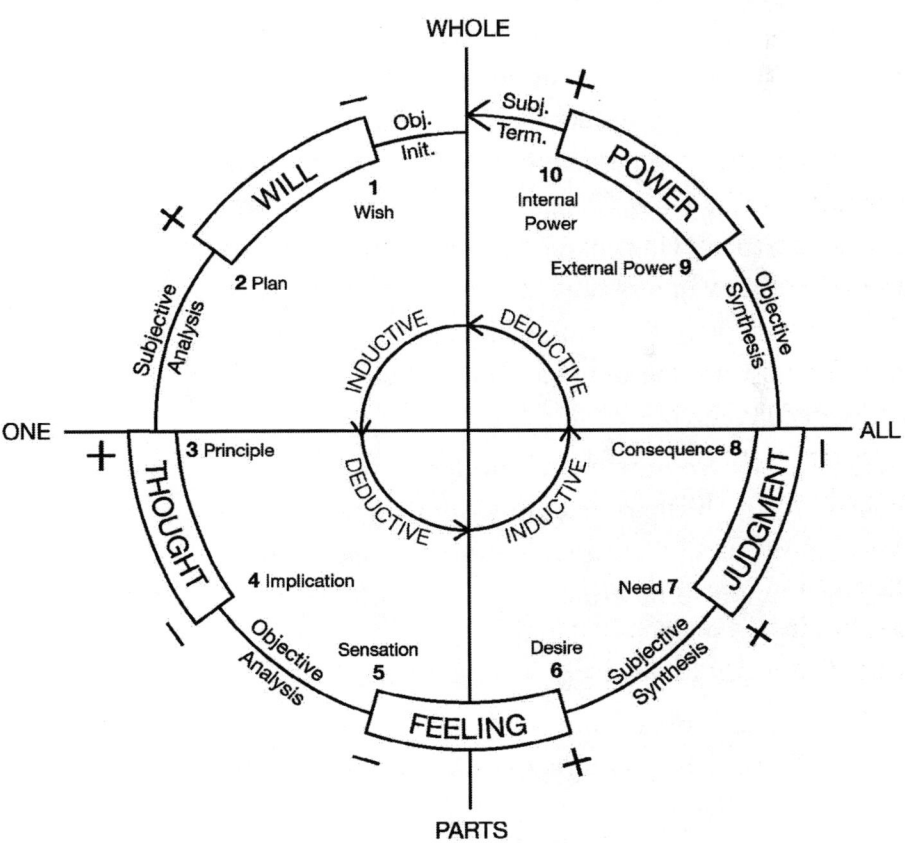

initial global wish into a specific personal power. The Cycle as a whole is thus a *wish-to-power* cycle, and we all continuously experience this perfectionistic drive. Our goal in any act of consideration is to achieve an understanding that will give us the power either to act immediately or to perform such an act in the future, so our *power* is either immediate or potential, but in both cases it is an *understanding*—by which I mean the integrated *physical and mental* learning that is the goal of a consideration and its penultimate point, which precedes our final decision to act or not act. Thus, our personal power is our understanding.

Impulses. As our focus advances in the Cycle, we experience the ten major epistemic ideas mentioned, each of which has what I call an 'impulse'. These congenital impulses are among the most important of our characteristics. They reflect the fact that an epistemic idea has only two possible directions of cognition; that is, we cognize it either by *projecting* (creating, sending out, transmitting) it from our internal reality or by *assimilating* (observing, taking in, receiving) it from our external reality. So most of us are by nature both creator-transmitters and observer-receivers, and usually an act of communication is not, as we say, a two-way street, but rather a four-lane highway, where both parties are at all times both sending and receiving.

These two cognitive directions are alternatives, but they are not choices. As our birth in space determines and as our natal chart indicates, we use only one of these two directions at each epistemic idea, and after birth each impulse functions in us naturally in that congenital direction only. I refer to these impulses as the *polarity* or *charge* of our reasoning at each defined point of the Cycle. If at any point we are impelled to send out a cognition, or transmit it from our internal reality, then we will say that the impulse is *projective* and has as a *positive charge* (+). But if we are impelled to take in at that point, or to receive a cognition from external reality, then we will say that the impulse is *assimilative* and has a *negative charge* (-).

Thus, an individual functions with either a positive or a negative charge at each of these ten major cognitive points, and is impelled to either transmit (project) or receive (assimilate) it, and cannot naturally do the opposite. The best we can do if we realize that one of our impulses is the opposite of what our standard defines as the logical charge at that epistemic point, is to impose on our reasoning some conscious artificial steps, or some explicated reasoning, that may negate some of its harmful psychologic or social effects. So if we have any ability to overcome such a point of illogic in our natural reasoning, it is due to our learning and language, which of course we use more often to rationalize our illogical decisions.

Systems and Phases. Our next question is, How do these ten sequential cognitions relate to each other as adjacent pairs in the Cycle? This is important because it is as pairs that they define ten intervals of considerational space—except that, since the Cycle is a helix and not a circle, in a single act of consideration one of these intervals works like two spaces. In *Figure 6* the Cycle is shown open at the top to reflect the fact that one half of the top space is connected to the prior act of consideration and the other half to the next act. This top space of the Cycle thus differs from its other intervals, for three reasons. First, no other interval is directly connected to any prior or later act of consideration or to any nonpsychologic event; they are all confined to reasoning about the current context. Second, its halves have opposite functions: starting or ending an act of consideration. Third, it is divided by our most powerful cognition, the complete percept by which we perceive real and whole events, or contexts of reference, and begin a reasoning act.

Nevertheless, all ten intervals of the Cycle are defined by a polar pair of epistemic ideas, and when we consider the charges of both these cognitions, as shown for the standard Cycle in *Figure 6*, we see that these ten spaces are of two kinds, depending on whether their two polar cognitions have like or unlike charges. From our metaphysics, which sees 'charge' as a matter of spatial direction, and from the familiar example of magnetic impulses, we will hypothesize that *like charges repel* and *unlike charges attract*. Subject to empirical testing, then, we will hold that the defining poles of each space either cohere as attracting ideas to form a tight system or they repel each other to prevent the formation of a system. The

Cycle thus has two basic kinds of psychologic space. In the four spaces bordered by cognitions of like charge, (- -) or (+ +), their repulsion moves our consideration rapidly from the first to the second pole. But in the six spaces bordered by unlike charges, (- +) or (+ -), their attraction delays our consideration, and we cannot move on in our reasoning until we have reconciled these opposite impulses.

I distinguish these psychologic spaces with the following names. The top interval of the Cycle is *the prime interval*, the halves of which in a single act of consideration are the *initiating* and the *terminating* intervals. The other five cohering spaces are our psychologic *systems*, and the four repelling spaces that connect these systems are our psychologic *phases*. The prime interval is of great psychologic significance, but we won't discuss it in detail in this work. It is a system when it relates two different events, or contexts, but in a single act of consideration each of its halves functions like a phase.

We normally move quickly across a phase, but not across a system. It takes a conscious effort to propel our reasoning out of each cohering system, and we exert that effort when we conclude that we have lingered there long enough to satisfy our present purpose. We each have some power to hasten, slow, or abort most acts of consideration, and we might linger in one system for several reasons—such as the importance of the context to us, our inability to handle that system's logic, a difficulty in grasping or reconciling its ideas, and the conflicts or harmonies between its ideas and those of the other systems.

Since the two cognitions of a phase have the same charge, we either transmit-transmit (+ +) or receive-receive (- -) there. So the reasoning direction of a phase is either outward or inward, and these impulse directions are the reality-referents of our old terms *subjective* and *objective* respectively. But the two cognitions of a system have opposite charges that impel us either to transmit-receive (+ -) or to receive-transmit (- +) there. So a logical psychologic system is both subjective and objective; that is, it is a polarity of opposite impulses as shown in *Figure 6*, so that one is a subjective projection from inside to outside and the other is an objective assimilation from outside to inside. This means that the natural function of a psychologic system, and hence of any formal intellectual or social system that we construct in imitation of it, is to reconcile some state of objectivity with some state of subjectivity. It is then the function of the phase that follows that system to store its reasoned conclusions in memory, as explained later.

As *Figure 6* illustrates, the memory function of the phases and of the prime interval show that we have three different states (kinds) of objectivity and three different states of subjectivity. This conflicts with the traditional hypothesis which holds, for no particular reason, that we have only one state of objectivity and only one state of subjectivity. This view of our psychologic systems and phases also lets us define two other terms that traditionalists know only as vague ex post facto descriptions: *consciousness* and its true opposite *subconsciousness*.

Consciousness and Subconsciousness. In a psychologic system, we need some time to reconcile its polar cognitions and then move on, so we must either make a conscious effort to complete the reasoning of that system or abort that act of consideration there. This is not so of a psychologic phase, for its repelling poles force us through it too quickly to notice the passage of any space there; we can store a memory there, but then we move on without focusing on its contents. So, by this factor of charge, the Cycle defines the five systems and the prime interval as the only intervals in which we are normally *conscious* of our reasoning.

Consciousness is caused by charge, but descriptively it is just a more intense focus, not much different from when we willfully strain our muscles in physical work. This extra intensity is required to reconcile a system's poles, the objective idea (-) and the subjective idea (+) that define it as a system. It is also why we can withdraw (recall) a past experience from the prior phase when we reach that system again in a reconsideration. It is only this extra time and focal force that lets us form a conclusion that can be stored in memory, much as photons paint on photographic film or as electric impulses fix a binary charge in a computer's memory. Our conscious systems create or recall specific images; our subconscious phases merely store them.

Our psychologic theory thus admits no hypothetical state of *unconsciousness*; that is, no 'unconscious' or 'collective unconscious'. We cannot have unconscious ideas or unconscious reasoning, because we define an idea as a psychologic impression, and if we have that impression, then some part of our body is aware (conscious) of it. So the issue is not whether we are aware of our ideas or our reasoning, for we are always aware of them in some sense; rather, it is whether we are aware of them enough to make them mentally tangible, which we must do to memorize or explicate them. The notion of unconsciousness doesn't contradict the notion of consciousness, it denies it. To propose an unconscious cognition is to claim, as rationalists do, that we can have a cognition (idea) that is not a psychologic impression (idea).

Strictly speaking, the notion of an unconscious realm of memories of any kind is absurd, but if one only means by this that something that was previously conscious is now forgotten, then it is just a poor choice of words. It is common knowledge, and not the discovery of any modern psychologist, that we humans can forget by excision, suppression, or disuse what we once knew consciously, and that prodding by ourself or another may help us recall it. But anything that we once concluded in our reasoning was a consciously formed tangible notion then; otherwise we couldn't recall it from our memory banks, not even with the best psychoanalyst to prod us.

The terms 'consciousness' and 'subconsciousness' don't refer to our epistemic ideas; they refer to our reasoning, or to the psychologic spaces that connect our conscious cognitions, and each of these spaces has a distinct function as a reasoning interval. Our reasoning in a system is cohesive, which is why we can make tangible products there that we can store in memory, but our reasoning in a phase is so fleeting that we can create nothing in it. And it must be the case that we store different kinds of memories in separate subconscious spaces, for otherwise all our memories would all arise to consciousness when we try to do any reasoning, which would then be impossible. The distinction here is between reasoning that we do or don't take extra time to notice. And we are only able to explicate our reasoning with symbols because our psychologic has these systems and phases and they function together; that is, we first create or adopt a tangible conclusion in a system, then we store it in a phase, and then we recall it in a system.

The Cycle's spatial conception of subconsciousness suggests that, contrary to traditional materialists, we are correct in claiming, as we all do in some way, that we have 'instinctive' or 'intuitive' faculties. Traditionalists are aware of our conscious systems because these are amenable to explication and mere descriptions, but our subconscious phases mystify them because they don't see our psychologic wholistically. If they did, they would see that some people, such as those we call 'psychics', have an exceptional sensitivity, or particularized intelligence, that gives them a greater power than most people have to sense their reasoning in the subconscious phases and to recall the memories stored there. Some people also have more strength than others in the functions of one or both halves of the prime interval, as noted below.

Our Five Conscious Systems. *Figure 6* shows the five systems as boxes and the four phases and prime interval as lines connecting them. After considering the most appropriate conventional terms for the functions of our five psychologic systems in the Cycle, I named them, in their natural order, our *will, thought, feeling, judgment,* and *power* systems, which I abbreviate as *W, T, F, J,* and *P.*

As I said, the prime interval differs from those five systems because it bridges any act of consideration to the prior and subsequent acts. So it is not a 'system of reasoning' in the sense that its reasoning is confined to only one context of reference. Its function is to store and relate *events*, and the stronger we are in this function, the stronger our instincts are. Its memory bank consists of many events, which we organize and reorganize as an hierarchic structure of events that are of greater or lesser personal importance to us. In its initiating half, we store perceived events and our instinctive responses to them; in its terminating half, we store our understandings, or developed powers. And in the Cycle's four other memory banks we store the consciously reconciled notions produced in the preceding psychologic system.

It is speculative but not unreasonable to further propose that the hereditary process somehow causes individuals to begin life with a set of specieal and cultural instincts already implanted in their prime interval's memory bank. This is the only reality referent that I can grant to Jung's poorly named notion of a 'collective unconscious', which is better called a specieal or cultural 'instinct'. Something similar may also occur in our other memory banks, the Cycle's four phases. All together, this would explain why so many false traditions persist in spite of our common logic, why it so difficult to uproot them in the public consciousness, and why so many old mystical proposals (such as god, spirits, soul, innate ideas, the unconscious, or other worlds or dimensions) seem plausible even to people who can consciously reason well.

It also explains why none of the sacred texts of our religions today reflect conceptions that were new when they were written. Given the extraordinary illogic—the proven contradictions, fictions, and lies—of all those texts, it is inconceivable that any one of them was solely the product of someone's conscious reasoning. Perhaps specieal or cultural instincts are not transferred through generations by inheritance, but it is hard to imagine anything else that can explain the persistence in humans over millennia of so many totally irrational notions.

The Impulse Pattern

The Consideration Cycle gives us a new and powerful analytic tool. Specifically, we can refer to a person's natal chart and determine the congenital charge at each of these major epistemic ideas, record these cognitive impulses to form a total pattern of ten charges, and so get the equivalent of a psychologic X-ray of that person. And even though this picture is derived from a natal chart, it is not just a snapshot of one instant, for it reveals how that person will handle those psychologic functions throughout life. I refer to the string of symbols that records these ten charges as an individual's *Impulse Pattern*.

To derive the Impulse Pattern, we refer to a natal chart and, using the astrological method explained in *Appendix A*, we determine the charge for each of the ten numbered cognitions in *Figure 6*. We then arrange these ten symbols in their numbered order there and consider them two at a time, which pairs them by psychologic system. Since there are two cognitions and two possible charges for each, a system has one of four impulse permutations: (+ +), (- +), (- -), or (+ -), and we can simplify the string of ten symbols by using only one symbol for each of those permutations. This will give us only five symbols in an Impulse Pattern, which we should always express in the logical order prescribed by the Cycle: W, T, F, J, and P.

We will symbolize the impulse of a system as follows. If both of its poles are positively charged (+ +), we will say that it is *projective*, and symbolize it with a single +. If both poles are negatively charged (- -), we will say that it is *assimilative*, and symbolize it with a single -. Otherwise the impulse is either (- +) or (+ -), and for each system one of these is the logically *balanced* impulse, symbolized with B, and the other is the logically *reversed* impulse, symbolized with R. As *Figure 6* shows, the balanced impulse in our will, feeling, and power systems is (- +), while in our thought and judgment systems it is (+ -).

Using my own natal chart in example, the string of ten symbols has six projective and four assimilative points, which in their logical one-to-ten order are (+ + + + + - - - - +). When we pair the adjacent symbols to get the systemic impulses, we get (+ +) (+ +) (+ -) (- -) (- +), and in the simplified form just described, we write this as (+ + R - B). So verbally we would say that I am *projective* in will and thought, *reversed* in feeling, *assimilative* in judgment, and *balanced* in power. And this tells you more about my character than you would now think possible.

The most extreme Impulse Patterns are the four in which all five systems have the same impulse. The most impulsive people are totally projective (+ + + + +) or assimilative (- - - - -), since these patterns have no contrary charge to balance and restrict the impulses. This gives us an objective definition of *impulsiveness*. Traditionalists call highly projective people 'impulsive' because they equate this term to excessive projections from the self, but highly assimilative people are also impulsive. Projective people eagerly want to give or do things to others, and assimilative people eagerly want to receive or take things from others.

A balanced (B) system is not impulsive, so our only *non-impulsive* people are those with the totally balanced (BBBBB) pattern, which occurs when all ten charges are as shown in *Figure 6*, our universal standard. People with six to nine cognitions of one charge are slightly to very impulsive. Those with five cognitions of each charge but no balanced (B) system have the totally reversed pattern (RRRRR), and they are *erratically impulsive* in all areas, because they are very slow in their systemic reasoning and yet always in a rush to get out of it. The totally balanced pattern is the most logical one, and the totally reversed pattern is the most illogical one, since the charge at all ten points is the opposite of the one in our standard. The two other extreme cases, (+++++) and (- - - - -), are only illogical at five cognitions.

The number of possible Impulse Patterns is limited, of course. Since the ten points can have either of two charges, the possibilities are 2^{10} permutations, or 1,024 distinct patterns. So with respect to this one congenital factor only, the Impulse Pattern, there are 1,024 basic character types. We are each born with one of those 1,024 patterns, and its impulses direct our natural reasoning, or logic, forever. As we mature, we can artificially compensate for some of their negative effects, but we cannot alter their charge, or the impulse they give us in reasoning.

Because our Impulse Pattern controls our logic and is inalterable, it reflects our most important innate characteristics. Our reasoning-mode and cardinal-idea preferences are also important, but they can be altered somewhat by relocation after birth. Other factors, such as our congenital intelligence and learning experiences, also affect how well or poorly we reason about things, but they don't influence our dynamic dispositions in reasoning—meaning the underlying logic or illogic that doesn't vary no matter what we reason about or when we do so. And since an intelligent person can share an Impulse Pattern with unintelligent people, even imbeciles, it is a mistake to assume that our 'intelligence' alone determines our logicality. In fact, it only influences our logic indirectly, by affecting how well we can see and explicate our natural reasoning. We can sharpen our reasoning and logic through learning experiences, but our basic dispositions in those functions are not learned, they are congenital, and they are determined first by our Impulse Pattern and then by our reasoning-mode and cardinal-idea preferences.

The Impulse Pattern is not all that we must know to understand someone's psychologic, but it is of primary importance in that effort because it is the dynamic background against which all other aspects of our nature operate and all of our later life experiences occur.

The rate of incidence of a particular Impulse Pattern, one case in 1,024, is not rare. We all know people who are excessively projective and won't stop to assimilate anything in their reasoning, and people who are excessively assimilative and reluctant to project anything from themselves. In our broadcast media, for instance, we see both bad interviewers who never let their guests finish a sentence because they are eager to project their own ideas, and good interviewers who seldom interrupt their guests and have a natural knack for 'drawing people out'. But we also know these character types from our own social and business circles. Surely we have all argued a point with a projective person who distorts something we said to make it something that they assumed we said, and we all know taciturn people who will give other people no words, or anything else for that matter, unless they are asked or compelled to do so.

These obvious differences among people and other animals—being highly projective, highly assimilative, or some combination of both impulses—have been described by biologists and modern psychologists with terms that are now widely used in ordinary speech. Specifically, some biologists classify animals as *alpha*, *beta*, or *omega* males, females, or pairs, and some modern psychologists classify people as *Type-A* or *Type-B personalities*. But we must reject these classifications because they are merely descriptive. The scientists who proposed them observed some behavior, described it, and then invalidly used these incomplete mere descriptions as if they were basic operative principles of human or animal nature. The real principle here is the innate impulse of people and other animals to project or assimilate, so the real issue is, What causes these impulses and their different degrees in organisms?

Another major social implication of the Impulse Pattern is that, in any system, only one of the four permutations is the logical one. This means that, by hypothetical count, only one-fourth of all people handle that system logically, while three-fourths do so with either half or total illogic. And if we extend this ratio to all five systems, we can see that those who wish to build a logical, sane, and just society must fight the massive wave of our species' irrationality. Indeed, it will be a miracle of human will if they succeed or if our species even survives much longer.

The Standard Impulse Pattern. We can list the 1,024 permutations of the Impulse Pattern, but this doesn't solve the problem of which of those patterns represents the universal standard of all human reasoning. To have such a standard, we must find the universally logical impulse for each of the ten cognitions, and we can only do this one point at a time, by making a speculative guess informed by our common logic and subject to confirming empirical tests.

For instance, take the first systemic point in *Figure 6*, labeled *wish*, which begins our will system. This is our first response to the whole event we have just perceived, and it cannot be logical to project here, because then we will be trying to tell the event what it is, when the only logical way to reason here is to let that reality tell us what it is. So we must conclude that the logical impulse at the first pole of our will system is to assimilate the perceived event objectively, and that the impulse of half of us to project our subjective notion of it is unrealistic and hence illogical. This is the only sensible way to proceed here, by asking which charge is universally appropriate for all humans at each of the ten points of the Cycle. It is not arbitrary or difficult to do this, since it can only be projection from inside us or assimilation from outside us, and anyone who uses reality as their standard of judgment will see that only one answer is logically acceptable at each point. I won't explain how I decided the logical charge for the other nine cognitions, for it is easy to see in the detailed discussions of our systems in the next chapter.

But it will help you to know the origin of the Consideration Cycle, meaning the problem that I saw for which it is the solution. In my early twenties, I began to sense clearly from my readings and social contacts that all intellectual disputes were psychologic, or decided by something other than the words being spoken. Whenever I tried to apply reason in a dispute, I noticed that most people were biased and couldn't be swayed by logic. But later, when I studied the traditional *moral, political, epistemic, metaphysical,* and *emotive* disputes (in that sequence, as it happens), I saw in each subject area that the most ardent debaters were polar-opposite extremists. And I saw that this fact was already reflected in the descriptive names by which disputants in these five areas were conventionally classified. Though a reconciliationist position was usually granted also, we have long been told that the antagonists in moral issues were *egoists* or *altruists,* in political issues *individualists* or *collectivists,* in epistemic issues *rationalists* or *empiricists,* in metaphysical issues *realists* or *idealists,* and in feeling issues *emotionalists* or *aesthetes.* So I was not alone in seeing that these polarized disputes recurred stubbornly and continuously in our intellectual history, but then I saw what apparently no one before me had noticed: that these polarities of views were somehow similar across all five of those major subject areas.

This wholistic perspective then led me to my notion of cognitive charge, for it made me ask why, across all intellectual works, there seemed to be one psychologic quality shared by egoists, individualists, rationalists, realists, and emotionalists, and an opposite quality shared by altruists, collectivists, empiricists, idealists, and aesthetes. My final answer was that the first five types were basically *projective* and the second five were basically *assimilative*. Perhaps this is what the pragmatist James sensed to reach his oft-quoted but merely descriptive distinction between 'tender-minded' and 'tough-minded' thinkers, though I think that his innate bias led him to apply these terms in reverse. Anyway, by 1971 I had constructed a formal explanation of these psychologic polarizations that at first I had sensed only vaguely, and that hypothesis was the Consideration Cycle, with its five systems and their impulses as shown in *Figure 6*.

As for my terms here, I will speak of the *charge* or the *impulse* of a unit cognition, but by the *impulse* of a system I mean both of its charges, and by *Impulse Pattern* or *pattern* I always mean the impulses of all five systems in their logical order. Only one of the 1,024 possible patterns is the Impulse Pattern of the Cycle itself, but this is not a normative pattern, because it is not determined by ex post facto count or statistics. Since its occurrence in individuals is no more or less likely than any of the other 1,023 permutations, it is not the *norm*, it is the *logically balanced* pattern, reached by the method described above.

I settled on this pattern of charges as our universal standard of logic because if the opposite charge was assumed at any point, it violates what is objectively necessary for all humans in the exchanges between their internal and external realities. I then tested this hypothesis over nearly four decades, with the help of friends and former students, and today we all consider the Cycle soundly confirmed in practice. I therefore take it to be the long-missing standard for judging people's innate logic or illogic, and hence their innate psychologic health or sickness.

Applying the Standard. We must avoid some confusions that arise because of the difference between reasoning about the Cycle theoretically and applying it to a real individual.

First, we must not confuse our standard's pattern, which is the universal pattern of our species in its present home and epoch of development, with the case of any individual with that same pattern (BBBBB), since real people have many other characteristics that modify their Impulse Pattern for better or for worse.

Second, since the hereditary process gives all humans their species' physical equipment, our individual variations of character and personality are circumscribed by our specieal nature, and so they cannot be total departures from the Cycle's standard pattern. This is why even people with an illogical impulse in a system understand that it is illogical when its error is explained to them. We can deviate widely from the Cycle's logic in a conscious system, because over time our conscious control lets us use our explicated reasoning to replace our natural logical reasoning with illogical reasoning, or vice versa, but such deviations are less marked in the subconscious phases. A phase is subconscious because in our standard it has two like charges, but this doesn't mean that people with unlike charges there can perform its function consciously; it only means that they are slightly more conscious of it, and slightly illogical there also.

Third, we should not confuse the terms *logical* and *reasonable*. 'Logical' means what is universally valid for us all, while 'reasonable' means only what is relatively valid for one or some of us. An individual or collective may act illogically and still act reasonably, in the given circumstances. Since what is universal precedes and implies what is relative, any logical act is also reasonable, but an act can be reasonable even if it isn't logical. The failure to observe this distinction has caused many arguments and serious miscarriages of justice. Traditionalists don't see it clearly because they don't distinguish our *thought* and our *judgment* systems, as the Cycle does. We have two standards for judging a person or collective, a universal standard of thought and a relative standard of judgment, and we must be clear as to which one we are using.

Our legal systems recognize this when they hold that 'insane' people are not responsible for committing an illegal act, but they usually apply this rule arbitrarily and don't consider every form of psychologic impairment. For instance, children, teenagers, and dull-witted people have undeveloped or damaged brains as well as inadequate experience or ability, so they can't judge a situation soundly. But unjust courts routinely punish them as severely, if not more so, as adults who are not so impaired and can play a productive role in their defense. Logic is the standard for all judgments, but in judging an individual case, the less-strict standard of reasonableness must take precedence, since the logic that applies for all humans cannot apply for anyone who, through no act or omission of theirs, is naturally impaired in that logic. Though a legislature must use the universal standard of logic, or thought, a court hearing a specific case must subordinate that logic to the relative standard of reasonableness, or judgment, and appeal courts must permit this.

Speed. A psychologic system functions in individuals with a speed that varies with the impulse. The *balanced impulse* (B) in a system leads one to proceed logically at a proper pace, receiving and transmitting in turn as its functions require. So any limitation that can be associated with a balanced system is caused by other factors, not the charges of its cognitions.

The *projective impulse* (+) makes one proceed in a system very rapidly and half illogically, since it is illogical at one pole. This is the impulse of precocious children who seem mature and accomplished in some area or areas of reasoning. [1] Those who are projective in a psychologic system hardly need it explained to them. Whether they are intelligent or not, they are too fast and closed in its functioning to listen tolerantly to slower people speak about it, and unless a personal need is involved, they don't want to assimilate what others say there anyway.

The *assimilative impulse* (-) makes one proceed in a system slowly and half illogically, since it too is illogical at one pole. Assimilative people say that they need time to 'study the matter', but what they really want is extra time to receive ideas from external sources at the system's subjective pole, where logically they should project their own ideas instead. Unlike projective people who answer a question quickly, they want to go to school or consult with a confidant or a socially approved reference before answering, and they often try to accumulate academic or professional honors to rationalize their right to speak to us as 'authorities'.

The *reversed impulse* (R) makes people slowest in a system. They proceed in its area backwards and with total illogic, since both poles have the illogical charge. At one pole they have the failing of a projective system and at the other they have the failing of an assimilative system. People with a reversed impulse can't get that system's reasoning straight, and (as explained in the next chapter) they reach their conclusions there through the logical error of begging the question. This inverted logic blocks their progress in the system, so they search for rationalizations with which to deny, or turn off, that area of reasoning altogether. They will go to schools for social advancement, but even if they achieve every possible academic honor, they make no forward progress on the issues of

---

[1] A good example is Shirley Temple Black, whose pattern is (+++-R). Her projective impulses in will, thought, and feeling made it possible for her to be, from the age of three, an unbelievably precocious movie star. And as an adult, she showed both the altruism caused by her assimilative judgment and the total illogic in power that made her a conservative and a Republican.

that system. Most of them avoid dealing with that system, but some give it much consideration, in which case they may be perceptive academics, judges, editors, or other kinds of critics. That is, since a reversal makes one a negativist in a system, intelligent people can use this innate negativism to develop critical powers there.

Congenital Pathology. The reversed impulse in a system is the chief indicator of arealism, irrationality, and certain types of insanity in individuals. Those with this psychologic impairment go to extraordinary lengths to impose their illogic on others, because the only way they have to 'defend' this innate irrationality is to claim that it is common to many others—which is true, but irrelevant. They can't build a logical construct in their reversed system and they fear that others will notice this, so they fabricate a substitute for it. I call such a fear-based artifice an 'avoidance structure', and many of our intellectual, social, and practical systems are manifestations of this. In its simplest form, it consists of a word or other signal that triggers a defensive mechanism or escape plan. But it can also be a harsh political agenda or any form of monastic retreat or means of keeping others at a distance, such as silence, fences, security forces or devices, or close associations with others with similar fears. It can also be a lifework; that is, a rationalizing intellectual system that offers convoluted reasons why we all should avoid, deny, transcend, or 'go beyond' that entire area of psychologic or social reality.[2]

A reversal in a system doesn't let people ignore its psychologic functions, but it prevents them from completing those functions. Moreover, while others store in a system's succedent memory bank healthy defense mechanisms and positive memories with constructive future uses, people

---

[2] The behaviorist Skinner is a case in point. In his book *Beyond Freedom and Dignity* (1971), he seriously proposed that we should all 'go beyond' those two 'meaningless' notions, freedom and dignity. Since I knew from the Cycle that *dignity* is our abstract self-concept and that the only real meaning of *freedom* is the power to achieve our wishes, I concluded while reading that book, before knowing his birth date, that he was reversed in his thought and power systems. And indeed his Impulse Pattern is (BR-+R).

with a reversal store rationalizations for denying or minimizing that system's natural functions in their psychologic. These include painful memories, grudges, and destructive or reclusive defense mechanisms, ready for use instantly when triggered by some arbitrary sign, alarm, or code word. Those who are either projective (+) or reversed (R) in a system have a psychologic need for shortcuts there, but the former use shortcuts for speed and the latter use them for denial. This is why, even though their motive differs, pathologically reversed and pathologically projective people both prefer abrupt, brutal, or military answers to social problems rather than discussion, compromises, or fair negotiations.

In its general psychologic sense, 'pathology' means deviation from healthy functioning. So I define *congenital pathology* as a significant deviation in one's Impulse Pattern, which means having the same impulse in three or more of the five psychologic systems. It thus has four forms, each of which is found in about 10% of us. Its most illogical form is three or more reversals (R). This produces a weak personality that makes one, in areas related to the reversed systems, irrational, past-oriented, manipulable, slow, negativistic, skeptical, cynical, fearful, and defensive. If such people are also selfish (+ or R in judgment), they are also bitter, untruthful, vulgar, sarcastic, cruel, vengeful, spiteful, intolerant, and impositional, as we see in the cases of Nixon (RR-R-), Milosevic (RRR++), and Bush II (R++RR). Not everyone with this pathology is socially harmful, but the only exceptions I have found are intelligent and unselfish (- or B in judgment) people who were raised with compassion and who later retreated to some insular world such as art, religion, science, jurisprudence, academia, or nature.

People with one or two reversals, about 66% of us, are similarly impaired, but to a lesser degree that is easier to control or disguise. They can develop *experiential pathology*, which is how we should now refer to the postnatal pathologies described by modern psychologists.

The other three forms of congenital pathology are excessive projection (+), assimilation (-), and balance (B). Having three or more projective systems makes one inordinately self-centered and unreceptive, or close-minded. This form is worst when it is combined with reversals, just as the reversed form is worst when combined only with projective systems. It is easier to manage if there are two balanced or assimilative systems, but harder to correct if there are four or five projective systems, as in the cases of de Gaulle (R++++), Ho Chi Minh (++++R), and Bill Clinton (B++++). Having a majority of assimilative systems makes one compulsively passive, taciturn, receptive, and acquisitive or greedy; examples are Napoleon (-B- -B), Grant (-B-+-), and Stalin (BB- - -). This form is also easier to handle if there are only three such systems combined with two that are balanced or projective. Finally, though we normally don't consider good logic to be a fault, a pattern with a majority of balanced (B) systems is pathological because it makes one excessively conventional. And that makes one illogical whenever the conventions that one adopts are unsound, which is the case with virtually all our traditions to date. Examples are George III (BB-B+), Krushchev (BBB++), Kissinger (+BBBB), and Bush I (+BBB+).

When we use the term 'pathological' without qualification, it should mean either the generic sense (any form of it) or the worst case (three or more reversals), as the context indicates. For the three less-severe cases, however, we should state the form we mean.

Psychologic Strength and Weakness. The four possible impulses of a psychologic system go from greatest strength to greatest weakness in this order: projective (+), balanced (B), assimilative (-) and reversed (R). For general purposes, I refer to a system with a (+) or a (B) impulse as a *strong system*, and one with a (-) or an (R) impulse as a *weak system*. But many other factors in a natal chart can contribute to making a system stronger or weaker.

Political Attitudes. This is an appropriate point to define eight of our most basic political terms (and their equivalents), because now that we are defining them psychologically, they are also useful in nonpolitical contexts. These terms, which previously were only subjectively described, are now objectively defined from the two charges of our power system. The congenital dispositions to which they refer are explained in the next chapter.

The charge at the first pole of our power system (external power) divides all humans into two hypothetically equal classes, *moderates* (-) or *extremists* (+); the moderates are usually *tolerant* towards others and otherness, while extremists are *intolerant*. The charge at its second pole (internal power) also divides all humans into two classes: *leftists* (+) or *rightists* (-), who we can also refer to as *individualists* or *collectivists* respectively. Taking both charges together, as they are in our power system, defines our four basic political attitudes, each of which is shared by a fourth of all people. A *progressive* (-+) is a moderate leftist, a *radical* (++) is an extremist leftist, a *liberal* (- -) is a moderate rightist, and a *conservative* (+-) is an extremist rightist. Or, in the terms of the Impulse Pattern, a *progressive* is balanced (B) in power, a *radical* is projective (+) in power, a *liberal* is assimilative (-) in power, and a *conservative* is reversed (R) in power.

Because all of these terms are now causally defined distinctions in the class of all humans, we must reject their traditional merely descriptive meanings. And because they are defined by an objective method that involves no subjective judgment of people's political dispositions, they have a general function that relates the formerly discrete studies of human *character* and *politics*. So we now have, for the first time, a valid bridge between these two contexts, and we can now use these old political terms in our psychologic discussions also. For example, 'liberal in thought' is no longer a complimentary phrase, since it now means the half-illogic of being totally assimilative in thought. Similarly, 'conservative in feeling' now means being reversed in feeling, 'radical in judgment' now means being projective in judgment, 'predominantly rightist' now means being either assimilative or reversed in three or more of the five systems, 'predominantly extremist' now means being either projective or reversed in at least three systems, and so on.

Memory. For millennia, the notion of 'mind' meant little more than our conscious explicated reasoning plus our memory, and 'idea' meant little more than one of the tangible visualizations (images, symbols, or statements) that we store in memory. But our 'memory' was only vaguely described, so we need to propose its definition.

In a psychologic system, we cognize each polar cognition in its turn, but at the second pole we reconcile these into a tangible *reasoned conclusion*, which we then store in the subconscious phase that follows that system. As in our metaphysics, which suggests that the smallest tangible form is two ultiparticles in double-helical motion, every tangible notion we form consists at first (before we join it to other tangible pairs) of two unit cognitions. So we can only memorize a tangible *compound* idea that we formed in a system, and we store this in the following phase, where we do not pause and so cannot create or edit our memories.

This new conception of our memory thus proposes six discrete memory banks: the four phases and the two halves of the prime interval. The names of these six intervals, three of which store different kinds of objective conclusions and three of which store different kinds of subjective conclusions, are shown in *Figure 6*. This conception thus rejects the traditional view that we have only one memory bank. That old view denies process, and it fails to explain how we form different kinds of memories in our psychologic and why they can all be stored in the same place, and thus it ignorantly assigns the same source and logical status to every memory.

The validity of any reasoned conclusion depends on the impulse of the system that yielded it; for instance, a reversed system yields bogus reconciliations, or rationalizations for jumping out of it to the next system without having reconciled its polar ideas. Our memory banks can't store unit cognitions; they can only store compound images, which can be complex or as simple as a single symbol. Only in our conscious systems can we recall, edit, and structure the conclusions stored in our memory banks, and our main criterion for storing them is their future usefulness to us. Our six memory banks develop over time, but not uniformly so, since our systems and phases usually vary widely in their strength and how intensely we use them.

Since our pragmatists don't reason analytically, they ignore the dynamic process involved and so continue to make the ancient error of equating our psychologic, or 'mind', to our memory. This is why so many human scientists today assume that anything of importance about us is linguistic and social rather than congenital and is mostly determined by our practical reasoning. That may be so of what we store in memory, but not of our psychologic process itself.

We know that our memory functions are improved when we create an external object, such as a writing, drawing, building, mathematical calculation, or work of art. This is so because that act, even when the object is not before us, concretizes and makes more useful what we previously stored subconsciously. This is a form of 'speaking to ourselves', and it is as much a function of a language system as is communicating to others. We construct formal systems from the material stored in our memory banks, and then in our reconsiderations our five psychologic systems test each of these constructs by correcting its errors and omissions, adding new images to it, discarding old ones, or changing its priorities, structure, and signals. This explicit individual operation is also the psychologic model for our *social traditions*; that is, of the collectives, customs, and institutions that imitate our memory banks with their own tangible rules.

But as we age, we do more reconsidering than new considering, and this focus on the past then hardens both our subconscious memory banks and the formal systems we constructed from them. And as this hardening increases, we engage less and less in new considerations in a psychologic system. Our traditional educators encourage this habit, but most of us succumb to it anyway because it is easier to use our bank of past conclusions in a context than to reason anew in it. We say, "I don't have to perform this system's reasoning in this case again, since I did this before and now I can just make a withdrawal from its succedent memory bank," and then we settle on a signal or code word that tells us when to do that thereafter. People of normal or high intelligence who age into this inflexibility become like people of low intelligence, because they have lost their inclination and power to use their reasoning as a moving process in the present.

This *involutionary* direction of reasoning, looking first to what we have already reasoned about and stored in a memory bank, blocks us from doing or accepting any new reasoning in that system. This is another flaw in Freud's psychic determinism: it denies our psychologic process by assuming that we all rely more on our tangible memories than on new reasoning. Whenever we call on our *personal traditions*, meaning our habits and stock of ready answers, rather than reasoning anew in a system, our reasoning in the next system begins with no force of intellect. There is just the simple stimulus-response mechanism of our memory banks, sans the systemic dynamics that formed and repeatedly tested our reasoning systems in our youth, when we often considered things in an *evolutionary* direction that freely allowed new motives, thoughts, feelings, beliefs, abilities, and associations to happen in us or to us.

This *hardening of the systems* occurs to us all as we age, but it happens sooner and more fully in anyone who has one or more reversed, or conservative, systems. We have all known children and young adults who are conservative in some psychologic area, so this hardening is not only age-dependent. It is caused sooner than usual whenever the impulse of a psychologic system is a reversal, for this forces one to reason backwards or to look for a shortcut to avoid reasoning there, and the shortest way is to call up something that one had previously learned and memorized. That is why many people with reversals value formal education and academic degrees. They rely blindly, with an almost unbelievable degree of unreasoned *faith*, on tangible memories, social traditions, their academic lessons, dogma, bibles, habits, all kinds of histories, and repetitive retrospective rituals. They also fill their memory banks with nonsense—with distractions such as the frivolous products of our news, sports, music, art, entertainment, and gaming industries—until it is soon the case, quite literally, that they are 'out of their minds', or disinclined to *reason* about anything.

Because our social constructs imitate our psychologic systems and their memory banks, this hardening also occurs in our societies, institutions, corporations, families, and so on. The *social memory* of any collective, meaning its traditions, rules, and bureaucracy, soon becomes dominant and allows no new reasoning to alter it. In primitive times, this social memory consisted of rituals and spoken stories, but today it is mostly written down in formal codes and histories that serve as the precedents, legal or otherwise, that close-minded bureaucrats substitute for the dynamic reasoning that characterized that institution at its birth and for a short time thereafter.

To put this psychologic hardening in its equivalent political terms, all of our social systems begin as a new event from *leftist* (progressive or radical) principles and actions, which is to say from our natural perfectionistic need for change and new thinking, but soon after their formation they become hardened *rightist* (liberal or conservative) constructs. Accordingly, there is no such thing as a rightist social or intellectual construct that was not born as a leftist construct or that is anything more than a reaction to it and a hardening and corruption of it. And any historical or political analysis that ignores this natural implicatory relation is invalid. Political rightism is subsequent; it is always reactionary and never creative, always rigid, inflexible, and ignorant of process, and hence always robotic and never human.

But in spite of its inflexibility and inhumanity, political rightism is inevitable as a psychologic era advances. This is partly because all new systems deteriorate and become inadequate in time, but mostly because rightist bureaucracy, the formalistic hardening of a social or political system, is simpler than continually refreshing earlier leftist principles through new reasoning. And this will not change until the core illogic of both forms of rightist reasoning, liberalism and conservatism, is widely known and generally accepted. The old expression, "That's how it has always been done, so it's good enough now," is just a rightist rationalization for not thinking freshly. It is far easier to use a tangible memory or written code than to reason from scratch in each case, so in both individuals and our institutions the letter of a rule soon replaces its initial spirit. But the rightist 'letter' is just a static memory, while the leftist 'spirit' is the moving process of current reasoning that causes all memories and speaks to what is real and fundamental in life, which is mainly the well-being of all individuals of all species.

The impulse of a psychologic system reveals an individual's logic there, but it also tells us something about the conclusions stored in its succedent memory bank. A memory bank that follows a balanced (B) system consists mostly of valid conclusions with appropriately assigned significance, while one that follows a reversed system (R) consists mostly of contradictory conclusions with inappropriately assigned significance.

But we can reach no general conclusion on the validity of the memories stored after a projective (+) or assimilative (-) system, other than to say that the former are filled mostly with one's own constructions and the latter with constructions adopted from others. The soundness of a memory bank that follows a projective (radical) system depends most on how logical the individual is, and the soundness of a memory bank that follows an assimilative (liberal) system depends most on how logical the adopted opinions or traditions are. And since the liberal (-) system depends on reasoning from multiple external sources, it is almost certain to be inconsistent, and hence unprincipled.

It is sometimes necessary in speech to distinguish the static systems stored in a memory bank from our dynamic psychologic systems. For instance, *belief* is one of our terms for a reasoned conclusion of our judgment system, so when we mean the tangible memories produced by our judgment system, we can speak of our beliefs or belief system rather than of our judgments or judgment system. Similarly, we can refer to the stored conclusions of our will system as *motivations*, to those of our thought system as *opinions*, to those of our feeling system as *desires*, and to those of our power system as *abilities*.

The prime interval is a special case. Our powers, or abilities and understandings, are stored in the subjective terminating interval that follows our power system, while significant events and our primary instincts are stored in the objective initiating interval that follows the complete percept. But whenever we are considering two or more logically related events, the entire prime interval functions like a psychologic system, because in this case we are also reasoning between two poles: a developed personal power and the new wish that it implies.

Other Implications. The Impulse Pattern and its four impulses also tell us much about our social problems. Two important examples of this are education and overpopulation.

Education. A student's success in formal education depends on the purpose of the school and its educators. If it is to demand the rote memorization of facts and different language systems, which is the purpose of most schools today, assimilative liberal students are favored; if it is to impart valid reasoning in a system, balanced progressive students are favored; if it is to promote creativity, projective radical students are favored; and if it is either to impart illogic (as in a religious school) or to help the most illogical, reversed conservative students are favored. And students will face this same bias later in their careers.

The problem is that traditionalist educators, who know little or nothing about human character, impose the same educational goals for all their students—even to the absurdity of standardized state or national tests, which are intended to serve governmental or corporate motives rather than the students' best interests. But the proper purpose of a school is not to teach everyone collectivistically; that is, in the same way and by the same tests and standards. Rather, it is to educate all of the *unique individuals* who attend a school, which cannot be done with any success if their innate character is not known. Therefore, as one part of the solution to bad education, a child should not be sent to a school without his or her natal chart, and every educator should know how to read that chart and how to design or select a distinct learning program for it.

Overpopulation. As our population grows, the total human force for all the forms of illogic or pathology defined by the Consideration Cycle increases. Only one in 1,024 of us are born with the totally balanced pattern, so the other 1,023 character types, or 99.9% of us, have from one to ten points of malfunctioning in our five systems. In a world of six billion people, then, only six million (a thousandth) are fully balanced in this respect. But since people can be more logical than illogical without being totally balanced, let us just say here that, because such a large majority of us are born with psychologic impairments, our species' currently high levels of illogic and insanity must be increased so long as our societies permit random births.

Many traditionalists believe that we can create a sane world by improving people with better education and other helpful social programs, but this is wishful thinking, for it doesn't address the real cause of our ignorance, which is congenital, and it couldn't be done on the scale we need anyway. Others have suggested that the social problems caused by our psychologically impaired majority might someday be solved through genetics, but at present genetics is useless for this purpose and later it will be a partial answer at best. And the extreme genetic ideal, cloning better people, is unworkable as now conceived, since even a clone will have a unique character and be psychologically healthy or not because of its time of birth, which cannot be duplicated. Genetic research for medical purposes is valuable, but genetic manipulations can never reduce our great majority of psychologically unhealthy people. But with a little will and discipline we can all do this naturally, for population engineering will be simple once astrological methods are improved and widely accepted. Moreover, assuming that most parents want their children to be psychologically and physically healthy, they would cooperate in these methods.

Traditionalists who reject astrological methods assume that our natural intelligence and good health come from genetic factors only. But from this weak assumption they cannot explain why so many intelligent or healthy people come from parents or grandparents who are unintelligent or unhealthy, or why intelligent or healthy parents can give birth to mentally impaired or physically deformed children. Something more than genetics is clearly at play here, and we shouldn't listen to any scientists who refuse to ask what it is.

The Consideration Cycle shows that our overpopulation is a measure of human decline, not of human progress. It is true that increased population is the chief cause of economic growth and steadily increasing national or corporate profits, but it is also the chief cause of our increasingly irrational societies and the destruction of our ecological system—which together threaten the eradication of our species soon, much sooner than would be the case if we humans could on the whole act wisely. At present, our goals should be (a) to halve our population to three billion, and (b) to leave virtually unused by us about a half of all the earth's land, air, and water. Contrary to the lies we are told, the greater profits produced by overpopulation are no blessing at all, and indeed our survival depends on our states and corporations abandoning profit as their first goal. They would still have important functions in society without that goal.

In 1960 our population was three billion and only forty years later, in 2000, it was six billion. Imagine, then, the world that our children and grandchildren will soon be facing when it is twelve billion. You might also reflect on your own role in causing and permitting these twin disasters that they shall suffer, overpopulation and ecological destruction, and then add this to the terrible fact I pointed out above: that as we mindlessly multiply ourselves, we also multiply our congenital psychologic impairments and the insanity of our collectives.

The threat of overpopulation doesn't lie only in the deterioration of our ecosystem, the destruction of tens of thousands of other species, and insufficient habitable land and consumable water and food for humans and other living things. It also lies in its psychologic consequences on us and our institutions. Long before there are twelve billion people, in fact it is already happening, our overpopulation and the shortages it causes will create uncontrollable criminality, thievery, and mass emigration from undesirable areas. Indeed, our respective nations must defend us from the harms of overpopulation by prohibiting virtually all immigration now. Healthy people try to solve their problems, not run away from them, and no nation needs more unhealthy people than it already has. But if a society does need immigrants, then each one should have to pass a *character* test, by which I do not mean a personality or educational test.

Even with the population increase of the past forty years, which witnesses of my generation can testify has dramatically worsened the quality of our lives, individuals are now less valuable to each other, as partners or in general; their rulers are more contemptuous of and dictatorial towards them; those rulers now consider genuine democracy an absurd notion; and their immoral motives and heinous crimes are widely tolerated, as they once were not, even as recently as the sixties. And the chief culprit in this picture—other than a public that is intentionally distracted from politics by inane amusements—is greed; that is, the quest for rising profits by nations, corporations, and individuals that is destroying us and our world.

But in spite of these great threats, people still think it chic to have more than two children. Surely one vital birth, or two at most, is the moral maximum for anyone today, so we should censure rather than congratulate those who impose on us all by intentionally having more than that. If individuals don't observe this limit voluntarily, then our governments will soon have no choice but to impose periods in which no births at all are allowed. And we must hope that in determining those periods they will consult with humanologists who, using astrology and other methods, can tell them with a high degree of reliability which time periods are most or least likely to produce psychologically and physically healthy children.

Chapter 6. Our Five Psychologic Systems

DISCUSSING THE FIVE SYSTEMS.

We must now consider how the five psychologic systems of the Consideration Cycle function and how we humans differ basically in that functioning. This takes us to the heart of our psychologic; that is, to the parts of it that we must know well to use the Impulse Pattern to analyze character. But note as we discuss each point on the Cycle below, that we are also explaining the meanings that our new theories assign to the planet that governs that point. I will therefore start including the planetary symbols in our discussions, because this will help you in your astrological work to associate the planets with the psychologic factors they affect.

Also, I am introducing a new symbolic notation for astrology, one that combines the planet's symbol with its charge. Thus, ☽- means 'the moon in a negative sign' or 'the moon with a negative charge', ♂+ means 'Mars in a positive sign' or 'Mars with a positive charge', and so on.

I suggest that this is a good point for you to read the texts of *Appendix A, Calculating the Impulse Pattern*, and *Appendix B, Tables of Individuals*.

Appendix A lists the major astrological symbols and explains how to calculate the Impulse Pattern from a natal chart. Its *Figure A* shows how the planets and zodiacal signs relate to the parts of the Consideration Cycle. If you have natal charts, you should now calculate your own Impulse Pattern and those of the people you know best, for there is no better way to follow the discussions in this chapter or to judge the Cycle and its Impulse Pattern. If you don't have your natal chart yet, you should still be able to determine your own impulse in each system from the descriptions that follow.

Appendix B will also help you follow the discussions below. Its tables constitute empirical evidence for my theories. We need fuller empirical studies, of course, but they require more time and resources than one individual can provide. You probably know something about many of the people listed in those tables, and this should be enough to convince you of the value of the Impulse Pattern as a psychologic tool. In any case, as you read each of the twenty systemic impulses below, four for each psychologic system, you should look for instances of it in these tables. But remember that no one impulse defines a real and whole person. Remember also that each of these twenty sections refers to a fourth of all humans of our psychologic epoch, so you should study them all with equal care if you wish to understand human nature in general.

To achieve our potential as an individual or a society, we must know both our strengths and our weaknesses. But most of us know our strengths rather well, so our main reason for wanting to understand human nature is to correct our faults and see the faults of others and our societies. Also, we all work hard to construct rationalizations that allow us to overlook or excuse our points of innate illogic. It is therefore necessary here that I give more attention to people's faults and weak impulses than to their virtues and strong impulses.

We will consider the five systems in their logical sequence in the Cycle, and the four impulses of each system starting with the stronger (B and +) ones and ending with the weaker ones (- and R). The impulse discussions overlap, because each charge at a pole (+ or -) is shared by two of a system's four possible impulses. Also, in the section title for an impulse I add a descriptive keyword for people with that impulse; for instance, "Planner" for one whose impulse in will is balanced (B) and "Conservative" for one whose impulse in power is reversed (R). These twenty terms are very useful in our discussions of people, as you will see most clearly with the eight that apply to the four judgmental (moral) and the four power (political) permutations.

To understand anyone's character, we must look at the whole pattern; in fact, we must consider the entire natal chart. But here we are considering only one impulse at a time, and this only tells us how that single impulse inclines people to certain dispositions in one psychologic area. It doesn't tell us how those dispositions are affected by all the other characteristics or if a given person uses them productively or destructively. It is your job to judge the whole chart.

Since the Impulse Pattern is analytic, it is necessarily incomplete, but it is not just added data about someone, it is essential dynamic information. Its logic or illogic affects every conclusion a person reaches in life, so my claim for the Impulse Pattern is not that it tells us everything about a person, but rather that we cannot explain anyone's character without it.

The Consideration Cycle is the theoretic standard that is missing in every human science, and so every practitioner in those sciences needs to know it. Its dynamic factors determine our reasoning in psychology, astrology, sociology, political science, and economics, and it gives us more valid classifications of people than traditionalists ever had. So it will change much in our discussions of people. For one thing, we will now be speaking less often of 'the human' in a universal sense, as in 'all humans are X', because we will no longer assume that all people share any given psychologic attribute—except this universal dynamic itself, our common logic.

1. Will [☽-, ♄+]

The impulse of our will system is determined at its first pole by the charge of the moon (☽) and at its second pole by the charge of Saturn (♄).

We must assimilate (-) rather than project (+) at our will system's first pole, because its function is objective, or to take in any external or internal event that we perceive. In the psychologic context, I call this first cognition a 'wish response'. By *wish* we usually mean a conscious imagining of some state of events we would prefer, but this implies projection and denies assimilation, which is to confuse the first pole of this system (☽-) with its concluding pole (♄+). A *wish* is our first response to a perceived event, and it is not logical (realistic) unless it is an assimilation. It is how we greet an event that we decide to consider further because it seems to have some relevance to us. But it is not a *desire*, which is the opposite kind of wanting, a passionate wanting, for there is nothing emotional about our will process. Our will is at first instinctive and then entirely cerebral and analytic.

The wish response is prompted by the prime interval and the complete percept, the cardinal idea that told us *that* something has happened, and our wish is then both a vague expectation and our passive decision to let this consideration continue so that we can determine *what* has happened. But half of all humans perceive events by projection rather than assimilation, and consequently—reminiscent of *Don Quixote* by Cervantes (RB-+B), who was reversed in will—they illogically interpret an event as being not what it is, but what they would prefer it to be. A projective wish response thus serves as a strict guardian at the gate of our will system, and indeed of the mind as a whole, preventing one from considering any event further that does not pass all of one's previously stored or instinctive criteria of personal interest.

We are perfectionists whatever charge we have at the first pole, for we will try either to assimilate (-) the event perfectly or to project (+) our own picture of it as more perfect than it is. Assimilative perfectionists like to test their objective awareness, while projective perfectionists are those we call 'creators' or 'dreamers', as the case may be. The latter want to change and order the events around them, which can be anything from their immediate environment to the state of the world. Intellectuals or political leaders who are projective here (☽+), and so are either projective (+) or reversed (R) in will, often force us to contend with irrational fictions like religious and political myths, but our world would be bland indeed if we were all assimilative in our wish function. There would then be no grand motives and no progress, for people would passively accept the events around them, even harmful ones. So this illogical impulse at the first pole (☽+) is both beneficial and harmful. But no benefits, other than possibly pleasing fictions, result if it is combined with the illogical impulse at the second pole (♄-).

At the second pole (♄+), we should project an idea from inside ourselves that meets what we have just taken in at the first pole, for this is how we begin the process from which we form our subjective will conclusions, or primary motivations and plans of purpose. We must project these conclusions because no one else can know what it is possible for us to achieve. Our will system is not our 'wish' structure; it is our 'I will do this' structure. Our reconciliation of its two poles, our wholistic wish and how we think we may achieve it, yields a personal plan regarding the initial event, and that plan is a reasoned conclusion that we may then store and retain in the succedent memory bank as a motive. My shorthand terms for the poles of our will system, as shown in *Figure 6*, are *wish* and *plan*, the idea-referents of which are polar opposites because their relation is direct implication; that is, a wish causes a plan.

By *shorthand term* I mean any keyword that unambiguously points to a specific epistemic idea in the Cycle, a term that we agree to accept as having only that cognition as its idea-referent. Any term can be a shorthand term if we agree on its idea-referent, and we should do this in cases that would otherwise require us to list several equivalent terms.

The logical relation of the two cognitions of a psychologic system is a *polar opposition*. This is our third type of idea opposition, for it is neither a *direct opposition* (180°) nor a *quadrantal opposition* (90°). Unlike the idea referents of, say, 'north-south' or 'whole-all', it is the opposition of two sequential ideas with an immediate causal implication, as in what we mean by term pairs such as 'wish-plan', 'concept-implication', or 'act-consequence'.

Our reasoned conclusions in will are our wholistic (analytic) motives, as opposed to the partialistic (synthetic) motives that we form in our judgment system. The chief function of our will system is to create a long-term *plan of purpose* (or strategy) with respect to the event being considered, which might be the event of our whole life. This is the direct opposite of a short-term *plan of action* (or tactic), which we form in our tertiary reasoning to achieve one of our partialized desires. Our will system's long-term strategy is thus the direct opposite of our judgment system's short-term tactics. Our primary and tertiary reasoning produce directly opposite types of wants, which I distinguish strictly with the terms *wish* and *desire* respectively. Only the gratification of our wishes can give us what we call 'happiness', an overall psychologic state that is not affected by gratifying our tertiary desires. For instance, you may desire a person for sex, but he or she might not make you happy in the long run. It follows that our life is best when our wishes govern our desires, or our will governs our feelings, and this is more likely to be the case with people whose impulse in will is strong (+ or B) rather than weak (- or R).

Now let us consider how each of the four impulse permutations works in our will system, ignoring the reconsiderations by which the other four systems influence it over time.

1A. BALANCED (☽-, ♄+). THE PLANNER. The hypothetical fourth of us who are balanced (B) in our will function handle the logic of their will system realistically without special effort. They take in an event as it is, and then project from themselves their personal possibilities regarding it, and so they shape a realistic, and nearly always culturally acceptable, long-range plan with respect to that event and their global wish regarding it.

These are our most realistic people in their wishes and plans of purpose, because they reconcile the polar extremes of their will system logically and then create a motivational system that consists mostly of healthy and sane long-range plans; that is, socially noncontroversial plans that they are capable of achieving. Their motives are conventional because they are not creative in wishing (☽-), though they are in their long-range planning (♄+). This is why they often work on the higher corporate or governmental levels, more often as advisors than chiefs, devising broad plans for preserving traditional ways and social institutions. Because they assimilate the status quo in social and personal matters, they don't 'rock the boat'; instead, they work with reality and our traditions as these are, so they are realists without being revolutionists.[1] What they wish to do, more perfectly than before if possible, is what others and their society expect of them. Subject to their other characteristics, they take their responsibilities seriously. They are manipulable at the first pole (☽) but not at the second (♄), so attempts by others to dictate their long-range plans will not succeed unless it is how they decided to proceed anyway.

---

[1] The pathological radical Bill Clinton (B++++) illustrates this well. With four projective systems he could have been a revolutionist, but being balanced in will, he has always depended on social approval, and the long-range motives that drive him were highly conventional from the start. So he devoted all of his creativity to maintaining an old and corrupt political system.

Advice to Planners. Your will system functions logically, but you tend to accept the external events you observe and the situations in which you find yourself just as they are. This means that, usually, the problem you pose to your will system is only the question of how to deal with that observed event or situation. It is thus very likely that your motivations and life plan are centered about how to deal with the status quo as it is or has long been, rather than with trying to change it to make it a situation that is truly worth the sacrifice of your time, energy, or life. So be more critical of the proposals of your elders or famous people of the past or present on what your life motives should be. Don't be a sheep; stop and ask if what they say, from their own motives, really is a goal to which you should dedicate your life. Take more time to judge it before you decide, for your talent at planning means nothing if it serves the wrong end.

1B. Projective ($\mathrm{\mathbb{D}}+, \hbar+$). The Creator. Those who are projective (+) in their will system are logical only at its second pole, in their plans. At the first pole, they fail to see the event they have just perceived for what it is, mainly because they don't want to 'waste time' by absorbing it fully. Their eagerness to get to their own plans of purpose causes them to give little attention to the initial event itself, so they develop these two bad habits at the first pole: hurriedly dictating to external and internal events what they think these are, and not accepting others' interpretations of them. This close-mindedness at the first pole ($\mathrm{\mathbb{D}}+$) works well when others are wrong and badly when they aren't, but in any case they have an incomplete and biased perception of the events they experience. But then they get realistic at the second pole ($\hbar+$), by projecting what they can personally do to achieve their usually unrealistic wish regarding that event, or subject. In effect they say, "Don't tell me what is happening, for I know what is really going on here, and I know exactly what I intend to do about it." We are usually referring to these will-projective people when we speak of 'willful' or 'strong-willed' persons.

The flaw of the projective impulse in a system is failing to receive at the pole that logically requires receptivity, and in the will system this means not seeing events for what they are. So fictional or more-perfect events are often posited at the start of an act of consideration, and then they are elaborated on in all the consideration that follows. This impulse in will leads people to assume full responsibility for their own life plan, as one should, but it also illogically inclines them to assume personal responsibility for external events that are beyond their ability to control. Thus, not only are creators the most willful and perfectionistic of people, they are also the most responsible, even to the point of psychologic harm, as in thinking that they must try to cure the world's ills. Nevertheless, unless their other characteristics prevent it, they are our most original wishers and planners of long-range perspectives and goals, our true visionaries, and they have no tolerance for imperfections of will (purpose, motives) in themselves, others, or society. They are strongly driven to become more mature personally and to help others and their society do so also.

The projective impulse in a system blocks all direct manipulation by others in that system, so people who are projective in will can only be manipulated indirectly, such as through an illogical impulse in another psychologic system.

Advice to Creators. One of the dangers to your psychologic health is that you can become dissatisfied with almost every event and situation you observe. Nothing that others propose, if you bother to listen to it, can escape your criticism, and little that they say is acceptable to you. This distresses you, but it doesn't make you a pessimist, for you see almost immediately how it could be improved. You tend to shape your life motives and long-range plans around improving the social or political circumstances that you personally decide are most in need of correction. Thus, you develop some plan for your locality or the world that you are determined to effect, and since it is seldom a conventional plan, you routinely put yourself in situations that require sacrifices and go unrewarded by society. Be careful in asking people who are close to you to share your goals, for they may not have either your interests or your will power.

1C. ASSIMILATIVE (☾-, ♄-). THE FOLLOWER. Those who are assimilative (-) in their will system are half logical there, in their wishes. At the first pole (☾-) they take in events as these really are, without rushing, so they join those who are balanced in will in being conventional and compliant in how they see events. But they differ from balanced people at the second pole ($\hbar$-), where they fail to project their own plans of purpose. Rather than subjectively asserting their personal possibilities regarding the perceived event, they turn outwards, usually to others they trust or to their culture's traditions or respected gurus, hoping to acquire external guidance in their planning, including their plan for their whole life. This unrealistic impulse gives them that common but inappropriate expectation that the outer world is somehow obligated to tell them what they should do with their life, what they should say to the world, or what their role in society should be. This other-dependence in will makes them manipulable at both poles, a weakness that can cause them to be irresponsible or unreliable.

At the second pole ($\hbar$), it is logical to say, "This is what I can do to achieve my wish regarding that event." But those who are assimilative at this pole, or (-) or (R) in will, say instead, "Help me, for my happiness depends upon what you tell me to do with respect to this event and my wishes regarding it." The illogic here is plain, for no one else can give you a sound plan that is suitable for you in particular. Only you can know truly what your own internal and external reality is, so you alone are responsible for your plans and motives. Even if you are given advice on this, no one else can take responsibility for what is under your daily control.

Obviously our life plan must come from our own projections, but since people who are assimilative at the second pole ($\hbar$-) externalize the subjective half of their will function as if it too was an objective issue, they make their purpose in life not what they have planned, but rather what others have planned for them. It is these people—those who are assimilative (-) or reversed (R) in will—who will go to Tibet to find a lama or who, like Marcello in Fellini's movie *8½*, seek out a religious leader to tell them the meaning of life and what will make them happy. But the answer to those questions is never outside our self. As Marcello learned, we must design our own life plan and then be responsible for whatever we have devised.

Those who are assimilative here are open-minded in the sense that they will fill their will system's succedent memory bank with many opinions by others on wishes and plans. But since they have no subjective basis for editing what they have taken in, they resist settling on any final life plan or motivation as binding on them. So while they are young, they search long and hard for socially approved sources of indisputable wisdom, which may be their parents or rulers or various academics, scientists, other gurus, or revered texts. This search leads many of them to build up inappropriate motivations, so that later in life, when their will system hardens, they have no plan of purpose that is not conventionally accepted by their society. And this, of course, leaves them with no natural will-defense against the motive manipulators all around them.

Our subjects won't revolt against their political rulers or their society's traditions, not unless the people they respect most do so first or an irresistible opportunity for personal gain arises. In any case, they will have no new wishes, purposes, or creative plans to offer society. They may be academics, but not intellectuals, for they propose no original theories, though they will search for others' original thinking if this could increase their own status or profits. Since 'assimilation' and 'acquisition' are equivalent terms, people with the assimilative (liberal) impulse in any psychologic system are naturally seekers, collectors, and hoarders in its functions.

Though it is illogical in will to assimilate others' plans of purpose at the second pole ($\hbar$-), it is also psychologically convenient, for it gives one a scapegoat for every motivational mistake one makes in life. So those who are (-) or (R) in will always assert, in the most important personal and social matters, that *they are not responsible*, or that the blame lies elsewhere. They are logically required to project their personal goals in life, but they don't, and they assume that this omission lets them off the hook for the sad condition of their psychologic realm and their political or natural environment. They take no responsibility for the condition of their society or the world because they don't even consider themselves responsible for their own life decisions.

In short, these followers don't live their own life; they live others' notion of what that life should be. They say early on, "What I want in life is not important, at least not as important as what others want me to do with it," and so they are forever engaged in a search for external surrogates—for relatives, friends, lovers, gurus, politicians, religionists, social authorities, or educators—who will give them ersatz solutions to the basic problem of our will, which is how to form a sound and meaningful life plan. But they must pay a price to those advisors, sometimes even their life or freedom. The assimilative charge here ($\saturn$-) leads them to settle on traditional work and a traditional way to live—one that was created by others, that is still approved by others, and that won't provoke disputes with their social institutions.

The life ambition of those who are assimilative in will, other than the gratifications they find in submitting to the will of others and in not being responsible, lies in quantitative expansion, or in wanting more instead of what is better. Since they cannot personally posit the qualitative plan (or meaning) that is the function of their will, they habitually ignore quality and focus on quantity instead. To them, terms like 'improvement', 'progress', and 'maturity' mean only numerical increase, and they follow the rules imposed by others mainly to ensure their future security. They are compliant 'team players' who follow the path laid out for them by more willful people, their 'coaches', but even on a team their impulsive opportunism will emerge in some form.

Advice to Followers. First, don't accept any metaphysics, plan of purpose, or long-range goal that is proposed to you by others or by the traditions of your culture. In other words, don't follow a herd; you are a real individual, so no artificial collective has a right to direct your life goals. Also, reality is not mystical; though it is vast and we cannot see it all, we see its laws in everything around us. When you consider your work or your life strategy, be alone and without references. Consult only your own thoughts, feelings, judgments, and powers, and remember that a life devoted to material gain, or excessive accumulations of any kind, is a life devoted to others' demands; this can make them happy, but not you. The purpose of your will system is to determine your place in the world, or how you fit in the whole picture, so if you deny your own will and uniqueness by letting others dictate your course, *you* have no place in that picture.

1D. Reversed (☽+, ♄-). The Denier. The will reversal (R) is totally illogical because it has the inappropriate charge at both poles. Once we know this impairment, it is easily detected in people and intellectual works, because its illogic causes one to propose some form of arealism, fantasy, or delusion, or the opposite of the realism of the balanced impulse (☽-, ♄+).

Those with a will reversal transmit rather than receive at the first pole and receive rather than transmit at the second pole. So the entire system fails to work for them and the conclusions (motivations, plans) that they store are illogical. At the first pole, they see a real event as what they wish it to be, and then they compound this denial of reality at the second pole, where they cannot project a personal plan of purpose to achieve that unrealistic wish. So they are forced to resort to denial or fiction in their primary reasoning, which pertains to the most fundamental issues of life. However, intelligent people with a reversal in a system can use their innate negativism there to develop their critical skills, which is why systemic reversals are common in academics, jurists, journalists, psychologists, and other types of critics.

The will reversal makes people contradictory in that they inappropriately assume responsibility for external events they didn't cause, but refuse to take responsibility for decisions that were within their personal control. Such people might say, "I will use my life to make this improvement of society, so now you must tell me how to go about it." This illogic causes confusion, so this reversal, like the other ones, indicates a self-defeating nature. In fact, the systemic reversals explain the many references in our literature to people who are possessed by a devil, demon, or dybbuk that sooner or later undoes what they want most to achieve in life.

Being subject to this illogic daily, our subjects try to 'turn off' their will system. They deny their will and the realities with which it deals; they may even deny their own survival, saying that it too is irrelevant. When we speak of 'a failure of will' we are probably referring to this inverted congenital impulse in a fourth of us. We see the extreme cases of it in those people who sacrifice or risk their lives; who destroy their health by the addictions, diets, habits, desires, games, or pleasures that their weak will cannot control; or who rationalize (universalize) their personal denial of reality or life—a task to which intellectuals with a will reversal can dedicate their entire working life. For instance, as *Table 14* shows, this is so of most theologians.

Bearing in mind that we are considering only one characteristic here and not anyone's total character, we find the will reversal (☽-, ♄+) in most people who commit suicide. It doesn't cause suicide, of course, but it does make it seem reasonable. And the forms of social suicide, such as war and the destruction of our natural environment, fit its illogic perfectly. That is, not only do people with a will reversal deny their own life and that of others, they are easily manipulated into doing so, especially if they have been indoctrinated to believe some fictional ideal. This is so also of those who are assimilative in will, but to a lesser degree.

Intellectuals with a will reversal are a great threat to us all, for they are arealists who insist that we should all 'turn off' our will, and reality, life, theory, and primary reasoning in general. They advise us to deny our will or to 'go beyond' reality to some transcendental state of pseudoreality. They say that we should all 'rise above this earthly coil' by denying our lives, invariably in the name of some fiction such as God, Country, or Revenge.

The source, as distinct from the form, of all mystical beliefs (including theism) is usually a weak (- or R) will, for this causes the denial of the only part of our psychologic that deals with reality: our primary reasoning. Since this denial becomes negativism in general, our subjects never doubt the fictions that they create or adopt, and if they were traditionally educated, they can't see this flaw for the congenital impairment it is. Instead, they assume that this 'natural' urging inside them is speaking truth to them. They 'feel' this illogic inside, so they assume that it is an objective truth about all humans, except that others don't realize this while they do, by some special gift. It is then but a short step for them to believe that they hear the voice of 'God' or 'the Devil', neither of which must speak to us logically. Bush II (R++RR) is a case in point.

My research shows that most theists and other mystics are among that 37% of people who have *two or more* reversals, and the exceptions to this rule are usually people who are weak in will.² We know from our common logic that these people are impaired. We must, for it is no accident that whenever our writers of fiction portray insane people, they make them religious or mystical fanatics, since this communicates clearly that these are characters who deny reality.

Following is a list of the chief illogical points about the will reversal. I number them here to facilitate comparisons with the reversal in the four other psychologic systems.

1. Arealism. Our subjects have no personal philosophy of life because they deny all primary reasoning and theory. A personal philosophy is initially structured in our will system, but their will system is confused and its memory bank is filled with illogical conclusions. The will reversal is a reliable sign of a mystic, an escapist, or anyone else who opposes theory and the primary reasoning that includes life prolongation (survival) through good health, environmental sanity, and peace. They are the first among us to seek escapes from reality, and so, as other factors dictate, they often become addicts of some kind, or they will immerse themselves overly in the fictions of theoryless science or equally meaningless (will-less) entertainment, such as novels, music, games, parties, movies, television, sports, and so on.

2. Antiphilosophy. The will reversal leads intellectuals to deny primary reasoning and begin reasoning from the secondary, tertiary, or quaternary mode instead. We hardly need the Cycle to see the will reversal in the work of theists such as More, Luther, Hobbes, Leibniz, Berkeley, and Kant, or in atheists such as the academic Russell and the existentialist Sartre. Such intellectuals always ignore the reality that we can only perceive and consider in our primary reasoning, where we construct our motivational and survival system, and they never offer us a theory of Reality, as distinct from repeating some old rationalizations concerning it.

---

² We can quantify the serious social problem of the psychologic reversal as follows. From the 1,024 possible Impulse Patterns, we see that only 24% of us have no reversals, while 76% of us have one or more: 40% one, 26% two, 9% three, 1% four, and 0.1% five.

3. Manipulation. People who need others to give them a life plan are manipulated by those others, be they parents, teachers, preachers, friends, media celebrities, or social, intellectual, or political leaders. This susceptibility to motivational manipulation, which often leads these gullible people to sacrifice their resources and some or all of their life, is characteristic of about half of a population, those who are reversed (R) or assimilative (-) in will. To adapt Barnum's old saw to this context: *You can fool half of the people all of the time.*

4. Self-Undoing. Because our will system determines our motives and a will reversal makes people unrealistic in this function, their understandings and decisions are self-defeating. And if we can live with their irrational acts for a while, we can bank on that fact. We see this flaw plainly in the three worst US presidents yet: Wilson (R-RBR), Nixon (RR-R-), and Bush II (R++RR), all of whom were pathological, were reversed in will, and were later undone by their own psychologic limitations. This self-undoing also occurs with reversals in the four other systems, but its effects are less global as we move from the will to the power system.

5. Academicism. In any system, the reversal often motivates people to pursue some kind of academic, juridic, journalistic, or critical career. In will, such work lets one inappropriately project one's own subjective opinion on what events mean (☽+), and then assimilate plans of purpose from respected others (♄-) and their society's sacred texts.

6. The Gap. The reversal causes one to fill the succedent memory bank with invalid conclusions that cannot later be objectively prioritized and consistently structured as a formal system, and consequently that system functions as a hole, or gap, in one's reasoning. Its memory bank cannot be logically ordered, since it consists of confused and contradictory memories that ensure only circular considerations when one tries to explicate its contents.

7. Inner Peace. Our subjects' total illogic in will makes any rationalization that denies that system seem like a godsend to them. They eagerly embrace such a lie or delusion as the path to what they call 'inner peace', but they don't realize that this 'peace' is only needed by impaired people, since healthy people have it naturally. They falsely universalize this unrealistic state that lessens their worries, and then they project it on us all, insisting that the only delusion here is our good health, because 'in reality' everyone shares their need for relief from this illogic.

8. Shortcuts. The will reversal impels people to seek shortcuts to avoid reasoning about their motives and plans because, as explained next, they are compelled to jump ahead to the system's second pole before completing the psychologic functions of the first pole.

9. Begging the Question. This is an important general aspect of any of the five reversals, but I didn't discuss it in the last chapter as such because it has two basic forms that are better explained in the context of two different systems, an open (-+) and a closed (+-) one. We can detect the reversal in a system by formal logic also, by showing that one consistently begs the question there. In fact, I consider a psychologic reversal to be the chief cause of that logical error, which our logicians have described but have not defined.

Many media spokespersons often say that a statement '*begs* the question' when they mean is that it *prompts* or *raises* a further question. Their ignorance here is in not knowing that 'begging the question' refers to a logical error, also known as a *circular argument* or as a *petitio principii* (petitioning the principle). As logicians describe this, it is the error of presupposing what one is trying to prove, or of asserting as an argument's conclusion what was already assumed in one of its premises. But the Cycle shows us that we can beg the question in the opposite way also.

I distinguish these two errors as *petitioning the premise* and *petitioning the conclusion*, and here we will use our psychologic term 'reversal' and the logical term 'begs the question' generically, to mean either or both errors. So 'begging the question' is now a psychologic term, for it means the circular reasoning that results from inverted reasoning in a system, as described below. Anyone can commit this error through oversight, but it is characteristic of people with a reversal because they consider the sequential poles of a system in the wrong order. And it is a common error, for in any system a fourth of us beg the question habitually, and over all five systems 76% of us do so somewhere in our psychologic.

The type of question begging depends on the type of system. In our two closed systems, thought and judgment, the balanced impulse is (+ -), and in our three open systems, will, feeling, and power, it is (- +). Well, a reversal makes one petition whichever pole should be positive (+) but is considered assimilatively (-) instead. So in a closed system one petitions the premise (the first pole), and in an open system one petitions the conclusion (the second pole).

The key to understanding a reversal is that it causes one to leap ahead to a system's second pole before one has reached a decision at its first pole. In judgment, for instance, it causes both the 'rush to judgment' by which social injustices are rationalized and the equally irrational 'leap of faith' that theologians say we must make to believe in theism and its myths. In both cases we are asked to suspend reality and replace it with a fiction. People with a reversal soon learn from their experiences with that system that they have the wrong natural impulse at its first pole, so they approach that pole with caution and temporarily suspend their reasoning there—or they *bracket* it, to use the term of Husserl (+R- -+), who had a thought reversal. But they know that they must return to that pole later to get it right, and this they do in a later act of reconsideration, after they have in mind a reasoned conclusion from the second pole, which is the very conclusion that they intend to 'deduce' later at the second pole after they revisit the first pole.

In the open will system (☽-, ♄+), people with a reversal (☽+, ♄-) petition the conclusion. They don't pause at the first pole to assimilate an event, because they project their own notion of that event there, but they can't do this in the first go-round, since projection is subjective and can't occur naturally at an objective assimilative point of the Cycle. So they suspend (or bracket) their reasoning there and leap ahead to the system's subjective point, the second pole where motives are normally projected. But here they face their second problem, which is that they can't personally project this plan because they are assimilative there. So they must suspend their reasoning at this pole too, while they search the external world, for as long as it takes, to find someone else's plan of purpose (motive) that seems to fit them. Then they return to the first pole in a reconsideration with this borrowed conclusion in mind, and now they project this adopted plan as their 'premise' at the first pole, or as the wish response that they should have assimilated. This begs the question because now one's premise *is* one's conclusion; the wish *is* the plan, though it is not one's own plan. Now, over two acts of consideration rather than one, the wish is an assimilation, but it is an assimilated *plan*, not an assimilated *wish*.

In the three open systems, one petitions the conclusion thusly: in *will* one searches outside oneself for a personal plan of purpose, in *feeling* for a personal passion, and in *power* for a personal ability. A common instance in will is when young people with the reversal try to decide their life work but don't, because they instead assimilate from their parents or other authority figures a life plan that they 'should' follow. After receiving this external advice, they reconsider the work that they wish to do and then falsely say, "This is what I wish to do with my life." But it isn't a wish, it's a plan. And since this adopted plan wasn't based on their unique nature and is often a short-term rather than a long-term plan, they will pursue occupations, usually many different ones, that are inappropriate for them and so cannot make them happy.

Advice to Deniers. See the advice to creators and to followers, both of which apply to you, though together they make you want to deny your will altogether. You do that by escaping (in any of the well-known ways) from the realities you face or by staying with them but turning off your will's primary reasoning. Either way, this feeds your problem rather than solves it. To compensate for your illogic here to the extent you can, you must (1) reject theism or any other form of mystical reasoning, (2) embrace a monistic metaphysics, (3) insist on knowing the theory behind any construct or ideology proposed to you, (4) study human nature, (5) avoid impaired people and irrational leaders, (6) at least every thirtieth year, or Saturn cycle, clearly define your future life strategy and your particular place in the whole of things, and (7) be tolerant of others' uniqueness and life goals. If you work on this, you will be less destructive and less inclined to quit your present situation or relations over minor issues. It will even help you control your temper, passions, and appetites, for the long-range wishes that are formed in a healthy will system dictate which short-range desires may be safely gratified.

2. Thought [☿+,♅-]

The impulse of our thought system is determined at its first pole by the charge of Mercury (☿) and at its second pole by the charge of Uranus (♅).

Our will system leads our reasoning into the subconscious phase of *subjective analysis*, and we exit that phase by cognizing the abstract concept, our second cardinal idea. This cognition is the defining essence of the initial event, our context, and it is the beginning of our conscious thought system as such. Thought is a closed system; its balanced impulse is (+ -), which means that it begins with a personal projection and concludes with assimilation from outside the self. This system thus works deductively from its first pole (☿+)—which is epistemically the abstract concept, logically a principle, and linguistically an abstract term—to its second pole (♅-), where we cognize the objective implications of that concept, principle, or term. My shorthand terms for our thought system's polar cognitions are *principle* and *implication*.

Our thought system thus begins with a powerful cardinal idea, the abstract concept that is our cognition and affirmation of our context's defining essence, such as its existence, oneness, space, uniqueness, or dignity. This derived concept is only logical if we project and affirm it, but at the second pole, where we deduce its objective implications, only assimilation is logical.

It is in this system that we organize and logically structure the parts of any whole we consider, including the reasoned conclusions of our four other psychologic systems. This explains, for instance, the conflict between the personal morals that we follow in practice and the moral codes that we propose universally for everyone to follow. The former are the particular class conclusions of our judgment system, while the latter are the universal conclusions of our thought system that apply to every case or class in that context.

It follows that if we want to know how well organized a person's reasoning is on the whole, one of the main indicators is the strength or weakness of his or her impulse in thought. But note that the implicatory chain of the Cycle is important here, for we can't understand how well the secondary reasoning of our thought system works from its impulse alone; we must also know the impulse of our primary will system. Being weak (- or R) in our will system limits our secondary reasoning even if our impulse in thought is strong (+ or B).

2A. BALANCED (☿+,♅-). THE REASONER. To be balanced in thought is to reason from a subjective principle or abstract term to its partialized and objective implications, which is to dissect a One into a Some or a whole into its parts. People with this impulse are natural *reasoners*, in the sense of 'reason' described as follows in *Webster's Dictionary of Synonyms* (Springfield, MA: G. & C. Merriam Co., Publishers, First Edition, 1942, 680).

> ...the term is often used in a very general sense to note the power of arriving at knowledge or truth by logical processes, whether one starts with observed facts, with principles regarded as axioms or necessary postulates, or the like; thus, in Kant's definition "pure *reason*" does not start with facts derived from experience or observation, but with truths derived through the medium of a higher intellectual power.[3]

People with this impulse (B) normally have no difficulty with deductive thinking, for they understand the thought process well, they can organize

---

[3] The Consideration Cycle agrees with Kant on this, that our reason is not a faculty that functions from our partialized observations and fact determinations, but one that leads us to them. However, it identifies the "higher intellectual power" that provokes this faculty, which Kant did not do, by holding that it is our primary reasoning, with its instincts and its will system. Though traditionalists have no grounds on which to make this distinction, the nouns *reasoning* and *reason* refer to different things: our reasoning is our psychologic, or common logic, and our reason is just one part of that entire process, our thought system. It is therefore incorrect to say, as many of their references do, that our *reasoning* is the use of our *reason*, a mere part of it. The verbal term 'to reason' is thus ambiguous, since it can mean to use our thought system only or to use any of the other parts of our psychologic, including our emotions. It is better to use more precise verbal terms when we mean reasoning in a specific psychologic system, such as 'to will', 'to think', 'to feel', 'to judge', or 'to decide'.

any ideas coherently, and they can communicate abstract notions effectively. They also have a strong sense of personal dignity (☿+) and their individual uniqueness. Unlike those who are assimilative at the first pole (☿-), they are not likely to appear insignificant, to embarrass themselves, to diminish their physical attractiveness or their status in others' eyes, or to act as buffoons professionally or in their private lives. But while it is appropriate to assimilate the implications of a principle, they are conventional in this function. So, unless they are projective (+) in will, they will apply their logical thinking to socially accepted tasks and will seldom upset their society's intellectual traditions with new conclusions or methods.

Advice to Reasoners. Be sure that any abstract notions you project in your secondary reasoning have been properly derived from sound primary reasoning, and that any implications drawn by you or others have been derived from sound universal principles, or theories. Take more risks in thinking; that is, challenge any principle that leads to inconsistent conclusions no matter how popular it is with academics or the public.

2B. Projective (☿+,♅+). The Speaker. This impulse is illogical only at the second pole (♅+), where one does not objectively assimilate what a principle implies. People who are projective in thought talk or write much, and have a strong sense of their personal dignity and uniqueness. They construct their thought system with little help from others or tradition, and, depending on other characteristics, their thought conclusions can be new and valuable or arbitrary and opinionated. Their illogic at the second pole (♅+) makes them overconfident in those opinions, which may be fictions that they equate to facts, and some of them can be so impressed with their subjective thought conclusions that they refuse to assimilate any factual evidence that might contradict these.

Being projective in any system is to be half illogical there, so this impulse in thought produces two different kinds of speakers. At one extreme there are the close-minded and opinionated people who use their reason as a weapon to 'mow down' all who oppose their subjective opinions, and at the other there are intelligent people who make good use of the creativity in reason that results from being projective at both poles of thought. This difference is usually indicated by the logic of the prior system, will. People who are weak (- or R) in will are confused and manipulated there, so they can't make their thought system sound even if they are balanced (B) in thought, and if they are projective (+) in thought, they will be opinionated.

Bush II (R++RR) is a paradigm of opinionation. Being projective in thought and reversed in will, his thoughts aren't structured by a sense of reality, theory, or personal motives, as distinct from the motives he was manipulated into adopting—first by his willful father (+BBB+) and then by his "higher father," the imaginary deity that he claims speaks to him and uses in lieu of logic. He projects thoughts freely and often; in fact, it is hard to quiet him or to get him to listen to anyone. But given his weak will, there is no logic there, so his thoughts don't *mean* anything, and he can only defend them with religious arguments or stubbornness in his arbitrary opinions.

The tables in *Appendix B* list many people who are strong (B or +) in both will and thought, as Bush I is, and they all think and speak with meaning. Though other characteristics also play a major role in this, strength in will and thought is commonly found in our best thinkers, exactly because a strong will prevents a strong thinker from denying reality and primary reasoning.

Advice to Speakers. You think fast and are eager to project your thoughts. Depending on your impulse in judgment, you do this either to help people with your thinking or to command or persuade them for your selfish ends. You may not realize that while you can develop a full line of reasoning in writing or formal speeches, you can't do this in normal conversations. That's why you usually try to dominate a conversation and close out others' opinions, and since this is often perceived as rudeness or opinionation, it can defeat your purposes. Resist your urge to interrupt people while they are speaking; let them finish their sentences, and try to hear them out fully even if you know what they're going to say. Curb your eagerness to be the first to say something, for this can make you a gossip; a wise rule is to have a good reason for speaking before you do. Also, what you want to say at first blush may be mistaken, for you often reach thought conclusions that impress you before they are tested. So you need to give more thought to what you intend to say and do more revisions of your writing than you initially think necessary.

2C. ASSIMILATIVE (☿-,♅-). THE LISTENER. The illogic of this impulse (-) is only at the first pole (☿-), where one should but doesn't subjectively project (affirm) either principles or one's dignity. People with this impulse begin thought without forming an abstract conception, and so they must adopt principles and abstract terms from others. Thus, their thought process always begins slowly, and it continues slowly too, for at the second pole they will, appropriately, take time to assimilate the implications of those principles.

Being assimilative at the first pole impairs people's sense of dignity and personal uniqueness because their self-concept is weak (☿-). It is contradictory to say that one's *self*-concept was adopted from *others*, and yet about half of all people, the assimilative (-) or reversed (R) in thought, try to do just that. Whatever sense of dignity they have is derived from what others say about them, so they seek praise and make much of public honors and award ceremonies by which their rulers or peers express approval for anyone. They are thus unreliable; not only because they lack a sense of personal dignity, but also because others can easily manipulate their thinking.

Our subjects are indifferent to theoretical issues, but they are still natural students, scholars, and researchers, just because they must adopt a principle from tradition or others (☿-) and then search widely for its objective implications (♅-). This, then, is the familiar *academic-scientific* disposition. It is illogical because one cannot adopt a universal principle from someone else without detaching it from its psychologic cause (that is, from the realism, theory, and motives of its creator), and consequently one has no way to decide if any universal principle is sound.

Because this total assimilation in thought makes our subjects dependent on the principles and opinions of others, they are collectors of both. For instance, Jefferson (+- -BB) was concerned all his life with collecting facts and building his library. Since our subjects, who include Jefferson and many other famous listeners, take principles from others rather than proposing their own, their intellectual energy is devoted to deducing further implications of those borrowed principles. This is a common focus among academics and journalists, especially those who deal professionally with thought or thinkers. If they become famous as intellectuals, as many have, it is due to some combination of plagiarism and diligent research in finding relevant principles or implications (opinions) offered by others.

This impulse thus makes one more conventional in thought than people with the other three impulses. Their thought system's memory bank consists entirely of traditional conceptions, learned historical or scientific facts, different language systems, and current public or peer opinions, which are the woof and warp of all their explicated thinking. They listen to principles and opinions, but since they have so few of their own, they speak cautiously and with many qualifications, and so they seldom express *themselves*.

The tables of *Appendix B* list many illustrious people whose social prominence derived from this weakness in thought: the theft or promotion (often without credit) of others' principles or deduced opinions, which dependence they usually succeed in disguising by their participation in academic or other collective intellectual efforts. Their passivity, lack of brashness, and team participation may lead others to like, praise, and reward them, but we mustn't assume from this that they are original thinkers. With respect to thought, their role is that of sponges, not creators.

Advice to Listeners. Don't allow your self-concept to be shaped by what others think of you or by what material or social distinctions you have achieved in the outer world, for that is a self-deceiving image. You must define your own essence, without relying on what others believe, even your peers at work. This is important for your health because our personal dignity, along with our will, is all that saves us from being manipulated and misused by others. You will be happiest doing work that doesn't require creative thinking, such as teaching others' thoughts or reporting them in the media. But always remember to be open and honest in admitting the sources of your assimilated thoughts; you didn't create them, but you can at least take pride in uncovering them and (if your will is strong) in seeing their relevance to a current situation. Unless you have a strong will and good judgment, you will collect opinions but be unable to edit them, or to decide which are best and which are worthless. Recognize this fact so that you don't fall into the manipulative trap of supporting opinions merely because they are popular or supported by socially recognized experts. Admit that this is not valid grounds for adopting any conclusion, and then put your research talents to the task of proving or disproving it.

2D. REVERSED (☿-,♅+). THE SKEPTIC. The reversal also causes academic or journalistic other-dependence in thought, since it too causes one to adopt principles from external sources at the first pole (☿-). But it is also illogical at the second pole, where one subjectively projects (♅+) rather than objectively deduces the implications of those principles. This bipolar illogic produces skeptics, or people who, because they cannot validly deduce any thought conclusions, have unusual or even weird opinions—which they still call 'facts', because that's what these would have been if they had been objectively deduced.

The general flaws of the will reversal apply here too. So, following the nine-point list above and bearing in mind that a strong (+ or B) will system lessens the impact of these negative effects, we can say the following of people with a thought reversal.

(1) They cannot structure a realistic and sound explicit system. (2) They are dedicated anti-intellectuals. Since they deny their own thought system, they try to deflect any issue of correct thinking to make it about emotive, personal, or practical issues instead. (3) They are easily manipulated by thinkers who are more logical or socially esteemed than they are. (4) Their illogic in thought is their undoing. (5) They prefer professions that are academic, journalistic, or juridic in nature because these require them to research others' thinking (principles and opinions) and to project their own arbitrary opinions (♅+) to their students or the public as if these were valid deductions from true universal principles. (6) When they try to present a complete line of reasoning, there is a hole

where the deductive logic of their thought system should be. (7) They are the leading advocates of mystical, scientific, or practical formal systems that extol the benefits of *not* thinking; that is, of suspending, transcending, or 'going beyond' thought, including one's self-concept, or dignity. Like those who are assimilative in thought, human individuality and dignity mean nothing to them; only the collective (or the culture or tradition) is important, and individuals who are not socially esteemed are irrelevant to them. (8) Because they want to avoid sound thinking, they seek shortcuts in reasoning or diversions that will fill their mind with nonsense instead. And (9) they consistently beg the question by *petitioning the premise*, which in our thought system is its first pole, or a principle or abstract term.

To beg the question in a closed system (thought or judgment) is to petition the premise rather than the conclusion, and I will explain this case now. People who are reversed (☿-,♅+) in thought cannot project at the first pole as they should, so in their initial thinking about a context, they must suspend consideration there and leap ahead to the second pole, where they will project rather than assimilate some thought conclusion (implication, fact, opinion) that is vaguely related to that context. Then in an act of reconsideration they revisit the first pole with this subjective opinion in mind, which they assume is an objective fact because it would have been that if they had deduced it from a universal principle. But on this second pass they still can't project a principle at the first pole, so they must look for someone else's principle to adopt (petition), and now this search is simpler, since they know just what they want the missing principle to imply. And this inverted process is question begging, since that principle was not chosen because it is a universal defining essence derived from a theory, but only because it implies the arbitrary personal opinion that they previously projected at the second pole.

Here's a familiar example of this error. Say that I have a thought reversal and so I arbitrarily conclude, from my own observations only, that the black people I know are intellectually inferior to other people I know. To defend this subjective opinion, I will search for a universal principle that implies this 'fact'. But all that I can find are mere opinions by scientists or other academics that are as arbitrary as mine, because these too are based on partialized observations and because no antecedent principle can be derived from consequent observations or statistics on those observations. But if I do find a scientist who proposes a 'principle' of genetics or statistics that appears to imply my opinion, I will argue that, "Because scientist X has said Y, it follows that black people are intellectually inferior." But this is not a premise and a conclusion; it is the same conclusion twice, the scientist's mere opinion and mine, and so my 'argument' is circular, or begs the question.[4]

Both forms of question begging result in ersatz justifications, or rationalizations, chief among which are opinion polls and the circular self-promoting awards that our academic, professional, entertainment, corporate, militaristic, and governmental institutions ceremoniously dispense. Polls can only tell us what people think or did, and never why they think it or did it or whether it is a valid thought or proper act, so they are essential tools for people with a reversal. The same is so of honors

---

[4] More generally, we coined the term *intelligence* in this sense to mean an attribute of *any* individual, so it is a universal term in the context of living organisms. But it is a vague descriptive term because we don't know all the factors that cause it in any organism. We also use it more narrowly in speaking of a hypothetical class of living things, let us say people, but here we can only mean the 'intelligence' of *all* people with no discrimination, or with no measurements of it. If we attempt to measure differences in 'intelligence' within that class, then our conception of it ceases to be a universal term and becomes just a back-formation yielded by question-begging. That is, the term then means 'a *range* of intelligence', a range that we can't identify without examining all the individuals of that class to measure this thing about people that we have never defined. But this is impossible, especially with a broad class such as a gender, race, or culture, so we must arbitrarily select a small 'typical' group in that class—a sampling that cannot truly represent the entire class unless (at the least) its members are of both genders, of all ages, and of all generations and other intelligence-defining time periods. But even if we ignore that insurmountable problem, we can't measure 'intelligence' until we have defined it, or know all of its causes, and some of these are congenital astrological factors, which are *abstract (or universal) factors that can never discriminate by class*. So, until we can define the term causatively, no one can propose a valid hypothesis, statistical or otherwise, on the so-called 'intelligence' of any gender, race, or culture.

and awards, which prove nothing but social acceptance. Their purpose is entirely collectivistic; it is to stage a public ceremony that begs the question of the worth of some person, property, or political program, because it asks us to accept a final evaluation on this on no better grounds than the subjective opinions of some group of people. These deceiving award ceremonies are common in our societies because people who are assimilative (-) or reversed (R) in a system can't function in that system without 'experts' or some peer or public consensus that either provides input (-) or supports their own arbitrary opinions (+).

Advice to Skeptics. Learn to distinguish between an abstract (universal) conception and the implications that follow from it, for this will help you see the illogic of your natural impulses in thinking as described above. Remember that facts are not asserted opinions, they must be proven to be facts, and that this requires objective testing. If you don't understand the illogic of your thought system, you will stop using it, and then you will be manipulated by the thinking and logic of others, which is probable because you lack dignity, or don't project your self-concept. There is no safe escape from your reason, so it is better to deal with it than to skip (or bracket) it. You may seek relief from your doubts by relying instead on your emotions—as many theists, athletes, performers, and artists with a thought reversal do—but remember that in these activities you are dealing with fictions, not facts, and that such escapes from reality can help no one (not even children). You can benefit by studying the reasoning of intellectuals who are strong (+ or B) in thought, and by finding the logical flaws in the works of those who are weak (- or R) in thought.

3. FEELING [♀-,Ψ+]

The impulse of our feeling system is determined at its first pole by the charge of Venus (♀) and at its second pole by the charge of Neptune (Ψ).

We store our thought system's conclusions in the subconscious phase of *objective analysis*, which leads us to the first pole of our feeling system. To be logical, we must assimilate the objective cognition at this pole

(♀-), which may be just sense data. Then at the second pole it is logical to project a subjective response (Ψ+), an internal decision regarding the pieces we have just taken in. Keywords for these polar cognitions of our feeling system are *sensations* and *desires*, or in some contexts *affections* and *passions*.

Our feeling system is an open system (- +), so it is illogical to project at the first pole or assimilate at the second pole. At the first pole, it is unrealistic to project our own sense (or aesthetic) criteria upon any external reality. Being projective in sensation (♀+) is like placing a strict guardian at the gate of our feeling system, an error that can also occur in the open systems of will and power. This appears to be a defensive measure, but because it cannot be controlled it leaves one undefended in the opposite way, by causing one to reject otherwise rewarding experiences. People with this impulse say, "You can come into my emotional ground only if you first meet my subjective aesthetic criteria." The illogic here is that a whole is being denied by an argument that applies only to some of its parts.

For instance, in choosing partners or friends, one may ignore important attributes and select only from the smaller pool of sensually pleasing people. Those who are properly assimilative at the first pole (♀-) also reject unpleasing sensations, but they are more tolerant of unpleasant sensations that don't signify danger, so they are less arbitrary and restrictive than those who are projective there (♀+). They choose partners for deeper reasons, such as suitability for their life plan or for safety, loyalty, kindness, intelligence, morality, and so on.

But assimilation is illogical at the second pole. This pole's function is appropriately selfish, because we must make a subjective decision on each objective part that we assimilated at the first pole. I refer to these decisions, the reasoned conclusions of our feeling system, as our desires or passions, or more fully as our *passion determinations*. These conclusions are binary in nature; we must either love or hate what we have just taken in, for if we are indifferent to a sensation, we form no feeling conclusion and the current consideration is aborted. There is no middle ground at this second pole; there is only the dualism of a passion—of our subjective pro-con or either-or reaction to a perceived part. To continue with our present consideration, we must decide here, subjectively, whether we *desire* to have or avoid that part. In this our feeling system is like our digestive system, for when we eat we have an internal reaction, a 'gut reaction' as we say, by which our body or any part of it either rejects or accepts what we have consumed.

Of course, our passion to have any concrete and complex thing, say a mate or friend, is a conclusion we reach over time, by separately considering many different attributes of that person. And contrary to a popular misconception on this, true and deep love for another person is not based solely on our judgment of that person's virtues. It is also based on a passion for his or her faults, which can also incite our desires, if only because of our own flaws.

Our desires (passions) are implied by our sensations (affections), which can only tell us what appears best on the surface. The poles of our feeling system are sharply divided by our third cardinal idea, our cognition of a part, which begins our synthetic reasoning by forcing us to decide whether that part is or is not good for us physically or psychologically. Our passion determinations can ratify or contradict our sensual determinations, but the only conclusion they can store in the succedent memory bank is a desire to have or avoid that particular part, along with some memory of the sensations that implied it.

I can now clarify a point mentioned in our discussion of will. Our *wants* are either *wishes* or *desires*, each of which is our first response to a percept, but to opposite percepts. A wish is a response to a whole event and a desire (passion) is a response to one or some parts of that event; a wish begins analysis and a desire begins synthesis; a wish is validly cognized by objective assimilation (☾-) and a desire is validly cognized by subjective projection (Ψ+); and a wish pertains to our survival and long-term objectives, while a desire pertains to our partialized pleasures and short-term objectives. Traditionalists confuse the terms *wish* and *desire* with each other and with our conventionally ambiguous term *need*, but in truth we can only validly associate a desire with our partialistic feeling system and a wish with our wholistic will system. *Every wish is a power wish*, and it is our principal want because it implies all the little wants, or desires, that arise subsequently in its context. To gratify a desire is to satisfy an appetite, or a partialistic and immediate want formed by our passions, but unless that desire was informed by a prior wish and act of will, its gratification gives us no power over broader events. And of course it is far easier to develop the narrow powers by which we satisfy our appetites than to develop the wholistic power over events that we must have to be happy.

Our lives are made needlessly difficult by selfish manipulators of various kinds who urge us to ignore our wishes and gratify our desires instead. In Book V of his *Laws,* Plato said of a state that "the greatest of all plagues [is] not faction, but rather distraction." This is true, and our distractions are what we desire, not what we wish for.

3A. BALANCED ($♀-,Ψ+$). THE HARMONIST. Those who are balanced in feeling have a logical emotive system, taking in freely with their senses at the first pole ($♀-$), and then at the second pole ($Ψ+$) projecting their passion response to what they have assimilated. Their tastes are conventional, so they usually defer to the aesthetic opinions of experts or their peers, but their inner responses to their sensations are personal and creative, and they will freely express their passions, or emotive choices, when it is appropriate. So all their subsequent synthetic reasoning is based on a feeling system that functions logically, without superficial biases. Nevertheless, the soundness of that system and its memory bank depends largely on the strength or weakness of the two prior systems, will and thought.

Advice to Harmonists. There are times and situations in which you just 'play it too safe' emotionally. That is, you tend to accept the tastes and emotional customs of your society or culture without question, and yet some emotional risk-taking can introduce you to new and rewarding people and experiences that harm no one.

3B. PROJECTIVE ($♀+,Ψ+$). THE EMOTIONALIST. The illogic of this impulse is at the first pole, where one projects subjective sensual or aesthetic criteria as if these were objective facts. This is the creative charge, suitable for sense-based designing or descriptive communication, but it is not realistic. This reality-distorting urge at the first pole ($♀+$)

then influences the projection of passions at the second pole. Those who are projective in feeling are highly emotive; their feelings are of immense importance to them, sometimes to the exclusion of all other experiences. They are romantics and they brook no interference from others or social customs in expressing their emotions, both their surface sensations and their deeper passions, and they often do so loudly and at socially inappropriate times. They become musicians, writers, performers, or exhibitionists whose private feelings must be heard, even if it means imposing these on others.

Had Shakespeare's Romeo and Juliet been real people, they would have been projective in feeling, for theirs was not a balanced love guided by their global wishes; it was an idealized love that denied all else, even life. But contrary to what our emotionalists and many psychologists assume, our emotions are not the whole of us and they are not our most fundamental faculties.

Whether a projective impulse in feeling is healthy or not depends on the systems that precede and imply it. Those who are strong in both will and thought have firm control over their emotive process and its memory system, whatever its impulse may be. But those who are strong in feeling and weak in those prior systems can unrealistically risk everything on their emotions, and this is so to a lesser degree when only their will is weak. Their mere desires—for pleasures, possessions, life after death, or gratifying their loves or rages—then become ersatz wishes, or substitutes for their will's global motives. They foolishly believe that their sensations and passions are the source of everything and therefore should be put before all other things.

Healthy or not, our passions cause the hypothetical ideals that we create in our scientific, artistic, or mystical pursuits, and also in our wasteful and frivolous activities, which consist of any work or entertainment that is not based on will (purpose) and thought. If one's will and thought systems are weak, this emotive projection on others becomes a social threat because it causes romanticism, theism, or other mystical escapes from reality that can destroy an individual or, if widespread enough, a society. Such people are perpetually adolescent, lustful, and inclined to create *ideals*, meaning the fictions that we create from a tertiary passion rather than from a primary (realistic) will intent. They function best as performers or artists of some kind.

Advice to Emotionalists. Try to remain calm, even in situations that upset you. Remember that while your superficial tastes and affections are objective issues (♀-) and can be discussed as such with others, your passion determinations are private matters (Ψ+) that are best not shared with strangers or with anyone you know who may not have your best interests at heart. Though our for-profit media routinely and offensively ignore this rule, letting people know your deepest feelings is more information about you than most of them want; it is also an imposition that most of them resent. Your passions are personal, and since they are subjectively derived, they mean nothing to others; indeed, the purpose of art is to transform passions into something that is objectively meaningful to everyone, which in the fictional arts can only be universal moral conclusions. So restrain your feelings, be a more private person, and find an objectively meaningful way to express your passions. And don't be misled by psychologists who say that our passions are primary rather than tertiary, for this is to confuse them with our instincts.

3C. Assimilative (♀-,Ψ-). The Sybarite. This impulse begins logically as the balanced impulse does, but at the second pole (Ψ-) one fails to make the required passion determination. Instead, like those with the reversal, one looks outside oneself to others or traditions, and asks, "How should I feel about that?" This is not a sensible question, of course, for as with our life plan, others cannot know which passions are best for us. For instance, the maxim that we must all love and honor our parents or our country is nonsense, because logically we can only love or honor those people or things that provoke our positive passions or earn our respect. No other person has any right to command our feelings, such as our love, loyalty, or respect, or to insist that we swear oaths or allegiance to any person or collective.

The assimilative impulse in feeling inclines people to accept public and peer opinion on emotive issues, so they are conventional in their aesthetics and passions. They eat, drink, inhale, watch, or hear what others expect them to take in, even if they don't like it, just because others are doing it or say that it is pleasurable or good for them. In this conventional way, then, they are sybaritic, or acquisitive in feeling. They collect sensations, passions, lovers, and the stimulants or objects that please them or evoke memories of their feelings, and they do so by searching far, wide, and often for these things throughout their lives. And of course, especially if their will or thought system is weak, they have no logical ability to decide if any person or thing they have collected is the best one for them. Their emotions are quantitative, not qualitative.

Unlike the projective emotionalists, sybarites are easily manipulated through their emotions. Their emotive defenses are slight because they have no 'guardian at the gate' at the first pole, and because their inability to project their passions at the second pole makes them dependent on others for determining these and unable to refuse unhealthy sensual stimulants. But if their will or thought system is strong, they usually mature past these youthful weaknesses in time.

Advice to Sybarites. Your problem is the difficulty you have determining what you love or hate (or wish to have or avoid), and this leaves you open to manipulation by the people to whom you turn for emotional guidance. It also leaves you continually in doubt as to what things or people suit you emotionally and what desires you should work to gratify in practice. Your postponement of emotional decisions often makes you a victim of external events—such as being led into unsuitable emotional relationships, joining groups or purchasing things that don't really satisfy you, and so on. In other words, your emotional indecision, or inability to project a subjective passion determination and to say that it is correct solely because it is yours, makes you vulnerable to any kind of sales pitch. You listen to commercials, to salespersons, to politicians, or to the appeals of would-be lovers who are inappropriate for you because you foolishly expect others to tell you or somehow indicate what it is that you should desire. You may learn better in time, but only from your past mistakes.

3D. REVERSED ($♀+,Ψ-$). THE SPECTATOR. This is the totally illogical impulse in feeling, for first one inappropriately projects affections, and then one inappropriately tries to assimilate desires. People with this impulse deny their feelings and the feelings of others, and consequently they also try to deny others' freedom of choice in matters of affection or passion. This reversal is common in strict parents, wardens, torturers, or others who get a perverse pleasure by preventing others from having what they like or desire. Like our emotionalists, they make much of their personal aesthetic criteria and have a strict guardian at the gate of their feelings (♀+). But like our sybarites, they fail to determine their own passions (Ψ-) and so they are easily manipulated emotionally and are often trapped in love or hate relationships. It takes them longer than other people to love or to hate people or things, but when they do, it is usually irreversible.

In effect, the reversal makes them detached spectators in emotive matters. They can be devoted to sensual pleasures, but they make no passionate commitment to those who provide these pleasures. Though they are empathetic, they often ignore others' feelings and in their discussions they don't allow that any feelings are worth considering. This is so less often when their impulse in judgment is (-) or (B), which makes them compassionate as well as empathetic. Intellectuals who are strong in will and thought—Einstein (+BR-R), for instance—live more easily with this reversal than others do because it lets them deny pleasures, passions, or interruptions that would distract them from their life purpose and thinking.

Now let us apply our nine general points to people with a feeling reversal. (1) They cannot structure a realistic and sound feeling system. (2) They are dedicated anti-emotionalists; that is, they deny their own feelings and try to divert any discussion of feelings to make it about abstract or practical issues instead. (3) They are easily manipulated through their passions. (4) Their handling of emotional matters is their undoing. (5) Though they prefer professions that remove them from emotive issues or emotional displays, they often work as artists, psychologists, or critics because this requires them at the first pole (♀+) to project their subjective opinions on aesthetic matters, and at the second pole (Ψ-) to assimilate and study peoples' passions, as Freud (+-RB-) and Ellis (+-RB+) did.

(6) When they attempt to present their complete reasoning on a context, their feelings are not mentioned. (7) Often, especially if this is their only reversal, they oppose theism and other forms of mystical reasoning because

it is based on emotional premises. They judge religions, art, and play by their social value only, and so, like the great novelist Tolstoy (B-RR-), they believe that any art or entertainment that lacks a larger social purpose is meaningless. (8) They devise or adopt rationalizations for avoiding emotive experiences, and if they have other reversals also, they may even be capable of unbelievable cruelties, as was the pathological conservative Eichmann (-BRRR). On the other hand, they are romantics and are empathetic. This is so because, like our sybarites who are also assimilative at their feeling system's second pole, they feel others' passions more acutely than their own. This ability can be an asset for social critics, psychologic therapists, writers of fiction or biography, and even, paradoxically, torturers or penalists, who can excel at their job because their empathy tells them what will pain people most. And (9) they beg the question in their feeling system by petitioning the conclusion.

The question begging of the feeling reversal works as follows. At the first pole, our subjects try to project sensations, or affections, but in an initial consideration (such as a first meeting with someone) they can't do this, so they must leap ahead to the second pole, where normally our passions are projected ($\Psi+$). But since they are assimilative ($\Psi-$) here, they must delay to research others' passions so as to see what a 'good' or conventional passion is in such a case. And having begged this conclusion, or adopted a passion from others, they return to the first pole in a reconsideration (or second meeting), and this time, rather than assimilating what is before them, they project some aesthetic criteria ($♀+$) that they believe imply the passion they adopted. And the result is emotional self-deception, for they loaded their argument by projecting only the criteria that imply that passion. In other words, they control the sensations that they allow themselves to experience so that the only 'passions' they can have are the collectivistic ones that are approved by their society or peers.

The feeling reversal produces emotional blockage or backwardness (immaturity), and this makes one a detached spectator in emotional matters. Unless our subjects know of their impairment and work to compensate for its effects, which is unlikely if they are weak in will or thought, they will build inverted, past-oriented, contradictory, prejudiced, and confused desire systems, and they will construct avoidance devices with elaborate rationalizations for escaping from emotional commitment.

As you see, the familiar inquiry in psychologic therapy, "How do you feel about that?" is only pertinent for half of us, those who don't project their passions because they are (R) or (-) in feeling. We must assert a personal desire at our feeling system's second pole, because we alone are doing this wanting. In our open systems (will, feeling, and power), the projective impulse at the concluding pole ($\hbar+$, $\Psi+$, $\odot+$) gives us human motives, passions, or strengths, while the assimilative impulse make us like sheep who follow the herd.

Modern psychologists have often described this emotional blockage in people, but the Cycle defines it, and it allows us to predict it without a therapy session. Moreover, it tells us that this is but one of the five kinds of psychologic blockage. The reversals in will, thought, judgment, and power yield similar blockages, two that are more fundamental and two that are less so, and each produces its own kind of denial and avoidance syndrome. A psychologic system affects one's final understandings and decisions according to its sequence in the Cycle, so personally the most serious reversal is that of the will system, followed by those of thought, feeling, judgment, and power. But the inverse order holds in our social world. There the rest of us have more reason to fear people with judgment or power reversals, because these two synthetic systems have a more direct effect on how people behave towards others.

Advice to Spectators. If you must deny your own feeling system, remember that this system is important to many others and speak of it accordingly. Don't try to escape from emotive experiences; rather, participate in them and make a conscious effort to determine what you really like or dislike about them. Then rid yourself of your dislikes no matter what your social situation is or what others say. The study of art can be helpful if you use it to make subjective decisions rather than merely aesthetic ones. Denying your passion determinations, which begin all synthetic reasoning, will impair your practical efforts by leading you to misunderstand the subjective basis of judgments, morals, and social rules. That is, it will make you too formal and a bit inhuman in dealing with people, and they won't be as comfortable with you as they are with others. Be clear with people with whom you have any kind of relationship so that they have no doubts what it is and isn't to you. You will be more comfortable with spectators or sybarites than with harmonists or emotionalists, but you will learn something from the latter types.

4. JUDGMENT [♂+,♀-]

The impulse of our judgment system is determined at its first pole by the charge of Mars (♂) and at its second pole by the charge of Pluto (♀).

The desires that conclude the functioning of our feeling system are stored in the next subconscious phase, *subjective synthesis*. This leads us to our judgment system, the opposite poles of which, in shorthand terms, are *need* and *consequences*, or equivalently in the traditional view of moral judgment, *egoism* and *altruism*. As in thought, the other closed system, the balanced impulse in judgment is projection at the first pole and assimilation at the second pole, or (+ -). Logically, at the first pole we must subjectively assert our own need, or plan of action, which is always passion based, and then at the second we must objectively assimilate and evaluate the consequences (on ourselves, others, and our environment) of acting on that need. This evaluation is the reconciliation of the two poles, a reasoned conclusion that we store in the succedent memory bank as judgments, beliefs, values, ideals, morals, hopes, or anxieties.

I call the first cognition of our judgment process a 'need'. This is no longer a specific desire; rather, it is a constructed general notion of that desire. Though conventionally we confuse the two terms, our feeling system's *desire* is our passion to have or avoid a specific thing, but our judgment system's *need* is to have or avoid all things like that one. And this need, or tertiary generalization, begins our judgment process, where we liken or contrast things in order to *evaluate* them. We must pluralize our desire (or passion) in this way before can we assign a value to it, because we can only value a class of things. A particular thing that we desire is what it is, and though it may have a price, as decided later in our quaternary reasoning, its *value* derives from its being a member of the class of all such things, or from its being a kind of thing that we have decided we *need*. Value is not price, but it implies an agreed price later.

In our judgment system, we evaluate the kinds of things that we desire to have or avoid, one kind at a time, and also the risks or costs of acting to acquire them, which become part of their value. We create a need by generalizing a desire, whereupon we speculate on the future acts we might perform to gratify that need and the possible consequences of performing each such act. This speculative (hypothetical) process of evaluation quantifies the degree of our need, and what we mean when we say that something is 'worthless' is that we don't need that kind of thing enough to assign a value to its class. The basic elements of a thing's value are that it is of a kind that is desired by one or more persons, that it is possible for us or others to acquire it, and that the consequences, the risks or costs, of acting to acquire it are acceptable to us or to others.

We determine this value subjectively for ourselves (♂+), and we assign it to the generalized need, and thus indirectly to the initial desire. And because our tertiary reasoning is generalized accretive reasoning, we tend to believe that whatever we personally value highly or lowly, with its risks, should be similarly valued by all. It is here in our judgment system that we tend to assume that our subjective valuation of a need has objective validity, and this is why, how, and where we begin to rationalize our needs, or contemplated acts. This judgment function tells us which classes of things we shall hereafter deem worth having or avoiding, and to what degree. So our passions lead us to our generalized needs and then to our quantitative judgments, where we create our evaluative prejudices as to what is or is not worthy, or valuable, what we do or do not need, and what we will or will not risk. And if our subcontext is a person, he or she is now considered by us only as a class, a descriptive kind. Our judgment system is thus the proximate source of our social biases and our later power decisions for or against entire classes of people.

It is only in our judgment system that we plan our *acts*, as distinct from our will's *motives*, and we use our arbitrary valuation, a subjective bias that we name with a class term, to tell us just how ardently or mildly we should act in the future in order to have or avoid a thing of that class. If this process seems confusing, it is only because our conventional terms for it are vague and fail to make the required psychologic distinctions, so let me clarify some of those terms now.

The subjective conclusions of our feeling system are our arbitrary *desires*, the direct opposites of the *wishes* that begin our will system; both are *wants*, but neither is a *need*. We often use the terms in these pairs as synonyms, but their idea-referents are distinct impressions, for we have two kinds of wanting and a kind of needing that results from each. To avoid the old ambiguities here, let us use *motive* to mean only a plan of purpose derived in our will system from a wish, and *need* to mean only its direct opposite, a plan of action devised in our judgment system from a desire. Our motives are our life-needs; they compose our essential life strategy, the framework that gives structure to all that we do later, at least until we consciously alter it in our will system. And our needs are our short-range plans, our relative and arbitrary tactics for gratifying the desires that we have generalized into class notions.

Both are driving forces within us, but if we are logical, our driving motives command the driving needs by which we decide how much we want or value certain kinds of things and how we intend to act in practice to get them. Our desires imply our needs, and we often judge that the risks or costs are too great for us to allow a particular desire to become a personal need. If so, we won't act on it, which means that, however strong the desire is, we don't need it. A need is not a desire; it is a speculative plan of action by which we hope to get or avoid some kind of thing.

The reasoned conclusions that we reach at the second pole of our judgment system (♀-) are the various forms of the fourth cardinal idea, the concrete concept, as described earlier. So what we store in our judgment's succedent memory bank are our quantitative methods of evaluation and our specific evaluations of the classes of things we have considered, and also our beliefs, ideals, morals, class terms, prejudices, hopes, anxieties, and hypothetical conceptions of any static state of beingness, or substance. The latter are the fabricated forms (or Forms) and other fictional beings (or Beings) that we hypothesize in our judgment system.

At the second pole we reach a conclusion on the probable internal and external consequences of a hypothetical act. In this speculative reasoning, we even imagine acts that are vile to us, for this is where we decide that they are detestable acts that we must avoid. From these judgmental conclusions we construct and store an editable list of what types of acts we believe we should aspire to do or should never do. But these conclusions are of two basic kinds. If we believe an act will have consequences on others if it is performed, then it is a *moral judgment*; otherwise, it is an amoral *value judgment*. We maintain this distinction in our belief system, where we store our judgmental conclusions, and we carry it forward into our quaternary reasoning when we create formal legal codes. These are traditionally divided into criminal and civil codes, which were initially the social equivalents of our psychologic moral and value codes.

We all have a personal value system and a personal moral system, but they are largely informal, since we explicate only parts of both and don't make either into a complete and consistent system. That work is done formally by secondary or tertiary intellectuals. The former are analytic reasoners, or theorists who use their *thought* system to propose universal moral principles; the latter are synthetic reasoners, or hypothesists who use their *judgment* system to propose a generalized *social code*, which is an explicit list of 'thou shalts' and 'thou shalt nots'. A social code is just an hypothesist's personal moral code that he or she explicitly transformed, point by point, by considering whether it would be better or worse for the entire society if—hypothetically, since this is impossible in reality—everyone had the same personal moral code. This method only produces fictions, but it is how most traditionalists reason about morality, and it is why they fallaciously conclude that it is height of morality to impose their personal moral code on others and for their state to do the same to its citizens through its legal codes.[5]

---

[5] The Consideration Cycle reveals some key distinctions that traditional ethicists and philosophic intellectuals have not made in their discussions of morality, but we can't pursue these issues here in our psychologic context. In my next work I will present my new moral theory, as the necessary foundation of my new political theory. It was derived from the Cycle, and though it confirms some ancient and modern conclusions on the subject, it is critical of most traditional moral views—especially those that see the source of morality as divine, mystical, or cultural rather than as psychologic.

Our needs are amoral when they first arise in us because we have not yet judged them. They are just possible actions, mere plans that are unperformed and are seldom performed later as they were conceived in our judgment process. Our expressions of need can reveal our arbitrary passion determinations and the relative creativity of our partialized imaginings, but they tell us nothing about how we might act after we consider their consequences. This is why it is invalid for a legal system to punish people for their plans to act rather than for their actual acts, and yet our traditionalist states do just that, because it is a way to control us by invading our psychologic, especially our moral reasoning.

In our tertiary judgment we evaluate potential acts, but we don't yet know how we will act at the quaternary point of decision, and we must consider all possible acts here, even the worst ones, so that we can compare 'right' and 'wrong' acts in our judgment and thought. So what we call our 'conscience' is not a mystical thing within us, it is just our common logic. It is the clash between the universal terms of our thought system—where we criticize, universalize, and order any judgments that we stored away earlier—and the specific terms of our judgment system. It is our moral regret, or the sense of contradiction that arises in our thought system whenever we act, as we all do at times, in a way that we think is wrong for anyone. We act from a judgment, and when that judgment contradicts a *moral principle* of our thought as to how everyone should act, we are uneasy in our minds, and that uneasiness is our sense of guilt, or our 'conscience'.

So we use our thought system to analyze and criticize acts that we or others have performed, and we use our judgment system to imagine and criticize acts that we may or may not perform. Together these two open systems function as the harsh critic, moral preacher, and stern editor within us that brooks no superfluity, laxness, or immorality in any of our six memory banks. But in this role they are subject to our will system's control or lack of it. It is a matter of our will that *economy rules* in our global motives, and this principle of parsimony influences our subsequent systems if our will system is strong. In that case, we will have a sharp *sense of the essential* that keeps us on track in all our psychologic functioning and doesn't let us tolerate contradiction, waste, confusion, or immorality in any psychologic system or any intellectual, legal, or socio-political construct.

In sum, we use our judgment system to generalize our desires into needs, to speculatively evaluate and quantify those needs, to imagine acts that will gratify them, to deduce the internal and external consequences of performing those potential acts, and to create explicit hypothetical standards of all kinds—such as our personal moral system and any general standards of behavior, language, performance, or work for ourselves and others—that we believe are more perfect or ideal. But we don't decide there what act we shall perform; this we do subsequently, since our decisions to act are quaternary and reductive, not tertiary and accretive. In judgment we merely consider the consequences of possible acts that seem relevant to us in the present context.

Before proceeding with the four permutations of judgment impulses, we need to objectively define, and so distinguish, three terms that are widely used in our common and academic discussions of human feelings and judgments. These are *empathy*, *sympathy*, and *compassion*, which conventionally are merely described terms that are used vaguely, ambiguously, or synonymously. Symbolically, our definitions hold that empathy is caused by ♆-, sympathy by ♂-, and compassion by ♀- in a natal chart; so those who have a projective charge instead for any of these tertiary planets will lack empathy, sympathy, or compassion respectively. Verbally, *empathy* is the assimilation (adoption) of others' passions, *sympathy* is the assimilation of others' needs, and *compassion* is the assimilation of others' objective situation as a consequence of natural events or of acts by themselves or others. But, following the dynamic of third-quadrant reasoning, note that our empathy is personal (one-to-one), our sympathy is generalized as any need is, and our compassion can only apply to a class of people.

Contrary to the traditional assumption, empathy (♆-) and sympathy (♂-) are illogical, because it is only logical to project our passions and needs. That done, we can then validly compare our needs with others' and decide whether our compassion is justified for the class of people with a specific need. If we are confused about this, it is because we generally admire people who act unselfishly, even when it is illogical. But acts are objective events, not subjective ones. It is objective *to express* our empathy or sympathy, and we consider this kindness, but *to be* empathetic or sympathetic is illogical, and whatever we may say, no one else can know whether we actually experienced those reactions or not.

We can now correct a false argument in traditional moral reasoning that relies on the confusion of those three terms. Selfish people rationalize their immoral or amoral conclusions by correctly observing that empathy and sympathy are personally illogical, but from these facts their conclusion that there is no objective basis for morality doesn't follow. Our subjective desires lead us to imagine subjective needs, or plans of action, but this doesn't mean that we should or will perform those acts in the external world. We must still objectively judge the consequences of each contemplated act, and in this it is only logical to dispassionately consider and compassionately evaluate (♀-) the effects of that act on all others.

4A. BALANCED (♂+,♀-). THE MORALIST. This impulse works logically as just described. One subjectively projects from one's passions a speculative need (or plan of action) at the first pole (♂+), and then objectively assimilates its consequences at the second pole (♀-). People with this impulse have no difficulty in handling their judgmental functions, though it does make them conventional at the second pole, or in their judgment's conclusions and memory bank, which is to say in their ideals, fictions, class terms, language in general, work methods, moral codes, and notions of the consequences that will follow various acts. If their other systems are mostly balanced or assimilative, they will follow their society's accepted standards and will try to exemplify these in their behavior. But in any case they are compassionate and are concerned with moral issues and with being fair in their judgments of others.

Advice to Moralists. Given the mistaken views of morality that we humans have preserved for millennia, it is fair to say that the fourth of all people who are balanced in judgment have been insufficiently critical of the bad judgmental conclusions of the other three judgmental types.

So if that applies to you, I advise you stop to accepting the conventional views on judgment in your society just because they are the prevailing ones, because when you do that you are betraying your society as well as yourself. For instance, you may support a religion (or all religions) because of the unproven claim that our moral reasoning depends on the 'words' of fictional deities or mythical religious figures. But in truth morality is a part of *our* reasoning, that of each individual, so the relevant issue in a debate is whether the people reasoning about moral issues are doing so in a healthy or impaired way. You should be leading the way in your society to common sense on judgment, justice, morality, and theism, so don't tolerate the absurd old views of your culture as regards this crucial human issue of sound judgment.

4B. PROJECTIVE (♂+,♀+). THE EGOIST. People with this impulse appropriately project a personal need at the first pole (♂+), but at the second pole they subjectively project (♀+) rather than objectively assimilate (♀-) the consequences of that need. The positive side of this impulse is creativity in judgment, or originality in organizing complex tasks consisting of many fragments and formulating general standards that in quaternary reasoning will become social codes, language rules, organizational efforts, or work methods. The negative side is that one has no point of objectivity in reaching judgmental conclusions. Generally speaking, our egoists exclude others and the outer world from their judgments, they fashion plans and rationalizations for selfish acts only, their values and beliefs are arbitrary and personal, and they have no wish to discuss moral issues objectively or to ensure that others are judged fairly.

Ordinarily, then, the creativity of this impulse is misused, so that it becomes not an aid to healthy reasoning, but a weapon against others. Any projective (+) system is self-oriented and leads to subjective conclusions, and in judgment this impulse precludes any fair and objective consideration of the value of things, of others' needs or values, and of the consequences on others of one's judgments, beliefs, and standards. Its illogical impulse at the second pole (♀+), which is shared by those who are reversed (R) in judgment, indicates people who have no compassion, who ignore their conscience, who will not admit to any error in what they believe or say, and who will bully others to get their way.

The moral maxim of our egoists is that we are at all times free to gratify our own needs, as we personally decide these, even if this means deceiving, stealing from, destroying, harming, or otherwise imposing on others. They believe that a society's legal system *should* be unjust, for they consider any legal system deficient if it doesn't allow them and other egoists to impose on and use for their own ends other people, other living things, and our common natural resources. This attitude makes them ardent supporters of the political forms of egoism—mainly capitalism and libertarianism, both of which cloak themselves in the language of *individualism* while they deny what that term really means: humanism, or equal rights and resources for all individuals.

Advice to Egoists. You need to reverse your illogic in all the respects just mentioned. In addition, your point of illogic in judgment makes you devalue others because you see their class and not their individuality and uniqueness, and you need to stop rationalizing this as the correct approach to judgment or morality. The fact that it is correct to assert your needs at the first pole doesn't justify imposing your second-pole beliefs, evaluations, or judgments on others just because they are yours. You can be mistaken, and you often are because you rush to judgment. So resist your urge to make an instant judgment, for this is in fact just your attempt to find a shortcut around fair deliberations and to preclude others from saying anything in rebuttal. If you must judge others, then give them a full and fair hearing first. But resist your impulse to seek work in society that requires you to judge people, because you have *no* natural ability to be fair, objective, or compassionate in those judgments, even though those qualities are just what you hope to find in anyone who is judging you. That's hypocrisy, isn't it? I say much in this book that can help you minimize the irrationality and immorality of your egoism, so take it to heart, and try to compensate for this innate flaw that gives most people good reasons to dislike you.

4C. ASSIMILATIVE (♂-,♀-). THE ALTRUIST. This impulse gives people the opposite nature in judgment. They are reluctant to assert their personal needs, they are not rude, crude, or pushy about their needs, and they are not bullies. They are considerate of others, and are often advocates for the needs of other people or living things, because they assimilate these needs and adopt them as their own.

Altruists have the correct impulse at the second pole (♀-), where, like our moralists, they have compassion, judge others fairly, and objectively consider the consequences of their needs. But they differ in being illogical at the first pole (♂-), where they adopt others' needs instead of projecting their own. And this means that they have no way to judge a need, because they won't assert it (♂+) on their own authority, as moralists (B) and egoists (+) do. It also means that most of the time that they spend at the second pole is spent considering the social consequences of others' needs rather than the personal consequences of their own needs.

Conventionally, *altruism* is a moral term, but we are using it here in a broader sense to mean a congenital disposition in all judgments, not just moral judgments. The conventional meaning of *altruist* is one who puts the welfare of others before his or her own welfare, but that is not quite what we mean by the term, not even in its moral sense. Obviously we mean that an altruist (- -) is the opposite of an egoist (++), but we don't claim that an altruist will necessarily put others' welfare first. In other words, while we can generally attribute selfishness to egoists, we cannot generally attribute unselfishness to altruists, for there are too many exceptions.

This is so because the assimilative impulse in any psychologic system is that of a collector, and the impulse in a system to acquire many things doesn't give one any personal ability in that system to subjectively distinguish the good from the bad things. To a collector of external things, everything in that class of things is relevant, because he or she has no subjective (+) basis for preferring any of them over the others. Consequently, in early life all altruists have an amoral disposition, because they can't assert on their own authority which of the many moral principles preached by their elders they should observe. And since they can't see why any moral principle is necessarily valid, they decide that no such principle is binding on them, and that they can behave immorally if they wish, subject only to the threat of punishment.

It follows that there are two main descriptive classes of altruists in human society. One consists of those who sooner or later mature enough to see that they must have some binding moral principles to guide them in their practical decisions, and the other consists of those who never mature to that point, and so remain amoral and untrustworthy until they die. Of the latter there is no more to say, but we cannot understand altruism as a moral attitude unless we consider the moral reasoning used by the former—many of whom, like Kant (RBR-R), are compulsive seekers for universal moral truths that they can claim are binding on all humans alike.

Only an altruist has both sympathy (♂-) and compassion (♀-), but since sympathy is illogical, this combination produces some unique psychologic conflicts in those altruists who search for binding moral principles. First, the total assimilation of their judgment impulse makes that search quantitative and collectivistic. Though some have countering characteristics, their most common moral view is, "We are social animals, not individuals, so nothing that we do is moral or justified unless it serves our society." This leads them to the self-deluding moral creed that we should each positively do what benefits others and not ourselves, and from there perhaps to the seductive but illogical conclusion of utilitarians that our acts should by judged by what benefits the greatest number of others. The utilitarians' basic error is that they fail to define *morality* psychologically. So to them, and altruists generally, that term means only a calculus, an objective quantitative process that, using very vague psychologic terms, they have stripped of all its causative subjective elements. This then leads them to deny any individual's natural right to have unique needs, or plans of action, based on personal judgments, and from there it is but a short step to the perverted view that we are all obligated to obey the customs and formal rules of our society even if these are immoral or have negative effects on us as individuals.

In other words, in trying to establish the universality of this illogical collectivistic and quantitative moral reasoning, altruists objectify and thus de-psychologize the personal process of needing. To them, only the 'needs' shared by all humans or by all members of their own society are worth considering. So because they fail to assert (project) their own needs, they assume that our needs and our moral reasoning itself are not psychologic issues at all. This then leads them to the absurd conclusion that our needs, and the values and moral codes we derive from these, are not really decided by us individually, but are instead determined by some god, natural Law, or cultural or evolutionary force that by some mystical means commands us all alike. There is such a force, of course, but it is just our common human logic, the basic parts of which vary naturally and often oppositely in individuals.

This collectivistic perspective gives altruists the deep conviction that a society's morality, as this is made tangible in its legal system, is more important than that of any individual. Many then believe that even guilty individuals should not be punished by a society if its legal system is unjust. They are correct on this, of course, because while it can be reasonable for an individual to disobey a social rule, it is never reasonable for a society to be unjust, since its rules are invalid if they are not impartial. Like our moralists (B), our altruists (-) believe that if people or legal systems cannot judge fairly, then they have no right to judge at all. And contrary to the common assumption that we all desire a just legal system, in fact only this half of us do. The other half, the projective (+) and the reversed (R), want an unjust legal system, such as we have always had.

Mature altruists hope to receive social approval for their efforts, but if they don't get it, they will still seek just, even ideal, societies. We see the social conventionality of altruists in the misguided assumption of the progressive Gandhi (+-B-B), who as a young man thought that he could help the people of colonial India by going to their rulers' homeland to study the egoistic legal system known as 'English law'. Many altruists make this mistake, which is why so many of them become lawyers, politicians, or other participants in their society's legal system. Some choose these professions because they are conventional in judgment and believe deeply that society must have just legal systems, but immature (amoral) altruists also gravitate to them because they usually pay well and permit sly thefts. Our altruists' assimilative impulse makes them want to acquire almost anything with a socially accepted value. While egoistic thieves might blast open a safe or start a war of aggression, altruistic thieves prefer indirect thefts, such as embezzlements and the many forms of theft and corruption that their legal system permits.

So it is fair to say that most altruists would reject the cure that Gandhi, with his projective will, found for himself, which was the surrender of all interest in material things. We see people's character best in their contradictions, and this is the defining contradiction of altruists. They all suffer this conflict between serving others totally and acquiring, legally or not, personal possessions with a socially determined value. And as the life choices of the variety of altruists listed in *Appendix B* illustrate, there are many different ways to deal with this conflict.

Advice to Altruists. Think hard on moral issues so that you can pass beyond your innate amorality sooner; that is, search for sound moral principles and then follow them in practice as often as you can. Resist your urge to assume that moral behavior consists in serving your society, in preserving its traditions, religions, or biases, in doing the greatest good for the greatest number, or in sacrificing yourself for others or any artificial collective. The first moral question is, What should I do to preserve myself and my health with the least possible harm to others or to nature? Then we ask subsequent questions that define our *moral responsibility*, a notion that traditionalists erroneously confuse with that of *social responsibility*. But these are not the same notions, for we must make a tertiary judgmental decision on our moral responsibility before we even consider the quaternary power issue of whether to obligate ourselves socially through promises or oaths to any person or artificial collective. If you are a traditionalist, you need to ensure that your obligations to other individuals or collectives (even your family) are always voluntarily assumed, so that they are not gifts, but negotiable exchanges of promises by both sides. In other words, there is no *universal* moral principle that dictates your subservience to or your personal sacrifices for any person or fabricated collective. Quaternary contracts are the only real basis of social cooperation, but since most people and all unjust governments want to have the fewest possible obligations to you, they will avoid negotiating a fair contract with you whenever they can. And they usually do this by insisting that you have some mystical *moral* obligation to accept all of the *social* obligations that they intend to impose on you unilaterally.

4D. Reversed (♂-,♀+). The Nihilist. The reversed impulse is totally illogical. At the first pole (♂-) one fails to project one's own needs, and so one has all the faults of an altruist; that is, one reasons about needs and values collectivistically and not individualistically, and one is dependent on others and so is subject to manipulation by them. But then this illogic is compounded at the second pole (♀+), where one subjectively projects rather than objectively assimilates the probable consequences of one's adopted needs. So in judgment our nihilists combine the faults of altruists (-) with the faults of egoists (+), without having the better part of either. And as a result, the judgmental conclusions that they store in their belief system consist mostly of fictions that cannot be substantiated.

Applying our nine-point list for the reversal, we can say this of the type. (1) They cannot structure a realistic and sound belief system. (2) Whatever their practical field, they can't create new realistic hypotheses for it. And because they can't judge people fairly, they become cynics who believe in unjustifiable hypotheses such as 'original sin' and 'people are no damn good'. (3) They are manipulated by those to whom they turn for help with their needs, or plans of action. (4) Their bad judgments are their undoing. (5) Their judgmental illogic leads them to work in some juridic, governmental, religious, academic, commercial, artistic, communication, or scientific field where as social authorities they can judge others from some preexisting social standard. Their motives in this choice are to impose on others their own subjective beliefs on moral or evaluative matters and, with some spite, to prevent healthier people from gratifying any needs that they assert on individual rather than on collective, or social, grounds.

(6) Their complete reasoning on any context either lacks judgment or is highly judgmental but invalid. (7) They have difficulty with systemic construction, or ordering fragments into cohesive new wholes, so their belief system is chaotic, which is sometimes called 'anarchic' or 'nihilistic'. So, unless they have a strong will, we won't find them, say, creating complete intellectual systems, organizing any complex venture, or conducting a symphony orchestra.

(8) Other factors permitting, however, they can be good critics of others' work, and can become proficient in creating rationalizations for

rushing to judgment or leaping to conclusions. Being projective at the second pole (♀+), as egoists are, they lack compassion, so they often become our typically cruel prosecutors or judges or their intellectual antecessors in jurisprudence. Their denial of judgment and their need to find shortcuts to avoid making full and fair judgments leads them to become hypocrites and to harbor class prejudices, which can then be used by others to manipulate them. They believe that a society's legal system is valid only if its first purpose is to dispense injustice; that is, only if it intends to be cruel and to deny justice to all classes of people except the most autocratic one, which they assume is beyond judgment by ordinary folk.

This contradictory view, that *justice is injustice*, is implied by every rationalization they create for their moralizing. Egoists share this view, but unlike our nihilists, they don't insist on establishing a more unjust legal system if the one that they have now works to their advantage. Since egoists (+) and nihilists (R) are both projective at the concluding pole of judgment (♀+), they have no compassion and cannot develop a sense of justice. Both see others only as members of descriptive social classes, and they know that, short of brute force, class prejudice is the fastest way to deny the needs of large numbers of others—especially their need for social justice, or protection from egoists and nihilists like themselves.

And (9) our subjects consistently beg the question in their judgments by petitioning the premise. Since they are assimilative at the first pole (♂-), they can't project a personal plan of action there as they should (♂+), so they suspend or 'bracket' that task and leap ahead to the second pole (♀-). But being projective (♀+) rather than assimilative there, they will arbitrarily assert some imagined consequences of their contemplated act, all of which are mere assertions of hope, or preferred outcomes. The judgment process is speculative for everyone, but those with a reversal use it to retreat to a fantasyland where they dream of the best possible outcomes, and their anxiety is always high because they know that their hopes are unrealistic ones.

This dwelling on hopes that are unconnected to any plan of action that could imply them is what we mean by 'wishful thinking'. Nihilists are habitual risk takers because they deny judgment and seize on this shortcut, this mere faith or hope that the best result for them shall occur. With this projected consequence in mind, they then return to the first pole in an act of reconsideration, and though they still can't project a personal need here, they now know the result they want, and this narrows their search for a plan of action to adopt. But these adopted needs are all socialized ones; for example, voting, praying, or gambling. They reason that if they perform some such social act ritualistically, the consequence that they imagine could occur, but then they distort this *could* into a *shall*, as in "If I vote, then my society shall be better," or "If I pray, then my prayers shall be answered," or "If I gamble, then I shall be rich." So their adopted need *is* the consequence they hope for, and that is begging the question.

Though a reversal can make one a good critic in a system, it also makes one avoid self-criticism there. In thought or judgment, it prevents one from doing the cleansing of cluttered internal systems that we must all do to keep them optimally functional. This is why when nihilists are given any judgmental authority in society, their orders make the existing mess worse, since nothing that they decide will alter any psychologic, intellectual, legal, or political system fundamentally enough to make it more logical, ordered, realistic, just, or sane.

We have seen that theism is invalid because it claims to be a primary metaphysics (theory of Reality) when it is not, and also that theists usually have a weak (- or R) impulse in will or in three or more of their five systems. And now we see that anyone with a judgment reversal will oppose fair judgments and support unjust legal systems. It is highly likely, therefore, that theists with a judgment reversal will support social injustices with the same fervor that they support their religion's inverted logic and supernatural myths. Given this fact and their history to date, it is plainly foolish of us to expect that any religion will help us to achieve justice in the world.

The difficulties that nihilists have with their judgment lead most of them to search for some rationalization by which judgment and morality can be denied altogether. We saw the negative side of this urge in the judgments of the liberal nihilist Hitler (B+BR-), and we all know the insanity of his political hopes, or 'dream'. And we saw its positive side, or its critical power, in the work of the progressive nihilist Nietzsche (++BRB), which was willful, thoughtful, realistic, and creative, even though it was in systemic disarray and illogically denied all moral reasoning, as nihilists do. Nietzsche exposed the hypocrisy of Judaic and Christian (and hence Islamic) moralizing, but he never defined moral reasoning, and ultimately he came to the absurd conclusion that we should deny or go beyond this real part of our psychologic.

Advice to Nihilists. Don't be amoral; that is, don't deny your judgment faculties or your moral reasoning, and don't look for shortcuts to avoid them. Follow the advice above for egoists and altruists, because you have the illogic of both. Though your inverted perspective can at times make you a good critic in the judgment area, it will be best for you to avoid work that requires judging others or giving them advice on moral or evaluative issues. You pose a great danger to others whenever you assume that you have the correct answers to those issues and must proselytize them, so never try to 'spread the word' on morals or other evaluations. You may be drawn to a religion because you want to spread a moral message that is socially accepted as irrefutable and universal, but if so then you have been blinded by the pseudometaphysics of theism, which in any religious form offers no such message. You harm yourself as well as others with your tendency to construct false rationalizations for action and false hypotheses in your science or other field of endeavor. A good rule to follow is never to rush to judgment and make it a habit to give everyone a full and fair hearing. This will counter your impulse to declare someone wrong or guilty rashly, and then to quiet them somehow so that they have no chance to refute you. Generally, your illogic in judgment leads you to create fictions and harbor unrealistic expectations of situations and others, and this sets you up psychologically for repeated falls when the realty of a matter appears later, as it usually does. It is most important for you to find people with good judgment (which you should now know how to do) who can advise you personally or who have written works that can help you understand this innate impairment of your logic.

Our Four Judgment Terms. As you see, I have given a name to each of the four basic judgmental dispositions described above. Previously these four terms were only merely described, but now that we have objectively defined them, they will improve our moral vocabulary. However, we must not forget that they now refer to the four judgmental attitudes and not to our moral attitudes only; that is, they refer to every kind of synthetic evaluation or speculation that we perform. I use conventional terms for our four impulses in politics in this same way, fully aware that politics is not all that we deal with in our power system.

The descriptive terms *egoist* and *altruist*, coined in the modern era, fit the judgmental attitudes caused by the projective (+) and assimilative (-) impulses, but no conventionally described terms are suitable for the judgmental attitudes caused by the balanced (B) and reversed (R) impulses, so I should explain why I chose *moralist* and *nihilist* for these dispositions.

I mean the term *moralist* in our new psychologic sense, and not in a philosophic sense. Three famous American moralists were the progressives Jefferson (+- -BB), Lincoln (B-+BB), and Franklin Roosevelt (-BRBB), who were the three best US presidents, notwithstanding their personal faults and the grave political mistakes that they all made. Moralists (B) form healthy but conventional beliefs and value and moral systems. They differ from nihilists (R) in that they are not negativists and, rather than trying to divide us, they try to heal breeches and resolve contradictions by putting chaotic things into order, which is one of their talents.

The term *nihilist* is appropriate for people with a judgment reversal. The judgmental sense of 'nihilism' in my Oxford English Dictionary is, "total rejection of current religious beliefs or moral principles," but this is a narrow description. I have defined it as the judgment reversal, so briefly it means *the denial of logical beliefs or moral conclusions*. This improves on the Oxford's description in two ways. First, we now know what it means to 'deny logical beliefs' because we now have a standard of human logic. Second, psychologic nihilism applies to all judgmental conclusions, not just to moral conclusions or theistic beliefs (which I don't call "religious beliefs" as the Oxford does because religions are corporations, not beliefs).

Moreover, these four new moral terms now allow us to define objectively two old common but vague psychologic terms: *selfishness* is the judgmental attitude of egoists (+) or nihilists (R), and *unselfishness* is the judgmental attitude of moralists (B) or altruists (-). The psychologic importance of our four judgmental attitudes is evident, but they are also socially important because they directly shape our pragmatists' different proposals on legal codes and political structures, all of which to date have put selfishness before unselfishness.

5. Power [♃-, ☉+]

The impulse of our power system is determined at its first pole by the charge of Jupiter (♃) and at its second pole by the charge of the sun (☉).

From our judgment system, we pass through the subconscious phase of *objective synthesis*, our third state of objectivity, where we store our beliefs and ideals, our evaluative and moral conclusions, and our concrete conceptions of substance, beingness, otherness, and static form. This brings us to our power system, where the balanced impulse is (- +), or assimilation at the first pole and projection at the second. My keywords for these poles in the epistemic context are *external power* and *internal power*, in the psychologic context *otherness* and *self*, and in the political context *collectivism* and *individualism*.

At the first pole of power (♃-), the world of otherness, we face practical questions such as these. Can this person be useful to me? Can this doctor cure me? Can this group help me? Will my state protect and help me? Can this animal, plant, mineral, or other thing be a resource for me? Can this Supreme Being give me all that I wish for in life? But then at the second pole (☉+) we must project what we can personally contribute to achieve our wishes. So our power system is where, in specific cases, we reconcile our changing notion of *all the power that we have not* (♃-) with our changing notion of *all the power that we personally have* (☉+). And this reconciliation is a tangible power conclusion, an *understanding* that we store in the system's succedent memory bank, briefly or for a lifetime.

Our power system is synthetic reasoning, so like our judgment it too is hypothetical and prospective. At the first pole, we don't consider things in their true nature or complexity, but only relatively, as class ideas or synthetic *beings* that we have fabricated from our own desires, needs, and evaluations. This is why a subjective bias always underlies our quaternary practical reasoning, where we are only interested in what there is about these external beings—such as other people or living things, our collectives or institutions, or imagined deities or mystical forces—that might help us achieve the motive of our present act of consideration. Every hypothesis refers to a static state of beingness, not to a real and whole process, so we are entirely practical here, considering a thing only in terms of its utility. We only consider the reality of a person or other thing when we *perceive* it as an event, but in our quaternary reasoning we *conceive* a thing as a member of a class of useful or nonuseful things, or as outer beingness that will either increase or limit our powers. Our deities are just such conceptions; fictional beings that we imagine could empower us, which is just what we request in any prayer.

In our early quaternary reasoning, our perspective is objective, so our view of other people in our power system will be cold and heartless unless our four prior systems made it otherwise. We cannot feel or judge in our power system, which works from the morals, values, and class terms of our tertiary reasoning. So if we are egoists (+) or nihilists (R) in judgment, we were born with an uncaring attitude to others, and this means that our social, political, or practical decisions will be selfish no matter what our impulse in power is.

The external sources of power that we cognize at the first pole include nature, sunlight, animals, plants, the nutrients we need, our relatives, partners, and larger collectives, and the works of others, and mystics will include here their imaginary deities, spirits, or magical forces. The internal sources of power that we cognize at the second pole are our congenital or acquired talents, abilities, physical strength, and intelligence. So at any given time our developed power system is the integrated whole of our internal power, by which we understand, decide, and act to achieve our primary wishes (☽-) and motives (♄+), as these were transformed in our tertiary reasoning into our desires (♆+), needs (♂+), and beliefs, hopes, or ideals (☿-).

The Cycle tells us that external power implies internal power, so if we receive blessings from nature and heredity (such as exceptional intelligence or health or compelling beauty) or gifts from other people (such as profits, an inheritance, or an elevation in prestige, fame, or employment rank), our potential for personal power is greater for those blessings or gifts. But it is only a potential, for no matter what advantages we receive from external sources, we may still fail to achieve greater understanding and personal power. We must ensure this development, or maturity, at the second pole by our own projections (☉+), for we cannot transfer the internal tasks of reconciliation, integration, and retention to any external thing.

We can refer to our power conclusions with equivalent terms such as *understandings*, *individual powers*, *potential powers*, or *abilities*, but whatever we call them, they are the integration of both our received gifts and our individual will to perfection. In the Cycle's entire wish-to-fruition process, it is only at this final cognition that we know whether we do or do not have sufficient personal power to manifest our original wish with respect to the event that we selected as our context. We may find here that our new understanding gives us the power that we first wished for or even more than that, or we may find that we don't have or can never have that power over events. In any case, we will revise our will system in our reconsiderations so that it accords with our new heightened or lessened expectation as to which wishes (☽-) it is possible for us to achieve (♄+). We all do this and we all must do it, because this direct implication from an achieved power to a new wish and will intent is how we join any act of consideration to the next related one. We learn much when we are young and we become stronger for that, but as we age we gain some new powers and lose some of our old ones, and as we experience these changes in our powers, we must change the motives in our will system accordingly.

There is an important political lesson for us here; namely, that if we let others restrict our personal powers, we are also letting them restrict not only our personal freedom but also our will system, which is the source of our sense of reality, our drive to survive, and our global motives, or plans of purpose. And if we are foolish enough to do that, we are giving others our freedom and life to dispose of as they wish. So, as a fundamental principle of all our social and political acts and constructs, we must insist that—regardless of any prior contracts we may have made—we have no debt or obligation to any person, corporation, or state that, without our free consent, tries to restrict us, weaken us, endanger us, or take our common or personal property. Our *freedom* is our power to act without restraints, so in a sense *our freedom is our power*, which we make anew every day. It is thus not something that our rulers have a right to bestow on us or not as if it was one of our civil liberties, over which they claim absolute power. Except on valid moral grounds, which in each case is the point to be proven and not just assumed, no artificial state or other collective has the right to restrict the powers or freedom of any individual.

On the other hand, we know that we cannot become stronger without the help of nature, other people, and other living things. It is thus our lot in life that we must struggle daily with the horns of our power dilemma: external power versus internal power, or collectivism versus individualism. We must oppose all unreasonable impositions on us by others, to be sure, but we must also accept our responsibilities to all the external sources of power that did or might help strengthen us. To be healthy, we must be self-reliant, but we can never be self-sufficient.

The descriptions of the four power impulses that follow are necessarily limited because a real person is not just a power type. In discussing any power disposition, we can't distinguish between those who are, say, strong or weak in will or moral or immoral in judgment, because we aren't considering how to merge the impulses of all five systems to understand the character of any real individual. We can only do that when we are interpreting a specific natal chart.

Note that each power attitude is shared by a fourth of all people because it combines the two impulses at our power system's poles, each of which divides all people into halves. The impulse at the first pole defines half of us as logical *moderates* (♃-) and half as illogical *extremists* (♃+), while the impulse at the second pole defines half of us as logical *leftists* (☉+) and half as illogical *rightists* (☉-). So our power attitudes are properly defined by reference to those four terms.

5A. BALANCED (♃-,☉+). THE PROGRESSIVE. This impulse makes one logical at both poles of the power system, so progressives are *moderate leftists*. As explained in the last chapter, they are *moderates* because they logically assimilate external power at the first pole (⊕-), and *leftists* because they logically project their personal power at the second pole (☉+).

As moderates (⊕-), progressives seldom impose their views on others. Like liberals, the rightist moderates, they usually are liked by others and accept their environment and situation, which makes them conventional in their views. Those who are projective in will are exceptions, for they are both conventional and rebellious, as were the progressives Jefferson (+- -BB) and Gandhi (+-B-B). This preference for conventional politics is why progressives are more often advisors than leaders, and even advisors to extremist (radical or conservative) leaders. As moderates, most progressives reject the violence favored by power extremists, but they rarely support nonviolence for its own sake. Absolute nonviolence is supported mainly by mystical liberals (-), not by realistic progressives (B). Gandhi, for instance, did not oppose violence to end political oppression; being a realist with a purpose, he simply understood that many Hindus would never use violence, not even to end British terrorism.

As leftists, or individualists, progressives are self-reliant; they try to increase their physical and mental abilities, and then they trust those powers. They are like radicals, their fellow leftists, because they work to improve themselves, but they are unlike our rightists because they don't unduly rely on the collectives to which they belong. They prefer not to ask for help from others, they try to be independent, and they don't expect power to come to them as a gift from others or otherness. What they do expect is to have greater power in the areas in which they work to perfect themselves, so they are natural learners, whether they are formally educated or not.

Progressives neither ignore nor worship the past. They accept the present, but they oppose unrealistic people who try to keep us in the past or who try to drag us back there by proposing old solutions to current problems. They look to the future to define its possible perfection, and this, along with their desire to learn, reflects their mature attitude to power. They see life as a process in which they are supposed to become better people with each opportunity, and they expect, as a matter of common sense, to find this perfectionistic drive in other people and in their societies.

This form of opportunism, looking for chances to make oneself or one's collectives more perfect, is as common in leftists (progressives and radicals) as it is rare in rightists (liberals and conservatives), which is why more leftists than rightists are dissident activists. Activism to correct social wrongs is what *responsible* people do—meaning self-reliant people who won't tolerate errors, won't wait for others to act first to improve things, or won't blame others for their own failures. The political principles to which progressives are naturally inclined can be classified as those of *toleration* (♃-) and *individualism* (☉+), but these principles have positive and negative forms, and which type is embraced depends on a progressive's other characteristics.

In any case, their political message is invariably an appeal for unity, because both socially and intellectually they are psychologically driven to bring all conflicts, contradictions, and disparate things into a single integrated whole, or total understanding.

Advice to Progressives. Your impulse in power makes your practical reasoning more realistic and logical than that of people of the other three types, so they often turn to you for political or other practical advice, which you are usually willing to give. The problem is that, as a moderate (♃-), you are too conventional, or too willing to tolerate the traditional ways in which your society sees and deals with personal and social problems. Leave room in your reasoning and your advice for creative new ways to handle those problems; otherwise, you will end up opposing progress, which you know we need continually. You also know that your childhood lessons included many fictions and lies, but if you lack creativity you might accept and repeat those distortions. You should participate more than you do in collective efforts for political improvement, and, generally speaking, you probably need to be more daring than you are.

5B. Projective (♃+,☉+). The Radical. The projective impulse makes one illogical at the first pole of external power and logical at the second pole of personal power, so radicals are *extremist leftists*. As such, their power functions are conflicted, because they reason correctly as leftists but incorrectly as extremists.

Their negative side is the extremism (4+) that they share with conservatives, for this impels them to impose on others or otherness. They believe that whatever doesn't fit the ideals of their judgment system must be changed. This is intolerance, of course, for tolerance of a thing means having no desire to change it. We all expect external things to fit the subjective standards that we derive in our judgment system, but extremists in power—radicals (+) and conservatives (R)—will criticize anyone or anything that doesn't fit those standards. This is why they become prejudiced, or dissatisfied with people or classes of people for not being what they believe these others should be. Extremists are our natural imposers, but they differ in how they try to control others. Radicals try to do it individualistically, or "Because I said so," and conservatives try to do it collectivistically, or "Because our society's rules or customs say so."

The positive side of our radicals' power system is the leftism (☉+) that they share with progressives, which often puts them in the thick of a struggle to make a present situation better and to oppose the rightists' refusal to change. Our attitude to change is only partly decided by our power system; a greater role is played by the preceding systems, especially our will. People who are rightists in all five psychologic systems always want to prevent change, though this is proportionately less so of those with fewer rightist (- or R) systems. But radicals, especially pathological ones, usually want to change everything, and as soon as possible.

As leftists, radicals are self-reliant and forward looking, so the subjects they study usually relate to self-improvement. Rightists, on the other hand, prefer to study subjects that confirm the traditional beliefs they have adopted—which is why, to the amazement of most leftists, they can be enthusiastic about repetitious religious rituals, social ceremonies, or historical retrospectives. Radicals dislike people who refuse to improve themselves or society, so they are intolerant of rightists. Speed and action are their bywords, so they seek shortcuts to solve practical problems. This rushing makes them rude or careless, almost as a way of life, and it makes many young radicals so eager to engage in adult activities that they cut their learning short.

In any case, radicals work hard to develop their personal powers, and in this they rely more on the speed of their practical reasoning than on organization and method, which is the way of our slower rightists. Indeed, most radicals dislike both social organizations and organization in their personal life. Unlike rightists, they don't need statistics or a carefully drawn blueprint to figure out what other people are trying to do socially or politically. If they are intelligent, they will know this instantly, and if not, they will assume that they do. Intelligent radicals are our most precocious and capable people in practical matters, and if this is a fault, then it is one that puts them out in front of the rest of us. The problem is that when they do become leaders, they don't build formal systems to institutionalize their insights, but instead leave this mundane work to others while they look for new things to improve. Still, they are creative in power, and they are always busy making deals or alliances to increase their personal power.

Whether they are intelligent or not, radicals prefer activities that require a fast mind. They 'think on their feet', as they put it, though often this is just 'rushing to a conclusion'. They also prefer one-way communication from themselves to others, and in that sense they are our natural dictators, leaders, or supervisors. Unintelligent radicals often join a police or military force or otherwise support rightist political programs against the people. This is so because, unlike intelligent radicals, they are easily exploited by conservatives who share their social intolerance, and because our traditional intellectual system can't help them to understand their true nature.

Radicals are often criticized for wanting 'too much change too fast', but this is usually just a digressive complaint by rightists who want to slow or prevent needed changes in society. Our proactive leftists are more creative, insightful, and prophetic in their social and practical visions than our reactive rightists are, since people who are always looking backwards can't predict anything correctly. Leftists (☉+) develop their personal powers better than rightists (☉-) do, and these include anticipating the future events that are most likely to follow from present trends.

Though radicals have many personal abilities, their lack of social skills restricts their success in their social or political objectives. A major reason for this is that their intolerance of others causes them to limit their socializing and work teams to people like themselves. There are three main types of radical cliques: (1) the intelligent moral fighters for individualism and the people's interests; (2) the 'cultural' rebels, meaning all of the apolitical types, which include hippies, addicts, sybarites, artists, fictionists, entertainers, athletes, physical laborers, and criminals; and (3) the police, militarists, prosecutors, and politicians who serve the thieving rulers of their society, mainly because they are innately violent and eager to harm others, and too stupid (self-defeating) not to know better. The common picture of a radical today, based largely on the great misunderstanding of the turmoil of the sixties by our media and academics, is as a member of the first group, the dissidents, but that is by far the smallest of these three radical cliques.

Another major reason why radicals fail is that, given their excitability, they often acquire addictions, such as alcohol or other narcotics. Some of their other failure-inducing tendencies are: rushing to a decision without adequate preparation or a clear blueprint; revealing their intentions prematurely with boasts or threats; openly displaying their intolerance for others; disdaining long-range plans and durable structures; refusing to appear conventional in grooming, dress, speech, or behavior; gratifying their own desires without regard for others' needs or what others think; offending others with their rudeness, abruptness, vulgarity, or self-centeredness; resorting to violence; and being unwilling to negotiate middle-ground solutions.

This is a formula for social failure that is difficult to overcome, and they only do so if they are strong elsewhere, mainly in will and thought. Conservatives have these same social flaws, but being dependent on others, they try hard to disguise them. This is why many conservatives are fastidious to a fault about their appearance, speech, and conforming to social customs and rules, which in turn is why they often have many friends and groups to support them.

Any victories that radicals achieve are usually tactical and not strategic ones. They dislike being in one place too long, so they let rightists control any organizations they have established. This is their greatest failing as social, commercial, or political activists, for it allows rightists to coopt their creative efforts and make these serve a contrary purpose. This is why a rebellion led by radicals soon comes to naught and is forgotten; it lives on only if progressives helped to give it a sound form or if it was coopted by rightists to be something it was never meant to be. We see the latter case in the antifederalists, those American leftists of the eighteenth century who created a new nation on bold new principles and then foolishly allowed rightist conspirators to write and ratify an elitist constitution for it. Much the same thing then happened in France also.

Radicals naturally focus on the future; their only interest in the past is in what they might learn from history to improve their current understanding. They are dissatisfied with the present, but they don't deny society entirely or withdraw from it as many conservatives do; rather, they try to improve it—for themselves or for others, as their impulse in judgment indicates. That impulse also tells us whether they see their role in society as being a benefactor or a bully. In either case, the first 'solution' they consider when they want to improve something is one that imposes on others. This is their basic contradiction; as leftists (☉+) they wish to be mature and more perfect, but as extremists (♃+) they assume that they can become this without treating others fairly.

Advice to Radicals. Recognize that your leftist political views are superior to those of all rightists, and then stop being their dupe. Liberals and conservatives will try to use your intolerance and your militaristic, macho, or vengeful dispositions (♃+) to get you to work against the basic principles of individualism (☉+) to which you are psychologically committed. Give your instinctive responses to events more reflection; don't assume that these reflect certain knowledge merely because they are *your* experiences, and find ways to slow yourself down and relax, without narcotics. Also, force yourself to listen carefully to what others say and to what *they* mean by it—and, if you can, resist interrupting them. Most important, though, stop thinking that your needs and activities automatically take priority over those of people around you, and that therefore you need not ask their permission before you impose on them nor thank them for their help if they give it. Your intolerance and rudeness towards others, which includes your refusal to allow that their reasoning might be more correct than yours, cause most of your social problems and intellectual limitations. Many of the rest are caused by your prosecutorial attitude to others (4+) and your rush to conclusions.

Stop associating only with people who have a crude, abrupt, or 'macho' social manner, for this clannishness to which you are inclined only feeds your own weaknesses. Also, unless you have countering attributes, you probably narrow your social and support circles unnecessarily by speaking impulsively, ignoring your appearance, and threatening people. And even though risk-taking excites you, you should avoid doing immoral work for any government, corporation, clique, or gang. If you must be a *politician, judge, prosecutor, investigator,* or *enforcer* in any sense of these words, try to be the fairest one in the world. This won't make your work easier and you may not succeed at it, but otherwise you will become a bully or a criminal, which will cost you your self-respect and might lead you to self-destruction. Your best course in any dispute is to champion the moral side, which is usually the weaker one.

5C. ASSIMILATIVE (4-,⊙-). THE LIBERAL. The assimilative impulse makes one logical at the first pole of external power and illogical at the second pole of personal power, so liberals are *moderate rightists*. As such, their power functions are conflicted, but in the opposite way from radicals; that is, they reason correctly as moderates and incorrectly as rightists.

Their positive side is the moderatism (4-) that they share with progressives. By itself, this disposition makes them reluctant to impose their views on others and willing to accept their environment and situation realistically. Unless most of their other psychologic systems are extremist (+ or R), liberals have an easy-going manner that contrasts sharply with the rude social style of most conservatives and radicals. Such liberals are appealing; they invite others to be their trusted friends, partners, or confidants, and they devote much effort to socializing.

But this healthy social impulse at the first pole is then corrupted by their illogic at the second pole, or by the rightism (⊙-) that they share with conservatives. Consequently, their social and professional relationships are usually insincere, since one can hardly be a good friend or partner if one's main motive in socializing is to receive or take things from others. Extremists (♃+) try to do this directly, while the moderate (♃-) liberals try to do it by indirect manipulation.

Though it is subject to their other characteristics, this psychologic dichotomy defines all *liberals*, and we should understand this whenever we use that term. Simply put, liberals are tolerant and fair towards others when a social issue doesn't affect their material interests, but not if it does or if it threatens their political interests, meaning the interests of any state, corporation, or other collective upon which they depend for their comfort or material success.[6]

Not all of my criticisms of liberals here are new. During the second quadrant of the modern era (1822-1912), 'liberal' replaced the older term 'Whig' in British and American politics, and in the fourth quadrant (1971-2008), liberalism was intensely attacked by Republican extremists (radicals and conservatives) who wanted to impose more-intolerant social policies in the US. As a result, many people stopped calling themselves 'liberal' and used 'progressive' instead, as if these terms were synonyms, which they aren't. Linguistic confusions like this always result when the key terms of a context are merely described rather than defined. Also, though it is not widely known, more than a century earlier Bruno Bauer (R-+-R)—an altruistic conservative and prominent neo-Hegelian, historian, and theologian—attacked European liberalism, and in doing so he anticipated all the major criticisms of liberals made in our time, and indeed his work

---

[6] Since my objective definition of the noun 'liberal' is any person born with an assimilative impulse in the power system, it contradicts most of the descriptive conventional senses (thirteen in one of my dictionaries) of the adjective 'liberal'. For instance, we can no longer use this adjective in any sense that means *generous*, *favoring progress*, or *favoring individual freedom*, since liberals are acquisitive rightists who put artificial collectives, which they oppose changing, before all real individuals. But we can allow any sense that suggests *open-mindedness* or *tolerance* if it doesn't imply one of those denied senses, and also *reform*, if by this we mean what liberals mean by it: an incremental superficial alteration that changes nothing fundamentally.

may have been their main source. He held, as my psychologic definition implies and the great number of liberal dictators in history confirms, that personal greed, which is a form of assimilation, is the psychologic motive behind all liberal proposals for social or political 'reform'.[7]

In spite of their friendly demeanor, liberals are often described by their critics as duplicitous, foxy, opportunistic, unreliable, two-faced, or sneaky; qualities that may explain the large number of successful liberal generals in history. This unreliability stems mainly from their double assimilation in power, which leads them to take in, collect, or befriend many different opinions, things, or people, the multiplicity and differences of which leave them continually undecided as to which are best. That is, they collect but they don't edit. It is this vacillation that motivates those liberals in politics, academia, or the media who take great pains, even to the point of lying, not to offend large groups of people. This is one reason why patriotic and religious fictions are preserved in a society even when they are long known to be false. This acquisitive impulse in power also makes liberals want everyone in their family or other collectives to be supplicants, with themselves as the ultimate controller and dispenser of all rights and resources. It is thus no surprise that they usually try to be the dictators of their families, businesses, armies, or nations.

As rightists, liberals are unsure of their personal powers, so they have a psychologic need for the input of others on practical issues. They ask external sources, "What is this all about?" and "How should I decide this matter?" This is what it means to be a collectivist, or other-dependent in power: one is reluctant to project a decision on any matter on one's own authority, and yet one doesn't trust anyone who does. Rightists are never

---

[7] Some liberal rulers of the past century are: Truman (BB-+-), Nixon (RR-R-), bin Laden (BR-R-), Chiang Kai-Shek (B+-R-), Dayan (BRRB-), Fox (B+R+-), Tojo (+RRR-), Hitler (B+BR-), Hussein (+-RB-), Lenin (+-BB-), Mao (+B+R-), Nehru (RRB+-), Petain (+-RB-), Pol Pot (R-+- -), Salazar (+RBR-), Stalin (BB- - -), Sun Yat-Sen (-B+- -), and Trujillo (RBB+-). As you see, this list includes some of the worst dictators of any time. The other three power types have also given us terrible rulers, but not as many and none worse than the liberals.

self-reliant; they are rule-dependent, friend-dependent, or even therapist-dependent. And yet they always doubt what their rulers, friends, or therapists tell them. This is why so many liberals become dictators in their various collectives. "No one knows anything," they reason, "So, since it could profit me, why I shouldn't I be the one who decides everything?"

In politics, liberals don't object to giving the people 'equal rights under the law', such as religious freedom or due process, provided that they have the ultimate power as judges, legislators, or executives to determine what those laws say and mean. In their family, club, business, church, nation, or union of nations, liberals oppose any policy that limits their ability to control all of its resources, which can only be done through centralization. The general issue of property and the specific issue of their own wealth are of immense psychologic importance to our assimilative liberals, and that is why liberals, like radicals, are born dictators.

The poles of our power system tell us to distinguish between social and political issues, and when we do we see what our rightists are about. In public, they debate *social* issues only—such as policies on abortion, immigration, welfare, education, the economy, the environment, and so on—and they divide sharply on these issues as moderates (liberals) or extremists (conservatives). But in private they conspire together without hostility to decide the all-important political issues—such as which individual rights are guaranteed or denied, who rules the government, who bears the burdens of supporting it, and who benefits most from it.

Liberals pretend to be progressives when they need leftist supporters, as they do in elective politics, but their greed and anti-individualism can make them as intolerant as any extremist. Of course, this depends on their moral disposition. For instance, unselfish liberals (moralists or altruists) prefer nonviolent solutions to personal or political problems, and if they are also mystics, they may even support absolute nonviolence, as the theistic moralist King (B+BB-) did. But then there is the contrary case of the theistic altruist John Brown (BBR- -), a liberal who chose violence over inaction to end slavery in the US. Note that both men, besides being liberals, were strong in will and thought. On the other hand, selfish liberals (egoists or nihilists), will use any degree of violence necessary to keep their property or profits. This may be another reason why many of the leading generals in history were liberals.

Being assimilative rather than projective in power, liberals are 'laid back' rather than 'on edge' as extremists are, and they are traditional and never creative in their politics. They not only observe the old ways, they also plagiarize intellectual, social, economic, and political proposals from old and new sources. They accept their society for what it is, and then try to benefit from it with the least effort possible. As other-dependent rightists, they have a compulsive need for collectives to support them, psychologically and materially. All rightists assume that their power comes from their external associations and not from what they have made of themselves.

This explains their opportunism. Leftists are self-reliant, so they are not constantly on watch for external events that may increase their power; they believe that they can achieve or summon up this power whenever they choose. But our other-dependent rightists fear that there may not be another opportunity to acquire the personal power that a present situation offers. So they conclude that they must seize each such opportunity before it passes, as if it was what rightist advertisers call 'a once-in-a-lifetime offer'. This externalized notion of their personal power makes rightists work hard to build, maintain, and defend all kinds of social, economic, and political structures. This is why more rightists than leftists vote in our pseudodemocracies. That's what collectivists do; they maintain the social systems that are psychologically and materially important to them. And those who also lack personal dignity will go even further by wearing or displaying flags, icons, corporate logos, or other symbols that publicize this weakness, their total dependence on artificial collectives.

Liberals say that they want to improve, or 'reform', things, but in fact they join conservatives in wanting to preserve every traditional system that they have studied and learned to manipulate. For instance, we rarely find a liberal lawyer or accountant proposing a basic structural change in their state's legal or tax code. Liberals study the old ways diligently and learn how to profit from them through academicism, plagiarism, and a show of compliance with established rules, traditions, customs, and conventions. As assimilative traditionalists they want no change, but as the most opportunistic and grasping of the four power types, they welcome any 'reform' that may increase their own wealth, status, or fame. And liberal intellectuals have written volumes of social and scientific nonsense to rationalize their collectivism, works that other liberals in academia and the media praise highly as being what we should all read and believe.

To understand a liberal, we need only extract all the meanings of the terms *assimilation* and *acquisition*. Their power dynamic shouts, "Come to me!" They judge anything good if it accrues to their accounts or personal credit and public reputation, and bad if it doesn't. They are the collectors of the power spectrum, far more so than leftists and even more so than conservatives, and their appetite for acquisitions knows no limit. As either owners or overseers, they want to have under their personal control more and more land, property, collectible items, fame and repute, wealth, children, servants, slaves, workers, friends, or lovers. As rulers, they want to control more nations and acquire more legal and military power than anyone else. They are our natural *accountants* in the broadest sense of this term, for they quantify every social, economic, or political policy that they consider and put quality in the back seat every time.

This is why they support highly centralized social structures, for the centralization of power makes their control, accounting, and thefts from the public easier. Their quantitative compulsion makes liberals want to incorporate all lesser collectives under ever-greater ones, under master collectives that can expand without limit, at whatever cost or means. They are the driving force behind the insane political and corporate globalization that is strangling the world today. Their fellow rightists, the conservatives, are less certain about this. They too want the security of centralization, a master collective with powerful rulers like monarchs or popes, but they also appreciate economy of scale, so they oppose the liberals' wasteful expansionism, or their additive 'at all costs' approach to every social or political problem. But liberals have no such qualms; they feel psychologically fulfilled with each new increase in size, power, or centralization that is achieved in their family, corporation, or government, merely for the fact of that addition.

Because all rightists, unlike leftists, look to their collectives for their security in life, they busy themselves with socializing in every sense. It starts in childhood with family, clubs, gangs, teams, parties, and college fraternal groups, and extends to the adult forms of socialization. Each such social activity is in effect just a rule system that tells them how to behave in different social circumstances. They are psychologically dependent on these fixed rules and are lost without them, which is why more rightists than leftists join the military, the clergy, or other rule-driven collectives. But rightists differ in this socializing as they age. The intolerant conservatives either restrict their socializing to other extremists or withdraw from some or all social activities, and consequently the liberal is our paradigmatic socializer.

All rightists see the source of new conceptions as external rather than internal, so they distrust any proposal for changing social rules, because they didn't create it and they can't trust their own logic in judging it. Conservatives deny a new proposal and liberals delay it to get the external opinion of 'experts' or to take a statistical poll to give them a quantitative reason for accepting it. But both distrust all individualists, because leftists make new proposals solely on their own authority as thinkers. Some people admire creativity and others envy and resent it, and the general rule on this is that the admirers are leftists (☉+) and the resenters are rightists (☉-).

As collectivists, rightists are inclined to deny the possibility of individual creativity, and this leads them to conclude that, since there is no such thing as a new notion, plagiarism can't be wrong. Since they see the collective as the reality and the individual as its insignificant consequence, they regard anyone's new conception as public property. This is also why they prefer to reason in groups or committees, where they can either steal another's idea on a topic or at least claim that they participated in its creation.

It follows that our scholars should be more cautious than they are in crediting any rightist's intellectual works or social proposals with originality. For instance, their unjustified praise for the liberal Marx (-+B- -) and the conservative Freud (+-RBR) did us more harm than good, though Marx had the leftist thinking of the progressive Engels (B+RBB) to help him. Many other rightists listed in our tables also achieved fame mainly for collecting and restating what others had said before them. The truth is this: that leftists are the first to make every logical and beneficial proposal for society. But we lose sight of this fact because rightists quickly distort these leftist notions and then conspire as academics to portray those distortions as superior.

Liberals like to exploit or find new uses for the talents of others, so they are often power brokers or agents of some kind, or mediators between 'the parties at interest', a term by which they equate private interests to the public interest. Conservatives are also acquisitive, but they lack the ease and tolerance, and usually the duplicity, that is required to be a successful mediator or agent. Liberals seek to please all sides well enough to net some commission or personal credit, their concern for which explains their familiar bias in social or legal disputes for the more wealthy, powerful, or famous party. Unless they have strong opposing characteristics, they are obsequious and acquisitive, and they epitomize the grasping professionals who dominate the legal, banking, brokerage, advertising, journalistic, medical, accounting, and political trades.

On the higher economic levels, liberals are among our history's greatest capitalists and socialists. Because it facilitates their thefts, they want all of a society's resources centralized under the control of either an absolutist state (the socialistic view) or some mammoth private corporations that are protected from their workers and the people by an absolutist state (the capitalistic view). From the people's perspective, it doesn't matter whether this centralization is done by the state, its central bank, corporate conglomerates, or an international alliance of corporations or nations, for in all these cases the people have no say at all in how the vast wealth produced by their labor and their common resources is being used by these centralists.

As natural assimilators, liberals are patient. They are found on the scene long after radicals and progressives, and even conservatives, have left it. They work tirelessly at managing the alliances and coalitions needed to maintain their collectives and social institutions. They can see if a change is coming, but instead of railing against it as conservatives do, they befriend it and coopt it while they try to get the most for themselves from it. But this takes time, so invariably their first response to any call for change—even by their friends, children, or lovers—is to delay a decision and counsel patience.

Liberals are taciturn opportunists, so they demand secrecy in all their personal relationships and social dealings. People who continually steal other people's ideas, time, rights, bodies, or property live in constant fear that others may steal what they have stolen. And while brutal police and military forces are the invention of intolerant extremists, it is the moderate but devious liberals who conceive and manage the secret police of their societies or corporations, and otherwise conspire to deprive us of our privacy, or sacred selfness. Such organizations as the FBI, CIA, MI-5, MI-6, DGSE, KGB, Gestapo, and the 'mind police' of any rightist state or corporation are liberal constructs, not extremist ones.

In both government and their homes, liberals want the power to pry into others' lives. In the last half of the modern era there has been an incredible growth in domestic and international spying agencies and networks, led by liberal dictatorships and liberal pseudodemocracies such as the US and UK. Taking governmental and corporate data collection together, and they are all but one already, no individual has any privacy today, and this means that no state or corporation respects any individual, a situation that most rightists consider ideal. They can now say, "At last, the individual is meaningless in society!" This is our collectivists' political agenda, not only in their state, but also in their family, clubs, and workplace.

In considering a proposal for action, liberals argue that efficiency requires a careful plan, but what they mean is that they need more time to ensure greater benefits for themselves. In their personal life, they will delay formal commitment to a lover, partner, or business deal until they are certain that they have the best they can get. The liberal impulse for acquisition is pure greed; many unselfish liberals overcome this fault, but selfish liberals who combine greed with their social tolerance are our greatest hypocrites. If they don't seek greater personal wealth, then they seek some other form of personal gain, such as public honors or an imagined 'place in history'.

Liberals see time as conservatives do; they prefer the past and fear the future. But as our natural acquisitionists, they accept the present as it is, and they believe that it doesn't need much change because they have studied it, adapted to it, and are usually doing well by it. If they aren't, then they will act like extremists to improve their situation.

Advice to Liberals. You need to control your appetites. Besides your greed—which can consume you if you are selfish, or (+) or (R) in judgment—any other assimilative systems you have will give you the appetites appropriate to their functions, as listed earlier. If you are selfish, you should avoid politics and fiduciary positions, and work instead in areas related to your stronger psychologic systems. It is therapeutic for you to practice charity for the poor and to get by with less yourself. Also, you will benefit much from any time you spend enjoying and protecting nature and wildlife. Exercise your other strengths as a power liberal, which are your tolerance, understanding of others, and ability to communicate with them or negotiate for them. If you work for a government or corporation, you will be better able to counter your collectivistic (anti-individualistic) illogic by working on its local rather than its centralized levels.

Two rules that can help you are (1) focus on individuals and not classes, and (2) judge qualitatively rather than quantitatively. These rules will help you see that each person is unique and has natural rights that no one should violate, and that bigger is not better. If you do work in politics, follow your moderate first-pole impulse and join with unselfish progressives. Let them decide your coalition's political goals, while you help them design its social programs, organize its collective efforts, communicate to the public, and raise funds. In any case, dissolve all your political alliances with conservatives (R). They share your illogic as a political rightist but not your logic as a social moderate, so they will obstruct your social goals and lead you further from common-sense solutions than you are naturally.

5D. Reversed (♃+,☉-). The Conservative. This impulse makes one illogical at both poles, or *reversed* in practical reasoning, so conservatives are *extremist rightists*; that is, they inappropriately project at the first pole (♃+) and inappropriately assimilate at the second pole (☉-). And since they are the most troubled and the most troubling of the four power types, we must understand their illogic. Actually, we have already considered the psychologic flaws of conservatives, because they have all the social illogic of radicals and all the political illogic of liberals, without having the radicals' good political sense or the liberals' good social sense. It only remains to consider what it means when these weaknesses are combined in one person.

Take *theft*, for example, which means stealing anything from others, such as their lives, property, work, privacy, identity, space, time, or labor. It has three basic psychologic forms, as follows. If radicals (+) are thieves, it is because they assume the right to gratify their needs by imposing on others, by using them or by taking what they want from them. If liberals (-) are thieves, it is because they are compelled to acquire things and have a deep belief that everything is collective property anyway. And if conservatives (R) are thieves, it is for both those reasons, so they cannot consider practical or social affairs without this double psychologic belief that they have a natural right to impose on and steal from others.

Only total progressives (BBBBB) have no congenital impulse to steal, which means that there is at least one thieving impulse in 99.9% of us. From this it follows that people who are not thieves have matured enough to control their congenital impulses and have the will to do so. Thievery described is immorality, but thievery defined is psychologic impairment. So a society's problem with thievery is not the problem of harsher punishments or more policing; it is the problem, which traditionalists ignore, of how to help individuals mature through our schools and other social institutions. And today no one needs that help more than our rulers and politicians.

Maturity is a conservative's main problem because a reversal indicates a psychologic area that one wishes to avoid and so will not develop. Specifically, conservatives cannot integrate their conclusions in their will, thought, feeling, and judgment systems into sound understandings and practical decisions in their power system. This problem is less severe when there is strength in the other systems to compensate for this concluding illogic, but it is hard to take compensatory steps when another system is also reversed, and it is nearly impossible for the 10% of all people who are pathological, or have three or more reversals.

Objective discussions with conservatives on their social or political proposals are difficult if not impossible because those proposals come not from a free intellect, but from psychologic impairments. The power reversal gives one no political skills, except perhaps a critical ability and the ability to influence others who are also socially and politically irrational. As the pathological *conservative* Luther (R+BRR) wrote ruefully, "In civil matters, I am such a child." This was an accurate self-description, but it applies to all conservatives to some degree because immaturity in social and political reasoning always results from the power reversal.

With Luther, we see this immaturity not only in his theism, but also in the fact that it was not he, but Frederick the Wise (B-BRB), the progressive ruler of Saxony, who created the Protestant Reformation, in part by manipulating Luther through his three reversals, or points of immaturity. That so-called 'reformation' happened first in Frederick's realm, Saxony, then in other northern German electorates and then elsewhere in Europe. But reflecting the judgment reversal, or the nihilism that Frederick and Luther shared, its real purpose was to allow secular monarchs in their separate domains to end the centralized political power of the papacy so that they could steal the wealth that the Catholics had stolen from the people over the preceding millennium.

Most conservatives, especially those who are weak in will and thought, cannot mature in their understandings and decisions because they build avoidance structures that deny their own power functions. They decide, usually in adolescence or early adulthood, that because they can't handle the logic of this system, they must try to turn its functioning off, and consequently they become negativists with respect to nearly all social or practical affairs. By early adulthood if not sooner, they are reacting almost automatically to any practical proposal with some form of negative response. This continual negativism, which annoys logical people, can take the form of instant denial, carping over words or details, randomly distorting the reality of situations, transcendentalism, physical retreat from society, withdrawal into fantasies or mysticism, usually theism, and embracing irrational political views that range anywhere from monarchism to classic anarchism (no rulers). The power reversal causes the denial, but its form depends on the conservative's other characteristics or traits.

Now let us apply to power conservatives the nine points of illogic that we applied above to people with the four other psychologic reversals.

1. *Arealism.* However they might reason to get to their power system, once they are there they cannot be realistic. At the first pole (4+), they have unrealistic expectations of others and otherness, and hence of societies, governments, and legislations. They foolishly expect their government and its legal system to cure all social ills. And those who are also weak in judgment cynically believe that people are sinful and so cannot be trusted to govern themselves. As extremists (4+), conservatives see others only as they want them to be, and not as they really are. For example, they may expect an employer to reward them for their diligent work or their mate to love them always and to help ensure their safety and security, and if they are later disappointed in these expectations, they don't see that the fault was theirs for not appraising the other person realistically at the start. And many conservatives are provoked by such disillusionments to immature, and sometimes severe, reactions or retaliations.

2. *Anti-explanation.* We have seen what a reversal in the other four systems causes one to deny, or be negative about. In will, one denies reality, purpose, and primary theory; in thought, one denies one's own dignity and uniqueness, analytic activity, and universal reasoning; in feeling one denies aesthetics and the important role of the passions; and in judgment one denies morality, realistic beliefs or hopes, psychologic reasoning, sound plans of action, and the need for compassion. In power, conservatives deny the need to complete their practical reasoning, to treat other people or living things fairly, to develop their abilities and understanding, and to explain their decisions or actions. For instance, conservative judges make their legal system increasingly more confusing and contradictory because, rather than fully analyzing an issue and explaining their decision on it, they rationalize that decision with any shortcut that comes to mind.

Similarly, conservatives cannot and will not develop or adopt a coherent political theory. They prefer no such theory at all, since its principles would expose their confused practical reasoning and might restrict their thefts. So instead they base their political conclusions on ex post facto descriptions and opportunistic maxims, which they mislabel as 'principles' to imply that they or their gurus had once reasoned validly from a political theory. Their intellectuals or academics devise hypothetical ideals that they claim have social or political significance, but that in fact are neither consistent nor based on sound theory.

All conservatives collect clever quotations to cite whenever an appropriate practical situation arises; even their intellectuals and academics speak to us not from sound theories, but in pithy mottoes. Their explanations are little more than repetitious references to false 'principles' or 'laws' that serve as their shortcut answers to current problems, and that they presume we all accept as valid. Some examples are *the free-market principle, traditional values, family values, religious values, divine will, the social contract, the general will, original sin, we the people, the American dream, the American way, god bless America, support our troops, united we stand, the criminal class, justice is punishment, the system works, the rule of law,* and so on. I could go on, but this list suffices to make my point, which is that conservatives habitually evoke their name for some unexplained and unproven hypothesis and use this as a substitute for the full reasoning that is needed to substantiate an hypothesis or justify a decision to act.

3. *Manipulation.* Since conservatives rarely create their own social or political proposals, we should understand that these probably have another source. This might be an honored traditional thinker, a spokesperson for an institution they revere, or someone they admire for superficial reasons (such as status, wealth, formal education, fame, military or professional success, and so on), but it will be someone they respect enough to become his or her messenger or stooge. They adopt others' social and political opinions because they can't reason well in their reversed system, and then they do what most collectivists do: join a herd of rightists and worship the Judas goats who lead it. People who can't produce original notions have few options; they must reason in committees, make new hash of old

leftovers, or become the dupes of more-original thinkers. To paraphrase Barnum again, with only a slight exaggeration, "You can fool all of the conservatives all of the time," and sharp opportunists do this to them continuously.

Let me say this again for the emphasis it deserves: any system in which one has a reversal (R) is a psychologic area in which one *is* manipulated by others. Unless one has withdrawn entirely from human society, there is no 'maybe' about it. This is also true to a lesser extent of the liberal, or assimilative, impulse (-) in a system.

4. *Self-Undoing*. Given this power impairment, individual conservatives never have long-term victories. They are their own undoing. Their most ambitious projects fail because they blindly follow the lead of political manipulators or because their own social and political reasoning is so confused and unrealistic that nothing they try in practice works for them. Add to this their unrealistic expectations of others, and you see both the social daze they are in and why they are compelled to follow the rules laid out for them by their elders or society. At the first pole (4+) they are as prosecutorial and inconsiderate of others as radicals are, and at the second pole (☉-) they need other people as desperately as liberals do. But unlike liberals, their rudeness, intolerance, and frequent outbursts turn people away, so they often end up alone, a prospect that most rightists fear. Social success is not easy for conservatives. It only comes if they start life with wealth, intelligence, or beauty, if they have strength in their other systems, if they join the right clubs, or if they are fastidious and cautious in their appearance, speech, and social dealings. But even then they can, at any moment, be their own worst enemy.

5. *Academicism*. Many conservatives are led by their illogic in power to become academics, jurists, writers, journalists, pragmatic gurus, religionists, or politicians. Such pursuits attract them because they require one to study and apply the thinking of others on practical subjects, but even if their study is extensive, as it often is, it is usually restricted to a narrowed field.

6. *The Gap*. Because they deny their power system and its logic, conservatives have a hole in their psychologic process, and unfortunately

it is at the end of it, where their integrated understanding of all matters would normally be. Logically speaking, they fall off a cliff. Since they can't structure their power system consistently, which logical people do to integrate many varied theories and hypotheses into a mature global view of life, that system gets increasingly cluttered and unmanageable, and people around them wonder if they know what they're doing. Soon they stop trying to organize or improve that system, and turn it off instead.

Since conservatives can't order the complexities of their practical reasoning, they must rely on others to do this while they escape from the distress that practical affairs cause them. But the more gurus they call upon for advice, the more confused they become, so they end up limiting their advisors to the one or few that they trust most. They can't deal with multiple sources of practical advice, since their inability to structure their practical reasoning prevents them from accommodating even a small plurality of views there.

Indeed, this is the psychologic source of their innate antidemocratic attitude. The essence of democracy is tolerance and an accommodation of the natural variety of personalities, opinions, beliefs, and cultures in a population. But conservatives are intolerant of others to begin with, and then they can't integrate multiple views in their reasoning anyway. As the old joke has it, they can't walk and chew gum at the same time. That is why they prefer dictatorial political structures where there is *only one* leader, viewpoint, way to behave, or cultural type, and *only one* set of social rules that allow no deviations from 'the norm' or the literal statements of it. It is also why they don't want change. In the US, for instance, most conservatives speak of their Constitution as if it was a holy and perfect document written by unselfish patriots, but the 'Founding Fathers' who actually devised it (in private) were self-seeking elitists who detested democracy. Reliable legal scholars have proven that, if we want democracy, that constitution must be totally revised. As it is, any oath to that document is just a promise to support the rich and oppress the poor.

The power reversal also explains our conservatives' stubbornness. People who can't follow and prioritize a number of mental tracks or subjects at the same time in a system are always immovable there, as Bush

II has demonstrated to us daily. Conservatives are rigid because to replace any notion that they entertain with a new one, they must consider both at once, and this they can't do without confusing the two. That is why they detest people who can do two things at once. It is also why unintelligent conservatives become rabid anti-intellectuals, while the rest prefer work as narrowly focused intellectuals, specialists, jurists, clerics, artists, or detectives or researchers of some kind who single-mindedly explore tangible ex post facto evidence or data.

Because of this difficulty in relating disparate things, they can't achieve an integrated understanding of reality, and this even applies to deep-thinking idealists such as the unselfish conservatives Berkeley (RBRBR), Rousseau (BBRBR), Kant (RBR-R) and Hegel (B-RBR).

7. *Inner Peace*. These limitations compel conservatives to seek 'inner peace', or surcease from the stress of dealing with their internal conflicts and other people who are not similarly limited. Their dislike of people who can do or think of two things at once is one reason why many of them avoid partnerships and become monks, nuns, hermits, academicians, jurists, fictional artists, or some other kind of escapee from society or reality. If it is true, as I've heard, that psychologic stress produces unhealthy hormonal imbalances, then those who withdraw from society or reality without using alcohol or other drugs are acting from their will to survive. But this inability to understand the practical world leads those with weaker wills to use narcotics or to adopt theism or other mystical notions for 'peace of mind'.

We can tolerate this if they don't try to impose their escapes from reality—their narcotics, deities, other fictions, or mystical rituals—on those of us who have no need for them or, worse yet, on our impressionable children. Conservative religionists often complain about smut and vulgarity in the media, but these are not as harmful to children or weak adults as their religious rituals, which profanely promise the impossible in order to keep us content with what should be unacceptable in our lives, politics, and societies. The goal of any religion or other cult is to keep its 'true believers' in a trance, as if they were drugged, so that they won't even try to see reality or improve themselves or their societies.

8. *Shortcuts.* Driven by their need to deny their power system, conservatives always search for shortcut solutions to social or political problems, and then they try to impose these on us too—usually with some slogan or rhetoric that implies that these are real solutions that were fully thought out by great intellectuals of the past, *which we now know never happened.*

9. *Begging the Question.* Since power is an open system (-+), a reversal (+-) there causes one to petition the conclusion. It is unrealistic to project rather than assimilate at the first power pole, so before conservatives know the others or otherness that they are considering at the first pole, they leap ahead to the second pole to anticipate the personal power they should project. But they can't project this conclusion at the second pole since they are assimilative there, so they must search the external world to see what others believe the appropriate power solution in that kind of situation to be. When they find a power that others or traditional texts say that they should seek in such cases, they return to the first pole in a reconsideration and apply this general rule to their reasoning about the externality they were considering there.

For instance, in deciding what they think another person should be or do, they ignore that person's nature and situation and beg the conclusion, by saying that he or she must be or do what some general social rule, such as a legal edict or divine 'commandment', prescribes for all such cases. This question-begging in power is why conservatives see their relationships to other people not as the unique cases that they are, but rather as some *general condition of relationship* that is caused by social rules or roles. Consequently, they assume that the general roles we play in society and the general rules that our society expects us to follow are all-important, while any individual to whom a role or rule is applied is insignificant. So now this other person *is* the general rule or social role that the conservative adopted from others, and this is question-begging, or petitioning the conclusion as to what that person should be.

This inverted reasoning—taking a social or cultural effect to be the cause of people's behavior with no theory or evidence to support that claim—is why conservatives, even more than liberals, insist that we must all do only what our society's rulers expect of us, rather than what is, in each case, right for us in practice and morally right in its effects on others.

Most traditionalists who witness an instance of this approach to others will assume that it is a personal projection of what a particular conservative wants of some particular person, but in fact it is a projection of some general rule that the conservative previously adopted from others. This projection is always inappropriate because it ignores the logically prior question of whether the person or thing in question ever could or would meet that general expectation. It is like expecting people to admire you before you know them well enough to know why they will or won't. This unrealistic expectation is your fault, not theirs, because even if you did consider some general grounds for social admiration, you never considered their nature or how, for their own reasons, they would be most likely to judge you.

Because this question-begging—this searching for an external general rule before the real person being considered has been understood—is how conservatives reason in all practical matters, they soon develop socially to be little more than walking and talking rule books. For the knowledge of a person or thing that they should assimilate at the first pole, they substitute their learned social conclusions on all such cases. Consequently, they never relate to another person as one human to another, because in every relationship they have they refer to their collectivistic education and to their bibles of inconsistent general maxims on human behavior or roles, which they can often quote by chapter and verse. So, as the old joke has it, a conservative man will say, "This isn't a woman, this is my wife," and a conservative woman sees her husband similarly. To a power conservative, the role or the rule is always more important than the other person.

Many of us see that conservatives reason in reverse in their social affairs and we are repulsed by their lack of common sense. And since they sense this reaction from the more logical people around them, they confine their social life to their own kind, to those who don't see the illogic of their collectivism and their social rule books. This cronyism is harmful to them, but it is natural. Most conservatives can say, "I have a rule for that situation," but it is never their own rule, which is why they are robotic 'groupies', or exactly what we mean by the term 'collectivist'. They are naturally drawn to governmental, juridic, medical, accounting, academic, journalistic, or other professions that are all alike in that they require their practitioners to legislate or interpret an existing set of general rules for individual behavior *without requiring them to understand human nature*. Nothing could be more illogical than this, and yet traditionalists just don't see it.

We have probably all witnessed instances of conservatives who are outraged because someone refuses to comply with their irrational expectation or with some general rule that they adopted from others and self-righteously express as a command. Traditionalists misunderstand this hostile reaction, for when they see conservatives expecting compliance—such as parents commanding their children under the threat of punishment or cops arresting, beating, or even executing someone on the spot for not obeying a minor regulation in their rule books—they assume that the expectation is personal. But it is not; it is always a group expectation. That's what the cliché "It's not personal" means: that the person being punished has violated some arbitrary rule of some artificial collective.

It is important to understand this distinction, because as traditionalists we will blame the cruel perpetrators we see, when the real cause is the unrealistic expectation of social conformity that all rightists share because of their assimilative impulse at the second power pole (⊙-). Our rulers may punish those perpetrators, but they never condemn the legal code, the bible, the academic text, or the educational system that teaches this irrational expectation of social conformity. Some social conformity is rational, but most of it is not, and that is just why we individuals must judge its rationality before we conform to it.

As most leftists know from personal experience, a traditional education is not about how we should reason, it is about how we must conform. This early indoctrination at home, at school, or at church is why most rightists feel justified in holding others to 'the letter of the law' without asking them if there is a good reason why they refuse to conform to it. Generally, and this is the great divide between them, rightists believe that a social rule must be observed just because it is a rule, while leftists believe that no rule should be observed if it is illogical or unjust, and that therefore an individual must personally judge any social rule before obeying it.[8]

Liberals are also illogical at the second pole, so they too didactically expect people to conform (at least in public) to traditions, customs, rule books, bibles, or 'social norms'. But they don't beg the question. As moderates (4-), they see realistically at the first pole what others are or are not willing to do. But then at the second pole they say, contradictorily, that nevertheless there are these 'good reasons' (which in fact are hypothetical conceptions) why we must all conform to our society's rules and traditions. Rightists simply don't see the illogic of presuming the right to impose rules on others unilaterally or of expecting blind conformity from others.

We should conform to general rules when they are sane and when it is in our best interests to do so, as it often is when we are children or infirmed. But to grant this in such cases is not to grant in other cases that anyone else has the right to decide what we should do or what our best interests are. As adult and sane individuals, we are always free to decide against our own best interests, as altruists often do, or to decide our interests in a unique way that others don't use. And if we delegate this right to another by election or appointment, this doesn't mean that we can validly obligate either our progeny or ourselves ever after. Since our consent is only validly given on our own authority, our right to withdraw it is perpetual and inalienable. Our present consent to a government or other collective is not a blank check to its leaders, and contrary to the fallacious hypotheses of a 'social contract' and 'the rule of law', people of prior generations never had the right to give *our* consent to our present government for us. The *right* to impose on others, which is a moral issue, is distinct from the *authority* to do so, which is a legal issue. And our common logic, in which judgment precedes power, tells us that the moral right to do so must be established for certain in each case before anyone can assume the legal authority to do so.

---

[8] At the Nuremberg trials after World War II, it was hypocritical of the Allies to punish Nazi subordinates for obeying the lawful orders of their leaders while they fully expected their own people to obey every rule imposed on them by their leaders without judging its morality.

Advice to Conservatives. Try to minimize the damage that your conservatism, or total illogic in your power system, does to you and others. To do this you must first understand these impairments and then try, on each occasion, to catch and correct your illogic in practice. If you work at this, you won't rush to conclusions or beg the question as often, and then you can begin to improve yourself. In the meantime, though this will be difficult given your intolerance and impatience, you have a moral obligation not to impose your illogic in power on anyone in your family, community, or society, which includes not voting for psychologically impaired people. If you are selfish (an egoist or nihilist), you should reconsider how you deal with children, since selfish conservatives usually mistreat or miseducate children.

Don't rely on alcohol, narcotics, or other forms of denial. Also, control your impulse to command people; don't cite rules to them, as if they had no choice but to follow some old code or slogan that you believe everyone should observe. Anyone can utter commands, but we all have the right to disobey them, subject to the risks involved, and we *should* disobey illogical or immoral commands no matter who utters them. Speak to others with requests rather than commands, and with politeness, respect if it is due or if you don't know that it isn't, and a willingness to hear their views. Do so without rude interruptions, vulgarity, or signs of contempt, for these reactions only display your own immaturity or intellectual limitations. Civil speech is as essential for healthy thinking as it is for healthy relationships. When we hear it from people we meet, it is our first sign that they are trying to mature, just as rude or vulgar speech is our first sign, a warning in fact, that the speaker has no intention of ever becoming a better person.

Your conservative political attitude can harm you and vast numbers of others now and in the future who are unknown to you. If you support any immoral collective—which today is virtually any traditional state, institution, business, or religion—you are supporting the enemies of real individuals and hence of humanity, and so you have no reason to respect yourself. And when you display any symbol of your allegiance to any nation or corporation, you are displaying your ignorance as surely as vulgarity or addiction does. Our dignity isn't derived from our patriotism or beliefs or our association with any artificial collective; it comes only from how we see ourselves and what we make of ourselves. You must respect yourself to mature, and to do that you must be moral in spite of the rulebooks or the immoral commands of your leaders.

In politics, remember that only the progressive principles are logical. So if you can't support progressivism—with its *individualism*, *tolerance* for others, and insistence on *true democracy*, which can only mean decentralized political authority—then your only responsible choice is to withdraw from politics altogether. Ignore the appeals for support from all liberal, conservative, or radical parties; support only healthy and mature leaders, as described above; and don't run for political office yourself or otherwise advertise your illogical social or political opinions. Your immaturity in politics means that you must leave it to others—preferably to progressives, who you are by nature least able to understand.

As positive goals, devote your efforts to your stronger psychologic systems, give direct aid to individuals in need, and support only trustworthy organizations that promote progressive politics, local improvements, or disaster relief anywhere, or that oppose legislation that harms individuals, classes, humanity, other species, or our ecosystem. But don't support centralized charitable corporations, for they are a symptom of our social and political problems, not a cure for them. Though our egoists and nihilists self-servingly claim otherwise, charity is our common duty. It is therefore properly a job for our governments, the failures of which we should not excuse by expecting help from private persons or corporations. Private parties are inadequate to the task, but even if they weren't, we should never allow them to define the common good for us.

Your power reversal makes you prefer old solutions to new social or political problems, but this makes no sense, for if there had been sound answers to our present problems in the past, we wouldn't have these problems today. New problems require new solutions, and romanticism can't help us find them. In general, you have more difficulty than others do in moving beyond past experiences that affected you positively or negatively. You must try to cleanse your memory banks of all grudges you harbor for past insults or immoral impositions, for otherwise they will keep you immature until the day you die. Sometimes forgiveness is appropriate, especially with people close to you, but even when it isn't, you mustn't let that past event injure you further. We don't forget harms done to us to forgive them; we do it to heal ourselves.

The blame for our illogical impulses belongs to nature, but once we know that we have a psychologic impairment, the blame is ours if we don't try to correct it or if we let it harm others. The most rewarding social activities for you are those that help others or nature without requiring a deep involvement with other people, politically or otherwise. As a collectivist, this emphasis on personal efforts isn't natural to you, but nevertheless it can help you build the confidence you have lacked since birth. Your plans needn't be ambitious, for anyone who acts morally, as defined by our common logic and not by any religious or historical text, helps to improve the world for everyone.

Chapter 7. Judgment and Power

The Hypothetical Judgment-Power System.

Our power system has greater significance in the Consideration Cycle than the other four systems because it is where we integrate all of our previous reasoning about a given context into a practical understanding. The integrative function of that system's second pole (☉+) is why astrological practitioners have always assigned more importance to the sun's position in a chart than to that of the other astrological planets. This was explained descriptively in the past, by saying that the sun is the center of the solar system or the largest body in it, but our theory explains it psychologically, by defining it as the controlling influence of the final cognition in every consideration we complete.

Practitioners have always looked to the position and condition of the sun in a chart to consider someone's total character. That is why 'sun-sign astrology' came into being, and though that simplified approach to astrology is incomplete, our psychologic theory justifies some extra emphasis on the sun's position. Sun-sign astrology can be misleading, but it is like our nonastrological discussions of people, where we put more emphasis on their quaternary behavior than on their primary motives, secondary opinions, or tertiary feelings and beliefs.

We know that we aren't speaking of a real person unless we have considered all of his or her attributes, but we also know that we can't do this perfectly, so our problem in each case is to decide how many of a person's attributes we must consider to achieve a level of definition and realism that is adequate for our purpose. Since each attribute that we add makes our reasoning more realistic, it is relevant to ask anyone who expresses an opinion about one person or people in general how many attributes they are considering. And though I have offered a comparatively simple psychologic construct that shows how people differ congenitally in their will, thought, feeling, judgment, and power systems, most people will simplify this even further in their general discussions by speaking of only the four power types—progressives, radicals, liberals, and conservatives—since these distinctions come closest to describing how people behave.

The problem with this, as I said, is that there are *selfish* and *unselfish* forms of each power attitude, as indicated by the impulse in judgment, so we should also note that impulse when we classify people by their quaternary power types or even by their sun sign. But many people will resist using hyphenated terms such as *nihilistic-progressive* (...RB) or *altruistic-conservative* (...-R), for while these terms are more accurate, they are too complex for nontechnical speech. So I thought that, rather than *combining* the judgment and power impulses in that way, it would be better to *merge* them as if we humans had a single judgment-power system. And indeed this hypothetical approach yields four simple, but still objectively defined, terms that can improve our general discussions of people because they refer to both our judgment and our power attitudes.

We can merge any two psychologic systems to make an imaginary polar system, but it can't have four poles, so we must merge only the first or only the second poles of the two systems. The first-pole method works for analyzing children who haven't yet developed their reasoning powers at the second pole of their systems, but for adults we must merge the second poles, since that is where they reach their reconciled conclusions in a system. Our hypothetical judgment-power system therefore ignores points 7 and 9 in the Cycle and considers only points 8 and 10.

Our hypothetical system is thus an open system (-+) that consists of the selfish-unselfish distinction in judgment (point 8) and the rightist-leftist distinction in power (point 10), so its first pole is controlled by Pluto (♀) and its second pole by the sun (☉). In the judgment system, we defined egoists (+) and nihilists (R) as *selfish* because respectively they put their own needs or the needs of their power clique before the needs of all others, and moralists (B) or altruists (-) as *unselfish* because respectively they give others' needs due respect or too much respect. In power, we defined *rightists* as liberals (-) or conservatives (R) and *leftists* as progressives (B) or radicals (+). We can now use those four terms to define our four judgment-power terms.

A *selfist* is a selfish leftist. That is, an individualist who is either an egoist (+) or nihilist (R) in judgment and either a radical (+) or a progressive (B) in power. So the last two symbols in a selfist's Impulse Pattern are one these four pairings: (++), (+B), (R+), or (RB).

A *humanist* is an unselfish leftist. That is, an individualist who is either a moralist (B) or altruist (-) in judgment and either a radical (+) or a progressive (B) in power. A humanist's Impulse Pattern concludes with (B+), (BB), (-+), or (-B).

An *otherist* is an unselfish rightist. That is, a collectivist who is either a moralist (B) or altruist (-) in judgment and either a liberal (-) or conservative (R) in power. An otherist's Impulse Pattern concludes with (B-), (BR), (- -), or (-R).

An *elitist* is a selfish rightist. That is, a collectivist who is either an egoist (+) or nihilist (R) in judgment and either a liberal (-) or a conservative (R) in power. An elitist's Impulse Pattern concludes with (+-), (+R), (R-), or (RR).

These four judgment-power types are a simplification from sixteen to four types. We use the sixteen subtypes to analyze individuals, but we can now use the four main types in our more-general discussions of people or character types. The 'J-P' column of the tables of *Appendix B* applies these four terms to each person listed, so you can see from the people you know best there just how psychologically and socially meaningful these newly defined terms are.

The meanings of our terms *selfist*, *humanist*, and *elitist* almost agree with our dictionaries' descriptions, except that here they are objectively defined rather than subjectively described. But I had to coin the term *otherist*. This is a variant of *otherism*, a nineteenth-century synonym for *altruism* that is here given a distinct, though partly similar, meaning. I chose 'otherist' because it says 'the opposite of a selfist' and because no conventional word means what I mean by it: a political rightist who is naturally moral and has compassion for other people.

Leftists differ as *humanists* or *selfists*. A humanist acts in the best interests of all individuals in the world, with no concern for the interests of their artificial collectives aside from how these affect individuals, while a selfist subordinates all other interests to his or her personal interests. Rightists differ as *otherists* or *elitists*, but since I have coined the first term and the second is only merely described in our dictionaries, I should explain how these two kinds of rightists differ.

Elitists form small private collectives to serve the selfish interests and power needs of a carefully delineated club membership. They are therefore our natural political conspirators; those rightists who for their own gain get together to devise secret plans to control the political and economic power of their society, if not also of other societies or all societies. And in the process, since they cannot allow a genuine democracy to exist, they try to coerce others in their society by making them fearful through lies, threats, or violence. *Otherists* are also rightists, but they are dedicated to the best interests of the collectives to which they belong, and they put these above their own interests and the interests of any individual or clique. Being either moralists or altruists in judgment, they are naturally inhibited, even in competing for internal control, from conspiring against the best interests of their collective's entire membership.

Nevertheless, both otherists and elitists are illogical collectivists and hence antihumanists, or anti-individualists. Otherists say, "My country, right or wrong," and elitists say, "My club, right or wrong," but all rightists care only for their own collectives and not for any individuals or other collectives. Otherists are unselfish, but as collectivists they put their family, club, team, school, religion, business, community, and nation before all other such collectives, and in defending their artificial collectives, as all rightists do, they will fight other collectives, deny individual rights, and act against the broader interests of humanity and nature. So otherists are our only genuine *patriots*, since humanists have more sense than to put any artificial nation before all the world's real individuals, and elitists and selfists are insincere when they do profess patriotism.

Though some rightists are not nationalistic patriots, all rightists are chauvinists for some collective or descriptive class to which they belong. Psychologically, a *patriot* is a partialist who has no concern for all humanity; one who says in effect, "You must support my collective because

I need you to do so." Well, leftists do join rightists to fight just causes or wars, but a *just war* can only be one that is fought for *self-defense* or for *humanistic ends*—that is, for the inalienable rights of all individuals, and *not* for any nation, religion, race, or other collective, or for any particular hypothetical form of government or economic structure.

Though otherist conservatives or liberals are more moral than elitist conservatives or liberals, this is not invariably so because of their illogic in power. That is, like humanist radicals, otherist conservatives usually undo any good they intend for others by their extremism (intolerance) at the first power pole, and they and otherist liberals usually undo any good they intend for others by their collectivism (antihumanism) at the second power pole.

Because elitists are selfish in judgment, they are more illogical than otherists. This is so even of those who tried to help others, such as these elitist conservatives in our tables: Hugo Black, Thurgood Marshall, Muhammad Ali, Oskar Schindler, Chiune Sugimara, William Godwin, Simone de Beauvoir, Michel de Montaigne, Mary Shelley, Stephen Hawking, Dorothy Day, and Mother Teresa. These people all had serious psychologic flaws to overcome. So while we may respect theists like Day and Mother Teresa for helping the needy, we know, if only from their theism, that they were not psychologically healthy, or realistic. Godwin (+-+RR) was even more the exception; being strong in will, he overcame his theism, left the clergy, and then wrote more common sense on people and politics than any rightist has in the two centuries since.

But they are exceptions; the general nature of an elitist liberal or conservative is better seen in these people in our tables. In government, (*Tables 1* and *3* only): Nixon, Bush II, John Ashcroft, James Brady, Andrew Card, Richard Clarke, Barry Goldwater, J. Edgar Hoover, Karen Hughes, Joseph McCarthy, Richard Perle, Condeleezza Rice, Nelson Rockefeller, Karl Rove, Kenneth Starr, Robert A. Taft, Charles E. Wilson, and Paul Wolfowitz. In the media (*Table 6*), Pat Buchanan, Father Coughlin, Steve Forbes, Tom Freidman, Christopher Hitchens, Adrianna Huffington, Brit Hume, William Kristol, Rush Limbaugh, Dennis Miller, Charlie Rose, and Ted Turner. And in academia (*Table 11*): Alan Dershowitz, H.L.A. Hart,

Marshall McLuhan, Samuel Morrison, Robert Nozick, Willard Quine, B.F. Skinner, and Leo Strauss, the Zionist father of *neoconservatism*, a term that means elitism even when it doesn't mean Zionism.

As for the leftist distinction, the *humanists* are usually concerned with the best interests of all individuals everywhere, while the *selfists* put their personal interests first.

The Generational Clash

Now let us consider an extremely important social aspect of human judgment to which only astrology can alert us. This is that the planet that determines the charge at the second pole of our judgment system makes an entire generation of humans either selfish or unselfish!

As *Figure A* in *Appendix A* shows, this planet is Pluto. Pluto's sidereal cycle is 247.7 years, so its twelve periods (its time in one sign and hence with one charge) have an average length of 20.6 years. Actually, due to the high ellipticity of its orbit, it is in one sign anywhere from 12 to over 30 years. Since this is a reasonable range for the purpose, I use Pluto's sign transits to define our generations in general, which are better defined in this objective way than by any hypothetical average age of child bearing or irrelevant statistics on population changes. Still, these are generations only as regards our judgmental and moral reasoning. Our feeling systems also differ by a generation of sorts; by Neptune's transit through a sign every 13.7 years.

Everyone born in a generation thus defined has this point of similarity in their judgment, and yet traditionalists in the human sciences have ignored this natural fact. What it means is that human generations alternate between one that consists entirely of humanists and otherists (H&O) and one that consists entirely of selfists and elitists (S&E). Accordingly, the continual struggle between the most and least selfish people in the world is at root a generational conflict.

This explains why, in judgment at least, children are more often like their grandparents than their parents. For example, most of the parents of the H&O generation of 1913-38 were born in the S&E generation of 1883-1913, so they were egoists or nihilists with no compassion. They may have been otherwise good people with a cultural sense of duty to their children, but they seldom put their children's interests first and often tried to use them only for their own ends. This caused these children to disdain, dislike, or even hate their parents and to flee the home scene whenever possible; perhaps to visit their grandparents, who were probably compassionate people born in the H&O generation of 1851-83. But their own children were probably born in the next S&E generation, 1938-57, so they may have been disappointed to see in them the self-centeredness they saw in their parents. However, Pluto's periods were shortening then, so those born in the last decade of this H&O generation may have had unselfish children born after mid-1957 who liked their parents but perhaps not their grandparents.

Psychologic and social analysts should need little help in drawing the implications of this generational fact, which brings into question not only our traditional assumptions about families, such as the foolish expectation that all children must love and honor their parents or vice versa, but also every study of siblings and every biography that discusses its subject's family history. There are always exceptions to the rule, as we have seen, since people are not governed solely by their judgment and may have other innate characteristics or acquired personality traits that minimize their selfishness. Even so, this fact puts a whole new light on all family relationships.

But it is also important in considering political relationships and world events, for everyone is negatively affected while an S&E generation controls their society. Selfish politicians and judges are plainly a danger to us, but so are the selfish professionals, bureaucrats, teachers, employers, clerics, merchants, and service people in society that we must deal with routinely. Life is far more difficult for everyone when compassionless egoists and nihilists constitute the majority of adults; it is especially hard to be a child or an elderly or infirmed person then.

The twelve sign-periods of Pluto's cycle vary in length because Pluto, which is usually beyond the orbit of Neptune, crosses Neptune's nearly circular orbit and travels inside it for about a fourth of its elliptical orbit.

The fact that Pluto is sometimes not the farthest planet from the sun explains why its recent sign periods are shorter than the average 20.6 years. Also, we can't give one date for its transition into the next sign because all astrological planets except the sun and moon go retrograde for a part of their cycle, and so, as seen from the earth, they appear to move backwards in the signs then. *Appendix C* lists all of Pluto's sign transitions from 587 BCE to 2254, but the dates given are only for its *first ingress* into a sign. Pluto later retrogrades back into the prior sign, goes forward again into its new sign, and may go back yet again, so its sign transitions are uncertain for some months around that date. Only a natal chart for the specific day and the steps explained in *Appendix A* for determining the Impulse Pattern can give us Pluto's charge for any individual born near the time of one of its sign transitions.

Pluto's sign transits from late 1724 to early 2043, rounded to the nearest January 1st, are as follows. The destructive, war-mongering, and compassionless S&E generations are 1725-37, 1749-62, 1777-97, 1822-51, 1883-1913, 1938-57, 1972-84, 1995-2008, and 2023-43, and the constructive, peaceful, and compassionate H&O generations are 1737-49, 1762-77, 1797-1822, 1851-83, 1913-38, 1957-72, 1984-95, and 2008-23. The new era began on January 25, 2008.

All the events of these periods, including people born during them, have the character of the time. A full history proves this, but it should suffice here to mention only the S&E generations that I will refer to here as the *constitutional*, the *fascist*, and the *baby-boom* generations.

Even if you were born after the sixties, you probably know from the media that the young selfists and elitists of the baby-boom generation (born 1938-57), in spite of the good advice of their unselfish parents and teachers (born 1913-38), made many bad judgments then. Well, they are still doing this today as the rulers of our governments and corporations across the world. And we are suffering now not only from their bad judgment as our rulers, but also from the effects of the harmful events of the Pluto-in-Leo transit in which they were born—such as World War II, genocide across the world, the Cold War, the Republicans' McCarthyism, the Korean War, extreme overpopulation, the herpes, aids, and narcotics epidemics, and the epidemic of certain cancers that strangely coincided with the invention of plastics, pesticides, and other chemicals.

The general point here is that we must attribute human events to two periods, not one. In this case, the Pluto-in-Gemini transit of 1883-1913 shaped the judgment of the fascist generation that was ruling the world when the Pluto-in-Leo transit of 1938-57 helped provoke the events just listed. Earlier, the fascist generation also helped cause the Roaring Twenties, financial swindles, organized crime, the Great Depression, and fascism as a formal theory.

So it is that, in being selfish with no compassion or logic in judgment, the elitist Bush II of the baby-boom generation is like the elitist Hitler of the fascist generation. Hitler flouted his intolerance as an anti-Semite and Bush his intolerance as a Christian religionist, and both lied continually, opposed individual rights, and invaded other nations just because they wanted to.

Though the Nazi party was ruled by evil people, Germans born before or after the fascist generation were not such beasts. They can no more be blamed for being ruled by the majority in their state than older and younger people today can be blamed for being ruled by an immoral majority in theirs. Rulers born in an S&E generation have *never* produced a sane and moral government or tried to preserve life and maintain peace and prosperity. This is an astounding historical fact, but it has been ignored by our political and intellectual leaders, and by voters too.

In 2004, the final nine Democratic candidates for US President were baby-boomers, and hence selfists or elitists. But it was impractical for the Democratic Party to offer a humanist candidate against the elitist Bush II, since most voters then were also S&E baby-boomers. Selfist and elitist voters won't tolerate the sane and compassionate message of humanist or otherist candidates because they actually want an immoral government that will empower the rich, oppress the poor, rape our environment, suppress dissent, wage wars, or impose the fictions and political agenda of religious corporations on everyone. And though their plurality has diminished since Reagan was elected president, they were still a significant force in the 2008 elections.

Twelve of the fifteen active presidential candidates of both parties at the end of 2007 were baby-boomers who should have been rejected from the start for being elitists or selfists. This leaves the otherist McCain (-B-BR) and the humanist Paul (- - - -B) from the pre-boomers, and the humanist Obama (-+- -B) from the post-boomers. But Paul must be rejected for embracing the fallacies of libertarianism, McCain for his conflicted three-term political perspective which makes him a confused maverick and (absurdly) a 'militaristic moralist', and both for supporting the Republican Party, which has been opposed to genuine democracy since its founding. Some of the rejected Democrats have strong will systems that give them good intentions, but their judgment is self-centered and that is a fatal flaw for any leader. As for Hillary Clinton (BRB+R), she is not as much at odds with the elitist Bush II as she pretends. Though they support opposed power cliques, both are elitists who conspire against the people for their different wealthy cliques, and neither of them can see the new era happening.

So our system identifies Obama as the best choice available among those candidates, even though (like all the others) he has no plan to change the elitist US Constitution that imposed corrupt federal and state governments on the people and legalized an inequitable distribution of wealth, resources, and essential human services. As a 60% rightist (liberal in three systems), he is almost certain to support rightist candidates and policies, and otherwise act against the best interests of the people. His desire to mix religion with politics is clear evidence of this weakness. Still, he is a humanist, an altruist and progressive-liberal with empathy and compassion, and the only one of the 2008 candidates who perceived that his generation doesn't have the bad judgment of the prior generation, and that, for some reason, we have entered a new psychologic era that demands new political conceptions. We must hope that he will take the pains to search for those new conceptions, for his three assimilative (liberal) systems won't help him create them.

Table 16 strikingly confirms my claims on this generational clash. That table, which is based entirely on timed birth data provided by the

French psychologists Michel and Françoise Gauquelin, shows that 96% of the major Nazi political and military leaders of World War II were selfists or elitists. Of the seventy-three names there, only three were not of the fascist generation, and they were not the worst of the Nazis. The humanists Churchill (BR+B+) and Franklin Roosevelt (-BRBB) were also born before the fascist generation, but most other Allied leaders in WWII were born during it. This includes the selfist radical Eisenhower (R++R+), the elitist conservative Patton (-+-RR), and the elitist liberal Truman (BB-+-), who needlessly dropped atomic bombs on Japanese civilians—not to end the already-won war with Japan, but to terrorize the world with US power. Japan would have surrendered just as quickly if he had demonstrated that bomb in an unpopulated area.

A table of world leaders today, most of whom are baby-boomers, would yield much the same results as *Table 16*. The main difference in these two S&E generations is that the baby-boom generation spanned 19 years while the more-deadly fascist generation spanned 30 years.

Needless to say, Jews of the fascist generation had the same judgmental impairments the Nazis had. This explains the elements of truth in the charges by some, such as Ben Hecht in his book *Perfidy*, that Zionist leaders betrayed all the Jews in Nazi Europe in their private bargains with Eichmann and other Nazi leaders that allowed many wealthy Jews to escape.

But there were exceptions then, such as (in *Table 7*) the conflicted elitist conservative-radicals Oskar Schindler (+BR+R), whose story was told in the movie *Schindler's List*, and Chiune Sugimara (B++RR), a Japanese diplomat in Lithuania who was sent home in disgrace because he disobeyed orders by issuing visas that allowed some 6,000 Jews to escape the Nazis. Both had strong will and thought systems and more leftist than rightist psychologic systems—characteristics that incline anyone, even elitists, to be governed more by universal principles than by the fads or insanities of their time. So all that we can fairly conclude is that *most* people born in an S&E generation are selfish, destructive, and militaristic; many are not because they also have other innate characteristics or acquired traits that allow them to control those impulses.

These same truths hold across every generation that historians can accurately describe, as we see with the three short generations that produced the US Constitution. The S&E generations of 1725-37 and 1749-62—which sandwiched the H&O generation of 1737-49 in which such people as Paine, Jefferson, and Hancock were born—produced the majority of adults from 1787 to 1789, when the antidemocratic US Constitution was conceived, written, and ratified, thanks mainly to the conspiratorial elitists Madison, Hamilton, and Washington.

Here is an excerpt from a fuller description of the adults of the 1780s that one respected historian assembled from many sources of that time. But for their temporal color, these words would apply just as well to any other S&E generation:

> By 1780 Patrick Henry "feared that our Body politic was dangerously sick." The signs of disease spread everywhere. Merchants and farmers were seeking their own selfish ends; hucksters were engrossing products to raise prices. Even government officials, it was charged, were using public positions to fill their own pockets. The fluctuation in the value of money was making "every kind of commerce and trade precarious"...and was putting a premium on selfishness. Everyone was doing "what was right in his own eyes," and "thus the whole of that care and attention which was given to the public weal is turned to private gain or self preservation." That benevolence among the people had not grown as a result of the Revolution was measured in the frightening increase in litigation.... Vices now seemed more prevalent than before the war. Virtue was being debased by "the visible declension of religion,...the rapid progress of licentious manners, and open profanity." Such symptoms of degeneracy threw the clergy especially into confusion. Instead of bringing about the moral reformation they had anticipated from victory, the Revolution had only aggravated America's corruption and sin. The Americans, they said in sermon after sermon throughout

the eighties, could only be an ill-tempered and unrighteous people, so soon forgetting the source of their deliverance from British tyranny. (Gordon S. Wood, *The Creation of the American Republic 1776-1787* [Chapel Hill: The University of North Carolina Press, 1969], 416-417.)

Conclusions for the New Era. For two reasons, because every other generation is a selfish one and because a majority in an electoral government is dictatorial, the only sane government that can be proposed is one in which no majority is permitted to impose its beliefs or rules on anyone with reasonable grounds for not consenting to them—such as refusing to support an immoral war of aggression and the immoral people who choose to fight it. And the fact that traditionalists cannot conceive such a government doesn't mean that no one can.

Also, we now have good reason to reject three lies that few have disputed. One is that we should support our political and military leaders and their troops even if they are engaged in immoral conflicts. The others are that *majority rule* is beneficial for the people and that it is what defines a democracy. In truth, it is neither of those things, so in the new era we need to define democracy correctly. We are fools if we trust, obey, or support any majority that consists of people with bad judgment, a character flaw that makes most people immoral and some of them inhuman.

Political theorists have long argued that a democracy can only work if the best people rule, but these were just empty words so long as no one understood human nature well enough to identify the best and the worst people among us. But now the theories and empirical evidence offered here prove that many people are born selfish, or innately disinclined to consider others, and this is sufficient reason to deny them a role in our governments, at least any supervisory role. That is not undemocratic, for democracy applies to the electors, not to the elected or to those they appoint or hire. It is just another wise criterion—like being citizens, of a certain age, apparently sane, and adequately educated—for allowing people to wield our great collective power.

Note that these psychologic facts cannot be explained by traditionalists through experiential or genetic factors, but are explained by astrological factors. Suddenly, then, at the very dawn of the new era, the role of astrology has become more important to society than it ever was.

We have seen here that the logic or illogic of our fundamental moral and political attitudes is determined by our congenital characters, and not by the form of the statements we make when we describe those attitudes *ex post facto*. People may be superficially irrational because of what they think or have been taught, but they are innately irrational because of when they were born.

We must be astonished by all those candidates, authors, media spokespersons, and other pontificators who claim that they understand our politics and know how to organize our societies properly when they haven't the slightest idea of why and how we humans differ innately in our moral and political dispositions.

Obviously, our basic social problem is that people must find a way to live together sanely even though they are born with those and other psychologic differences, but they will never do so until someone has soundly explained those differences to them.

Chapter 8. The Natal Chart

Realistic Astrology

The purpose of this chapter is to explain the main ways in which *realistic astrology*, meaning the astrology that follows from the theories of this work, differs from traditional astrology. So I am not trying to teach astrology here, but only a new way of practicing it. Accordingly, I must assume that my readers are not beginners. They should know traditional astrology, its methods and symbols, the three coordinate systems (the *ecliptic*, *equatorial*, and *horizon* systems) used by astronomers and astrologers for their celestial measurements, the elements of a two-dimensional astrological chart, and what each element refers to in three-dimensional reality.

The theory of realistic astrology is similar to that of humanology as outlined in Chapter 4. Its new and essential point is the equivalence of the parts of any cycle, astrological or not, to the corresponding parts of the Consideration Cycle. The cardinal points of the Cycle, our *epistemic cycle*, are the complete percept, the abstract concept, the partial percept, and the concrete concept, and these correspond to the cardinal points of the astrological cycles as follows. In *the annual cycle*, or zodiac, they correspond to 0°♑, 0°♈, 0°♋, and 0°♎ respectively; in *the daily cycle*, or a chart cast for a specific place and time of day, to the projections on the ecliptic that we refer to as the cusps (beginning points) of the 10th, 1st, 4th, and 7th houses; and in the cycle of any *astrological planet*, meaning any object that moves around the earth and displaces our spatial field, to its *north point*, *ascending node* (☊), *south point*, and *descending node* (☋).[1]

---

[1] The ascending node (☊) is where any planet's path crosses the ecliptic moving north of it, and the descending node (☋) is where it crosses it moving south of it. I call the points of a planet's cycle that are farthest north or south of the ecliptic its 'north point' and 'south point' respectively, and for astrologers this means the geometric projections of those points on the ecliptic (zodiac).
(continued)

It follows that the Consideration Cycle's vertical axis of particularity corresponds to the 0°♑-0°♋ axis of the annual cycle, to the 10th-4th house axis of the daily cycle, and to the north-south axis of any planet's cycle. And the Cycle's horizontal axis of universality corresponds to the 0°♈-0°♎ axis of the annual cycle, to the 1st-7th house axis of the daily cycle, and to any nodal (☊-☋) axis. Epistemically, then, the first three axes correspond to particularity in our reasoning and to natural reasoning, while the latter three axes correspond to universality in our reasoning and to explicated reasoning. These correspondences also hold for the quadrants of those cycles, which we will number as we did the quadrants of the Consideration Cycle. The Cycle's first quadrant corresponds in the annual cycle to the space from 0°♑ to 0°♈, in the daily cycle to the space from the 10th house cusp to the 1st house cusp, and in any planetary cycle to the space from its north point to its ascending node (☊), and so on counterclockwise.

The Basic Problems

A full astrological theory must answer these five questions: Which cycles are real and not imaginary? Which real cycles should we use? How can we objectively divide any cycle into parts? How can we know the psychologic meanings of those parts? And how can we determine the true beginning point of each cycle, which we must know to relate discrete cycles?

The Zodiac. Our first problem is to decide which *zodiac* to use, for this is an ambiguous term. There is the *tropical zodiac* and the *constellatory*

In traditional astrology, 'north node' and 'south node', or ☊ and ☋, mean the ascending or descending nodes of the moon's orbit, but in realistic astrology we will avoid these terms because we need to apply them to all planets. That is, since we see every planet's cycle as a house system, we must use some new symbols. For instance, '☽☊' means the moon's ascending node, '♄☋' means Saturn's descending node, '♂N' means the north point of Mars' cycle, '♆S' means the south point of Neptune's cycle, and so on.

zodiac. Some practitioners call the latter 'the classical zodiac', but this implies that it came first, and that is not known for certain. People observed the stars before they conceived of a zodiac, but that doesn't tell us which zodiac came first because they also observed the four seasons. This issue is irrelevant anyway, since our reasons for using the tropical zodiac have nothing to do with which one came first.

The tropical zodiac is our annual cycle, or the ecliptic (sun-earth) plane, divided into twelve segments of 30° each, starting from *0° Aries*, or the vernal equinox, which is the real point at which the sun and the ecliptic ascend north of the earth's equator. Astronomers calculate this point precisely each year to time our seasons and adjust our clocks and calendar. The tropical zodiac is a *plane*, while the constellatory zodiac is a rough *band* of fixed stars that were arbitrarily grouped to form the twelve *astrological constellations*. These constellations don't span exactly 30° in space, their stars are not neighbors in three dimensions, and their hypothetical beginning point, also called '0° Aries', is arbitrarily determined. We therefore have no reason to use these twelve fictional groups of stars or the mythical 'Circle of Beasts' based on them.

The term *sign* is also ambiguous in traditional use, for it can mean one of the 30° segments of the tropical zodiac or one of the twelve imaginary constellations near the ecliptic. To avoid this ambiguity we will call the former a 'sign' and the latter an 'astrological constellation'.

About 1800 years ago these zodiacs coincided in space, which made interpretive distinctions between them slight for centuries before and after that time. But because of the precession of the equinoxes, these zodiacs have separated so that their 0°♈ points are now about 25° apart in the heavens. Since this is nearly a whole sign, they are now antithetical, and so we must discard the fictional one. The constellatory zodiac is used in Asia, mainly India, but in the West it is used only by a small number of arealistic practitioners. We don't use it in realistic astrology because, unlike the tropical zodiac, it is not a real motion system as defined by our metaphysics. Thus, the notion of a coming *Age of Aquarius* is nonsense to us. Also, the Impulse Pattern, our powerful new method for determining major congenital characteristics, is based on the charges acquired by the planets from the signs of the tropical zodiac, and if we determined this by the astrological constellations instead, we would lose the individual and statistical significance of this valuable new method. So in realistic astrology, the term *zodiac* means the tropical zodiac only.

Dividing the Zodiac. The next question is, Why should the zodiac have *twelve* signs, or 30° divisions? We accept this practice for two reasons: first because its 90° quadrants are objective natural facts, the seasons, and second because dividing each quadrant into 30° segments was a good synthetic guess by ancient astrologers. This second reason may seem insubstantial, but further reflection shows that it is valid.

Our psychologic theory holds that after we see an event's objective facts with our analytic reasoning, we can only continue our reasoning with tertiary speculations, or the natural hypothetical reasoning that characterizes every art or science. And the Cycle tells us that all of our synthetic reasoning, even when it seems unrelated to psychology, begins with our tertiary reasoning about our own psychologic—specifically, with our passions and needs, from which we consider psychology in general and then create the quaternary languages of our arts and sciences. So with any relative issue it is always the case that *our initial belief is merely a subjective guess*. It is a valid guess if our prior analytic reasoning was sound, but even then we can't know if our statement of it is true or false until it is proven in practice. In fact, that is why we create any science: to gain this confidence by transforming our subjective guesses in its subject area into objectively proven facts. So when astrologers make valid guesses and then verify these guesses with empirical evidence, as they have done in this case, they are only doing what all scientists do.

Accordingly, until physical or psychologic evidence to the contrary appears, it will be a premise of realistic astrology that this synthetic guess by ancient astrologers to divide the zodiac's quadrants into 30° sectors is sound. We know, of course, that this could not be the case unless that guess reflected some as-yet-unknown fact of nature pertaining to particle motion, but the task of explaining that natural fact does not belong to astrology or psychology. Since this mystery pertains to external rather than internal space, it can only be solved by our physical scientists. But they have ignored the problem, and many of them have even ridiculed astrologists and psychologists for not having solved this and other physical mysteries for them.

The quadrants of a real motion system are natural facts, and so are their *midpoints*. A cardinal point has one spatial direction, but a quadrant has two, and both are equally in effect only at the quadrant's midpoint. Before that point one direction dominates and after it the other one does. These are real differences in spatial direction, so we have objective grounds for dividing a quadrant further, and some astrologers proposed that we should divide the zodiac into eight 45° parts. The problem with this 45° solution, though, is that it is based on essentially the same reasoning that supports the empirically proven 30° solution.

Take the first quadrant of a compass in example. Moving CCW from north, its first 30° segment mostly lies in the north and moves eastward, the second 30° barely distinguishes north and east, and the third mostly lies in the east and moves southward. These spatial differences are objective reasons for accepting the ancient 30° signs, and we could consider the point proven if physicists explained in their terms what I call the 'charges' of the 30° segments of any real cycle. But until then we must accept the 30° signs for the empirical reasons given. *The only property of a motion system that tells us how to divide it is a change in spatial direction*; otherwise we can only divide it objectively by combining it with other motion systems that share its space, as I did in identifying the intermediate ideas of the Consideration Cycle by reference to the ten planetary cycles. But since this merging of cycles is synthetic reasoning, we cannot trust its conclusions until we have tested and verified them in practice.

A related issue is that soon after the 30° signs of horoscopic astrology were accepted, some astrologers proposed that each sign should be divided into 10° sectors called 'decanates'. Any change in spatial direction within a sign is real, but we must reject this notion of a sharp 10° demarcation because there is no theoretic basis for it and the psychologic arguments offered for it are few and too vague to be tested.

The Quadruplicity. The fact that the three 30° signs of each zodiacal quadrant (or season) differ for natural reasons means that the old *quadruplicity* of astrology is realistic. This is the claim, previously unsupported by any theory, that the spatial distinctions between the first, second, and third signs of a zodiacal quadrant relates those three signs to the respective signs of the other three quadrants. A quadrant's first sign is its *cardinal sign* (♑, ♈, ♋, or ♎), the second is its *fixed sign* (♒, ♉, ♌, or ♏), and the third is its *mutable sign* (♓, ♊, ♍, or ♐). From our spatial analysis we can validly infer that the cardinal sign is the *initiation* of a new direction, the fixed sign is the *immobility* caused by indecision over the quadrant's two directions, and the mutable sign is the *transformation* to the next direction, or cardinal sign. These same three meanings also hold for the *houses* of any other cycle, so the traditional quadruplicity is also used in the daily cycle, where each quadrant is divided into three houses, equivalently named its *angular*, *succedent*, and *cadent* houses.

The Triplicity. But this reasoning does not let us keep the ancient *triplicity*, which is as great a mistake as any in traditional astrology. Since ancient astrologers had no theory of astrology, they couldn't see why the quadruplicity is valid, so from the mathematical fact that it was a fourfold division of the zodiac, they assumed that it would also be valid to claim that a threefold division of the zodiac shows sign similarities. Then they assumed that their four sets of three signs, called 'trigons', could be assigned psychologic meanings from their simplistic view that the world consists of only four elements, which of course is not so. Hence their fictional trigons: *fire* (♈, ♌, and ♐), *earth* (♑, ♉, and ♍), *air* (♒, ♊, and ♎), and *water* (♓, ♋, and ♏).

Realists need an analytic, not a linguistic, reason to conclude that signs have common features. The quadruplicity is based on real events, changes in spatial direction, but the triplicity is not. The old claim that we can classify the signs by rotating an equilateral triangle around the zodiac is absurd, for this is our doing, not reality's. The triplicity may help novices memorize which signs are related by a 120° angle, but it has no interpretive value. For instance, most traditionalists hold that the 'element' of the sign on the third-house cusp indicates a native's preferred mode of travel (earth, water, or air), and sometimes this seems to apply. But who travels in fire? There must be another explanation for any case where this rule seems to hold.

And indeed there is a partial truth in the triplicity, one on which our Impulse Pattern also relies. This is that there is a factor shared by the six traditional 'masculine' signs that compose the air and fire trigons, and an opposite one shared by the six traditional 'feminine' signs that compose the earth and water trigons. Most of the meanings proposed for each trigon by traditionalist authors are accounted for by this factor of positive (+) or negative (-) charge, which we discussed at length earlier. This is so even in the 'mode of travel' example above, for the restless projective (+) signs make one prefer fast travel, while the passive assimilative (-) signs make one prefer slow and safe travel. Some traditionalists have described the fire signs as *ardent, aggressive, creative, masculine, keen, rash, easily excited, impulsive, animated, vital, intense*, and so on, but these words also describe the projective impulse that the 'fire' and 'air' signs share. And they have described the earth trigon as meaning *practical, cautious, nervous, worried, feminine, agitated, collectivistic, stable, mundane*, and so on, but these terms also describe the assimilative impulse that the 'earth' and 'water' signs share.

The chief damage done by the triplicity scheme is that it distorts the meanings of the signs. To see this, compare any traditionalist's comments on the trigons to *Figures 6* and *A*, which show the meanings of each sign in terms of its dynamic position in the Consideration Cycle.

For instance, a major psychologic error made by astrologers who use the triplicity is the claim that the signs of the water trigon—Cancer (♋), Scorpio (♏), and Pisces (♓)—are related by 'emotionality', or an equivalent term. Well, that is so of Cancer, which corresponds to the part of our psychologic (♆, or point 6) that governs our subjective passions. But 'emotionality' does not apply to Scorpio or Pisces. The first 24° of Scorpio corresponds to an objective, not a subjective, part of the Cycle. So most of this sign has nothing to do with inner reasoning, but is instead about cold opportunism and collectivistic reasoning (♃, or point 9). It may influence otherwise passionate people to be stubborn fighters for their collectives (family, club, nation, religion, and so on), but this doesn't show their emotionality, it only shows their collectivism and psychologic dependence on their collectives. Pisces also isn't emotional; its reasoning is subjective, but it is subjective analysis, not subjective synthesis. It corresponds to the phase of the Cycle between points 2 (♄) and 3 (☿) where we do realistic, analytic, and reductive reasoning, such as planning, denial, and affirmation. But that reasoning is entirely cerebral; it has no emotional element at all. Every human has emotions, but we can't claim that a chart factor governs our emotions unless we first have a sound psychologic theory that distinguishes these from other inner elements. Note, for example, how differently these 'water' signs affect one's approach to music: Cancer makes it expressive and romantic, Pisces makes it abstract and dry, and Scorpio makes it practical—that is, social, patriotic, religious, or otherwise chauvinistic.

The Beginning of the Zodiac. The fact that ancient astrologers used the intersection of the ecliptic and equatorial planes to calculate 0°♈ precisely doesn't mean that this point is the *beginning* of the zodiac, or ecliptic plane. Anyone who thinks that it is should be able to tell us what natural fact implies that conclusion, but no one can do this, because the beginning point of the entire zodiac, unlike that of the four seasons, is not defined by any objective reality.

In our metaphysics, as *Figure 5* shows, we define the *beginning point* (cardinal point 1) of any motion system's cycle as the point where object P intersects the forward direction of C's orbital motion about O. One could argue on the analytic level that this selection is arbitrary, and it is, because we don't know where *P* was when its motion system was created. But if we mean which cardinal point begins each complete spin in an already-formed motion system, then we can only resolve this issue scientifically; that is, with hypothetical guessing and testing. So I proposed that definition synthetically, or speculatively, and not analytically, because in interpreting charts over decades I observed, in every real astrological cycle I use, that only this selection is correct in its tertiary psychologic correspondences.

Is this valid reasoning? Yes it is, because every synthetic speculation in any art or science is at root psychologic, or tertiary. So the fact that I created the Consideration Cycle lets me deny the traditional beginning points of our cycles and affirm my selections. This standard of all human reasoning shows the psychologic meanings of the four cardinal points of any cycle—in other words, the Whole, One, Parts, and All of it. But those who have no epistemic standard can only guess at those psychologic meanings, and then they have no way to verify their guesses.

Actually, what I realized first here was not that 0°♑ begins the zodiac, but rather that its traditional beginning point, 0°♈, could not be its beginning, since that point is psychologically equivalent to the abstract concept, or to the start of the Consideration Cycle's second quadrant. I therefore concluded that the zodiac must begin at 0°♑, or the cardinal point 90° before 0°♈.

If Aries was the first sign, then 0°♈ would be psychologically equivalent to the *complete percept* and would mean *particularity*, *wholeness*, and *realness*. But no practitioners attribute those meanings to Aries. I'm sure most would agree that, among other things, Aries means *conscious abstract reasoning* and *projection from the self* and Capricorn means *instinctive, wholistic response to assimilated events*. As quadrantal opposites, these signs have nothing in common but their cardinality. Capricorn means *beginning* and hence perception, particularity, wholism, and realism, while Aries means *conception* and hence dualism and derived universal conclusions; Capricorn leads the way in space and Aries leads the way in 'time', or in analytic thought about spatial events that have already occurred. A thought (♈) never comes first in our reasoning; it always follows the whole event (♑) that provoked us into thinking.[2]

---

[2] As we would expect from his natal chart and Impulse Pattern, the theist and rationalist Descartes (-RB++) put this issue backwards in his famous *cogito*. Because he was weak in will, reversed in thought, and had five of his ten planets in Aries *and* in its corresponding house, he was impelled to say, "I think, therefore I am," which of course is a conceptualist's claim that everything starts from our secondary reasoning, or thought. He should have said the converse, "I am, and therefore (given what I am) I think."

Untimed Charts. Another problem in astrology is how we should cast a chart when we know an event's date, or the sun's position in the annual cycle, but not its time of day, or the zodiacal position of the daily cycle's cardinal points. A true horoscope incorporates the annual and the daily cycles, so if we don't know the time of day we must make a partial horoscope that shows only the zodiac and the planets' approximate position in it. Practitioners deal with this problem of untimed charts in two ways.

The first way is to draw the chart for noon. Since the houses of this *noon chart* can be off by as much as 180°, they are meaningless, but at least this method ensures that the planets' positions are no more than twelve hours off from their positions at birth, which is why we use a noon chart to calculate an Impulse Pattern when we don't know the birth time. Twelve hours seldom makes a difference with nine of the astrological planets, but it might with the moon, which can move as much as 15°, or half a sign, in a day.

The second way is to use a *solar chart*, where one assumes that the zodiacal position of the sun is also the ASC of the daily cycle and then takes that point to be the cusp of the first house, from which equal 30° divisions are marked on the zodiac in counterclockwise order as the cusps of the other eleven houses. This yields the *solar house system*. Though we must use a noon chart to get the Impulse Pattern for an untimed birth, previously solar charts were preferred, both because statistics showed that most births occur near sunrise and because practitioners found that the solar houses have some meanings that are like those of the houses of a timed chart. But this doesn't mean that a solar chart's houses are valid substitutes for the houses of a timed chart; it only means that both are psychologically meaningful, and this is so because the solar 'houses' emulate the signs. Since the sun never ascends above or descends below the ecliptic, which is its own cycle, it cannot define a house system, but its annual cycle does define the twelve signs, which our metaphysics holds correspond to the twelve houses of any other cycle.

THE HOUSES

Though we must accept the correspondence of the daily and annual cycles, we must deny these other assumptions of traditionalists on the daily cycle: (1) their claim that the ASC is its true beginning, (2) all of their proposals on how to divide the daily cycle into houses, and (3) their belief that since the daily cycle is a single cycle, a horoscope has only one house system.

1. Just as we held that 0°♈ begins the second quadrant of the zodiac, so we must hold that the ASC begin the second quadrant of the daily cycle. Psychologically, the ASC reflects the nature of our self-concept, uniqueness, and dignity, but the Cycle tells us that we can't have these personal *conceptions* until we have first had the *perception* of our self as a real and whole event. In other words, "I am, therefore I think." So our theory requires us to hold that the true beginning of a chart's daily cycle is not the cusp of its 'first' house, but rather the cusp of its 'tenth' house. This change doesn't alter most of the traditional house meanings, but it is important because it determines how we are to correspond the houses of the daily cycle to the signs of the zodiac and to our psychologic cycle, which is the source of all meanings.

Unfortunately, this change of beginning point gives us a linguistic problem that doesn't arise with the annual cycle because, unlike the signs, the houses have ordinal names (1, 2, 3, and so on). With the signs, I can say that Aries is the fourth sign and not the first, and everyone who learned traditional astrology still knows what 'Aries' means. But if I say that the traditional first house is really the fourth house, and so on around the daily cycle, I am stripping the old number-names of their literal ordinal meaning. And this is confusing in two ways. It is confusing to use ordinal words like 'first' and 'second' while having to understand that sequentially they now mean 'fourth' and 'fifth'. But it is also confusing for those who learned traditional astrology to have to remember that our new first house now means what the old tenth house meant, our new second house now means what the old eleventh house means, and so on.

My first thought here was to follow the Cycle in our naming, but then I realized, from my own practice, that it would be less confusing for those who learned astrology the old way to use the wrong ordinal names than it would be to interpret a chart that uses new house names that mean a different house. And since no astrological software today lets the user decide how to number the houses, we would have to correct our computer-printed charts manually. Therefore, we will call the sequential first house of the daily cycle 'the tenth house', its traditional name, and so on for the other houses of the cycle. This linguistic confusion is regrettable, but it is not our fault, for we are only correcting an error on beginning points made by ancient astrologers. Someday perhaps, when realistic astrology is widely accepted, we can agree to rename the houses either with the literally correct numbers or with a set of nonordinal names.

2. In realistic astrology, we agree with most traditionalists that, like the signs, there must be twelve houses. But we oppose every traditional way of dividing the daily cycle to define those twelve houses spatially. There are two basic types of house division: an *equal house* system and a *quadrant system*.

Equal-house systems have two main forms. The basic form, which is what we mean by '*the* equal house system', divides the daily cycle into twelve 30° divisions starting from the ASC. A variant of this form is the solar house system described above. The second form, the *whole sign* system, is from the Vedic astrology of India, and it may be the oldest twelve-house system. Its 30° equal-house system begins not at the ASC, but at 0° of whichever sign contains the ASC. This is simple because it gives each sign a full 30° correspondence to one house, but it is erroneous because the cusp of a house is not the whole house, and testing confirms that a sign that covers even a few degrees of a house rules those degrees.

But many practitioners reject the equal house system because it is based on a chart's horizon axis and ignores its meridian axis. By starting from the ASC, it usually creates two 'tenth' house cusps (its own tenth house plus the MC) and two 'fourth' houses cusps (its own fourth house plus the IC). This subordinates the MC-IC axis to the ASC-DSC axis and otherwise confuses interpretation. I agree with this criticism, and add to it my epistemic objection that the equal house system favors conceptualistic (explicated) over perceptualistic (natural) reasoning. The Consideration Cycle regards its vertical and horizontal axes as equals, except as to priority, which it assigns to the vertical (perceptual) axis.

Given these flaws, most astrologers rejected the equal house system in favor of a *quadrant system*. The quadrant systems give the daily cycle's four cardinal points equal importance—except as to priority, which traditionalists assigned to the ASC because of its correspondence to 0°♈, which they assumed was the beginning of the zodiac. But since these critics had no theory, they saw the problem of domification (house-division) as merely a question of how to divide each quadrant of the daily cycle into three parts, and in this they took different quaternary (mathematical) paths. Some got eight houses by dividing the quadrants at their midpoints, but most insisted on twelve houses, so they devised the quadrant systems.

The earliest of the quadrant systems appears to be the one that bears the name of *Porphyry of Tyre* (c.233-c.309), though it was reported (and probably not originated) a century earlier by Antiochus of Athens, who also reported the false notion of the decanates. Here one divides each quadrant of the daily cycle into three equal parts. The later quadrant systems were just proposals for dividing the quadrants into three parts by other mathematical methods. But none of these could be proven to be superior to the simpler Porphyry system; they were just different guesses by quaternary reasoners. They include, in what is probably their chronological order, the *Alchabitius, Campanus, Regiomontanus, Meridian*, and *Placidus* systems, with the latter being the most widely used system in Western astrology today. In the twentieth century, the *Koch, Topocentric*, and *Krusinski* systems were proposed. Our formalists like to say that there are two types of quadrant systems, those that divide *space* and those that divide *time* into three parts, but since time is space, this distinction is meaningless. We won't consider the quadrant systems here because, as explained next, we have a sound reason to reject them all as a class.

3. In realistic astrology, we reject the equal house systems because they denigrate an axis of the daily cycle, and we reject all of the quadrant systems because they create a fictional cycle by hypothetically merging two real cycles.

Ordinarily, what we mean by 'the daily cycle' is one motion system, where P is a selected place on earth that turns about C, the earth's center. As the earth turns, the place—with its meridian (the longitudinal plane perpendicular to the equator) and its horizon (the plane 90° from the place that is perpendicular to its zenith-nadir axis)—turn with it, so that the cardinal points of the daily cycle move around the zodiac as the day progresses. But a two-dimensional horoscope doesn't show the reality here, which is that a place's meridian and horizon planes belong to two different motion systems, each of which has a distinct polar axis. The equatorial system yields the daily cycle's MC and IC, and the horizon system yields its ASC and DSC, and the fact that these two systems and their cardinal points move together as the earth rotates is irrelevant. So anyone who combines these two systems to make hypothetical quadrants that can be divided into three houses is invalidly proposing a fictional system.

The error here is like claiming that you and I are not distinct motions systems because we are both subject to the earth's daily turning. This deprives us of our uniqueness as real events solely on the basis of class reasoning; that is, we are not unique because we can be described as belonging to the class of all terrestrial objects that turn as the earth turns. But we are unique because we each have a unique position (and zenith) on earth. Similarly, though we can lump the equatorial and horizon systems together as members of this 'as-the-earth-turns' class, they are different events in space. It is therefore invalid to claim that they are a single whole event that we can divide into parts as we choose.

So a premise of realistic astrology is that a horoscope's daily cycle consists of two house systems, and is not a fictional system that combines them. One of these house systems is based on the intersection of the meridian plane with the ecliptic and the other on the intersection of the horizon plane with the ecliptic. Technically, we can call the former 'the meridian house system' and the latter 'the horizon house system', but after

I assigned psychologic meanings to them, I thought it better to refer to the former as *the passive house system* and the latter as *the active house system*. I used these names because I found in practice that the meridian system refers to *what happens to us* regardless of our choices or acts, while the horizon system refers to *what we choose to do* given that situation. And the passive system (or vertical axis) functions before the active system because a situation must exist before we can make any choice regarding it.

But for the name problem, this new method is simple enough. Both house systems follow the proven division of the zodiac into twelve 30° signs, and the *literal* (or sequential) first house of each is the *nominal* 'tenth house' by the traditional name. We draw the active house system by dividing the zodiac counterclockwise into twelve 30° houses starting at the ASC, and we draw the passive house system similarly starting from the IC. So the ASC is the cusp of the active system's nominal first house and the IC is the cusp of the passive system's nominal first house, and the beginning point of each house system is the cusp of its nominal tenth house.

This is my solution to the ancient problem of domification. One difficulty I had in reaching it was to determine whether the nominal first house of the passive system should start from the IC or the MC. To solve this, I had to find in reality a principle that applied to all such cases. Traditionalists usually say that the ASC is the zodiacal point where the *eastern horizon* (meaning the half of it that faces *east*, or towards the sun) intercepts the ecliptic, but this east-west distinction doesn't give us a principle we can use for the IC-MC case. A better way to put it is to say that the ASC is where the horizon *ascends north* (♌) of the ecliptic, and the DSC is where it *descends south* (♒) of the ecliptic—with the understanding, of course, that we are to determine what 'ascend' and 'descend' mean by moving counterclockwise along the horizon.

Let us accept this traditional definition of the ASC and DSC, including its assumption of counterclockwise motion, which our theory requires for the terrestrial system anyway. This gives us the principle of our active (horizon) house system, which to be consistent we must follow to define our passive (meridian) house system. So if we move along the meridian of a place in a counterclockwise direction, we see that it *ascends north* (☊) of the ecliptic at the IC and *descends south* (☋) of it at the MC. Therefore, in our passive house system the IC is the cusp of the nominal first house and the MC is the cusp of the nominal seventh house.

Our theory tells us that we can also make such a house system for the cycle of any planet except the sun, and we must follow our house principle in these cases too. This means that a planet's ascending node (☊) is the cusp of its nominal first (or literal fourth) house, that its descending node (☋) is the cusp of its nominal seventh (or literal tenth) house, and that its cycle's true beginning point is its south point. As for the sun, its cycle is the ecliptic, so its 'houses' are the signs of the zodiac, which begin at 0°♑, or the winter solstice. But the sun ascending north of the *equator* is not the same thing as another planet ascending north of the *ecliptic*, so while the signs and houses do correspond, their correspondence is less complete than that of the like-numbered houses of any other cycles.

It is not incorrect in a horoscope to add the house systems of every planet, but this is more analysis than we normally need. I won't discuss the planets' house systems here for that reason, but I must mention this key interpretive point: the meanings of the houses of a planet's cycle are subordinate to that planet's meaning in the Consideration Cycle. A planetary house system is therefore just an analytic tool for better understanding how that one planet works in a chart, and accordingly I reserve this technique for a chart's dominant or most important planet or planets.

I named this domification method *the passive-active method*, or *the PA method* for short. It yields twenty-four houses in all, and the houses of its two systems correspond exactly in a chart only when the MC and the ASC are 90° apart. *Figure 7*, which assumes that special case, shows the correspondences of the active (horizon) houses to the passive (meridian) houses, which for the cardinal houses are A10 to P7, A1 to P10, A4 to P1, and A7 to P4.

Let us consider the A10 to P7 overlap in example, using simple meanings for the tenth and seventh houses; say, one's *social status* (career and reputation) and *partnerships*. Taken alone, the A10 house shows how one's social status is affected by one's own choices and acts, and the P7

Figure 7. The Two House Systems Compared

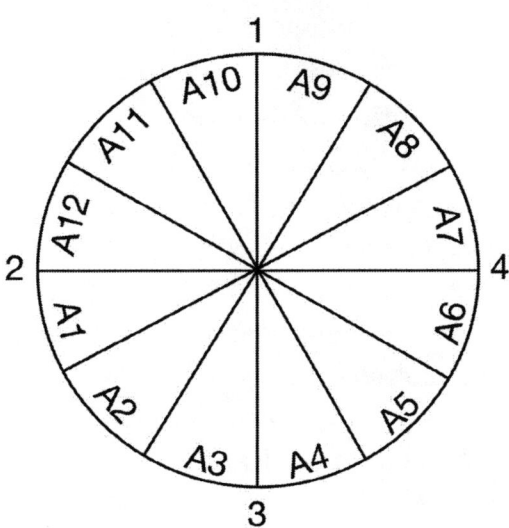

The Active Houses

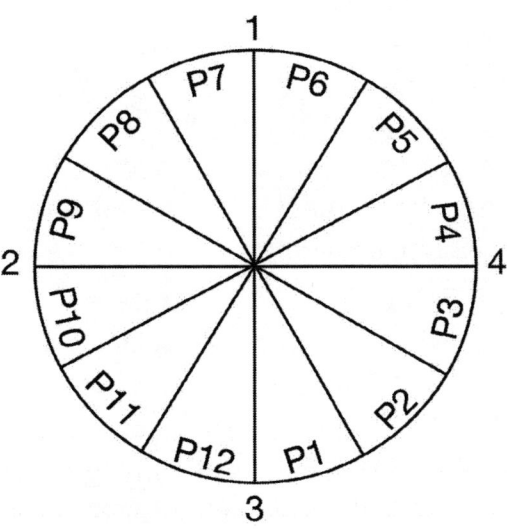

The Passive Houses

house shows how one's partnerships are initiated, influenced, or terminated by external circumstances beyond one's control. These are important distinctions that cannot be made in traditional astrology, but the PA method shows us more than that, for the space that A10 and P7 share, if any, also indicates how one's partnerships (of any kind) will passively affect one's social status (career, reputation) regardless of what one does, and conversely how one's active tenth-house choices will passively affect one's seventh-house circumstances. And of course the signs and planets affecting this overlap range will shade these meanings in their different ways.

But sometimes there is little or no A10-P7 overlap, because the quadrants of the daily cycle are usually not near the 90° angle assumed in *Figure 7*. For instance, Jefferson's MC-ASC angle was 69°, so only 9° of his A10 house overlapped P7. Its first 21° overlapped P6 instead, which is why his active 10th house was continually affected by 6th house matters—such as work, value and moral judgments, and health conditions—that were beyond his control. On the other hand, Einstein's MC-ASC angle was 119°, so most of his A10 house overlapped his P8 house, which meant for one thing that his choices in career and status were affected by 8th house social and cultural conditions beyond his control—such as his family, the respect received from his peers, and his need to leave his homeland, Germany, just because he was a Jew.

First-quadrant angles ranging anywhere from 60° to 120° are common, so normally any one of three adjacent passive houses can overlap all or part of any active house, and vice versa. But even though these overlaps occur in many charts, the shadings of those houses by signs and planets create great differences in individual charts.

Traditional astrology cannot account for these distinctions, but surely it matters much whether the events governed by the houses are caused by external factors or a native's own acts. For example, good or bad health (sixth-house matters) or fame or obscurity (tenth-house matters) can have either or both types of causes. Traditional astrology has no way to explain and study this important distinction, but we can do so clearly because the PA method distinguishes the meridian and the horizon systems, or the passive and active houses.

I can't list the meanings of every P-A overlap here because to do this properly requires a separate work, but this shouldn't matter, because it is a valuable exercise for you to make this active-passive distinction yourself as you interpret charts. What I can do here in a reasonable space is to list my understanding of the twelve house meanings *before* this passive-active distinction is applied. In fact, I must do this because the Cycle requires us to reject some old house meanings that have led traditionalist practitioners into interpretive errors. And because I omit this distinction here, the house meanings listed below will also apply to the corresponding signs, since a sign doesn't have an active and a passive form.

I'm sure you know, even if some traditionalist authors don't, that any house meaning is judgmentally neutral, and that it only acquires a positive or negative meaning as a result of shading by other chart elements—such as a planet that occupies it, the aspects between that planet and other planets or significant points, the planets that rule or oppose it, the charge of those planets, and the sign or signs in which that house occurs. As for the latter case, we have always known that a sign strengthens a house if it is its corresponding house, but now we also know that it weakens a house that is directly or quadrantally opposite to its corresponding house.[3]

I assume that I need not repeat in each case below the basic dynamic point that any angular house means *initiation*, any succedent house means *immobility*, and any cadent house means *transformation*. Nevertheless, the PA method requires the following interpretive change from the current practice on this issue.

---

[3] For instance, when the corresponding sign Aries is on A1 or P1, as it is in Descartes' natal chart, this strengthens one's self-concept and one's ability to handle abstract concepts and other first-house matters. But when Libra, which corresponds to the nominal 7th house, is on A1 or P1, it is antithetical to their first-house purposes. For one thing, it weakens one's self-concept because it is the sign of otherness; for another, it causes the native to confuse concrete and abstract concepts, which is the error made by people who take their fictional beliefs or hypotheses to be universal facts of nature. The quadrantal opposites Capricorn and Cancer also defeat first-house purposes, though each does so in a different way.

Traditional practitioners conclude something about a native's character by counting how many planets in a chart are in cardinal, fixed, or mutable signs, and then something similar (if not identical) by counting how many planets are in angular, succedent, or cadent houses. But in realistic astrology we see all cycles as dynamically similar and we know that each quadrant of any cycle begins with a *cardinal idea*, so we handle this differently. First, we discard the old terms *angular*, *succedent*, and *cadent* because they are redundant, and we use the terms *cardinal*, *fixed*, and *mutable* for the houses as well as for the signs.[4] Then, as if signs and houses were the same thing, which they aren't, we count the number of planets in the signs and in both house systems, for a total of thirty instances (if we use ten planets). If one of the three types dominates the other two in this count, then we know that the native is mostly a *cardinal*, *fixed*, or *mutable type*, which tells us respectively whether he or she is most inclined to initiate things, to preserve things as they are, or to overturn what is old and prepare for the new.

The following sections on each house include new meanings implied by the Consideration Cycle and old meanings reported by traditional authors that the Cycle confirms. I end each section by explaining why we must reject the italicized meanings that were offered by some traditionalist authors, who I see no reason to name. It should not surprise us that the Cycle supports many house meanings given by ancient astrologers, for this is but one of many indicators in our world's literature that the natural logic of the Cycle has long been characteristic of humans. But note how all the meanings that I propose or accept are now logically related, thanks to the Cycle, and how each house is logically dependent on the houses that precede it. This tells us that we cannot understand any house fully until we have considered the preceding houses, going from the first to the last, or from the nominal 10th to the nominal 9th house.

---

[4] It is true that these six italicized words tell us if our context of reference is a house or a sign, but this is irrelevant since we always add the word 'house' or 'sign' to them anyway. So there's no reason why we can't speak of, say, 'a fixed house' as well as of 'a fixed sign', for we mean the same quality in either case.

1. Tenth House (or ♑). Root psychologic meaning: instincts and conscious awareness of events, or of what is really happening now. Basic dynamic: perceiving whole events, whether real or imagined.

This is the house of primary instincts, awareness of danger, objective realism, global perceptions, true beginnings, wholistic reasoning (whether real or fictional), outer-world activities, meeting others, leadership, piloting others through difficulties or obstacles, assuming responsibility for others, wishing, ambition, perfectionism, and skepticism towards anything or anyone who is unrealistic. It is present-oriented; it governs objective physical, intellectual, or scientific explorations, and hence study, pioneering, detection, and investigating. It represents the public space and the public at large, so it is the house of business and governmental affairs, of diplomacy, of socializing and social affairs on any level, of the social elite or mere celebrity, of performing or suffering investigations, and of one's reputation or status in society.

We look to the tenth houses (A10 and P10) to see how others perceive the native in a wholistic sense, and this is usually a superficial picture. It is thus the house of fame or infamy, celebrity or obscurity, honors or punishments, police matters, public trials, public statements, the public media, and any implied or psychic means of communication. That is, it does not govern explicit communication, but rather what one presumes is communicated by a global impression, including gestalt appearance, facial expressions, body language, and other gestures. P10 often overlaps A1, in which case one's self-concept and dignity are involved accordingly.

The tenth house reflects the source of one's life and one's support and security in the outer world. Therefore, in youth or so long as it is the case, it represents the mother or the father, or perhaps both parents or anyone else who performs a parental function. It pertains to all ancestors as the source of one's occurrence, so it also means one's physical and cultural heritage, or 'roots'. It governs our wishing (as defined earlier) and the state and condition of our happiness—which means the possibility of achieving our wishes, and hence our general state of contentment or dissatisfaction with the status quo or our present power over events.

Reject *moral responsibilities*, for while assuming responsibilities is a tenth-house matter, the morality of doing so is not. One's moral sense begins in tertiary reasoning (judgment) and it is perfected in secondary reconsiderations (thought). Also reject *political power*; involvement in politics is indeed a tenth house matter, but having power is an eighth and ninth house matter.

2. Eleventh House (or ♒). Root psychologic meaning: reductive reasoning and long-range or global planning of one's life and social goals. Basic dynamic: the reduction of a real and whole event to its personal significance.

The eleventh house reflects the nature and quality of the native's life plan and analytic-reductive reasoning in general. Here the objective realism of the tenth house has become subjective realism, or how one will personally cope with external events including nature, one's society or culture, politics, economics, public perceptions or investigations of oneself, and so on. It represents mental reflection on objective events that have occurred, especially those that affect one's place in the world, the development of one's culture or society, and an understanding of recent events in the light of history. It thus governs historical investigations of any kind, such as psychological or archeological inquiries, and dealing with abstractions or the unemotional psychologic drives, such as securing 'a place in history' or ensuring the survival of oneself or one's culture, family, or closest friends.

It is the house of close friends and of forming private (or even secret) associations, collectives, or clubs that are intended to help one achieve one's primary motives or long-range goals. It is therefore the house of allies and cohorts in general, and also of secret plans relating to personal or political conspiracies. Thus, it shows one's 'sense of honor', meaning how one deals with one's debts to individuals who either helped one personally or worked on a shared goal. Since this is a fixed house, the native will be unyielding in the long-range purposes indicated by the chart elements that influence it. P11 often overlaps A2, so the alliances or conspiracies involved often reflect active concerns for finances, proselytization, and so on.

Reject *wishes*, since our definition of this term applies to the tenth house only. Reject *acquaintances* for vagueness, since the eleventh house refers only to people who can advance or hinder one's long-range aspirations, and this excludes mere acquaintances. Reject *social life* for vagueness; having friends and socializing are different things. Socializing is a tenth-house matter, or in special senses a seventh- or eighth-house matter. Reject *hopes*, since hoping is a tertiary matter of speculative belief, and not the eleventh-house planning of life goals from one's understanding of reality. Reject *groups with a charitable or humane aim* because a house meaning is judgmentally neutral; the eleventh house is about any club, friendship, alliance, or coalition that works to advance private long-range motives, even if its purpose is not charitable or humane. That phrase—like *progressive* politics, social *reform*, and political *power*—expresses a judgment, when it should just state the subject that is to be judged in interpreting a chart. For the same reason, reject *new forms of social expression or relationship*; a native might propose new forms of it or might do what most people do, which is to rely on the old forms.

3. Twelfth House (or ♓). Root psychologic meaning: internalization, or withdrawal into the subjective analysis of events and any plans relative to them, and denial or negativism generally; conceiving oneness, separations, and aloneness. Basic dynamic: subjective reduction of a whole to nothing or next to nothing (one, existence, essence).

The twelfth house reflects our subconscious awareness of the essence of things, including the universal principles or limitations that are caused by nature or by one's society, race, culture, or life plan. It governs any form of denial and the consequences of that denial, because analytic reduction can be taken all the way to nothingness. It is in this sense, denial, that the twelfth house means death, the awareness of decay or dissolution, social conflicts on any level, all forms of negativism, imprisonment or hospitalization, destructive rulers, revolutions, poverty, maiming, or murder. For the same reason it also means loss, such as the loss of people who are close or just the loss of their help. It thus reflects secret sorrows, unseen problems, and being deprived or depriving others of life, liberty, property, sanity, physical health, faculties, or body parts.

This house is the main indicator of how one's personal enemies or any public (impersonal) political, commercial, or competitive conspiracies are likely to harm the native and of how a native may prevent or mitigate that harm by positive acts. Generally speaking, it means one's stored resources or accumulated debts; that is, both what one has and what one owes.

Because twelfth-house denials can include the denial of reality, a negative emphasis of either A12 or P12 can indicate theism and other forms of mysticism, spiritualism, hallucinations, delusions, illusions, fictions and fictional stories, and anything *occult*, which simply means hidden. This is especially so when P12 overlaps the subjective passions of A4. More often it overlaps A3, which means that the native gives expression to twelfth-house internalizations in some form of tangible analysis, design, or language—such as writing, mathematics, or music.

The twelfth house is the house of psychologic, astrological, philosophic, macrocosmic, microcosmic, genetic, psychic, or internal medical investigations, especially of a cerebral nature, so we can look to the chart elements that shade the twelfth house to see whether the native's mental investigative faculties are strong or weak or healthy or impaired.

This house governs all hidden matters and secrets in general, and hence hidden sources of personal support or of enmity and opposition. It is the house of hidden political or commercial schemes by oneself or others to either accomplish or defeat anyone's eleventh-house plans of purpose. Its shadings by other chart elements show the ability or inability to enlist others to join one's cause or to deceive others through secret conspiracies or with lies, rationalizations, or other fictions. It also governs the use of universal reasoning to resolve inner or social conflicts or to deny superficial distinctions. Generally, it shows us how the native ends primary reasoning and prepares for secondary analysis and objective study.

Reject *self-undoing*, not because it doesn't apply, but because it is ambiguous and doesn't include limitations imposed by others who are close or remote. It could mean the twelfth-house denial of the realism of primary reasoning or of tenth- and eleventh-house affairs, but it could also mean the self-undoing that results from the illogic of any psychologic reversal. Reject *fate* and *destiny* for vagueness (see Chapter 4). Reject *the unconscious (individual or collective)* and *karma* for being descriptive notions that have never been supported by realistic definitions, or causative propositions. Reject *the individual dissolves his relationship with the past cycle, proceeding to the next*, because this is inferred from the traditional misunderstanding of where the annual and daily cycles begin.

4. First House (or ♈). Root psychologic meaning: affirmation of life and thought; sensing the essence of things as universal laws. Basic dynamic: conceiving uniqueness and personal dignity, and defining dualities.

The first house governs self-reliance in general and personal initiatives. Psychologically, an emphasized first house indicates awareness of the essential self; that is, of one's self-concept, dignity, uniqueness, individuality, identity, or character—which are extensions of the twelfth-house conception of oneness per se. This is where we see how a native truly conceives of his or her congenital nature, or character, as opposed to his or her developed personality. The self-image that we shape in the first house is derived from the reductive reasoning (wishes, motives, and analysis) of the three prior houses, and it changes slowly. And because we think that this is what we are from birth, it shapes our notions of what we can or can't do in life.

By extension, this house also indicates the countenance or other aspects of appearance that reveal one's self-image to others. Though we look to the tenth-house to see how the whole person is displayed to the world, we look to the first house to see how one conceives of oneself, and this can be communicated to others, some others at least, whether one wishes it or not. It reflects a native's picture of his or her self as apart from all others or otherness, or as detached from one's environment and from one's society, race, culture, family, and other collectives. The signs and overlapping houses that influence A1 or P1 tell us much about the native's essential nature and basic self-conception, but the planets in those houses (if any) reveal this best.

The first house is where we reflect on the universal man or woman, so strength in this house inclines one to favor individualism as against collectivism, although other chart elements can support this or conflict with it. It also governs one's deductive reasoning or conscious realization in general, the externalization of abstract concepts into symbols or expressed ideas, true essences, one's sense of the essential, and any product of reduction or abstract conceptions.

But because it means dualism—such dichotomies as affirm-deny, one-zero, either-or, spirit-substance, and so on—it is also the house of personal uncertainty, skepticism, and social unreliability, even to the point of criminality if A1 or P1 is negatively shaded by other factors. A first-house or Arian emphasis often indicates a rebel of some kind; that is, an individualist who disdains not only collectives, but also their social or moral rules, just because these partialized commands by others have no universal or personal significance. The traditional view is that an emphasis here or in Aries indicates rebellion because this house and sign begin their cycles and rebels want new beginnings. But in fact they mean this for another reason: because within their range we do universal reasoning, the direct opposite of the synthetic reasoning of the seventh house or Libra that produces a collective's partialized rules. Rebelliousness can be caused by one's first-house uniqueness of thought or sense of independence as an individual, but it can also be caused by one's twelfth-house denials, and in the latter case the first house indicates how one lives with the consequences of those prior denials. Of course, other chart factors can make such natives highly conventional, in which case they are still rebels, but their rebellions are confined to a few social or ethical rules or to narrow contexts, such as intellectual or scientific pursuits.

Reject *personality*, since this is the house of the opposite concept, our congenital character. Reject *natural disposition* for its vagueness. Reject *the body* and *worldly outlook generally*, for the whole body and one's whole perspective is a tenth-house perception. Reject *conditions at birth* and *the start of things*, for these phrases imply 'true beginning' which applies only to the tenth house. The traditional confusion on this may be due to the common overlap of A1 and P10. Reject the term *ego* because it ambiguously implies two different notions: egotism or egoism. Egotism is a first-house impairment of thought, or self-concept, while moral egoism is a tertiary impairment of judgment. Reject *sensual experiences*, for these follow from first-house thought. Reject *life* or *outlook on life* for their vagueness, but keep them in the sense that this house is where one's life is affirmed—in A1 by oneself, and in P1 by others, by external events, or by one's actions in the overlapping house (usually A3, A4, or A5). Reject *subjective viewpoint*, for while the first house begins from the subjective analysis of the twelfth house, its dynamic is outer directed; it is about deducing objective facts and externalizing one's thoughts.

5. Second House (or ♉). Root psychologic meaning: pursuing the consequences of one's existence, self-concept, uniqueness, and expressing the implications of one's abstract concepts or universal principles; hence the products of one's deductions and individuality, including one's physical senses and speech. Basic dynamic: extending the One to a Some or the unique to a kind, hence sense-based classification and naming.

The second house pertains to our thought system only initially; after that, it is all about drawing the implications of the abstract concepts of the first house and objectively analyzing those implications. It is thus the house of all the external tangible things that result from our self-image and the deduced conclusions of our thought system. This broad statement is more precise than the traditional statements that relate this house to little more than money matters. Obviously what we earn from our mental labors is a tangible product of our thinking and so is included in the meaning of the second house, but there are many such products that have nothing to do with money. Every opinion we have or object we create from our thought system is a second-house product, as is our physical appearance to the extent that we shape it to make it accord with our current self-image.

As a fixed house that deals with our secondary opinions (and not our tertiary beliefs), its negative shading by other chart factors indicates opinionation and stubbornness in thought, while its positive shading may mean that the native is a fount of knowledge, but in the sense of isolated facts rather than total understanding. This house covers most of the subconscious phase of objective analysis, so it represents any place, from our minds to our libraries, where we store our thoughts or their products—such as words or other symbols, deduced facts or opinions, and money or personal possessions. Like the seventh house, where we store the products of objective synthesis, it is a material house, so its positive shadings show material reasonableness and generosity, while its negative shadings show stinginess, profligacy, or unreasonable generosity.

Because the second house reflects the retention of our money and other property, its positive or negative shading also indicates the gain or loss of these things—either in A2 by one's own acts or in P2 by others or external events. This house corresponds to the phase of the Cycle that rules division and hence the expansion, extension, or increase that division produces. Besides an increase in property, this also means cellular division and growth, and hence breeding humans or other animals or organisms, horticulture, agriculture, and the seeding of plants or ideas. P2 most often overlaps A5, which (for one thing) means that acting to breed children, a fifth-house matter, will have passive effects on one's opinions, finances, and other second-house matters. Children seen objectively as extensions of oneself are a second-house matter, but children seen subjectively as the product of passion and sex are a fifth-house matter. When negatively shaded, the second house indicates the lack of increase or growth, the loss of money or property, impotence, failure in any type of farming activity, and the spread of diseases.

Since our five senses expand our personal reach, the second house governs them and the technological devices that improve or replace them. In both natal and continuous horoscopy, we look to the condition of the second house to see the strength, weakness, or loss of sensual abilities. The dynamic of this house is objective analysis with the senses, which prepares one for the scientific, artistic, or sybaritic pursuits that sensual analyses imply. It represents not only words and other symbols, but also the means by which we externalize them, including our marks, gestures, and voice. Taurus corresponds to the second house and its symbol (♉) represents the throat, and indeed an emphasis in this sign or house often indicates a singer or speaker.

Reject *values and priorities* because these have nothing to do with the second quadrant; we determine values in the third quadrant and priorities in the first or third quadrant. Reject *loss or gain* for its vagueness; every house governs something that can be lost or gained, and since every house is value neutral, it only means loss or gain because of other chart elements that affect it. Similarly, reject *health* because all houses relate to some aspects of our health, and good or bad health depends not on the houses, but on how they are affected by other chart elements.

6. Third House (or ♊). Root psychologic meaning: studying and ordering material resources, thought conclusions (opinions), sense data, and how people or things are related or correspond. Basic Dynamic: relating and organizing thoughts and sense impressions.

The third house refers to all the implied consequences of the objective analysis of the second house. So it pertains to constructs based on words, sense impressions, dissections, separations, growth, expansion, accumulated money, and stored facts, opinions, or possessions. Its function is to compare, relate, and order those thoughts or things. This house tells us how the native arranges the parts of a whole, and its condition in a chart (how it is affected by other chart elements) can indicate whether this means order or chaos or beauty or ugliness. For better or worse as those shadings indicate, if those parts are tangible objects, they are aesthetically ordered; if they are words, scents, sounds, tastes, or visual images, they become poetry, perfumes, music, prepared foods, or drawings. And if they are universal ideas, they become ordered theoretical or scientific constructs.

It is the house of *correspondence* in both senses of that term: relation and communication. In the former sense, it pertains to people who are somehow like oneself, such as siblings, other relatives, or neighbors, and to one's community and local environment; accordingly, it governs travel over short or medium distances. In the latter sense, it is a house of study—not of second-house matters (facts, words or other symbols, opinions, sense impressions, or other data), but rather of how we relate and organize these objective things and communicate our views on them. So it also the house of writing, teaching, advertising, and spreading news or gossip by any means, but locally rather than globally. It governs all modes of explicit communication, and hence 'the media' and 'the press' and all the technological extensions of second-house speech or opinions.

Third-house communication can be theoretical, academic, scientific, or artistic. As art it will pertain to facts, thoughts, or the physical ordering of material things, when it is more aptly called 'design' or 'craft' rather than 'art'. We construct fictions, or stories in any medium, in the next quadrant, so third-house art is not about telling stories; it is about such activities as designing clothes, tools, rooms, furniture, houses, landscaping, and organizing sounds or words to compose music, poetry, nonfiction, or short messages such as notes or letters. Since the third house corresponds to the end of the analytic half of the Consideration Cycle, it is past-oriented, so it reflects one's interest in history, with emphasis on comparing different periods, individuals, or other things over time. Other chart factors aside, biographies and creative histories are as close as its writings come to story-telling. In its academic form, it governs informal teaching or teaching fundamental things of general value, so it differs from the ninth house which governs formal teaching that prepares people for a broad understanding or for specific professions.

The third house also indicates if the native pursues sensual pleasures much or little, and the chart elements affecting it show which pleasures are preferred. It governs shopping, or buying things with one's money, and bartering or negotiating with one's possessions. Analytic reasoning ends here; all that follows is synthetic, or constructive and future oriented.

Reject *traveling* for vagueness; the modes of travel are ruled by the third house, but long-distance trips or globe-hopping are ruled by the ninth house. Reject *education* for being too general; teaching and learning apply to the third house, but they do so only in the forms just specified. Reject *the mental equipment with which we are born*, for while the third house uses that tenth- to first-house mental equipment, it is mainly a physical house. Also reject vague terms such as *the lower mind, superficialities, everyday matters, mental inclinations and abilities*, and *minor impressions made upon the physical brain*. There is no 'higher' or 'lower' mind, for these are just descriptive terms; there is only reasoning that is objective or subjective and more or less fundamental. What we learn in the second quadrant is more objective than what we learn in the third quadrant and more fundamental than what we learn in the third or fourth quadrants. Ninth-house knowledge (understanding) can be superior to third-house knowledge (facts), in the sense that knowing the whole is superior to knowing the parts, but only if its prior analytic theory and facts are sound. As our intellectual history testifies profusely, ninth-house understanding that lacks analytic soundness, such as a knowledge of religions or other mystical 'philosophies', is false, and being false is worse than being superficial.

7. Fourth House (or ♋). Root psychologic meaning: emotive response to sensual intake, one's environment, and the effects of the past; discriminatory selections based on the passions. Basic dynamic: subjective focusing on a part or parts for further consideration.

The fourth house indicates how the native responds to any third-house matter, such as sensual stimulation, teaching, or explicit communications, including the advice of elders in childhood and youth. It deals with past events, a third-house issue, only in the sense that it is a subjective response to them. It refers to the home and home life because that is a narrowing (by oneself in A4 or by others or external circumstances in P4) of one's third-house community or local environment down to one's private and subjective space. It thus refers to all the objects in one's private space and to any possessions that are kept close because they elicit a specific passion. The fourth house also means land or other property associated with one's private space, at home or elsewhere, and so it governs dealing with land or real estate in general.

Similarly, it also reflects our diet, since (like sense data) we take in food in the third house and then decide in the fourth house whether it is or isn't good for us and whether we desire to have it or avoid it. Our third-house food choices are sybaritic, meaning that we eat something because it tastes and smells good, with no regard for its later internal effects. But a fourth-house food choice is passionate; we decide to eat something because we love it, and we love it for internal reasons such as easy digestion, nutritional value, or how it makes us feel.

This is so with love partners also. Other chart factors aside, a strong and positively shaded fourth house or seventh sign (♋) leads one, soon enough if not initially, to dislike the flirtations and promiscuity of the third house. It inclines one to prefer having one partner who is deeply loved and deeply loving. This may describe a *romantic*, but not the *romanticism* of the fifth and sixth houses (or ♌ and ♍), where a passion is transformed first into a general need and then into a fictional ideal.

As the house of the desires that begin our tertiary reasoning, the fourth house is associated with those schools of modern psychology that emphasize the passions or one's emotional reactions to third-house experiences. These schools attempt to explain people solely in fourth-house terms, such as how their personality was affected by their relatives, home scene, early-life experiences, or passion determinations. But we realists reject this partialistic view, for we know that our development is not written on a blank slate, but rather on our congenital character, which does far more to determine our present personality than our postnatal experiences ordinarily do. Still, we can look to A4 and P4 to see the source of the experiences that those psychologists assume, on little more than anecdotal evidence, can affect the personality of some persons.

The fourth house is where we see the *effects* of any real and whole *cause*, so if our context is a person's life, it refers to the effects of that life, which means one's estate or anything else that one may leave after death for specific others or posterity. For the same reason, it refers to one's subjective responses to all past events, whether recent or historical.

The fourth house (or ♋) is a private subjective realm, and since there are three basic states of subjectivity, it shares this quality with the twelfth house (or ♓) and the ninth house (or ♐). It also shows how one actively achieves (in A4) or passively acquires (in P4) *inner* security. And so, as with the tenth house drive for outer security, it refers to anyone—parent or parents, friends, spouse, children, lovers, or others—who once provided or now provide that inner feeling of emotional security. These effects on the personality also extend to what one learned from one's elders and to what, for any reason, one subjectively prefers to study or read. As the beginning of our synthetic reasoning, this house shows the desires that drive all of our speculative or practical acts, and its shadings by other elements will show whether those passions are or are not healthy for us or beneficial for our society.

Reject *the beginning of life* for vagueness as to which kind of 'beginning' is meant, for that term has four senses: *beginning* (♑/10ᵗʰ), *conception* (♈/1ˢᵗ), *formation* (♋/4ᵗʰ), and *birth* (♎/7ᵗʰ). The fourth house means only formation, which is constructing new things from a piece or pieces of an existing whole. Positively a formation could be the growth of muscles or mental acuity, and negatively it could be the beginning of a tumor or epidemic. Reject *hereditary influences or tendencies*, since all hereditary effects are in us when our life begins, and so we must look to the tenth house for these. The fourth-house (or ♋) effects on a native are all postnatal. Reject the old notions of *later years, the state of things at the close of life*, and *the end of life*. The Cycle tells us that the ninth house (or ♐) shows the end of a life or of any other whole event we consider. The twelfth house can also mean 'the end of life' because it reflects willful denial (A12) or external circumstances that deny (P12), but denial aborts a cycle prematurely, it doesn't end it naturally. Thus 'end of life' conditions and death are twelfth-house matters when some form of denial is involved, and eighth-house matters when they result from externally imposed limitations, including the lack of proper care by others or institutions. Otherwise, 'the end of life', death, and old age are ninth-house matters. And the fact that the fourth house relates to what one leaves behind after death doesn't mean that it refers to death or the native's old age, for these meanings would contradict its fundamental meaning, which is formation.

8. Fifth House (or ♌). Root psychologic meaning: subjective synthesis, creative fabrications, transforming passions into general needs, idealizations, and subjective evaluations of the worth of people, things, or ideas. Basic dynamic: expanding on the emotions.

This is the house where the native assigns a subjective value to things and devises short-term plans for achieving specific or general personal desires, so it is where one's needs are prioritized according to their perceived worth. Its main focus is on the worth of things, but it also rules the native's tactics and the people or resources needed to perform those short-term actions.

It is the house of 'make believe' because its reasoning is subjective synthesis, which is always arbitrary and speculative. It reflects the fictional arts, all forms of story-telling in words, music, drama, graphics, sculpture, and so on. It also governs intellectual, scientific, or mystical speculation, probability hypotheses, all physical, intellectual, scientific, social, or financial risk-taking, and any form of wishful thinking, including theism or other forms of mysticism and magic. It is the house of gambling, games, sports, play, leisure time, love affairs, and pleasure-seeking, but in a deeper, or more subjective, sense than second-quadrant sensual stimulation.

The fifth house governs creative expression, especially in those ways that involve bodily display or any type of story telling. This can mean creating stories for any medium of art or entertainment, but it can also mean crafting fictions, rationalizations, or lies for any purpose.

Many traditionalists call it the house of 'true love', and this is so if one means by that a love based on sex or another passion that one desires never to surrender. A 'true love' might live on throughout later life simply because it was arrested in this fixed house. An emphasized fifth house indicates romanticism and idealism in one's reasoning, but other chart factors could make one either persistent or variable in such beliefs.

This house reflects one's offspring since they are the products of passion and the need for sex, and its shadings indicate the ability or inability to procreate. A5 commonly overlaps P2, and often children are the unintended second-house consequences of the first house, or one's self. But the fifth house also refers to children that one supervises, cares for, teaches, or plays with. Fifth-house reasoning is the reasoning of children and immature adults, so a planet in this house shows how the native deals with children, and many planets in it show a preoccupation with children or with childish, fictional, speculative, physical, pleasurable, or risk-taking activities.

If A5 or P5 is negatively or excessively emphasized in the chart, the fixity of this house may arrest the native's personality in its development, usually soon after puberty. This third-quadrant immaturity—which starts with the fourth house passions, home, parental figures, and formative teachings and continues in the fifth house with sexual activities, play, fictions, and unrealistic reasoning—is one of the congenital causes of homosexuality in either gender. Other factors also play a role, of course, since most immature people are not homosexual and many heterosexual relationships are also based on immaturity. But immaturity, or arrested development, is a necessary condition for adult homosexuality, which (in the sense that doesn't mean a total life style) is just the extension into later life of sexual play that is common among adolescents.

In general, we know immature adults from their continued devotion to the fifth-house activities that preoccupy adolescents—such as sports, the cinema, the theatre, other entertainment media, story-telling, music, dancing, games, gambling, parties, social functions, gangs, clubs, sex, pornography, alcohol, drugs, biased criticisms of people or things, excessive physical training or exertions, physicality per se, exhibiting one's body or talents, displaying one's religion, politics, or other personal beliefs, and participating in activities with children.

Reject *sensations* for being second-house experiences, or the opposite of the deeper passions that drive fifth-house matters. Reject *generative powers* for vagueness; it could mean creative powers, virility, tissue regeneration, the eighth- or ninth-house senses of power, or something else. Reject *self-expression* for ambiguity; this term confuses the third-house expressions of our essential self with the fifth-house displays of our body, talents, or creative products. Reject *casual relationships* for not being always the case. I called these 'casual friendships' above, meaning the short-term relationships that we initially form only to gratify our desires or a tactical goal. But these can last as long as the initial passion or need continues. In fact, anyone who is at first just a friend or a convenience for us can become a lifelong companion.

9. Sixth House (or ♍). Root psychologic meaning: objectifying subjective synthetic reasoning (such as one's needs, plans of action, hopes, ideals, and beliefs), considering the possible consequences of performing acts related to them, and forming class notions and terms. Basic dynamic: extending a thing's parts to a hypothetical concrete conception.

The sixth house shows how one prepares to concretize one's ideals, speculations, or plans of action, including bringing people or other resources together for practical goals. Its condition indicates a native's routine work activities—which can be for oneself or for others as an employee, subordinate, helper, coworker, or to serve others or the public in general. It shows if one is a strong or weak coordinator or organizer, and if one is physically or mentally capable of the work one undertakes.

Physical work is a strain and mental work is a source of stress, and both can cause illness; stress is also caused by the anxieties that arise in this house due to excessive speculations, hoping, or risk-taking. The sixth house is thus an indicator of physical or mental sickness and anxiety, and it tells us if the native's functional machinery works well or needs repair. If A6 overlaps P4, the native probably prefers to work at home or some other private place.

Above all, though many traditionalists ignore this function, the sixth house (and ♍) is the house of *judgment*, which we considered earlier, so it refers to judgments, critics, and judges. It takes the subjective evaluations of the worth of people or things in the fifth house and objectifies them to reach general conclusions on values or morals. We cannot have success in sixth-house matters like health, morals, or work if our judgment is poor, which will happen if other chart elements negatively shade this house or if one's judgment system is impaired by impulse.

One's psychologic sense of *duty to others* arises in the sixth house (or ♍), and it does so in everyone, though immoral or selfish people usually deny their obligations to others with harmful avoidance structures. The sixth house is where, voluntarily or not, we work to achieve our needs or meet our duties to specific others, to groups, or humanity in general. On the one hand it refers to one's employment or subordination by others and to any kind of menial work we must do, and on the other hand it refers to our own employees, servants, helpers, dependents, or subordinates.

The sixth house refers to the products of our mind and body. In the former case, it shows the ways in which we objectively explain and formalize our creative mental products. In fact, it is the house of explanation, so if it is negatively shaded by impulse, signs, or planets, one will not explain one's acts or judgments to others or one will lie about them, but if it is positively shaded, one will try to explain the reasons for one's acts or judgments. As for the body, this house refers not only to its waste products, but to every other kinds of waste also, and hence to the medical and sanitation professions, industries, or methods that deal with waste of any kind. It also shows a native's innate proclivity to good or bad personal hygiene or dietary practices.

But in all these respects—daily work, anxiety, sickness, health measures, and one's critical, moral, or objective judgments—the sixth house causes conflicts with others. This is why it also reflects the enemies we make in the course of our work or service to others, in expressing our beliefs or criticisms of others, or in trying to meet our personal needs. People take offense at our criticisms of them, especially when these are true, but they can also dislike us because they have conflicting hopes and plans with respect to any work or service goals that we share with them, or because their subjective beliefs on morals, values, ideals, work methods, or other judgments conflict with ours.

Emphasis in A6, P6, or Virgo indicates that the native is imaginative, future-oriented, anxious about future events, and inclined to ignore or denigrate the past, as the planets, impulses, signs, or overlapping houses will indicate.

Reject *private enemies* for vagueness, since it could mean personal or impersonal enemies, and only the former are sixth-house enemies. It is also said that the sixth house reflects *secret enemies*, but this term applies more to the subjective twelfth house, which reflects conspiracies to deny our motives or long-range plans, either by people we know or, more often, by total strangers (such as the governmental or corporate agents who try to steal what we own). Since the sixth house *objectifies* the subjective processes of the fourth and fifth houses, our enemies in its affairs are all people who we know from our home, school, work, or community who openly express to us or to others their dislike for our judgments, morals, beliefs, work efforts, or plans of action.

10. Seventh House (or ♎). Root psychologic meaning: cognizing objective states of being (substance, total form) and how people or things are alike by association, hence class-based cognitions and reasoning, and the construction of ordinary or specialized languages. Basic dynamic: the practical application of substances or idealized conceptions.

The seventh house is where we store our concrete conceptions of tangible external realities. It is where we consider, by class comparisons, what we are or are not in the concrete sense of our personality, or present state of being. Here we also consider humanity and its needs, and, in descriptive class terms, how other humans are like us or unlike us.

Two points that traditionalists miss is that this house is about form and accumulation. As the realm of form and formalistic reasoning, it is the house of languages, rules, jurisprudence, ideal governments or work methods, formal agreements or disagreements, all scientific, academic, and mystical disciplines as constructs, and the surface appearance of things. In the latter respect, it joins both the tenth house (event appearance) and third house (design) in dealing with attempts at beautification, cosmetics, and adorning the body or anything else with things of value, decorations, or messages (advertising). As the realm of accumulation, it is the house of storage, savings, exchanges, and all forms of commerce, bartering, negotiation, or bargaining.

The meanings *marriage* and *partnerships* remain for this house, but not as broadly as it is traditionally put, for it means these things only in the sense of formal agreements that bind people and obligate them to follow expressed rules. A relationship can exist without agreed rules, but a seventh-house relationship exists only if words are said, contracts are signed, or rules are written that define some concrete relationship, legal collective, moral obligation, or formal duty. The chart elements that shade this house usually indicate the type of person that one prefers as a formal partner (A7) or that one will encounter by chance (P7). Positively, it is the house of solemn oaths; negatively, it is the house of insincere promises, false contracts, and those meaningless rituals, oaths, or pledges of allegiance that our ill-conceived governments or other artificial formal collectives demand of us.

The seventh house corresponds to the part of the Consideration Cycle where we form language systems from our class-based words, numbers, musical notes, or other symbols. So, like the third house, it governs communications, but third-house messages (such as letters, poetry, or designs) are less formal. Seventh-house messages are not directed to specific individuals, but to specific classes of people or to all humans. They convey one's ideals, fictions, beliefs, morals, tertiary hypotheses of a scientific, psychologic, or mystical nature, formal warnings, notions on proper work methods or social organization, or the rules of a collective. We can distinguish it from the third house by saying that it is the house of proselytization rather than of communication. It governs public messages to any class of people, such as political or religious messages and advertising or publishing in general. But since its content was previously created by subjective tertiary reasoning, the proselytizer and the creator are often not the same person, which is why the seventh house (or ♎) also indicates opportunism or plagiarism.

The relationships indicated by this house pertain only to people with whom we have made formal seventh-house agreements. For instance, if you marry a lover (fifth house) or start a business with a relative (third house) or friend (eleventh or fifth house), your chart refers to that person in the seventh house as well. Formal agreements can result from a friendship or family relationship, but more often they result from a proposal by one party to an unrelated party that a formal union between them will have mutual benefits. Thus the seventh house also reflects our attitude to opportunism and competition, for our benefit or that of others, as our impulse in judgment indicates. Similarly, relationships with our twelfth- or sixth-house enemies only become seventh-house relationships if they lead to overt hostility—such as revolutions, wars, coups d'état, riots, civil disobedience, personal or class-action lawsuits, criminal or civil trials, slander, gossip, libel, physical fights, oral or written disputes, legal separations or divorces of any kind, proxy fights or other ownership contests, and so on.

On the constructive side, however, this is the house of cooperation, and hence of politeness, tact, diplomacy, etiquette, kindness, and civility in speech and manner. These social gifts are essential to maintain cooperation, commerce, and formal unions, but most people of an S&E generation (♀+) lack these social graces because they are born without compassion.

Reject *all direct close personal relationships* and *realizing the nature of relationship* for their imprecision. The seventh house does not refer to 'all' relationships but only to formal ones, which excludes many of our 'close' ones, and in it we only 'realize the nature of' formal relationships. Reject *open enemies*, a sixth-house matter; the seventh house is not about our sixth- or twelfth-house enemies, it is about open hostilities with anyone, enemy or not. Reject *individual character and humane tendencies*; the former because the seventh-house concept of our uniqueness is our present personality and not our innate character, and the latter because humaneness is a judgment and every chart sector is neutral until we judge it. People with a seventh-house emphasis might be humane or might be deceitful opportunists, and both types are common in seventh-house fields such as politics, law, advertising, and religion. As *Appendix B* confirms, humanism is a function of planetary charges, not of chart sectors; specifically, it is unselfishness in judgment (☿-) and individualism, or leftism, in power (☉+).

11. Eighth House (or ♏). Root psychologic meaning: awareness of one's personal limitations and of one's dependence on real or imagined external sources for help. Basic dynamic: reducing external reality to the people and things that are personally useful.

The eighth house, which is the house of external power, is self-contradictory. It is *the help-and-limit house*, because we can't get help from external sources without getting restrictions too. It is about how others or otherness help us or limit us, in a reductive sense. Once we dismiss our mystics' absurd claim that their fictional deities or spirits can help or punish us, we see, first, that we are most helped and limited by nature, especially the local or regional environment to which we are presently confined. Next comes the help received and limitations imposed by others—not by all others (a seventh-house notion), but reductively by formal collectives, meaning humans who are organized to help or restrict individuals like us. So the 'help-and-limit' nature of this house (or ♏) means what we receive from our near environment, our social collectives, and individuals who are acting for or against us in a social role.

This is the house of all the formal collectives or artificial legal entities that we construct from the rules of the seventh house, which are more often arbitrary than objective. It pertains to every natural or social form through which external power reaches us. It reflects individuals who help and limit us. Usually these are people who don't know us personally or who are acting as agents of a collective or a formal profession, such as police or doctors, but otherwise they are the relatives, friends, acquaintances, enemies, or competitors of the other houses. Here the general opportunism of the seventh-house is reduced to the specific collectives, institutions, and methods through which people exploit others or nature. This led traditionalists to equate this house to destruction, when in fact it reflects the scorpionic dichotomy of construction and destruction.

Given this dichotomy, the eighth is the house of mystics, politicians, academics, and scientists who hypothesize that our lives are controlled by external factors such as fictional gods, constitutions or other legal precedents, hypothetical forces such as our history or our racial, cultural, or artistic heritage, a collective unconscious, genetics, or endless evolutionary progress. However much these people may help us, their collectivistic hypotheses on our nature and situation do even more to limit us. Politicians strongly influenced by this house (or ♏) will with one face swear that they mean to help us, and with their other face act to limit or destroy us.

Traditional texts call the eighth house 'the house of death', but this association applies only because its root meaning is *external power*, which limits us. It doesn't mean internally caused limitations, for these are shown in the three subjective areas of a house cycle. As "all the power that we have not," the eighth house represents nature and its forces, other people or living things in our society or environment, and all governments, corporations, or other formal collectives that affect us, any of which can cause us to die or to have to deal with death. And since these sources can benefit us too, this is the house of value or money received from a death or from any collective, and of the recuperative powers dispensed by nature or medicines. Traditionalists often call recuperation 'regeneration'; this is acceptable if we mean cellular regeneration, but not if we mean new lives, as in the mystical hypothesis of reincarnation. This fiction led some to say that the eighth is a house of 'birth', but no fixed house can mean any type of beginning.

The eighth house is not 'the house of death', but only a house of some causes of death and of dealing with death personally or professionally. On the personal level, it shows the external events or conditions that limit our personal power so severely that our life will be terminated later as indicated by the ninth house, which is a house of death. It also shows whether we ponder about death, perhaps by speculating on alternatives to it like heaven or reincarnation. Such fictions led some to call it 'the house of the occult', and indeed many mystics have eighth-house emphasis in their charts, but then so do many nonmystical scientists and professionals.

This house refers to those who deal with death routinely, such as doctors, morticians, spiritualists, agents of religious corporations, political assassins, murderers for profit, agents of a state such as police and other law-enforcement officials, all military personnel, spies, informers, coroners, and judges. It is the house of government, corporations, banks and markets and other financial institutions, clubs, courts of law, and armed forces of any kind. In general terms, it governs any form of restricting people as individuals or of defeating people who oppose a specific collective. All collectives work to suppress individuals, and most do so by imposing rules, imprisonment, fines, or poverty, or by dispensing death, defamation, injury, or disease. This is the house of legacies, inheritances, and laws or judgments related to death, but it is not the house of funerals or commemorations, which are tenth-house ceremonies that follow death.

As *Figures 2b* and *3* indicate, the entire fourth quadrant has a reductive dynamic. The seventh house means a beginning in the sense of birth, or completed form, and that born thing is then reduced through the eighth and ninth houses to death, which prompts a new event in the tenth (or literal first) house. The seventh house also means all humanity, an All that is reduced in the eighth house to mean only the collectives that affect us, which are then further reduced until, in the ninth house, we are referring to the individual only.

The traditional terms *birth*, *death*, and *beginnings and endings* just don't apply to the eighth house. Also reject *sexual relationships and deeply committed relationships of all kinds*, because the former are fifth-house matters and the latter is a judgment. Eighth-house and fifth-house matters are associated only because A8 often overlaps P5, but physicality and sexual activities don't pertain to the eighth house itself; they affect it only passively. This house is where we deal with the formal commitments made by seventh-house contracts or rules, but we can't call these 'deep' until we judge a specific chart. Reject *expansion of relationship*, for the eighth house is purely reductive; it reduces all humanity to those who are close enough to us to help or harm us through their social roles or their collectives' rules. Formal relationships that continue into the eighth house don't expand, they involute, and 'expanding a relationship' by adding people to it gives us a new seventh-house relationship. For the same reason, reject *expansion of world view*, for the eighth house is where we reduce our world view to what affects us personally or is of practical use to us.

12. Ninth House (or ♐). Root psychologic meaning: reaching an understanding and decision on an issue, developing a sense of one's personal physical and mental powers and preferred forms of activity, and completing things. Basic dynamic: learning for understanding rather than for facts, terminating events, and preparing for new events.

To understand the ninth house correctly, we must have considered all the previous houses, because this is where we integrate their elements and complete a line of reasoning. Like the tenth house, it is a house of wholistic reasoning. Its function is to reach an integrated understanding of an issue, decide on it, and anticipate the new events or conditions that will result if one acts on it. Some might describe this anticipatory ability as 'intuition', but I reserve that term for fourth-house anticipations and use 'instinct' instead when I mean the wholistic reasoning of the prime interval, the halves of which fall in the ninth and tenth houses. I also assume from the available evidence that we can be born with stronger or weaker instincts than others have, that we can develop these further through experience or formal learning, and that we also inherit some instincts from our ancestors. In any case, the ninth house indicates whether one's instinctive ability to anticipate future events or conditions is strong or weak, and how decisive one is or is not in terminating events and moving on to new ones.

The ninth house governs completed intellectual achievements. It governs higher education as traditionalists say, but more generally it governs any personal achievement that enhances an individual's power, even if it is not publicly recognized through a tenth-house ceremony.

Its functions reflect the third kind of subjectivity in the Cycle. This is not subjectivity in its first-quadrant *mental* sense (subjective analysis) or its third-quadrant *physical* sense (subjective synthesis), but rather in the terminating sense that combines our mental and physical faculties in decision and action. Other chart elements will show whether the native prefers (or is better at) mental or physical activities or both. So the ninth house (or ♐) should not be interpreted, as it so often is, as just an intellectual area, for it is often emphasized in the charts of physically powerful athletes or combatants. This is true also of the fourth and fifth houses (or ♋ or ♌), but the physical activities associated with these houses require less mental ability.

The ninth house reflects one's *wholistic learning* and hence one's *freedom*. When I said earlier that our only real freedom is our personal power, I meant that any other sense of the term, such as being independent or unrestricted, is partialistic. Because we live in a world of others and otherness, we either have personal power or we are not free.

The essential point about the ninth house is that it reflects the natural end, or completion, of any cycle, and since in one sense 'completion' means achievement, it reflects our personal achievements. But in another sense 'completion' means death or any other form of termination. As I said, the eighth house only shows the causes of death, and the twelfth house is associated with death only because one of its meanings is the denial of an event by will. But the ninth house means death in a broader sense because it means the natural end of a cycle, and so it is where we say, "This is finished," or "The breath goes now." Note also that A9 often overlaps P6, in which case sixth-house health and work matters play a passive role in promoting or delaying death or other ninth-house terminations, such as resignation or retirement from a job or task.

Epistemically, the ninth and tenth houses correspond to wholistic reasoning, while the third and fourth houses correspond to partialistic reasoning. So traditionally the ninth house is said, in opposition to the third house, to govern long journeys and foreign countries, as well as one's remote relatives or relatives of one's relatives. The tenth house reflects our entire environment, so it refers to foreign nations, international affairs, diplomacy, and dealing with remote events. The ninth house means this also, except that, unlike the objective tenth house, it is personal and subjective. Accordingly, the ninth house reflects our personal travel to foreign nations or other remote places, as well as to our personal achievements in dealing with anything pertaining to global or international affairs, relations, trade, or wars and other conflicts.

Reject *foreign countries and cultures* and *worldwide contacts* to whatever extent these mean objective tenth house matters, since the ninth house cannot mean anything that is not personal and subjective. Reject *writings* for vagueness; ninth-house writings are those that are prepared for publication and broad public distribution in the tenth house, as distinct from third-house writings that are private or have a smaller audience or are intended for self-expression, narrow or local distribution, fourth-house passion gratifications, or to explore scientific, philosophic, or theistic hypotheses. Reject *invention*, unless this only means novel ways of understanding and behaving; otherwise we invent mental or physical things earlier in the Cycle, long before we apply them in our ninth-house decisions to act.

Reject *religion* for irrelevance and ambiguity. The irrelevance is that we can associate the ninth house with the term 'religion' only in the same sense that we associate it with any other professional discipline or area of academic study. The ambiguity is that most people use 'religion' to mean both a theistic belief and a corporation that speaks for a theistic belief. A religion in this latter sense, a formal business, is not governed by the subjective and personal ninth house, but rather by the objective eighth house which governs all collectives. And if by 'religion' one does means a theistic belief, then this has nothing to do with any fourth-quadrant house, since we create or adopt all of our beliefs in the third quadrant. Traditionalists who make this claim assume that when the ninth house is emphasized by tenanting planets, the native has 'religiosity' in some sense. But this doesn't follow, as a broad review of timed natal charts shows. If you examine many timed charts of theists or religionists, you will find, as I have, that their ninth houses (counting both A9 and P9 instances) are just as often void of planets as not, and that this same inconclusive result occurs when we examine the timed charts of many nontheists. In short, this traditional association cannot be statistically supported.

The Body Parts. I haven't mentioned the parts of the body that are traditionally associated with the houses and signs, for two reasons. Medical astrology is an important subject, so I believe that any astrologer who writes on it should have much medical knowledge, which I do not. Also, in the texts I have seen on that subject, I couldn't confirm the proposed associations statistically. We sorely need a large database of individuals with timed birth data that indicates the natives' major illnesses and whether these were congenital or experiential and fatal or not. But even more than that, we need a realistic astrologer with physiological knowledge who will devise, test, and propose a new and sound hypothesis on the subject. At present, we have only some ancient and modern guesses on it, mere descriptions that sometimes apply but that, like the four ancient elements, have no theoretical basis and have not been supported by empirical testing. The most familiar of these is the simplistic illustration that relates some body parts from head to foot to the signs from Aries to Pisces.

Nevertheless, I will mention the traditional associations, though I caution you in their use. The following is a composite of the views of two prominent astrologers as to which body parts are governed by which houses or signs: **10/♑** knees and spleen. **11/♒** lower legs, calves, ankles. **12/♓** feet and toes. **1/♈** head and face. **2/♉** neck, throat, and ears. **3/♊** arms, shoulders, collarbone, hands, lungs, and nervous system. **4/♋** the breast, stomach, and digestive organs. **5/♌** the heart, sides, and upper back. **6/♍** bowels and solar plexus. **7/♎** loins, ovaries, and lower back. **8/♏** bladder, sex organs, and the generative system. **9/♐** liver, hips, thighs, and hams.[5]

---

[5] I formed this composite from Alan Leo's 1911 work *How to Judge a Nativity* (London: L.N. Fowler & Co. Ltd.) and Llewellyn George's 1910 work *A to Z Horoscope Maker and Delineator* (St. Paul: Llewellyn Publications), both of which were printed in many later editions. Leo's work associates these parts with the houses and George's work with the signs, but both accepted the correspondence of the signs and houses. Later astrologers adopted these views with little criticism, but astrologers are cautious in their use because they are incomplete and unsupported by theory or testing.

Planetary Rulership

Undoubtedly the worst case of bad synthetic guessing in traditional astrology is its illogical conception of the planetary rulership of the signs and the houses. And yet this ancient scheme—as amended by modern-era astrologers after the planets Uranus, Neptune, and Pluto were detected—persists in the science, apparently for no better reason than blind faith in tradition. There is no theory or empirical support anywhere in the traditional literature for its arbitrary claims that the planets rule certain signs and houses, and that in other signs they can be 'exalted' or in their 'fall' or 'detriment'. And the old notions of 'dispositor' planets and a 'chart ruler', no matter what rulership scheme they are based on, cannot be meaningful.

The most widely used form of that old scheme today is probably this one, which has ten planets ruling twelve signs or houses. ♄ rules ♑ and the 10th house. ♅ rules ♒ and 11. ♆ rules ♓ and 12. ♂ rules ♈ and 1. ♀ rules ♉ and 2. ☿ rules ♊ and 3. ☽ rules ♋ and 4. ☉ rules ♌ and 5. ☿ *also* rules ♍ and 6. ♀ *also* rules ♎ and 7. ♇ rules ♏ and 8. And ♃ rules ♐ and 9.

Some astrologers still accept this old scheme because it sometimes seems to work, but even with the wide availability of computers in recent decades, they never tested it rigorously. They can't, actually, because you can't test which planet functions best in a sign or house if you don't have a psychologic theory to tell you what the planets, signs, and houses mean. Meaning is psychologic; it is not a detached fact of reality that can be inferred from mere observations.

But in realistic astrology our hypothesis on planetary rulers is supported by a metaphysics and an empirically verifiable psychologic theory. *Figure A* in *Appendix A* shows our basic planetary rulership scheme for the signs. This is essentially the same scheme as our Impulse Pattern, so if we deny or revise it, we will also have to deny or revise the Impulse Pattern.

When I first considered this issue, I had only the Consideration Cycle and the Impulse Pattern as shown in *Figure 6*. Then I applied the Cycle to a horoscope's annual and daily cycles by aligning their beginning points, and I speculated that the charges required by my psychologic theory were determined by the planets' position in what the ancients called the 'masculine' and 'feminine' signs. I then had to decide which planet determines the charge at each pole of each psychologic system, and I did this by trial and error, testing the planets' established meanings against the Cycle until I reached the rulership solution in *Figure A*. If this were an astrological textbook, I would take the space needed to explain why I assigned the ten planets in the Cycle as I did and why I believe that my rulership scheme is the best one, but given the other goals of this work, my earlier comments on the Cycle and the planets must suffice.

My rulership solution can be refuted either by creating alternative theories that imply a different scheme or, more simply, by testing the Impulse Pattern in practice. If it holds up in that testing, then you have good reason to accept it and its rulership arrangement. If it doesn't, then the failure of the traditional scheme requires you either to create a new theory and rulership hypothesis or to reject the whole notion of planetary rulers until someone else creates one.

Though I had no doubts about the planetary rulers as shown in *Figure A*, I sensed in my interpretive work that we needed more rulership distinctions than it gave us, so I didn't assume that the problem was solved. The purpose of that figure was only to apply the Impulse Pattern to the signs, not to propose a complete solution on rulership. It gives each planet rule over a tenth of the 360° cycle, or of 36° rather than the traditional 30° range that requires a duplicate rulership for two signs and houses. Traditionalists achieve their one-sign-to-one-house fiction by adding the rule that whichever planet rules the sign on the cusp of a house rules the entire house. But in realistic astrology we apply planetary rulership to a cycle's degrees, not to its signs or houses, so that each planet, in the logical order of the Cycle, rules a 36° range.

But then my suspicion that we needed further distinctions to give us a smaller range of rulership than 36° was supported by my domification solution, the PA method. This tells us that there are twenty-four houses in the daily cycle, twelve in the horizon system and twelve in the meridian system, and that these two motion systems begin at different points in the zodiac. It follows that a timed chart has two rulership schemes, not one. It has ten *active rulers* and ten *passive rulers*, with the planets of each set following the Cycle's logical order. In our standard rulership pattern, which assumes a chart with 90° quadrants, the passive set begins 90° before the active set, giving us twenty planets around the cycle rather than ten. Thus, each 18° segment of the cycle has both an active and a passive ruler, which differ in the same way that an active and a passive house do. *Figure 8* shows this standard, with the passive rulers on the inner circle.

Though this figure speaks for itself, it may help to mention a few of its parts. We see that the 36° segment from 0°♑ to 6°♒ is ruled actively by the moon, and that its first 18° is passively ruled by Pluto and its last 18° by Jupiter. One difference in the meaning of these 18° segments is that one's active wishing (☽) is passively influenced in the first segment by *all humanity* (♀) and in the second by *specific collectives* (♃). So a planet in the first segment is a global and humanistic influence in the chart, while one in the second segment is a narrowed collectivistic influence. Applied to the houses instead, these segments would mean, for instance, that one's active choice of career (10th house) is passively influenced either by the needs of all people (♀) or only by the needs of the collectives (♃) to which one personally belongs.

For simplicity, I will speak now only of the signs. A passive rulership by the sun is fitting for Pisces, a sign that influences conspiracies for personal power even as it works to prevent any open appearance of such power. The passive rulership by Saturn of 24°♉ to 12°♊ is appropriate also, since this 18° second-quadrant segment is strong in the natal charts of hard-working system builders (♄)—such as Wagner, Hegel, Kant, Dostoyevsky, Russell, and many others—while less ambitious thinkers have no emphasis there. Indeed, perceptive analysts have noticed the great difference between the first 12° of Gemini and its last 18°, which is passively ruled by ☿ rather than ♄. The passive rulership by Uranus of the 36° segment between 18°♋ and 24°♌ explains the association of this third-quadrant segment with mystical and scientific reasoning; the former where the active ruler is ♆ and the latter where it is ♂.

Neptune's passive rulership of the fourth-quadrant sign Libra, which is actively ruled for its first 18° by Pluto and for its last 12° by Jupiter, corrects the traditional misunderstanding of that sign, which also has a sharp division in its meanings. Traditionalists agreed that a native with a strong Libran influence is oriented to others, but they never noticed the break at 18°♎ (like the one at 18°♑) that alters this orientation from all humanity (♀) to specific collectives (♃). And they don't even mention the subjective passions (♆) that clearly influence Libran people. In fact, they deny this passionate quality twice over; first by the old air trigon that erroneously associates Libra with cerebral reasoning, and second by their old rulership scheme, which by giving rulership of Libra to Venus attributes to it superficial affections rather than deep passions.

Also, the 36° segment from 6°♏ to 12°♐ is greatly clarified when Mars' energy and physical urges are seen as passively conjoined with the active force of Jupiter up to 24°♏ and with the active force of the sun from there to 12°♐. This explains the physicality, athleticism, self-orientation, and competitiveness of most people with strength in that 36° segment, and also why many traditionalists believe that Mars ruled Scorpio as well as Aries. It doesn't rule Aries, a sign that is more mental (☿) than physical (♂), but it passively rules much of Scorpio. And Mars is a far better active ruler of the partialistic sign Leo than the wholistic sun is. Finally, I don't see how we can doubt that the collectivistic Jupiter plays a passive role in late Capricorn and most of Aquarius, that the mental and dualistic Mercury influences Gemini and Cancer as well as Pisces and Aries, and that the critical and sensual Venus influences Leo and Virgo as well as Gemini.

This rulership proposal is a speculative scientific hypothesis that needs more testing than I can give it alone. Nevertheless, I'm sure you will find in your practice that this new scheme, which proposes an active and passive ruler for each 18° segment of a cycle, corrects the errors and omissions of the old scheme, even as it confirms those parts of it that seemed to be correct.

Chapter 8. The Natal Chart

Figure 8. The Rulership Pattern

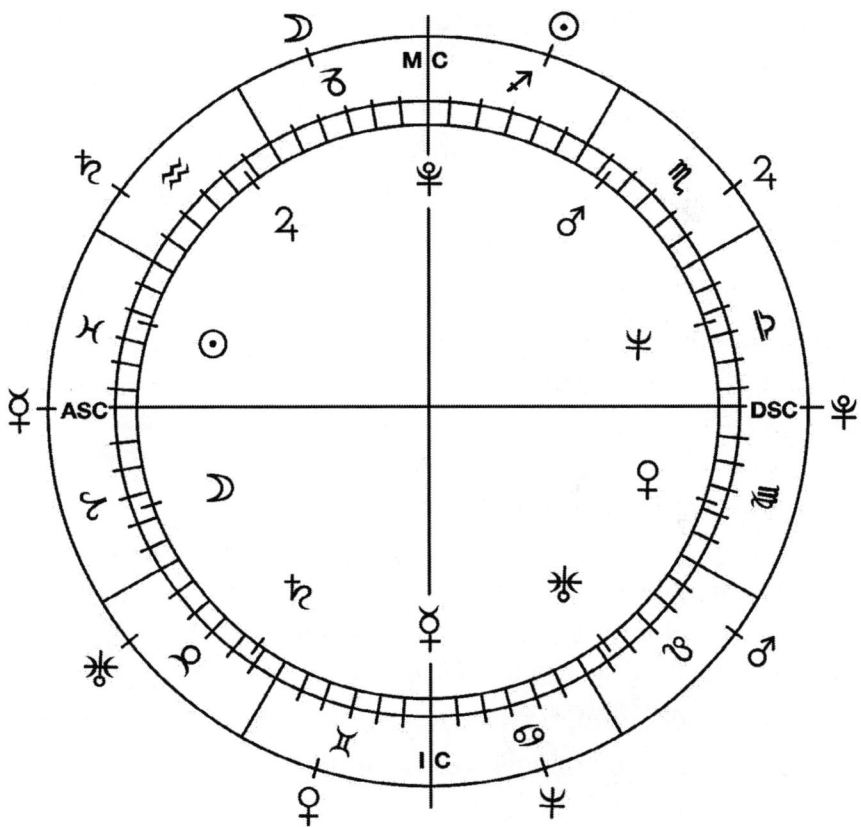

Outer Cicle = Active Rulers; Inner Circle = Passive Rulers

Planetary Aspects

When modern engineers showed that a motor has points of greater or lesser stress depending on whether its spinning armature is respectively at the 45° or 30° harmonic, they probably didn't realize that this echoed the hypothesis of ancient astrologers on the aspects (angles) between a chart's planets, as later modified by Kepler and other astrologers. Over at least two millennia, astrologers have empirically proven their speculative notion on the 'soft' and 'hard' aspects; namely, that the effects of the 'soft' angles of the 30° harmonic (mainly 30°, 60°, 120°, and 150°) are generally harmonious, while those of the 'hard' angles of the 45° harmonic (mainly 45°, 90°, 135°, and 180°) are generally stressful. These rules are variable because other aspects or chart elements can mitigate them, but they hold when considered as single factors.

Accordingly, I use the nine standard aspects of traditional astrology: those eight and 0°, the conjunction. But I reject all the other aspects that astrologers tried to introduce from their quaternary mathematical reasoning, such as the 36° *decile*, the 40° *novile*, the 51°25' *septile*, the 72° *quintile* or *bidecile*, and their 'bi-' or 'tri-' forms (80°, 102°50', 144°, and 154°15'). These aspects were never supported by theory or by rigorous empirical testing. Their proponents agreed that the ancient hypotheses on the four soft and four hard aspects have been proven, but then they illogically surmised that this must be so because the 30° and 45° harmonics are mathematical divisions of the 360° circle by the numbers 12 and 8 respectively. This led them to assume that if they divide a circle by other numbers—such as 5 (the quintile set), 7 (the septile set), or 9 (the novile set)—the resulting angles must also be psychologically meaningful, and then, with no psychologic theory to guide them, they guessed at the meanings of those aspects. But why stop there? If this formalistic reasoning is valid, then we should also use aspects based on dividing a circle by 10, which adds 36° and 108° to the others, and by 11, which adds a set based on 32°43'38.18", and so on.

Our metaphysics gives us all the theory we need here, by telling us that stress in a motion system has only one cause: a sharp change in spatial direction. The sharpest directional change is at 90°, or at each cardinal point of a motion system, so this is the most stressful angle, and the less-abrupt change at the 45° midpoint of a quadrant is also stressful, though less so. But it is not valid to suggest, as some formalists have, that 22.5° is also a valid aspect because it too is of the 45° harmonic. This claim misses the essential point, which is that our conclusions here should be reached not from mathematical fictions, but from the reality of changes in direction. But there is no sharp change of direction within a quadrant's 45° halves, where all the soft aspects fall, so these angles (including 22.5°) are not stressful. The next question is whether the 30° harmonic (30°, 60°, 120°, and 150°) is more harmonious than other angles in each half-quadrant, and this can only be settled with empirical testing, which confirms the old hypothesis. So, until we have a theory that contends otherwise and is proven in practice, we must accept ancient astrology's nine standard aspects and its time-tested orbs for their effective range.

Another formalistic, or quaternary mathematical, conception that we must reject is that of *the Arabic parts* and aspects from them. We shouldn't complicate our work by introducing fictions to a natal chart, for it is hard enough to consider all the chart elements that do have counterparts in reality. I'm sure those fictional 'parts' seemed necessary in the psychologic vacuum that existed when they were first proposed, but they are useless now that astrology finally has a psychologic theory.

I won't discuss the nine standard aspects or their allowable orbs here because I have few disagreements with tradition on them, but I will mention the following points because in the texts I have read they were either ignored or inadequately discussed.

1. The conjunction (☌) is the aspect of *creativity*. Conjoined planets work as a single force rather than as separate elements, so the native handles their discrete functions instantaneously, in a unique way that most people don't use. Whether that is a logical or a socially beneficial way varies with each chart, but in any case the conjunctions in a natal chart tell us all about the native's creativity. If a natal chart has no conjunctions, the native has no natural creativity, and conversely if it has many conjunctions, the native is highly creative. The type of creativity is indicated by the conjoined planets and the sign and house segments where the conjunction occurs, and

conjunctions in different chart segments indicate multiple creative areas.

2. Two conjunctions need special comment: those of the sun with either Mercury or Venus, the two *inferior planets* that are closer to the sun than the earth is. Their *superior conjunction* with the sun (☉☌☿ or ☉☌♀) occurs when the sun is between the planet and the earth, and their *inferior conjunction* (☉☌☿℞ or ☉☌♀℞) occurs when the planet is between the sun and the earth and is in retrograde motion. The effects on us of the superior conjunction are strongest and best, and those of the inferior conjunction are weakest and worst. Indeed, in recent decades (and not earlier it seems) it became routine for astrological forecasters to note that Mercurial or Venusian matters go badly when the planet is retrograde. Well, this is so in a natal chart also.

In the case of Mercury, a study of many charts shows that its superior conjunction with the sun is a necessary (though not sufficient) condition for mental brilliance of the Mercurial kind; that is, strength in deductive logic and in abstract, essential, realistic, universal, and graphic reasoning. But even its superior conjunction is diminished in its positive effects when a native's thought system has a weak impulse (R or -). On the other hand, its inferior conjunction, or retrograde Mercury in general, is a reliable indicator of a native's illogic, idealism, mysticism, or other form of disinterest in realism, theory, or abstract Mercurial reasoning, and it sometimes reflects serious mental damage or deficiencies.

If you check the charts of people whose work you know, you will find that this indicator puts them into three basic groups: the most logical (☉☌☿), the most illogical (☉ ☌☿℞), and those who are unexceptional either way in Mercury's functions because it has no sun conjunction. But in the latter case, its powers are better or worse, respectively, according to its closeness to a superior or inferior conjunction. You can confirm this point negatively also, by examining the charts of people who you know had or have mental deficiencies. In any case, like a thought reversal, a retrograde Mercury is sufficient reason to doubt, if not reject, the opinions or constructs of any intellectual, academic, or public speaker.

The case of Venus is dynamically identical; it differs from the sun-Mercury conjunctions only as its functions differ from Mercury's. Its superior conjunction improves the native's physical attractiveness, senses, voice, aesthetic sense and appreciation of beauty, sense of order, linear reasoning (which is essential for writing and music), critical abilities, and so on through the Venusian functions. And its inferior conjunction denies or limits those things.

3. Similar rules holds for the six *superior planets* (♂, ♃, ♄, ♅, ♆, and ♇). Taken alone, they function at their best when they are conjoined to the sun and at their worst when they are in opposition to the sun. More generally, they function better when they are on the far side of the sun, poorly when they are on the same side of the sun as the earth, worse when in retrograde motion, and badly when they are in square (□) to the sun. Still, much depends on the other chart elements, especially whether the sign they occupy gives them the logical or the illogical charge.

4. Our metaphysics clarifies the meanings of the opposition (☍) and square (□) aspects, since it tells us that two planets in direct opposition (180°) share a dimension, while two planets in quadrantal opposition (90°) are in different dimensions, or worlds. So, except for a planet in opposition to the sun, a square puts two planets in greater conflict than an opposition does.

The most important meaning of the opposition stems from this sharing of a dimensional axis, and that meaning is not contradiction or conflict; it is *actualization*, for good or for ill. What is actualized depends on the planets, signs, and houses involved. For instance, the native will cause things to happen in matters ruled by the opposed active houses, and will benefit or suffer from external events in matters ruled by the opposed passive houses. In a predictive chart, the opposition means that things pertaining to those four houses shall happen, and the matter is often completed when the aspect passes. So an opposition is stressful, but its results are not always negative since it sometimes actualizes an event that the native wanted. Conversely, a natal chart with no opposition indicates that the native has difficulty actualizing or completing things, and will probably do so only when oppositions occur in his or her postnatal charts.

Traditional texts agree that the square means stress and conflict, and some even say that it is the worst aspect, but they miss the psychologic meanings that follow from the fact that the two planets are literally in different dimensions; namely, that each planet ignores the other one as if it was in another world. This means that their respective functions in the native's logical process are detached. Thus, the square is more dichotomous and internally divisive than any opposition except a sun opposition. Like systemic reversals, either or both of these flaws are common in the charts of those who modern psychologists describe as 'schizophrenics'.

Though the square's negative effects are due to the detachment of the logical functions of the planets, a positive effect can result if the native has a strong mind, for such people are able to hold the planets' distinct functions apart so easily in their reasoning that each is better analyzed and understood for that detachment. In such cases, then, we must add *analytic power* to the meanings of a square, and consider it increased as the number of squares increases. And conversely, a natal chart with no square aspect indicates that the native lacks this analytic power.

PLANETARY DISTRIBUTION

In interpreting a natal chart, it is important to note the distribution of all ten planets in the chart. As far as I know, this was first emphasized by Marc Edmond Jones in his 1941 book *The Guide to Horoscope Interpretation* (Stanwood, WA: Sabian Publishing Society). Though his works reflect most of the traditional errors mentioned above, on this subject they are a good point of departure for a theoretically based study by realistic astrologers.

Jones rightly proposed that we must begin our interpretation of a chart from a wholistic perspective, by which he meant interpreting the overall pattern formed in the chart by all ten planets. He then described the seven basic patterns of planets that he considered significant, which he named the *splash, bundle, locomotive, bowl, bucket, seesaw*, and *splay* types.

His thoughts on this were later summarized by Michael R. Meyer in *A Handbook for the Humanistic Astrologer* (Garden City, NY: Anchor Press/Doubleday, 1974). Meyer—an acolyte of Dane Rudhyar, an arealist who mislabeled his views as 'humanistic astrology'—agreed with Jones on these *planetary patterns*, which he took pains to distinguish from *planetary formations*. The latter had been proposed by earlier astrologers; they are formed when three or four planets are linked by different kinds of aspects, giving us the *grand cross*, the *grand trine*, the *T-square*, the *mystic rectangle*, the *trine divided by sextiles*, and so on. Most practitioners know what these terms mean, so I won't explain them here, but two points should be mentioned.

First, the interpretive importance of the planetary formations and of our taking a wholistic perspective requires realistic astrologers to use an *open chart form*, different types of which are widely used in Europe. The key feature of an open chart form is that it has a spacious circle at the center of the chart in which to draw lines of different kinds or colors between the planets to show their aspects clearly. This shows the formations graphically and makes them unlikely to be overlooked in interpretation, as they often are when one of the older chart forms is used.

Second, in describing his planetary patterns, Jones recognized the interpretive importance of the planets' distribution in the quadrants and the hemispheres. The four distinct hemispheres of the Consideration Cycle, illustrated in *Figure 2*, are *analysis* (quadrants I and II), *synthesis* (III and IV), *reduction* (I and IV), and *accretion* (II and III). I mention this because the number of planets that occupy a quadrant or a hemisphere tells us which parts of the Cycle are dominant in the native's character, regardless of Jones' descriptions of the planetary patterns. If you recall, I said in Chapter 2 that on the issue of epistemic priority we humans are divided into realists, rationalists, empiricists, and formalists, and these reasoning modes correspond to the quadrants of the Cycle and therefore to the quadrants of the various cycles in a chart.

So, if some planets occupy one of the first quadrants in a chart, the native is to the degree indicated a primary reasoner and hence a realist, initiator, and theorist, while a planetary emphasis in the later quadrants indicates that the native is a secondary, tertiary, or quaternary reasoner instead. But a *relocation chart*, which is a natal chart except that it uses the longitude and latitude of the new place rather than of the birthplace, changes the chart's cardinal points, quadrants, and houses—more sharply so if the move is east or west than if it is north or south. Therefore, when a person moves after birth, the relocation chart must replace the natal chart for all interpretive purposes, natal or predictive. But since such a chart cannot change the planets' zodiacal position in the natal chart, a person's Impulse Pattern is never changed.

The relocation problem also applies to Jones' planetary patterns, but only as regards their house, quadrant, or hemispheric positions. He never mentioned how relocation could affect the meanings of the planetary patterns, but this is not important if we are using the current relocation chart for our analysis. It is very important, however, if we are doing a psycho-historical study of the life of someone who moved often or far from his or her birthplace.

Chart Interpretation

Most astrological texts tell beginners how to proceed in interpreting a natal chart; start with this or that chart factor, they say, then move on to these, and so on. Well, the Consideration Cycle changes this random advice by showing us the logical way to proceed.

The old advice to start by considering the chart as a whole is sound, so we should first note the location of the chart's angles in the zodiac, the planets' patterns, and the Impulse Pattern as a whole. *Then we must follow the logic of the Consideration Cycle.* We start this by considering the Midheaven (MC) and the active and passive tenth houses, then the factors that affect the Cycle's first planet, the moon, then those affecting Saturn, and then the will system as a whole. We then proceed in this way through every planet, phase, and psychologic system of the Cycle, ending with how the sun connects to the moon, or to new events. During this process, we must consider the planets' formations and what I call 'aspect paths'. Our goal throughout is to understand the native's character, because everything that follows birth is wholly or partly determined by it.

Let us not overlook ethics. If we agree to read anyone's chart, for compensation or not, we must do our best to be realistic, honest, and objective. And, but for public figures who have not consulted us personally, everything we are told or see in a chart must be kept confidential.

The Aspect Path. This new psychologic approach to interpretation leads us to an important new technique. After we consider the first planet (☾), the question arises as to how, logically speaking, the native gets from there to *the next planet in the Cycle's sequence* (♄), then to the next (☿) and so on, ending with how one gets from the last planet (☉) to the first one (☾) in a subsequent consideration. And the answer is that these psychologic connections are made only through the aspects; specifically, through the simplest or, failing simple, the most harmonious *aspect path* available in the chart. Therefore, our preparations for a natal chart interpretation must include writing out, preferably near the wheel, the full aspect path for every planet pair.

Doing this is important, because if two sequential planets of the Consideration Cycle are not linked in the chart by an aspect or aspect path, their logical functions will operate independently. And this means either (a) that the poles of a psychologic system are disconnected, which will make that system work much like a reversal, or (b) that two sequential systems in the Cycle are disconnected, which creates a gap in one's entire reasoning process. An *aspect* and an *aspect path* are usually different things. They are identical only when there is a direct aspect between two logically sequential planets in the Cycle, say, ☾☌♄ or ♆☍♂. Otherwise, an aspect path is a chain of three or more planets, each of which is linked to the next planet by a standard aspect.

For instance, here is the path taken by Washington (B+BRR) to get from Uranus to Venus, or in psychologic terms from the conclusions of his thought system to the beginning of his feeling system: ♅□☉⚺♄☍♀. Uranus square (□) the sun means that these two planets didn't recognize each other, and even though his sun was smoothly connected to Saturn by the semisextile (⚺), he could only get from Saturn to Venus through an opposition (☍). This was not a smooth and easy path, as were the direct paths by which he got from will to thought (♄✶☿), and from judgment to power (☿☌♃). Jefferson (+- -BB) also had a difficult thought-to-feeling aspect path: ♅□☉△♂□♀. What both these paths signify is that, even though neither of these men had a feeling reversal, they couldn't find an easy bridge by which to reason from their thought conclusions (or opinions) to their feeling process. It was not a complete disconnect because there was an aspect path, but it was one that caused them psychologic distress.

Complications arise when there is more than one aspect path between the same two planets. In this common case we should write only the *favored path* on the chart; that is, the one that the native comes to rely on exclusively. Lacking reliable testimony by the native to the contrary, we must assume that this is the *most direct* path, meaning the one with the fewest aspects or, if that doesn't apply, then the *most harmonious* path, meaning the one with the most soft aspects. And when 'most' doesn't apply, quantitative ties should be settled by the strength of the aspects.

For instance, the sun-to-moon path that Jefferson used was his harmonious ☉△♂△☽ path, and not his ☉△♄☌♃□☽ path, the square of which blocked his reasoning and forced it to take the easier path. Any intermediary planet in an aspect path interjects its home psychologic system and functioning between the two sequential planets that define the path. In this case, ☉△♂△☽, we see that even though Jefferson was by impulse a moralist and a humanist, he always referred to his own needs and personal evaluations (♂) whenever he went from one act of consideration to the next (☉ to ☽). Though his good judgment usually allowed him to subdue his personal needs on major social issues, those needs were nevertheless the chief means by which his enemies manipulated him into supporting their elitist, antidemocratic policies.

Table 1 shows that the US has had six pathologically reversed presidents. The first was Madison (BRRR-) who, with his fellow elitists Washington and Hamilton, was largely responsible for the content and ratification of the elitist US Constitution. Echoing the illogic of his three reversals, *six* of his ten planets (☽, ♄, ♅, ♀, ♇, and ♃) have *no* aspect path to the next planet in the Cycle. This is so of any planet with no aspects, but he had no such planets, so we would miss this weakness if we didn't write out his full aspect path. This deep illogic permitted his immoral opportunism and vacillating loyalties, most notably his continual betrayals of his humanist 'friend' Jefferson to Jefferson's natural enemies Hamilton and Washington.

The sixth pathological US president, the conservative-radical Bush II (R++RR), has three planets (☽, ♄, and ♀) with no aspect path to the next sequential planet. This means, first, that the poles of his will system are internally disconnected, and that consequently his functioning in his four subsequent systems (thought, feeling, judgment, and power) has no connection to his will or to any life goals he may have formed there. In feeling, the disconnect between his initial affections (♀) and concluding passions (♆) in effect gives him a fourth reversal; that is, he will play or he will emote, but these activities are unrelated to each other.

Afterword

Our psychologic theory holds that we have five conscious psychologic systems, five subconscious phases, or memory banks, and a psychologic interval that combines the functions of each. This rejects the old view, as some physiologists have also done recently, that we have a single 'mind' that controls all of our functions. It proposes instead that we have distinct psycho-physiological centers, whether located in the brain or elsewhere in the body, that independently control different functions, and that certain external events can affect those centers individually without having any direct effect on the other ones. They have indirect effects on the others, of course; physically through the body's integration as a total system, and psychologically through the Consideration Cycle's logical sequence.

And though this proposal of discrete functions is a revolution against our traditional intellectual system and its *mind*-body dualism, it is just what astrology has proposed about us for millennia. So it is no surprise that the Cycle and astrology work well together; the only surprise is why traditionalists continue to insist, in spite of all the evidence to the contrary, that we humans have a single mind-dictator that controls our body and behavior, and that we have much personal control over it. In fact, since we had no choice at all in forming our innate character, we have a smaller role than most of us imagine in deciding how our personality develops after birth.

This is regrettable, but it is the case, and it means that any control we have over what we become in life or leave behind after it depends on our ability to understand our self. This is hardly a new thought, for every seer through the ages has said in some form that we must know our self. But while their ancient maxim "Know thyself" means well, it is misleading. First, 'know' is ambiguous, for it doesn't mean that we should know more *facts* about our self; it means, in Plato's sense of the word, that we should *understand* our self, as a whole. Second, since only the Whole of Everything *is what it is*, every relative thing within it, our self included, is that plus its relations to all the other parts of that Whole. So to understand our self we must also understand other people, other living things, and the inanimate objects on earth and beyond it that can affect us. The correct maxim, then, is *"Understand human nature."*

And when we do understand people truly, we see what this work's theories and tables of individuals have proven; namely, that most of the beliefs that determine the destructive and self-defeating behavior of the vast majority of humans are not the result of their free, independent, and rational reasoning, but rather of the congenital psychologic impairments that prevent them from seeing the irrationality of the traditional assumptions they are taught to embrace. It follows that we will never have the sane societies we need to preserve our species and the other living things on earth until enough of us learn to accept these plain truths: that most people, by virtue of their innate character, have no right to advise us or to lead us, and that we must understand human nature well enough to identify the relatively few people around us who are capable of giving us sound advice.

Of course, that understanding will be only the first step in our battle for world sanity, for after we have solved the intellectual problems involved, we must solve the social and political problems and then institute those solutions in sane governments across the globe. But given all the selfish or deluded people who will array themselves against us in that goal, it will require a united exercise of human will such as our species has never before displayed.

Most realists know, as our mystics and idealists do not, that we humans have three urgent needs today. First, we must change our antiquated political structures so that they are truly democratic, which means politically and economically decentralized to the maximum degree possible. Second, we must halve our present population, or return it to what it was only five decades ago, so that we no longer overstress ourselves, our earth, and our limited natural resources. And, third, we must preserve intact, meaning unused by humans, about a half of all the world's land, air, and water. Some claim that we are masters of the earth, but if that were true, we would be its protectors rather than the very cancer that is destroying it.

If we don't make progress soon in all three of these goals, we may not make it through the new era (2008-2254), at least not in any way we would now consider acceptable. In fact, I predict that our species will be more severely tested by human and natural catastrophes later this century than it has been for millennia. This means that we have much less time than we now assume, probably only the next three to four decades, to establish sane governments that will prevent the human-caused disasters and begin the environmental programs that will mitigate the natural ones.

Appendix A: Calculating the Impulse Pattern

A correct Impulse Pattern depends on a correct natal chart. Whatever wheel the chart uses to show the planets' positions on the ecliptic plane, it will also show the celestial longitude of the ten planets, expressed in degrees and minutes (and perhaps seconds) of arc within the 30° of the indicated sign; for example, ☽ 28°♌54′. This gives you the *planet in sign* (here the moon in Leo) that you need to determine that planet's *charge*.

According to my theory, a planet's charge is determined by the ancient astrological distinction between 'feminine' and 'masculine' signs, but I reject these gender terms, for it is more precise to refer to the signs as alternately *assimilative* (-) or *projective* (+). I also differ from traditional astrology by seeing the true beginning of the zodiac as 0° Capricorn, the point 90° behind our astronomers' annually calculated point of 0° Aries. Thus, the six assimilative signs and their symbols are *Capricorn* (♑), *Pisces* (♓), *Taurus* (♉), *Cancer* (♋), *Virgo* (♍), and *Scorpio* (♏), and the six projective signs are *Aquarius* (♒), *Aries* (♈), *Gemini* (♊), *Leo* (♌), *Libra* (♎), and *Sagittarius* (♐). *Figure A* below shows these signs in their zodiacal order.

A planet's charge is negative (-) if it is in an assimilative sign, and positive (+) if it is in a projective sign. That's simple enough, but there's a complication, which I call 'anticipation'. Early astrologists noticed this sign anticipation and so spoke of 'the cusp' between two signs, which they held to be a range of one or two degrees before and after 0° of a sign; a range within which they assumed that there was some vague mixture of the meanings of the two signs. But I reject that reasoning and propose these precise anticipation rules, which have been well tested as regards the Impulse Pattern and seem to hold for all other interpretative purposes also.

The general rules. If the moon is in the last degree of a sign (at or after 29°00′), its charge is changed to that of the next sign. But the other planets move more slowly than the moon, so they get the charge of the next sign only if they are at or past 29°20′ of their sign.

The Retrograde rules. As seen from the earth, all planets other than the sun and moon appear to move backwards in the heavens during a part of their cycle, and this retrograde motion (symbolized after the planet's zodiacal position with '℞' or with 'S℞' for stationary-retrograde) changes the second general rule in two cases. *Case 1*: if a retrograde planet is in the last degree (29°xx′) of its sign, its charge is changed to that of the following sign if it *does not* move back to less than 29°20′ of its current sign in the next thirty days. *Case 2*: if a retrograde planet is in the first degree (00°xx′) of its sign, then its charge is changed to that of the previous sign if it *does* goes back to less than 29°20′ of that prior sign within thirty days. You need an ephemeris to apply these thirty-day rules, but sometimes the planet's position thirty days later tells you if the sign should be changed.

After we determine the correct charge of all ten planets, we need to know which planet determines the charge of each of the ten epistemic points around the Consideration Cycle, as shown in *Figure A* and as numbered in *Figure 6*. Point 1, the first pole of the will system (keyword *wish*) is given the charge of *the moon* (☽), then each point in turn is given the charge of *Saturn* (♄), *Mercury* (☿), *Uranus* (♅), *Venus* (♀), *Neptune* (♆), *Mars* (♂), *Pluto* (♇), *Jupiter* (♃), and *the sun* (☉). Accordingly, the impulse of the will system is determined by the charges of ☽ and then ♄, of the thought system by ☿ and then ♅, of the feeling system by ♀ and then ♆, of the judgment system by ♂ and then ♇, and of the power system by ♃ and then ☉.

As an example of the entire procedure, consider President Zachary Taylor's natal chart. The astrological software I use prints the celestial longitude of the ten astrological planets in the following order, which is not the order we need, but I expect that all astrology software will be calculating the Impulse Pattern for us soon: ☽ 04°♉09′, ☉ 03°♐07′, ☿ 29°♏05′, ♀ 00°♑37′, ♂ 14°♏21′, ♃ 29°♒43′, ♄ 20°♑32′, ♅ 15°♋56′℞, ♆ 13°♎52′, ♇ 09°♒30′.

(1) The first step, *always*, is to note if any planet is in the last (29°xx′) or first degree (0° xx′) of a sign and whether or not it is retrograde. Taylor's

chart has two 29° planets that are not retrograde, ☿ and ♃, so by our second general rule, ☿'s assimilative (-) charge in Scorpio is not changed, but ♃'s charge in Aquarius (+) is changed to the charge of Pisces (-).

(2) Next, we write the charges of all ten planets in the order of the ten epistemic points of the Consideration Cycle, which is this planetary order: ☽, ♄, ☿, ♅, ♀, ♆, ♂, ♇, ♃, ☉. Writing Taylor's ten charges in that order gives us: - - - - - + - + - +.

(3) Then we pair that string of ten charges. This yields the five pairs (- -) (- -) (- +) (- +) (- +), which respectively are the impulses of Taylor's *will, thought, feeling, judgment,* and *power* systems. And when this is shortened as described in the text, his Impulse Pattern is (- -BRB). Of course, before long you'll be calculating the Impulse Pattern quickly each system in turn.

Planetary Cycles. Scientists who do statistical studies of people (or other organisms) over periods greater than a year cannot have accurate results unless they consider, at the least, the effects on human nature of our four slowest planets. Dividing a planet's sidereal cycle by twelve gives us its average period in one sign, and hence with one charge. I discuss the great importance of this fact in the case of Pluto in *Chapter 7*, in the section entitled *The Generational Clash*.

Here are the four longest cases. The charge of Pluto (♇), which is in one sign for an average period of 20.6 years, determines the logic or illogic of the conclusions (second pole) of our *judgment* system. The charge of Neptune (♆), which changes sign regularly every 13.7 years, determines the logic or illogic of the conclusions of our *feeling* system. The charge of Uranus (♅), which changes sign about every 7.0 years, determines the logic or illogic of the conclusions of our *thought* system. And the charge of Saturn (♄), which changes sign about every 2.5 years, determines the logic or illogic of the conclusions of our *will* system.

To complete the data for shorter-term analyses, the average sign-period of Jupiter (♃) is one year, of Mars (♂) 57.2 days, of the sun (☉) 30.4 days, of Venus (♀) 18.7 days, of Mercury (☿) 7.3 days, and of the moon (☽) 2.3 days.

Figure A. This figure shows the Consideration Cycle with the sequence of the ten astrological planets and the twelve astrological signs superimposed on it. A principle of my astrology theory is that no planet or sign can have any meaning that is not derived from these points or intervals of the Consideration Cycle, as discussed in the text. In fact, my psychologic theory proposes that nothing can have any *meaning* to us except through the Cycle. I created that theory with no reference to the pragmatic science of astrology, for I saw from the first that its practitioners had never objectively defined any of the merely descriptive meanings that they had assigned to a chart's elements over millennia. My psychologic theory, on the other hand, objectively defines the distinct meanings of the ten planets, the twelve signs, the twelve diurnal divisions called 'houses', and the quadrants and hemispheres of a chart. And if my attempt at this has failed, it means that someone else must now develop new metaphysical, epistemic, and psychologic theories that will give all things, including the elements of an astrological chart, their real meanings.

Figure A. The Consideration Cycle with Planets and Signs

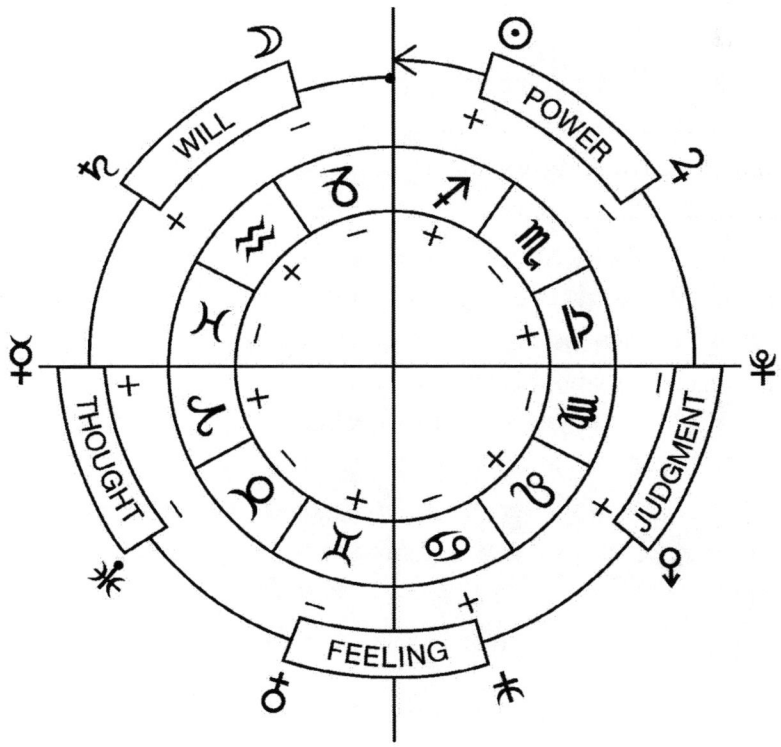

Appendix B: Tables of Individuals

The Impulse Patterns of 875 individuals are provided here, in sixteen distinct tables to permit class analysis. The following list shows the number of names on each table, but these include 40 duplications since some people belong in more than one class.

Table 1. US Presidents (43)
Table 2. US Supreme Court Justices Appointed Since 1900 (53)
Table 3. US Governmental Figures (105)
Table 4. US Non-Government Political Figures (55)
Table 5. US Revolutionary Figures (31)
Table 6. US Media Figures (78)
Table 7. World Political Figures (126)
Table 8. Philosophic Intellectuals (26)
Table 9. Political Intellectuals (36)
Table 10. Political Literary Figures (30)
Table 11. Academics and Scientists (84)
Table 12. Business Leaders (66)
Table 13. Religionists and Other Mystics (73)
Table 14. Theologians (16)
Table 15. Non-Governmental Assassins or Murderers (20)
Table 16. Nazis of WW II Era (73)

UNDERSTANDING THE TABLES

The Date Issue. The first four columns of the tables are *Number*, *Name*, *Birth Date*, and *Died*. The fifth column is data that varies with the table, such as the person's political party, birth place, affiliation, field, or ideology. The main complication here is with the birth date, which must be correct for a correct chart and Impulse Pattern. There are two basic problems.

First, the date is not always available. This may be due to lost birth records, especially in past centuries. Often we know the date of a famous person's death, but not the date of birth, and some people won't disclose their birth data voluntarily. In Table 10 we might like to know the Impulse Patterns of Shakespeare, Dante, and Molière, but we have to guess at their birth dates from other records, and that would mislead us.

Second, our traditionalist encyclopedias and biographical references are lax to the point of negligence in their editorial policy regarding birth data. Some report the year only, while others merely echo a date taken from another source, often without specifying that source or indicating the date's accuracy or the calendar used. For instance, in its articles on people, the Encyclopedia Britannica often ignores the issue of calendar changes in presenting birth or death dates. Also, nonastrological references rarely mention the birth time even when it is known, and many fail to mention the birth place or else they do so too loosely to determine its longitude and latitude, which is needed to calculate an astrological chart.

This sloppiness stems from the disdain for astrology of many US academics, an ill-considered attitude that is less extreme in Europe and Asia. For centuries astrologers had to maintain their own birth records of famous people as best they could, especially since religious corporations, whose first business is mysticism, controlled almost all academic institutions. Astrologists today owe much to the efforts of the French psychologists and statisticians Michel Gauquelin (1928-1991) and his wife Françoise (b.1929), who collected much data on European births for their research. Michel's book *The Scientific Basis of Astrology* (New York: Stein and Day, Inc., 1969) is still required reading in the field. Another noble attempt was made by Lois Rodden (1928-2003), who digitized the birth data that she and others had collected. The result is a filterable database (sold at *astrodatabank.com*) of about 30,000 persons with birth and biographical data; many of the births are precisely timed, and the data sources are discussed and rated. I used this database when I could, but its over-emphasis on socially irrelevant sports and entertainment celebrities makes it of less value than it could have been for serious psychologic, social, or medical studies, so I was often forced to use our inadequate academic references.

The calendar problem is severe as regards many persons born after the Gregorian calendar replaced the Julian calendar in Europe in 1582 and before the former finally became the global standard, when Greece converted to it in 1923. The astrological software that I use treats all dates entered in it up to October 5, 1582 as Julian or Old Style (OS) dates, and all dates from October 15, 1582 on as Gregorian or New Style (NS) dates, and that requires some dates between 1582 and 1923 to be converted to the NS date.

The Encyclopedia Britannica tells us that Italy, France, Luxemburg, Spain, and Portugal converted on that date, losing ten days on their calendar. But all nations did not convert then, mainly because of issues related to religious holidays. In 1584, the Catholic German states converted, and Switzerland did so piecemeal from 1583 to 1812. In 1699 and 1700, Denmark, Holland, and the Protestant German states converted. Britain and its colonies made the change only in 1752, when the day after September 2nd was designated September 14th, the difference now being eleven days rather than the ten that it was at first. Sweden converted in 1753, Alaska in 1867, Japan in 1873, Egypt in 1875, China in 1912, and the nations of Eastern Europe did so variously from 1912 to 1917. Complicating the situation in France, the Republican calendar was used from September 22, 1792 to January 1, 1806. Russia converted to the Gregorian calendar in 1918, but then the difference had to be twelve days, so that the day after February 1st was named February 14th. I found more details on the web at *tondering.dk/claus/calendar.html*.

Speaking now only of those cases where the birth would have been initially recorded with an OS date, I handled this situation as follows. The birth date shown in my table is the date I used to calculate the Impulse Pattern shown. Whenever this date could have been OS but was given by all references with no indication of OS or NS, I put an asterisk after the year to note the uncertainty. When any reference specified that the date it gives is NS, I used that date and put an 'n' after the year. I did this also where I could deduce from other facts just which calendar applied for the date given by all references, none of which specified OS or NS. If we know that the date was taken from written birth records before the conversion, it will be OS, but if the individual was the source later, it will probably be the NS date, since people start using a new calendar to which they are legally subject immediately.

The Time Issue. In the small unnamed column after the additional data column, I indicate with a '*t*' if the time of birth is known. But this notation doesn't mean that the time used is exact, though it is in most cases, especially for births in Europe, where recording the time on a birth record has long been the rule. When the time is unknown or its accuracy is doubtful, I calculate the chart for noon. Though in natal analysis we lose knowledge of a person's character when the time of birth is not known within a half-hour or so, a noon chart seldom yields an incorrect Impulse Pattern. This is so because a planet's charge is determined by the sign it is in, and because the fastest planet, the moon, stays in the same sign for 2 to 2 ½ days.

I indicate the use of a noon chart in three ways: (1) if the moon could not possibly have been in a sign other than it was at noon, I leave this space blank; (2) if the moon's sign could have differed if the actual birth time was sufficiently *before* noon, I put an '*a*' there, for *am*; and (3) if the moon's sign could have differed if the actual time was sufficiently *after* noon, I put a '*p*' there, for *pm*. In these two latter cases, the moon would have the opposite charge from the one in the Impulse Pattern shown. The charges of the other nine planets are seldom affected by a 12-hour difference, but in such a case (and I recall only one here), we should assume an earlier or later time if we can objectively judge which charge fits the person's life and statements better.

The charge of the moon determines the charge of the first pole of the will system (W), so if it is incorrect because the real time is unknown, only the will system's impulse is incorrect. A simple rule tells us quickly how the will impulse would differ if the moon at the actual time was not in the sign it was in at noon. If an '*a*' or a '*p*' appears in this space, first note if the will impulse that is shown is *strong* (+ or B) or *weak* (- or R), and then understand that a different charge for the moon would change the will impulse shown to the other strong or weak impulse.

The Impulse Pattern. The next five columns, labeled W, T, F, J, and P, show the calculated Impulse Pattern for the five psychologic systems, as explained in the text and *Appendix A*.

Political Attitude. This column, labeled 'Attitude', is the impulse in power only, shown here in two columns to allow a count of the power leftists and rightists. Here and in the next column I abbreviate the four political attitudes as *Rad*, *Lib*, *Con*, and *Prog* (or *Pro* in combination).

Political Perspective. Next is the 'political perspective', by which I mean one's overall disposition to practical matters as revealed not just by the power system, but by all five systems. The name of the perspective tells us more about a person's political dispositions than the power attitude alone does, so it is the better indicator when we are considering the political dispositions of specific individuals. Accordingly, I use it consistently for this purpose from *Chapter 6* on.

The three columns under this heading allow a count of how many people listed are *leftist*, *conflicted*, or *rightist* in their perspective. The name of our political perspective has one, two, or three terms, as determined by these four rules. (1) We refer to any system's impulse by using *progressive* for B, *radical* for +, *liberal* for -, and *conservative* for R. (2) If the power impulse is the only repeated impulse in the Pattern, then the perspective has the same name as the power attitude. (3) Otherwise, any impulse that occurs more than once in the Pattern is also a part of the perspective's name, and the name of the power attitude is always its first term. (4) If that rule requires a three-term name, then the impulse of the *will* system is its second term.

If rule (2) doesn't apply, the perspective's name will be a hyphenated term or combination abbreviation; if it does apply, I distinguish the perspective from the attitude with italics or with the qualifying term 'straight'. For example, in *Table 1* in the Leftist column under 'Perspective' we see that the only *progressives*, or straight progressives, are Lincoln and Franklin Roosevelt, and that the only straight radicals are Tyler, McKinley, Hoover, and Clinton. In the Rightist column, we see that the only straight liberals are the Generals Jackson and Grant, and that the only straight conservatives are Garfield, Cleveland, Theodore Roosevelt, and Wilson.

Those two end columns also show the four *two-term* labels that are wholly leftist or rightist. The leftist labels are 'ProRad' for progressive-radical and 'RadPro' for radical-progressive, and the rightist labels are 'LibCon' for liberal-conservative and 'ConLib' for conservative-liberal. In these cases, the leftism or rightism of the power system is reinforced by the other systems, so there are no psychologic conflicts in one's *political* reasoning. But there are conflicts in one's *social* reasoning, since each of these four perspectives is partly moderate and partly extremist.

The middle column here, labeled 'Conflicted', is a very important political and psychologic indicator, for it shows the eight *two-term* and the twenty-four *three-term* perspectives that are conflicted. The two-term labels comprise the four that reflect leftist-rightist conflicts (ProLib, LibPro, RadCon, and ConRad) and the four that reflect both leftist-rightist political conflicts and moderate-extremist social conflicts (ProCon, ConPro, RadLib, and LibRad). All such two-term psychologic conflicts cause confusion in people's practical reasoning, and a common, if not universal, result of this is that they are opportunists or untrustworthy in their practical behavior. They often embrace one set of social or political opinions in their youth and change to the other set in mid-life, and perhaps back again in old age, but usually they hold these contradictory opinions at the same time and jump to one or the other as their needs dictate.

An excellent example of the two-term conflict is the progressive-liberal Jefferson (+- -BB), who equivocated on such major issues as slavery and the federalist-antifederalist dispute over the provisions and ratification of the US constitution. As a 60% leftist (3 of 5 systems), he had always opposed the "infamous practice" of slavery, but as a 40% rightist (liberal), he profited from it throughout his life and blamed its continuation alternately on providence or the political opposition of others. We must expect such hypocrisy from anyone, even a moralist like him, who has a conflicted political perspective. A part of his conflict was that he was a leftist progressive (B) in judgment and a rightist liberal (-) in thought. This means that his intellectual and moral parts were continuously in conflict, and that his rightist thinking, which was usually borrowed from others he knew or read, often overturned his innate good judgment.

Politically, his progressive views until age 33—when he wrote the *Declaration of Independence*, the key parts of which were borrowed from Locke, Paine, and Mason—were discarded in his forties as regards the elitist 1787 Constitution. His liberal side dominated his reasoning then, so he was seeing true democracy and individual rights as less important than his own political status and property, including his slaves. He gave no direct support at all to the leftist antifederalists who rejected this constitution because it lacked a bill of rights, though as a leftist he had always championed those inalienable rights. But privately he did write to Madison and Washington from Paris urging them to correct this intentional omission from their new constitution and to heed "the general voice from north to south, which calls for a bill of rights."

This raises an important question that historians never answered about him, which is *Why* did he accept Washington's request to serve in Paris for those crucial years in which the ultimate fate of the revolution was to be decided in Philadelphia and in the States' ratifying conventions? Did he strike a bargain to absent himself in exchange for the General's future support for his career, or was he duped into leaving by the conspiracy of Madison, Hamilton, and Washington, elitists all? Both seem likely to some degree. In any case, he didn't support the antifederalists on individual rights. Instead, he just echoed his liberal 'friend' Madison by saying that since we can never win all the rights we want, we must be satisfied with half the loaf—although, of course, what the liberal-conservative Madison (BRRR-) wrote in the final Bill of Rights was far less than half of the individual rights that a genuine democracy would protect. In fact, it was an intentional emasculation of the great *Virginia Declaration of Rights* that was written by George Mason (-B++B) and ratified on June 12, 1776 by a state convention that Madison and Jefferson attended.

But Jefferson vacillated to the leftist side also. For instance, when he was Vice-President and had no role in the Federalist administration of Adams I—which was long ruled from New York by Hamilton through

Adams' cabinet members—he anonymously opposed in writing the Federalists' Alien and Sedition Acts and defended states' rights as against the powers assumed by the federal government with those acts. And in 1816, after his presidency, his progressivism resurfaced and he strongly defended local governments as against centralized federal or State rule, saying among other things that the wards (or townships) of America "have proved themselves the wisest inventions ever devised by the wit of man for the perfect exercise of self-government."

Thus, Jefferson was at times a leftist and at times a rightist. His liberal (-) impulses in thought and feeling gave him a thirst for wealth, sensual pleasures, and tangible possessions, a tendency to plagiarism and opportunism, and hypocrisy on slavery and on the need for absolutist centralized government that his good judgment had opposed at first and then again late in life. As president, we also see his left-right conflict in his Louisiana Purchase, for as a liberal he more than doubled the nation's territory, but as a moralist and progressive he did so without war.

All the three-term perspectives have a '1-2-2' form, where the first term refers to the power impulse, the second term to the duplicated impulse that includes the will system, and the third to the other duplicated impulse. This type of psychologic conflict indicates one who is *very confused* in his or her basic social and political assumptions and behavior, far more so than those with a two-term conflict. It is the sign of a natural maverick or flip-flopper; that is, a person who works for one political program, then switches to another, and perhaps back again to the first or to yet another one, and without ever understanding why.

For instance, the humanist Thomas More (RBRB+) was a confused *RadConPro* (radical-conservative-progressive), which is why he was beheaded by the elitist conservative-radical Henry VIII (+B+RR). More was a leftist in power, thought, and judgment, but a rightist in will and feeling, and those two reversals made theism and martyrdom seem reasonable to him. Also, he was an extremist in will, feeling, and power, but a moderate in thought and judgment. Like others with a three-term perspective, he was a maverick because he couldn't reconcile these competing impulses, and so he couldn't reach a consistent political position when he needed it most; that is, his rightism and theism restricted his leftist realism and humanism. A true realist wouldn't sacrifice his or her life for any mystical conception.

In the 2008 campaign for US President, two of the prominent candidates were mavericks with a three-term perspective; namely, McCain (-B-BR) and Biden (BRBR-), neither of whom should be elected or appointed to any public office. They try to hide their basic confusion and opportunism by posing in public as having unshakable convictions, but if they ever agreed to write out the political principles they embrace, you would see their stark contradictions plainly. Every day they are 'winging it' and there's no telling where they will be next on any issue. For instance, McCain calls himself a 'straight talker' because he can't call himself a straight thinker.

Anyone with a three-term political perspective, even if it has no reversals, is seriously confused psychologically, intellectually, and politically. These cases are over 6% of the people in our tables, but taken with the two-term perspectives that are also conflicted, they are over 49% of all the cases. And if this conclusion from our tables can be validly extended to the entire population, it means that, contrary to an analysis by power attitude alone, in their overall perspective *half of all people are neither rightists nor leftists*, but rather are naturally confused over fundamental social and political issues and are unpredictable in practice regarding them.

The hypothetical normal distribution for the three 'Perspective' columns is 25.2% leftist, 49.6% conflicted, and 25.2% rightist. Rounded, this means that any strictly rightist or leftist message by a politician or party appeals to only 25% of the population. The remaining 50%, who are called 'the uncommitted' or 'the undecided' when in fact they are psychologically conflicted, are indifferent until they have been swayed to one side by the arguments of the rightists or the leftists, and they are unreliable in their commitment to that side thereafter.

<u>Political Type</u>. The political type gives us an overall picture of a subject's personal and social nature before we analyze its parts. One might

be a leftist or rightist by attitude (power) and still have the opposite cast to one's overall disposition, and the perspective doesn't always suffice for this since it could be determined by as few as two systems. Each half of the type's two-term name refers to a majority of the systems. The first term tells us whether three of more of the five systems in the Pattern are *leftist* (B or +) or *rightist* (- or R), and the second term tells us whether three or more of the five systems are *moderate* (B or -) or *extremist* (+ or R).

The most logical type is 'LM', for *leftist moderate*, which means that most of the five systems are leftist and, in a separate count, most are moderate. The better-known cases in *Table 1* are Jefferson, Adams II, Lincoln, F. Roosevelt, Truman, Carter, and Bush I. 'LE' means the half-illogical *leftist-extremist* type, such as Washington, Eisenhower, and Clinton. 'RM' means the half-illogical *rightist-moderate* type, such as Grant, Kennedy, L. Johnson, and Reagan. 'RE' means the worst case, the totally illogical *rightist-extremist* type, such as Adams I, Madison, Monroe, Van Buren, T. Roosevelt, Wilson, Nixon, Ford, and Bush II.

<u>Judgment-Power.</u> The 'J-P' column indicates whether one is a *humanist, otherist, selfist,* or *elitist*. These revealing moral-political terms are objectively defined in Chapter 7.

<u>Empathy and Compassion.</u> The last column, 'E/C', shows if the subject has empathy (e), compassion (c), both (ec), or neither (•). As discussed in Chapter 6 under *Judgment*, my theory defines *empathy* as the assimilative impulse at the second pole of the feeling system (point 6 of the Cycle), so only those who are assimilative (-) or reversed (R) in feeling are naturally empathetic, or receptive of others' passions. It defines *compassion* as having the assimilative impulse at the second pole of the judgment system (point 8 of the Cycle), so only those who are assimilative (-) or balanced (B) in judgment are naturally compassionate.

These indicators are invaluable, because they tell us, reliably, whether one who speaks to us really does have empathy for our pains and pleasures or compassion for our general situation. People who lack both empathy and compassion (•) as herein defined, have no natural ability to be concerned for others, and their decisions don't reflect the best interests of other people or living things. Conversely, people who have both (*ec*) cannot live their lives without being naturally concerned for others and otherness. In the other two cases, those with empathy alone (*e*) will naturally care only for people or living things close to them, while those with compassion alone (*c*) will naturally care only for classes of people or living things, including humanity as a whole. So empathy is personal and compassion is general, and we should remember that humanists and otherists are compassionate, while selfists and elitists are not.

Summary. Below the lines of individual data, the columns are totaled and evaluated. Directly under the listing of Impulse Patterns is a summary that shows how often each impulse (B, +, -, or R) occurs among all the people listed there. Since these are small lists, I take a variance of 4% or more from the 25% mean to be significant, and I indicate these low or high cases, if any, on the left, after "Impulse Deviations from Norm." The bold-faced box below the count of all impulses is of special interest because it gives us the *typical pattern* of the individuals in that table, the significance of which varies with the relative narrowness and completeness of that table's class of subjects. Moving right, I show the number and percentage of the leftists and rightists in attitude, and of the leftists, rightists, and conflicted persons in perspective. Then the *Type*, *J-P*, and *E/C* columns are summed and analyzed.

COMMENTS ON THE TABLES

These tables are provided mainly to show the psychologic process of the individuals listed, but their class summaries sometimes yield general conclusions that are well worth knowing.

Table 1 is a complete and narrow list, so its typical pattern (- -+RR) tells us something real about US Presidents as a whole. This type is rightist-extremist, the worst type, and its 80% rightist perspective is that of a conservative-liberal. It indicates those who have a weak will, are manipulable, adopt their motivations and thoughts from others, are emotive and project their feelings on others, are amoral nihilists in judgment, and are irrational in social and political matters. If people with this elitist judgment-power combination (...RR) also lack strength in their will and thought systems and still become politicians, as is the case here, they are irrational, conspiratorial, and amoral in practice. Also, only a handful of our presidents were even good persons, which shows how little ability the electorate has to distinguish between the best and worst candidates. We cannot expect to have a 'good president' under our elitist constitution and the later subversions of it by all three branches of government, but if we are speaking of persons rather than of presidents, the best were no doubt the eleven humanists listed.

The other thirty-two were on balance not even decent men, and the worst by far were the six pathological rightists with three reversals. Ignoring the elitist *conservative* Garfield (-+RRR) who served less than four months, the other five were all ardent opponents of democracy, and hence champions of the rich. In power, two of them, Madison (BRRR-) and Nixon (RR-R-), were liberals, while the rest were conservatives. We all know the elitist conservative-radical Bush II (R++RR), for he plagued us all recently with his illogic, Jesus-based mysticism, domestic and international terrorist acts, opposition to democracy and individual rights, bullheadedness, dimwittedness, lack of compassion, and support for unrestricted thefts from the people by the superrich. But perhaps he learned some lessons in immoral rule from the two otherists in this psychopathic group, who were just as irrational as the elitists. I refer to the straight conservatives Theodore Roosevelt (BRR-R) and Wilson (R-RBR), who have been favorably described by rightist historians in spite of being racists, militarists, opposed to democracy, oppressors of the people, and defenders of oligarchic rule by the superrich through powerful private trusts and those two private corporations that we call 'the major political parties'. Teddy Roosevelt is widely credited with breaking up Rockefeller's Standard Oil monopoly, but scholars rarely note that the only reason he did this was to help the anti-Rockefeller monopolists in his own elitist clique, and that at all other times he was a staunch defender of the trusts as against the people. Nevertheless, Wilson was by far the more fanatic of the two.

Wilson is widely praised for starting the League of Nations, but he should be condemned for this attempt to impose on all the people of the world a centralized government that was, and that in the form of the United Nations still is, *totally* undemocratic. He was an Anglophile who called the elitist British system "perfected party government." He lied to the people ceaselessly, promising reforms and peace while enriching the trusts, forcibly suppressing honest populist movements in the western and southern states, establishing private *party* rule nationally and locally over every formerly democratic governmental function, and completing the program of his immediate predecessors McKinley, Teddy Roosevelt, and Taft to establish in the southern states—for the first time ever, since it was not there before, not even when slavery was legal—the segregation of the black and white races.

No less evil was his invention of false reasons for the US to enter World War I. He proclaimed that war to be necessary to 'save the world for democracy', but this was a lie, for it was solely about supporting one nation with a constitutional monarchy (Britain) in a war against another nation with a constitutional monarchy (Germany). In his twisted mind, we had to enter that war to help Britain's aristocrats defeat Germany's aristocrats. He also intervened militarily to suppress popular revolts against brutal dictators in Latin America, filled his cabinet with racist machine politicians from the South (who hadn't had such federal power since before the Civil War), strengthened his national party, and instituted a broad reign of terror in the US.

To that end, he proposed and signed the Sedition Act of 1918, which forbade Americans to use "disloyal, profane, scurrilous, or abusive language" about the US government or its flag or armed forces during wartime, and which allowed the Postmaster General to deny mail delivery to any newspaper or other publication that advocated peace or otherwise opposed his government. Thus, like most pathological conservatives, he had no respect for Amendment 1 or for any other amendment of our elitist Constitution that was intended to protect individuals from their governments. In his terrorist campaign against all opposition to his Democratic Party, a private corporation, he created a vast network of official federal and local agencies and private vigilante groups (including boys clubs) that spied on, beat up, tarred and feathered, imprisoned, or murdered citizens for expressing opposition to his falsely justified intervention in Europe's war, and even for refusing to purchase the so-called 'Liberty Bonds'. His Attorney General boasted in 1918 that never before in our history has this country been so thoroughly policed.

I mention these instances of evil government (which is any government that serves itself rather than the people) because, as any objective observer can see, the public has been broadly miseducated in US history by rightist scholars, teachers, and media spokespersons, and because if I don't counter that perpetual academic conspiracy, my claim that the Impulse Pattern is a reliable predictor of good or evil officials will seem to the public to be incorrect. But not only is my new psychologic theory sound, *we cannot preserve democracy without it* (or a better theory). The foremost political thinkers of history have said that the chief failing of every form of democracy yet proposed is that it requires the people to know how to determine the best and the worst persons among them, and yet we have never had a way to do that. But we do now, and now that we can choose among candidates wisely, a democratic government is no longer the threat to social sanity that it was in the past. We need only publicize each candidate's character, and teach everyone why they shouldn't vote for any selfist or elitist.

I made tables for the three US Senates elected in 2002, 2004, and 2006, and though it was unnecessary to include them here, it is worth noting that the typical Impulse Pattern of all three (++BRR) have the same elitist reversals in judgment and power as the typical US President. This is not surprising, since both the presidency and the Senate were designed in our constitution to be elitist institutions, and indeed both have worked diligently to suppress democracy ever since.

Table 2 lists the 53 Justices of the Supreme Court appointed since 1900. This table is extracted from my larger table of all 110 Justices, and its number column starts with 58 because it is based on the order in which each Justice took office. The full table, which I plan to provide in a later work, is useful for legal scholars who wish to evaluate the logic of specific Supreme Court decisions. This makes it clear that the most illogical decisions in the Court's history were made by rightist and selfish courts, while the best were made by leftist and unselfish courts.

Table 3 consists of a variety of people who hold or held some government office, so it has an even balance of types with no significant class conclusions, except perhaps that 60% of these people were selfists or elitists, the very people who don't belong in a sane government.

Table 4 lists noteworthy people of all kinds who participated in politics without holding a major governmental office. Given the variety of individuals here, the summary is not significant.

Table 5 is a short but significant list of American revolutionists. It could be made longer, but only with difficulty, since the birth data for known federalists and antifederalists in the standard references are inadequate. Most references show only the years of birth and death, and don't mention the calendar used when the date is ambiguous. By 'federalist' I don't mean a member of the later Federalist Party of Washington and Adams, but rather anyone who supported the antidemocratic constitution drafted by the 1787 convention and worked for its ratification by the states before the Bill of Rights was added to it in 1789. An 'antifederalist', then, is one who opposed that 1787 document and its ratification by the states. Most rightists, being collectivists and anti-individualists, favored the original draft as it was, without a bill of rights, while most leftists detested it because it did not protect individuals and their local governments from the absolutist powers given to the newly centralized federal and state governments.

This leftist-rightist conflict between antifederalists and federalists is just as my psychologic theory predicts, and the few deviations are due to the complexity of an individual's character or situation. That theory is largely confirmed by the predominance of power leftists among the antifederalists and power rightists among the federalists. Thirteen of the federalists listed were power rightists while only four were leftists; three of whom were opportunistic selfists, while the one humanist (John Jay) was conflicted in perspective. The eleven antifederalists listed include only one rightist, the otherist Gerry, and a few years later Luther Martin took a contrary position for political reasons. And of the three equivocators listed, two were conflicted as to leftism and rightism. Let me add that no prior psychologic theory can yield a similarly sound explanation for these opposed moral and political views in anyone, let alone in disputants of past centuries.

Table 6, with its typical pattern (RR+++) or (RRR++) and low number of balanced (logical) systems, confirms what we already know about our opportunistic media as a whole. That pattern is radical-conservative in perspective, and, like that of the conservative-radical Bush II, it is 100% extremist, opinionated, and compassionless. It shows rushing to judgment and superficial practical reasoning that ignores all theory and principles, as well as the feelings of others. There are more leftists than rightists on this list, and by two-to-one more extremists than moderates. It makes sense that projection is more common than the other impulses among media people, but it is unfortunate for us all that balanced reasoning is least common in the class.

Table 7 lists some world political figures, and they too confirm our theory. The 100% extremist (+ or R) rulers in this table are Augustus, Ben-Gurion, de Gaulle, Ho Chi Minh, and Milosevic, who compare in that respect with two US Presidents: Eisenhower and Bush II.

Our theory tells us that the worst political leaders as far as the people's interests are concerned are rightists, and that because of their greed the moderate liberals are often as bad as the extremist conservatives. The elitist conservatives here include Augustus, Czar Alexander III, Batista, Elizabeth I, Henry VIII, Ho Chi Minh, Koizumi, Louis XII, Louis XVI, Robespierre, and Tito. The elitist liberals include bin Laden, Tony Blair, Catherine the Great, Chiang Kai-shek, Cromwell, Fox, Tojo, Hitler, Mao Tse-tung, Lorenzo de Medici, Nehru, Salazar, and Trujillo. The otherist conservatives include Arafat, Indira Gandhi, Gladstone, Marcos, Mubarak, Nassar, Rabin, and Sharon, and the otherist liberals include Dayan, Hussein, John the Steadfast, Lenin, Louis XIV, Petain, Pol Pot, Stalin, Sun Yat-Sen, and Trotsky.

Among leftists, our theory holds that the most logical and moral leaders are the humanist progressives, and that the worst leftists are the selfists. The selfist progressives here include Beria, Bolivar, Brandt, Hugo Chavez, Deng Xiaoping, Duvalier, Frederick the Wise, Kim Jong-Il, Mussolini, Netanyahu, Putin, Röhm, and Sukarno. The selfist radicals include Ehud Barak, Ben-Gurion, Franco, De Gaulle, Kim Sung Ju, Krushchev, Louis XIII, Louis XV, Milosevic, Lord North, and Richard III. The progressive humanists listed here were generally better leaders than the radical humanists, but of course a conflicted perspective can complicate our judgment of any leader. For instance, the progressive-liberal Napoleon (-B- -B) was better at first than later, when in spite of his humanism he gave in to his pathological liberalism (or three assimilative systems) and decided to conquer the world and control its riches.

Table 8 lists intellectuals with a philosophic interest. This is a short list because reliable birth data isn't available for most people born before the classic era, and of course I excluded those many academics who are called 'philosophers' because of what they study rather than what they create. The typical pattern here is (BBR- -) or (BBR-R), both of which indicate, by the greater strength in will and thought, persons who prefer analytic to synthetic reasoning and so prefer to deal with universal issues rather than with partialized class issues or practical matters. This is one of the tables that supports my theory's conclusion that most idealistic intellectuals will have the illogic of multiple reversals, while the most realistic ones will have no reversal or one at most. Note that 50% of these intellectuals have both empathy and compassion, which is one reason why most of them put the need to solve the riddles of the ages before personal gain.

Table 9 lists nonphilosophic intellectuals who focused mainly on the issues of political structure or individual rights. Not surprisingly, 70% of these political intellectuals are either humanists or otherists, while only 30% are elitists or selfists. Moreover, this is the only one of our tables in which the number of unrealistic reversals is significantly less than the mean. Here too, as with the philosophic intellectuals, a high percentage, 42%, have both empathy and compassion. Note that those who adopted the label 'anarchist' as Proudhon had misdescribed it were mostly progressives, and not true anarchists in the original sense of 'no rulers'.

Table 10 lists some major literary figures who were concerned with social and political issues. Since a broad range of political views is reflected here—from the fascism of the elitist and pathological liberal-conservative Pound (RRR+-) to the individualism of the humanist progressive-liberal Conrad (-B-BB)—this table yields no significant general conclusions, except that 83% of these writers were born with empathy or compassion or both.

Table 11 is significant only generally, because it includes people in so many different academic or scientific fields. The typical pattern here is complex, as you see, but it reflects the rightism, or liberal assimilation, that we know to be characteristic of the academic class as a whole. Adler is the only total progressive (BBBBB) in our tables, and indeed he writes with the predicted combination of near-perfect logic and pathological conventionality. Not surprisingly, the guru of American neoconservatives, the German Zionist and liberal-conservative Leo Strauss (+RBR-), who taught at US colleges from 1938 on, was a compassionless elitist—as were the Nazis from whom he fled and the young US neocons of the baby-boom generation who followed his misguided lead.

Table 12 lists people who have had success in business. Here too the range of interests is too broad to yield many valid general conclusions, but the typical pattern (RRB+-) or (RR++-) is just what we would expect for this class. That is, our practical 'men and women of action' invariably deny primary and secondary reasoning, or theory and essential issues, but they are synthetically creative and, like many power liberals, they can credit their wealth to their greed and to what they inherited, borrowed, or stole from others. A high 59% of them have the conflicted political perspective that is typical of unprincipled opportunists, though a few of the humanists here did try to make their businesses serve broad social purposes. Many of them established 'charitable' foundations that did more harm than good, since their true purpose was to preserve rightist and elitist governments.

Note that the creative entrepreneurs listed here have more strong (leftist) impulses than weak (rightist) ones, while the rest have the same lack of creativity that is found in all rightist governments. And it is no surprise that the selfist Disney (RR+RB) was pathological, since his creations, which harm more than help children, reinforced the immature desire to escape from reality that the reversals cause in people of any age.

Table 13 lists religionists and other mystics, and here there are some meaningful general conclusions. First, the significant deviations from the mean, few balanced systems and many reversals, confirm the congenital illogic of the class. As for the reversals, the extreme cases (four reversals) are the mystic Blavatsky and the Ayatollah Khomeni. The other pathological, or less-than-sane, cases shouldn't surprise you; they are Bakker, Richelieu, James Jones, Kerri (a Nazi), Mother Teresa, Olcott, Pius XII (the Pope whose acts in WWII were rightly criticized by Jews), Joseph Smith (the founder of Mormonism), and Ste. Bernadette.

The typical pattern here is (-RR- -), which indicates a weakness in will, the denial of thought and personal desires, altruism in judgment, and a pathological liberal (collectivistic, expansionistic, acquisitive, and opportunistic) bias. The liberal passivity in power causes one to assume that personal power comes from external sources only, such as other people or imagined deities, spirits, or forces. But no less significant than the high number of reversals here is the abnormally low occurrence of the balanced impulse, the only impulse that imparts unimpaired logic to our reasoning. And, as we would expect of religionists whose social mission is to impose their unrealistic beliefs on others, their dominant political type is the worst one, the rightist-extremist.

Table 14 lists 16 prominent theologians. Here we can say for certain, as we can't of all the religionists, that their theism was sincere. The typical pattern here is (RBR-R) or (R+R-R), which is pathologically conservative and shows strength only in thought, which is why they were theologians rather than just religionists. These patterns also show a denial of personal will, Reality, metaphysics, primary reasoning, and theory; a feeling reversal by which one begs the question of the passionate source of one's beliefs; an assimilation in judgment that makes one a compassionate altruist, denier of people's personal needs, and a receptacle for accepted traditions and others' beliefs; and a power reversal that causes one to deny one's own abilities and to assume that all control over events, as well as all the blame for them, lies outside the self. The power reversal also causes the irrational collectivism, or anti-individualism and antihumanism, that characterizes every religion.

As with the religionists in the previous table, the rightists in attitude dominate over the leftists, 69% to 31%. Here too the dominant (44%) type is the rightist-extremist, the worst type, while there are only two leftist-moderates, the best type; namely, Scotus and St. Francis, who are often described as 'realists'. Both these tables confirm that the main reason why people become theists, religionists, or theologians is that they are innately illogical, or psychologically impaired.

Table 15 is a short list of twenty assassins, murderers, or serial killers who held no major governmental office, though the former may have been the agents or dupes of people who did. The typical pattern here indicates a rightist who is both weak in thought and projective in will and judgment. Note especially that *none* of these persons are humanists or straight progressives, and that the extremist projective systems dominate. 75% are selfists or elitists, five are otherists, 65% are power rightists, and 55% have no empathy or compassion. But if we look at some of the other tables, we find these same innate impairments in those far-worse murderers who performed their immoral deeds as heads of state or high officials in a government or religion.

Table 16 exists only because the Gauquelins collected and published detailed birth data for the major criminals of the Third Reich. The typical pattern here, (RBB+-) or (R-B+-), is that of an elitist liberal who denies will, theory, and reality, is conventional in thought, and is highly judgmental. Since the elitist liberal-progressive Hitler (B+BR-) was strong in will and thought, he was a natural leader for German-speaking people of his selfish generation.

Because its class of subjects is narrow, this table confirms some of my theory's main conclusions. First, as the summary indicates and as no one disputes anyway, Nazi Germany was a rightist state, not a leftist one. But it was a liberal state, not a conservative one; in fact, it is a perfect picture of the expansionist and anti-individualistic extremes to which liberals are prone wherever they are. Also, it might surprise us to see that 96% of these seventy-three Nazis were either elitists (60%) or selfists (36%), but this is due to the simple fact, explained in Chapter 7, that people of that 30-year generation had to be either egoists (+) or nihilists (R) in judgment. There are only two humanists and one otherist in this table, and the humanists are the industrialists Krupp and Keppler, who were successful in business before the Nazis came to power. Only those three, who were born in the prior generation, had any compassion; all the others did not, which is why morality and justice were considered irrelevant and were denied in Nazi Germany and the many other fascist states of that time.

Appendix B: Tables of Individuals B-22

Table 1. US Presidents

No.	Name	Birthdate Mo	Birthdate Day	Birthdate Year	Died	Data	W	T	F	J	P	Attitude Leftist	Attitude	Attitude	Perspective Leftist	Perspective Conflicted	Perspective Rightist	Type	J-P	E/C
1	Washington, George	2	22	1732n	1799	Federalist	t	B	+	R	R			Cons		ConRad		LE	Elitist	·
2	Adams, John	10	30	1735n	1826	Federalist	t	R	+	R	–			Lib			LibCon	RE	Elitist	·
3	Jefferson, Thomas	4	13	1743n	1826	Dem-Rep	t	+	–	B	B		Prog			ProLib		LM	Humanist	ec
4	Madison, James	3	16	1751n	1836	Dem-Rep	t	B	+	R	R			Lib			LibCon	RE	Elitist	e
5	Monroe, James	4	28	1758	1831	Dem-Rep	t	–	–	B	–			Cons		ConLibRad		RE	Elitist	·
6	Adams, John Quincy	7	11	1767	1848	Dem-Rep	t	B	+	B	R			Lib		LibPro		LM	Otherist	ec
7	Jackson, Andrew	3	15	1767	1845	Democrat	t	R	+	–	–			Lib			Lib	RM	Otherist	ec
8	Van Buren, Martin	12	5	1782	1862	Whig	t	–	–	B	B		Prog			ProCon		RE	Selfist	·
9	Harrison, William	2	9	1773	1841	Whig	t	+	+	B	–		Prog			ProLib		RM	Humanist	ec
10	Tyler, John	3	29	1790	1862	Democrat	t	–	+	+	+		Rad		Rad			LE	Elitist	·
11	Polk, James	11	2	1795	1849	Democrat	t	B	–	R	R			Cons		ConPro		RM	Selfist	·
12	Taylor, Zachary	11	24	1784	1850	Whig	t	–	–	R	B		Prog			ProLib		LE	Elitist	e
13	Fillmore, Millard	1	7	1800	1874	Whig	t	B	+	B	B			Cons		ConPro		LE	Otherist	ec
14	Pierce, Franklin	11	23	1804	1869	Democrat	t	+	+	R	B		Prog					LE	Humanist	ec
15	Buchanan, James	4	23	1791	1868	Republican	t	B	+	+	B		ProRad			LibRad		LE	Elitist	·
16	Lincoln, Abraham	2	12	1809	1865	Democrat	t	B	–	B	–		Prog					LM	Humanist	c
17	Johnson, Andrew	12	29	1808	1875	Democrat	t	B	+	–	–			Lib		LibPro		LM	Otherist	c
18	Grant, Ulysses	4	27	1822	1885	Republican	t	–	–	+	–			Lib				LM	Otherist	c
19	Hayes, Rutherford	10	4	1822	1893	Republican	t	R	–	R	B		Rad			RadLib		RM	Humanist	e
20	Garfield, James	11	19	1831	1881	Republican	t	–	+	R	R			Cons			Cons	RE	Elitist	ec
21	Arthur, Chester	10	5	1829	1886	Republican	t	B	–	+	+		Rad			RadCon		RE	Selfist	e
22	Cleveland, Grover	3	18	1837	1908	Democrat	t	R	–	R	R			Cons			Cons	RE	Elitist	·
23	Harrison, Benjamin	8	20	1833	1901	Republican	t	B	B	R	B		Prog			ProLibCon		RM	Selfist	e
24	McKinley, William	1	29	1843	1901	Republican	t	B	R	R	R		Rad		Rad			LE	Selfist	·
25	Roosevelt, Theodore	10	27	1858	1919	Republican	t	+	+	B	+			Cons			Cons	RE	Otherist	ec
26	Taft, William	9	15	1857	1930	Republican	t	R	R	R	R			Lib		LibConPro		RM	Otherist	ec
27	Wilson, Woodrow	12	28	1856	1924	Democrat	t	B	–	B	B			Cons			Cons	RE	Elitist	ec
28	Harding, Warren	11	2	1865	1923	Republican	t	R	+	R	R			Cons			ConLib	RM	Otherist	c
29	Coolidge, Calvin	7	4	1872	1933	Republican	t	–	–	+	B			Cons			ConLib	RM	Otherist	c
30	Hoover, Herbert	8	10	1874	1964	Republican	t	R	+	R	R		Rad		Rad			LE	Humanist	ec
31	Roosevelt, Franklin	1	30	1882	1945	Democrat	t	+	+	B	B		Prog					LM	Humanist	e
32	Truman, Harry	5	8	1884	1972	Democrat	t	B	+	B	R			Lib		LibPro		LE	Elitist	·
33	Eisenhower, Dwight	10	14	1890	1969	Republican	t	R	+	+	+		Rad			RadCon		LE	Selfist	c
34	Kennedy, John	5	29	1917	1963	Democrat	t	B	–	R	B		Prog			ProLib		RM	Humanist	e
35	Johnson, Lyndon	8	27	1908	1973	Democrat	t	B	+	R	–			Cons			ConLib	RM	Elitist	e
36	Nixon, Richard	1	9	1913	1994	Republican	t	R	R	–	B			Lib			LibCon	RE	Otherist	e
37	Ford, Gerald	7	14	1913	2006	Republican	t	+	+	B	–			Lib		LibRad		LM	Otherist	e
38	Carter, Jimmy	10	1	1924		Democrat	t	–	–	R	B		Rad			RadLib		LM	Humanist	e
39	Reagan, Ronald	2	6	1911	2004	Republican	t	B	+	B	+		Prog			ProLib		RM	Selfist	e
40	Bush, George H.W.	6	12	1924		Republican	t	+	B	B	R		Rad		RadPro			LM	Humanist	c

Table 1. US Presidents

							B	+	+	+	+	+	Rad		Rad				LE	Selfist	·
							R	+	+	R	R	R	Prog	Cons		ConRad			RE	Elitist	·
							p	–	+	–	–	B			Rad	ProLib			RM	Humanist	ec
41	Clinton, Bill	8	18	1946	Democrat																
42	Bush, George W.	7	6	1946	Republican																
43	Obama, Barack	8	4	1961	Democrat																

Table 1. Totals & Analysis

	B	13	10	6	12	11	20	23	8	23	12
	+	6	10	13	8	9					43
	–	15	13	13	9	11	L	R	Leftist	Conflicted	Rightist
	R	9	10	11	14	12	47%	53%	19%	53%	28%

Total Names= **43**
Total Impulses= 215

Impulse Deviations from Norm **Slight**

Maximum Value 15 13 14 12
Typical Pattern – – + R R
(Tied Count) – –

Type Summary
LM	8	19%
LE	9	21%
RM	14	**33%**
RE	12	28%
	43	100%

E/C Summary
E&C	14	**33%**
E Only	10	23%
C Only	7	16%
Neither	12	28%
	43	100%

J-P Summary
Humanists	11	26%
Otherists	10	23%
Selfists	9	21%
Elitists	13	**30%**
	43	100%

n=NS date   t=timed birth

APPENDIX B: TABLES OF INDIVIDUALS B-24

Table 2. US Supreme Court Justices Appointed Since 1900

No.	Name	Birthdate Mo	Birthdate Day	Birthdate Year	Died	Data		W	T	F	J	P	Attitude	Perspective Leftist	Perspective Conflicted	Perspective Rightist	Type	J-P	E/C
58	Holmes, Oliver W.	3	8	1841	1935	1902-1932	t	R	B	B	R	+			ConPro		RE	Elitist	•
59	Day, William R.	4	7	1849	1923	1903-1922		+	R	B	–	–	Rad	Cons			LE	Selfist	e
60	Moody, William H.	12	23	1853	1917	1906-1910	p	R	+	R	+	B				LibCon	RM	Otherist	ec
61	Lurton, Horace H.	2	26	1844	1914	1910-1914		–	–	R	–	B		Lib			LE	Elitist	•
62	Hughes, Charles E.	4	11	1862	1948	1910-1916, 1930-1941 CJ	t	+	+	B	B	B	Prog	Lib			LM	Humanist	c
63	Devanter, Willis V.	4	17	1859	1941	1911-1937		B	R	–	–	+	Rad		RadLib		RM	Humanist	ec
64	Lamar, Joseph R.	10	14	1857	1916	1911-1916		–	–	–	B	B	Prog	Lib	ProLib		RM	Humanist	ec
65	Pitney, Mahlon	2	5	1858	1924	1912-1922		–	–	R	B	B	Prog		ProLib		RM	Humanist	ec
66	McReynolds, James C.	2	3	1862	1946	1914-1941		R	R	R	–	–	Prog		ProCon		LM	Humanist	c
67	Brandeis, Louis	11	13	1856	1941	1916-1931		R	R	B	B	+		Lib		LibCon	RM	Otherist	ec
68	Clarke, John H.	9	18	1857	1945	1916-1922		+	+	B	R	–		Lib			RM	Otherist	ec
69	Taft, William H.	9	15	1857	1930	1921-1930 CJ	t	R	R	R	–	B		Lib	LibConPro		RM	Otherist	c
70	Sutherland, George	3	25	1862	1942	1922-1938		R	R	B	–	–			LibConPro		RM	Humanist	c
71	Butler, Pierce	3	17	1866	1939	1923-1939		+	B	R	B	–	Prog		ProCon		LM	Otherist	c
72	Sanford, Edward T.	7	23	1865	1930	1923-1930		+	+	R	–	+	Rad		LibPro		LE	Humanist	c
73	Stone, Harlan F.	10	11	1872	1946	1925-1946 CJ		R	+	B	–	B	Rad				LE	Humanist	ec
74	Roberts, Owen J.	5	2	1875	1955	1930-1945	a	–	R	R	–	+				Cons	RE	Otherist	c
75	Cardozo, Benjamin N.	5	24	1870	1938	1932-1938	a	R	R	R	R	R	Rad	Cons			LE	Humanist	ec
76	Black, Hugo	2	27	1886	1971	1937-1971	t	+	+	B	–	+				Cons	RE	Elitist	•
77	Reed, Stanley F.	12	31	1884	1980	1938-1957		B	R	R	–	R	Rad	Cons		LibCon	RE	Elitist	e
78	Frankfurter, Felix	11	15	1882	1965	1939-1962	a	–	–	R	B	R		Lib		ConLib	RM	Otherist	e
79	Douglas, William O.	10	16	1898	1980	1939-1975		R	+	R	B	+	Rad				LE	Selfist	ec
80	Murphy, Frank	4	13	1890	1949	1940-1949		R	+	R	+	–	Rad				LE	Selfist	•
81	Byrnes, James F.	5	2	1879	1972	1941-1942		+	+	B	R	+		Lib	LibPro		RM	Otherist	ec
82	Jackson, Robert H.	2	13	1892	1954	1941-1954	a	B	–	–	B	B	Prog	ProRad	ConRad		LM	Selfist	•
83	Rutledge, Wiley B.	7	20	1894	1949	1943-1949	p	+	+	B	B	R			LibRad		LE	Elitist	•
84	Burton, Harold H.	6	22	1888	1964	1945-1958		+	+	R	+	B	Prog		ProCon		LE	Selfist	•
85	Vinson, Fred M.	1	22	1890	1977	1946-1953 CJ	p	R	+	B	B	B	Prog		ProCon		LE	Selfist	•
86	Clark, Tom C.	9	23	1899	1977	1949-1967	p	B	+	+	R	+	Rad	Rad			LE	Selfist	•
87	Minton, Sherman	10	20	1890	1965	1949-1956		–	–	R	R	B		Lib		Lib	LE	Elitist	•
88	Warren, Earl	3	19	1891	1974	1953-1969 CJ	t	+	+	R	R	–	Prog	ProRad			RM	Selfist	e
89	Harlan, John M. II	5	20	1899	1971	1955-1971	a	+	B	–	+	B					LE	Elitist	•
90	Brennan, William J.	4	25	1906	1997	1956-1990	p	R	+	+	R	R	Prog			ConLib	RM	Selfist	•
91	Whittaker, Charles E.	2	22	1901	1973	1957-1962		–	B	+	R	–		Cons		LibCon	RE	Elitist	•
92	Stewart, Potter	1	23	1915	1985	1958-1981		B	R	+	R	–	Rad	Lib			LE	Humanist	ec
93	White, Byron	6	8	1917	2002	1962-1993	a	R	R	+	–	B	Prog		ProCon		RE	Humanist	c
94	Goldberg, Arthur	8	8	1908	1990	1962-1965		–	+	B	+	R	Rad	Rad			LE	Selfist	e
95	Fortas, Abe	6	19	1910	1982	1965-1969		–	–	–	+	+	Rad				LM	Selfist	e
96	Marshall, Thurgood	7	2	1908	1993	1967-1991	p	+	–	–	R	R			RadLib	ConLib	RE	Elitist	e

Table 2. US Supreme Court Justices Appointed Since 1900

#	Name																				
97	Burger, Warren	9	17	1907	1995	1969-1986 CJ	p	–	B	–	R	R		Cons	ConLib	RM	Elitist	e
98	Blackmun, Harry	11	12	1908	1999	1970-1994		B	–	R	+	–		Lib	Lib	RM	Elitist	e
99	Powell, Lewis F. Jr.	9	19	1907	1998	1972-1987		R	B	–	R	R		Cons	Cons	RE	Elitist	e
100	Rehnquist, William	10	1	1924	2005	1972-2005 CJ	t	–	–	+	B	+	Rad		RadLib	LM	Humanist	c
101	Stevens, John P.	4	20	1920		1975-	t	–	B	+	R	R		Cons	ConLib	RM	Otherist	c
102	O'Connor, Sandra D.	3	26	1930		1981-2006	p	R	+	R	–	+	Rad		RadCon	RE	Humanist	ec
103	Scalia, Antonin	3	11	1936		1986-	t	–	B	B	R	R		Cons	ConPro	RM	Otherist	ec
104	Kennedy, Anthony	7	23	1936		1988-	t	R	B	R	–	+	Rad		RadCon	RE	Humanist	ec
105	Souter, David	9	17	1939		1990-	t	–	+	–	R	R		Cons	ConLib	RM	Elitist	e
106	Thomas, Clarence	6	23	1948		1991-	t	+	R	B	R	R		Cons	Cons	RE	Elitist	.
107	Ginsberg, Ruth B.	3	15	1933		1993-		B	+	–	–	–		Lib	Lib	RM	Otherist	ec
108	Breyer, Stephan	8	15	1938		1994-	t	R	–	R	+	+	Rad			RE	Selfist	e
109	Roberts, John G. Jr.	1	27	1955		2005- CJ		–	B	+	+	B	Prog		RadCon	LM	Selfist	.
110	Alito, Samuel A. Jr.	4	1	1950		2006-	p	–	B	+	R	+	Rad			LE	Selfist	.

Table 2. Totals & Analysis

Total Names= **53**
Total Impulses= 265

Impulse Deviations from Norm **Balanced Low**

	B	8	20	8	8	11	27	26		14	22	17
	+	12	10	18	12	16	53	53				53
	–	17	10	11	17	13	L	R		Leftist	Conflicted	Rightist
	R	16	13	16	16	13	51%	49%		26%	42%	32%

Maximum Value
Typical Pattern

17	20	18	17	16
–	B	+	–	+

Type Summary

LM	7	13%
LE	16	30%
RM	18	34%
RE	12	23%
	53	100%

E/C Summary

E&C	15	28%
E Only	12	23%
C Only	10	19%
Neither	16	30%
	53	100%

J-P Summary

Humanists	14	26%
Otherists	11	21%
Selfists	13	25%
Elitists	15	28%
	53	100%

Italized names appeared on a previous table(s).   *t=timed birth; p or a= Will system differs if pm or am birthtime*

APPENDIX B: TABLES OF INDIVIDUALS   B-26

Table 3. US Governmental Figures

No.	Name	Birthdate Mo	Birthdate Day	Birthdate Year	Died	Data	W	T	F	J	P	Attitude	Perspective Leftist	Perspective Conflicted	Perspective Rightist	Type	J-P	E/C
1	Agnew, Spiro	11	9	1918	1996	Republican	t B+	B	B	B	–	Lib		LibPro		LM	Otherist	c
2	Ashcroft, John	5	9	1942		Republican	t B+	+	B	R	R	Cons			Cons	RE	Elitist	e
3	Babbitt, Bruce	1	27	1938		Democrat	. B–	R	–	B	R	Lib			Lib	RM	Otherist	ec
4	Baker, James	4	28	1930		Republican	t –	–	R	–	R	Cons			ConLib	RM	Otherist	ec
5	Baruch, Bernard	8	19	1870		Democrat	t +	+	B	B	+	Rad		RadLib		LM	Humanist	c
6	Bennett, William J.	7	31	1943	1965	Republican	a +	B	R	R	–	Rad				LE	Selfist	•
7	Biden, Joseph	11	20	1942		Democrat	t B+	B	B	B	+		Rad	LibProCon		RM	Elitist	c
8	Black, Shirley Temple	4	23	1928		Republican	t R+	B	+	+	B	Lib		ConRad		LE	Otherist	e
9	Bloomberg, Michael	2	14	1942		Republican	t R+	B	+	R	+		Rad	RadCon		RE	Selfist	e
10	Bradley, Bill	7	28	1943		Democrat	p +	+	B	R	–	Cons				LE	Selfist	•
11	Brady, James S.	8	29	1940		Republican	t B–	–	–	–	+	Lib			Lib	RM	Elitist	e
12	Brown, Jerry	4	7	1938		Democrat	t B+	R	B	B	R	Rad		RadLib		LM	Humanist	ec
13	Bryan, William J.	3	19	1860	1925	Democrat	t +	+	–	B	R	Lib		LibRad		LM	Otherist	e
14	Bundy, McGeorge	3	10	1919	1996	Democrat	t B+	+	+	R	–	Lib		LibProRad		LM	Otherist	c
15	Bush, Jeb	2	11	1953		Republican	t B–	–	+	+	B	Prog	ProRad			LE	Selfist	•
16	Card, Andrew Hill Jr.	5	10	1947		Republican	t B	R	–	+	B	Lib		LibRad		LE	Elitist	e
17	Cheney, Dick	1	30	1941		Republican	t B–	–	+	+	B			ProLib		LM	Selfist	e
18	Clark, Wesley	12	23	1944		Democrat	t R+	+	+	+	–	Prog		LibRad		LM	Elitist	e
19	Clarke, Richard	10	30	1950		Republican	t –	–	+	+	R	Lib				RM	Elitist	•
20	Clinton, Hillary	10	26	1947		Democrat	t B+	B	+	B	R	Cons		ConPro		LE	Otherist	e
21	Colby, William E.	1	4	1920	1996	Republican	t +	R	+	B	R	Cons		ConRad	ConLib	LE	Humanist	•
22	Cuomo, Mario	6	15	1932		Democrat	t B+	–	–	R	+	Cons		RadLib		LM	Elitist	c
23	Daley, Richard J.	5	15	1902	1976	Democrat	t –	–	B	B	R	Rad	RadPro		Cons	RE	Selfist	ec
24	Daschle, Thomas	12	9	1947		Democrat	t B+	+	R	B	R	Rad	Prog			LE	Humanist	e
25	Davis, Jefferson	6	8	1808	1889	Confederate	t +	+	B	+	–	Prog				LM	Elitist	•
26	Dean, Howard	11	17	1948		Democrat	a R+	+	+	B	B	Rad	Rad	LibRad		RE	Selfist	c
27	Dean, John	10	14	1938		Republican	t B+	B	B	R	R	Prog	Prog	RadProCon		LM	Selfist	•
28	DeLay, Tom	4	8	1947		Republican	t R+	B	R	R	+	Rad		ProCon		LM	Selfist	•
29	Dodd, Christopher	5	27	1944		Democrat	t +	B	–	B	+		Rad			LE	Selfist	c
30	Dole, Robert J.	7	22	1923		Republican	t B–	–	+	R	–	Lib		LibPro		LM	Otherist	e
31	Dukakis, Michael	11	3	1933		Democrat	t R+	B	B	B	B		Rad	ConRad		LE	Otherist	e
32	Edwards, John	6	10	1953		Democrat	t +	–	–	B	+	Cons				LE	Selfist	•
33	Ehrlichman, John	3	20	1925	1999	Republican	t R+	B	B	B	–	Rad	Rad			LM	Humanist	c
34	Feingold, Russ	3	2	1953		Democrat	a B+	+	+	+	–	Prog	Prog	LibRad		LE	Elitist	•
35	Gardner, John W.	10	8	1912	2002	Republican	t B+	B	B	+	+	Rad	RadPro			LM	Humanist	c
36	Gephardt, Richard	1	31	1941		Democrat	t R+	B	+	B	B	Prog	Prog			LM	Selfist	ec
37	Gingrich, Newton	6	17	1943		Republican	t +	–	R	B	B	Prog	ProRad			LM	Selfist	e
38	Giuliani, Rudy	5	28	1944		Republican	t +	+	+	R	+	Rad	Rad			LE	Selfist	e
39	Goldwater, Barry	1	1	1909	1989	Republican	t B–	–	R	–	–				LibCon	RM	Elitist	e
40	Gonzales, Alberto R.	8	4	1955		Republican	t R+	B	+	R	+	Rad	Rad			LE	Selfist	•

Table 3. US Governmental Figures

#	Name					Party														
41	Gore, Albert Jr.	3	31	1948		Democrat	t	B	R	B	+	Rad		RadPro			LE	Selfist	•
42	Graham, Bob	11	9	1936		Democrat	p	–	B	B	+		Cons		ConPro		RM	Otherist	ec
43	Graham, Lindsey	7	9	1955		Republican		–	R	R	R		Cons			ConLib	RM	Elitist	•
44	Greenspan, Alan	3	6	1926		Republican	p	B	B	B	B		Cons			Cons	RE	Otherist	c
45	Hagel, Chuck	10	4	1946		Republican	t	+	+	+	R	Prog					LM	Selfist	•
46	Haldeman, H.R.	10	27	1926		Republican	t	B	R	R	R		Cons			ConLib	RM	Otherist	c
47	Helms, Jesse	10	18	1921	1972	Republican	t	–	–	–	–				RadProLib		LM	Humanist	•
48	Hoover, J. Edgar	1	1	1895		Republican	t	–	B	B	+	Rad				ConLib	RM	Elitist	ec
49	Huckabee, Michael	5	31	1955		Republican		R	B	R	+		Cons		ConPro		LE	Selfist	•
50	Hughes, Karen	12	27	1956		Republican	t	B	R	R	+			Rad	ProLib		RE	Otherist	c
51	Humphrey, Hubert H.	5	27	1911	1978	Democrat	t	–	–	–	+	Prog					RM	Selfist	•
52	Kemp, Jack	7	13	1936		Republican	t	R	B	+	R		Lib				RM	Otherist	ec
53	Kennedy, Edward	2	22	1932		Democrat	t	B	B	B	B		Cons		ConPro		LE	Otherist	e
54	Kennedy, Robert F.	11	20	1925	1968	Democrat	t	–	–	R	R		Lib		LibPro		RM	Otherist	ec
55	Kerrey, Bob	8	27	1943		Democrat	t	+	B	+	+		Cons		ConProRad		LE	Elitist	c
56	Kerry, John	12	11	1943		Democrat	t	–	–	B	B	Rad					LE	Selfist	•
57	Keyes, Alan	8	7	1950		Republican	t	R	R	+	+	Prog					LM	Selfist	•
58	Kissinger, Henry	5	27	1923		Republican	a	B	B	B	B	Prog			RadLib		LM	Humanist	ec
59	Koch, Ed	12	12	1924		Democrat	t	+	B	B	+	Rad			ProCon		RM	Humanist	e
60	Kucinich, Dennis	10	8	1946		Democrat	t	B	–	B	B	Prog					LM	Humanist	c
61	La Follette, Robert M.	6	14	1885	1925	Rep/Progressive	p	–	B	B	+	Prog					LM	Selfist	•
62	LaGuardia, Fiorello	12	11	1882	1947	Republican	a	B	R	R	R	RadPro			RadLib		RM	Humanist	ec
63	Leahy, Patrick	3	31	1940		Democrat	t	–	B	–	R					Lib	RM	Otherist	c
64	Lee, Robert E.	1	19	1807	1870	Confederate	a	R	B	B	B	Rad			ConPro	Cons	RM	Otherist	e
65	Levin, Carl	6	28	1934		Democrat	p	B	B	–	B		Lib			Cons	RE	Elitist	ec
66	Lieberman, Joseph	2	24	1942		Independent	t	R	B	R	R	Rad			ProLib		RM	Humanist	•
67	MacArthur, Douglas	1	26	1880	1964	Republican	t	+	+	–	B	Prog			ConLibPro		RM	Otherist	ec
68	McCain, John	8	29	1936		Republican	t	B	B	B	B	Rad			RadConPro		LE	Humanist	c
69	McCarthy, Eugene	3	29	1916		Democrat	t	R	R	+	+		Cons		LibRad		RE	Elitist	•
70	McCarthy, Joseph R.	11	14	1908	1957	Republican	t	+	R	B	+	Rad			RadLib		RE	Selfist	•
71	McClellan, George B.	12	3	1826	1885	Democrat	t	B	B	B	R	Rad			ConPro		LM	Otherist	ec
72	McGovern, George	7	9	1922		Democrat	t	B	B	B	R		Cons		LibProCon		RM	Otherist	e
73	Mitchell, John	9	5	1913	1988	Republican	a	–	–	–	–		Lib		LibPro		LM	Humanist	e
74	Moynihan, Daniel P.	3	16	1927	2003	Democrat	t	+	+	+	+		Lib				LE	Elitist	•
75	Palin, Sarah	2	11	1964		Republican		R	R	+	R	Rad		RadPro		ConLib	RE	Humanist	ec
76	Patton, George	11	11	1885	1945	US Army	t	–	B	R	B		Cons		ProLib		RM	Elitist	•
77	Paul, Ronald	8	20	1935		Republican	a	B	B	B	B	Prog			RadLib		LM	Humanist	e
78	Pelosi, Nancy	3	26	1940		Democrat		–	+	+	R	Rad					RM	Selfist	ec
79	Perle, Richard N.	9	16	1941		Republican	p	R	B	+	R		Cons		ConLibRad		RE	Elitist	e
80	Powell, Colin	4	5	1937		Republican	a	B	R	R	R	Prog		Prog			LM	Humanist	ec

Table 3. US Governmental Figures

#	Name				Party															
81	Rayburn, Sam	1	6	1882		Democrat	t	R	–	–	–	–						RM	Otherist	ec
82	Reich, Robert	6	24	1946		Democrat	a	–	R	+	R	R					Cons	RE	Elitist	e
83	Reid, Harry	12	2	1939		Democrat	p	+	–	B	–	B			Lib	Lib	LM	Selfist	
84	Rice, Condoleezza	11	14	1954		Republican	t	–	R	B	+	R	Prog		Cons	Cons	RM	Elitist	
85	Richardson, William	11	5	1947		Democrat		+	B	B	+	R			Cons	ConLib	LE	Elitist	
86	Rockefeller, Nelson	7	8	1908		Republican	t	B	B	+	R	R			Cons	ConRad	LM	Elitist	
87	Romney, Willard Mitt	3	12	1947		Republican	p	R	–	R	–	+			Cons	ConPro	RE	Elitist	
88	Roosevelt, Eleanor	10	11	1884		Democrat	t	B	+	–	R	+	Rad		Lib	LibCon	LE	Selfist	
89	Rostenkowski, Dan	1	2	1928	1962	Republican	t	B	–	B	–	–			Lib	LibPro	LM	Otherist	ec
90	Rove, Karl	12	25	1950		Republican	t	B	–	B	–	–				LibPro	LM	Elitist	
91	Rumsfeld, Donald	7	9	1932		Republican	p	+	+	B	+	R		Rad	Cons	ConRad	LE	Otherist	ec
92	Sanders, Bernard	9	8	1941		Independent		R	–	+	B	R			Cons	ConRad	RE	Elitist	
93	Schroeder, Patricia	7	30	1940		Democrat	t	B	–	–	+	B	Prog			ProLib	RM	Selfist	
94	Schwarzenegger, A.	7	30	1947		Republican	t	B	R	B	+	B	Prog				LM	Selfist	
95	Starr, Kenneth	7	21	1946		Republican		–	+	B	R	R		Rad	Cons		RE	Elitist	
96	Stevenson, Adlai	2	5	1900		Democrat	t	–	+	B	+	+	Rad			ConRad	LE	Selfist	
97	Taft, Robert A.	9	8	1889		Republican		B	+	R	R	+				RadCon	LE	Selfist	
98	Thurmond, Strom	12	5	1902	2003	Republican	t	R	+	R	R	+		Rad		ConPro	RE	Selfist	
99	Ventura, Jesse	7	15	1951		Reform/Independent	t	R	B	B	B	R				ConPro	LE	Elitist	
100	Wallace, George C.	8	25	1919	1998	Democrat	t	R	+	B	B	+			Cons	ConRad	RM	Otherist	ec
101	Watson, Thomas E.	9	5	1856	1922	Populist		–	+	–	–	R		Rad	Cons	RadCon	LE	Selfist	
102	Webb, James H.	2	9	1946		Democrat		–	+	+	R	+			Cons	ConPro	RM	Elitist	
103	Wellstone, Paul	7	21	1944	2002	Democrat		R	+	R	R	R			Cons	ConRad	LE	Selfist	
104	Wilson, Charles E.	7	18	1890	1961	Republican		R	B	B	R	R			Cons		RE	Elitist	
105	Wolfowitz, Paul	12	22	1943		Republican		B	R	+	B	+			Cons	ConPro	LE	Elitist	

B	35	20	40	26	19
+	20	30	20	32	28
–	26	36	24	17	22
R	24	19	21	30	36

	47	58	28	55	22
	(Power Only)	105	Leftist	Conflicted	Rightist
	45%	55%	27%	52%	21%

Table 3. Totals & Analysis

Total Names= **105**
Total Impulses= 525

Impulse Deviations from Norm   **Slight**

Maximum Value
Typical Pattern

B	–	B	+	R

t=timed birth; p or a= Will system might differ if pm or am birthtime

Type Summary
LM=	28	27%
LE=	31	30%
RM=	27	26%
RE=	19	18%
	105	100%

E/C Summary
E&C	23	22%
E Only	22	21%
C Only	20	19%
Neither	40	38%
	105	100%

J-P Summary
Humanists=	16	15%
Otherists=	27	26%
Selfists=	31	30%
Elitists=	31	30%
	105	100%

APPENDIX B: TABLES OF INDIVIDUALS   B-30

Table 4. US Non-Governmental Political Figures

No.	Name	Birthdate Mo	Birthdate Day	Birthdate Year	Died	Data	W	T	F	J	P	Attitude Leftist	Attitude	Attitude Rightist	Perspective Leftist	Perspective Conflicted	Perspective Rightist	Type	J-P	E/C
1	Abernathy, Ralph	3	11	1926	1990	Baptist Activist	t	R	B	+	–	R		Cons			Cons	RE	Otherist	c
2	Addams, Jane	9	6	1860	1935	Activist/Feminist	t	–	R	R	–	R		Cons			ConLib	RE	Otherist	ec
3	Ali, Muhammad	1	17	1942		Activist	t	R	B	B	R	R		Cons			Cons	RE	Elitist	•
4	Barton, Clara	12	25	1821	1912	Red Cross	t	B	B	B	R	R		Cons		ConPro		RM	Otherist	ec
5	Bauer, Gary	5	4	1946		Rep. Activist	p	R	+	+	+	R		Lib		ConRad		LE	Elitist	•
6	Boudin, Kathy	5	19	1943		Weather Under.	p	B	B	R	–	R		Lib		LibPro		RM	Elitist	e
7	Brown, John	5	9	1800	1859	Activist	p	B	B	R	–	B				ProLib		RM	Otherist	ec
8	Browne, Harry	6	17	1933		Libertarian		+	+	B	–	–		Prog			LibCon	LM	Humanist	ec
9	Burros, Don	3	5	1937		Nazi	t	R	B	R	R	B			Lib			RM	Otherist	c
10	Chavez, Cesar	3	31	1927	1993	Activist	t	B	B	B	B	B	Prog	Prog				LM	Humanist	ec
11	Chomsky, Noam	12	7	1928	1998	Activist	p	+	+	–	–	B		Prog		ProRadLib		LM	Otherist	ec
12	Cleaver, Eldridge	8	31	1935	1998	Leftist-to-Rightist		R	R	R	R	–			Lib		Lib	RM	Otherist	ec
13	Colin, Frank	11	3	1944		Nazi	t	R	+	R	–	B			Lib		LibCon	RE	Elitist	•
14	Darrow, Clarence S.	4	18	1857	1938	Defense Atty.	t	R	–	+	–	+		Rad		RadLib		RM	Humanist	ec
15	Davis, Angela	5	26	1944		Activist	t	+	R	–	–	+	Rad	Rad				LE	Selfist	•
16	Davis, Rennie	5	23	1940		Activist	t	R	–	R	–	B		Prog		ProCon		RM	Selfist	e
17	Debs, Eugene V.	11	5	1855	1926	Socialist	t	B	R	–	–	–			Cons	ConLib		RM	Otherist	ec
18	Dohrn, Bernadine	1	12	1942		Weather Under.	p	R	B	R	R	R			Cons	Cons		RE	Otherist	ec
19	Duke, David	7	1	1950		Nazi	t	R	B	B	–	–			Lib			LE	Elitist	•
20	Dworkin, Andrea	9	26	1946		Feminist	t	+	+	B	B	B	ProRad	Prog		LibRad		LE	Selfist	•
21	Friedan, Betty	2	4	1921		Feminist	t	–	+	+	–	+		Prog		ProLib		LM	Humanist	c
22	Garrison, William Lloyd	12	10	1805	1879	Activist	t	+	R	R	–	B		Rad		RadCon		RE	Selfist	ec
23	Garvey, Marcus Moziah	8	17	1887	1940	Activist	a	+	+	+	R	B	ProRad	Prog				LE	Humanist	•
24	Gold, Ted	8	13	1947	1970	Weather Under.	a	B	–	B	R	B	RadPro	Rad				LE	Selfist	•
25	Goldman, Emma	6	27	1869	1940	Anarchist	t	+	–	–	–	+					Lib	LE	Selfist	•
26	Groppi, James E.	11	16	1930	1985	Cath. Activist	t	R	R	R	R	R		Lib			LibCon	RM	Otherist	c
27	Hayden, Tom	12	11	1939		Activist	t	B	–	R	+	+		Rad		RadLib		RE	Selfist	e
28	Hoffa, Jimmy	2	14	1913	1975?	Labor Leader	t	+	R	R	R	B		Prog		ProCon		RE	Selfist	e
29	Hoffman, Abbie	11	30	1936	1989	Activist	t	B	B	B	B	+		Rad		RadLibPro		LM	Humanist	ec
30	Horowitz, David	1	10	1939		Leftist-to-Rightist	t	B	R	R	–	–			Lib	LibProCon		RM	Elitist	e
31	Jackson, Jesse L.	10	8	1941		Baptist Activist	t	R	R	B	+	B		Lib		RadLib		LE	Selfist	e
32	Jones, Mary (Mother)	5	1	1830	1930	Labor Organizer	a	B	R	R	R	+		Rad				RM	Elitist	e
33	Jordan, Vernon	8	15	1935		Lawyer	t	–	B	B	+	B	Rad	Prog			Lib	RM	Humanist	ec
34	Kerry, Teresa Heinz	10	5	1938		RepDem		+	B	–	–	+		Prog		ProLib		LE	Selfist	e
35	King, Martin L.	1	15	1929	1968	Baptist Activist	t	B	+	B	R	B		Prog	Lib	LibPro		LM	Otherist	ec
36	Kunstler, William	7	7	1919	1995	Defense Atty.	t	B	B	B	–	B		Prog	Lib	LibPro		LM	Otherist	c
37	Lewis, John L.	2	12	1880	1969	Labor Leader	t	B	B	B	–	B		Prog		ProLib		LM	Humanist	ec
38	Lindbergh, Charles	2	4	1902	1974	Nazi Supporter	t	+	R	B	+	+		Rad		RadCon		LE	Selfist	•
39	Nader, Ralph	2	27	1934		Activist	t	R	R	R	–	R			Cons		Cons	RE	Otherist	ec
40	Newton, Huey	2	17	1942	1989	Activist	t	–	B	R	R	+		Rad		RadCon		RE	Selfist	e

Table 4. US Non-Governmental Political Figures

#	Name					Role																			
41	O'Hair, Madalyn Murray	4	13	1919	1999	Atheism Activist	t	+	B	B	B				Prog	Prog		LM	Humanist	c
42	Parks, Rosa	2	4	1913		Activist		R	+	R	R	B			Prog	ProCon		RE	Selfist	e
43	Phillips, Wendell	11	29	1811	1884	Activist	a	+	B	+	B	B			Prog	ProRad		LM	Humanist	c
44	Poynter, Ralph	3	21	1934		Activist		+	R	B	+	B			Rad		RadCon	LE	Humanist	ec
45	Reed, Jack	10	20	1887	1920	Author, CLP		+	R	–	R	B			Prog		ProCon	RE	Selfist	e
46	Reuther, Walter	9	1	1907	1970	Labor Leader		–	–	–	R	R		Cons				RM	Elitist	e
47	Rockwell, Geo. Lincoln	3	9	1918	1967	Nazi	t	–	R	+	–	R		Cons			ConLib	RE	Otherist	c
48	Rubin, Jerry	7	4	1938	1994	Leftist-to-Rightist	t	+	B	–	R	–		Lib		ConRad	Lib	RM	Elitist	e
49	Rudd, Mark	6	2	1947		Weather Under.	p	B	R	B	R	B			Prog			LM	Selfist	•
50	Seale, Bobby	10	22	1936		Activist	t	–	B	–	–	R		Cons			ConLib	RM	Otherist	ec
51	Sekulow, Jay A.	6	22	1956		Jews for Jesus		–	+	B	R	+			Rad			LE	Selfist	•
52	Steinem, Gloria	3	25	1934		Feminist	t	+	R	R	B	+			Rad		RadCon	LE	Humanist	ec
53	Stewart, Lynne	10	8	1939		Defense Atty.		+	B	R	+	+			Rad			LE	Selfist	e
54	Thomas, Norman	11	20	1884	1968	Socialist	a	B	+	R	+	–		Lib		LibRad		LE	Elitist	e
55	X, Malcolm	5	19	1925	1965	Activist	t	–	–	+	–	–		Lib			Lib	RM	Otherist	c

Table 4. Totals & Analysis

	B	14	21	9	8	15	29	26	10	28	17
	+	17	11	12	8	14		55			55
	–	11	8	17	20	15	L	R	Leftist	Conflicted	Rightist
	R	13	15	17	19	11	53%	47%	18%	51%	31%

	17	21	17	20	15
+	B	–	–	B	–
–			R		

Total Names= **55**
Total Impulses= 275

Impulse Deviations from Norm **Slight**

Maximum Value
Typical Pattern
(Tied Count)

E/C Summary		
E&C	19	**35%**
E Only	15	27%
C Only	9	16%
Neither	12	22%
	55	100%

Type Summary		
LM	10	18%
LE	13	24%
RM	19	**35%**
RE	13	24%
	55	100%

J-P Summary		
Humanists	13	24%
Otherists	15	27%
Selfists	16	29%
Elitists	11	20%
	55	100%

t=timed birth; p or a= Will system differs if pm or am birthtime

APPENDIX B: TABLES OF INDIVIDUALS   B-32

Table 5. US Revolutionary Figures

No.	Name	Birthdate Mo	Birthdate Day	Birthdate Year	Died	Data	W	T	F	J	P	Attitude	Perspective Leftist	Perspective Conflicted	Perspective Rightist	Type	J-P	E/C
1	Adams, Samuel	9	27	1722n	1803	Antifederalist	B	+	–	–	B	+	Rad		RadPro		LM	Humanist	ec
2	Burr, Aaron	2	6	1756	1836	Antifederalist	B	B	B	B	R	+	Rad		RadPro		LM	Selfist	·
3	Clinton, George	8	6	1739n	1812	Antifederalist	–	–	–	–	–	+	Rad			RadLib		RM	Humanist	ec
4	Gerry, Elbridge	7	17	1744*	1814	Antifederalist	B	B	B	B	B	R		Cons			ConLib	RM	Otherist	ec
5	Hancock, John	1	23	1737n	1793	Antifederalist	t	B	B	B	–	+	Rad		RadPro		LM	Humanist	c
6	Henry, Patrick	5	29	1736n	1799	Antifederalist	+	+	B	B	R	+	Rad		Rad		LE	Selfist	·
7	Lee, Richard Henry	1	20	1732*	1794	Antifederalist	B	+	+	+	R	+	Rad		Rad		LE	Selfist	·
8	Livingston, Robert R	11	27	1746*	1813	Antifederalist	a	B	+	–	B	+	Rad		Rad		LE	Humanist	ec
9	Martin, Luther	2	9	1748*^	1826	Antifederalist	a	R	+	+	B	+	Rad		Rad		LE	Humanist	ec
10	Mason, George	12	11	1725*	1792	Antifederalist	p	–	B	+	+	B	Prog		ProRad		LM	Selfist	ec
11	Paine, Thomas	1	29	1737*	1809	Antifederalist		B	B	B	–	+	Rad		RadPro		LM	Humanist	c
1	Jefferson, Thomas	4	13	1743n	1826	AF, later Fed	t	+	–	–	B	B	Prog		ProLib		LM	Humanist	ec
2	Chase, Samuel	4	17	1741*	1811	AF, later Fed	p	B	B	R	–	B	Prog			RadLib		LM	Humanist	ec
3	Randolph, Edmund J	8	10	1753	1813	AF, later Fed		–	–	B	R	+	Rad					RM	Selfist	·
1	Adams, John	10	30	1735n	1826	Federalist	t	R	R	B	+	–		Lib			LibCon	RE	Elitist	·
2	Cushing, William	3	1	1732*	1810	Federalist		B	R	+	R	R		Cons		ConRad		LE	Elitist	ec
3	Ellsworth, Oliver	4	29	1745*	1807	Federalist		R	+	B	+	–		Lib			LibCon	RE	Otherist	·
4	Franklin, Benjamin	1	17	1706n	1790	Federalist	t	–	+	B	+	–		Lib		LibRad		LM	Elitist	ec
5	Hamilton, Alexander	1	11	1755*^	1804	Federalist		–	–	B	R	+		Lib			Lib	RM	Elitist	·
6	Iredell, James	10	5	1751*	1799	Federalist		+	B	+	B	+	Rad		Rad		LE	Selfist	·
7	Jay, John	12	12	1745*	1829	Federalist		+	R	–	R	+	Rad		RadLib		RE	Humanist	ec
8	Johnson, Thomas	11	4	1732*	1819	Federalist		R	B	B	R	R		Cons			Cons	RE	Elitist	·
9	King, Rufus	3	24	1755	1827	Federalist		R	B	+	R	B	Prog		ProRad		LE	Selfist	ec
10	Madison, James	3	16	1751n	1836	Federalist	t	+	+	+	R	+	Rad		Rad		RE	Elitist	·
11	Morris, Gouverneur	1	31	1752n	1816	Federalist	t	+	R	R	B	R		Rad			LibCon	LE	Selfist	·
12	Paterson, William	12	24	1745*	1806	Federalist		B	B	R	R	R		Cons		ConPro		RE	Otherist	ec
13	Pinckney, Charles	10	26	1757	1824	Federalist		–	B	–	B	R		Lib		LibPro		LE	Elitist	·
14	Rutledge, John	9	18	1739*	1800	Federalist	p	R	R	+	B	R		Cons		ConPro		RM	Otherist	ec
15	Sherman, Roger	4	30	1721n	1793	Federalist	p	+	+	B	B	R		Cons		ConRad		LE	Otherist	ec
16	Washington, George	2	22	1732n	1799	Federalist	t	+	+	R	R	R		Cons		ConRad		LE	Elitist	·
17	Wilson, James	9	14	1742*	1798	Federalist		B	–	R	–	–		Lib			Lib	RM	Otherist	ec

Table 5. US Revolutionary Figures

Table 5. Totals & Analysis

B	11	8	10	8	4	17	14	13	11	7
+	9	11	7	6	13					31
−	6	6	8	7	7					
R	5	6	6	10	7					
						L	R	Leftist	Conflicted	Rightist
						55%	**45%**	**42%**	35%	23%

Total Names= **31**
Total Impulses= 155

Impulse Deviations from Norm   **Projection High**

Maximum Value   11 11 10 10 13
Typical Pattern   B + B R +

° ° ° ° °

E/C Summary
E&C	13	**42%**
E Only	1	3%
C Only	2	6%
Neither	15	**48%**
	31	100%

Type Summary
LM	8	26%
LE	11	**35%**
RM	6	19%
RE	6	19%
	31	100%

J-P Summary
Humanists	9	29%
Otherists	6	19%
Selfists	8	26%
Elitists	8	26%
	31	100%

n=NS date <=1/30 is also suggested, but same pattern
*=Date given by all references, with no OS/NS designation
^=year in question, but this is more likely   t=timed birth; p or a= Will system differs if pm or am birthtime
Italized names also on a previous table(s)

APPENDIX B: TABLES OF INDIVIDUALS   B-34

Table 6. US Media Figures

No.	Name	Birthdate Mo	Day	Year	Died	Data	W	T	F	J	P	Attitude		Perspective Leftist	Conflicted	Rightist	Type	J-P	E/C
1	Alterman, Eric	1	14	1960		Columnist/Author	a	R	R	–	–	R	Rad		Rad			RE	Otherist	ec
2	Anderson, Jack	10	19	1922	2005	News Columnist	t	–	B	–	B	+	Prog				Cons	LE	Humanist	c
3	Beatty, Warren	3	30	1937		Actor/Producer	t	–	–	B	+	B	Rad		Rad	ProLib		LM	Humanist	ec
4	Berstein, Carl	2	14	1944		Journ/Author/TV	p	+	+	B	+	+	Rad		Rad			LE	Selfist	·
5	Blitzer, Wolf	3	22	1948		TV News	p	+	B	+	+	+		Cons				LE	Selfist	c
6	Brinkley, David	7	10	1920	2003	TV News	a	–	B	–	–	B	Rad			ConLibPro		RM	Otherist	e
7	Brokaw, Tom	2	6	1940		TV News		+	–	–	+	+	Prog					LE	Selfist	·
8	Brooks, David	8	11	1961		W.Times/TV		R	+	–	–	B		Cons				RE	Humanist	ec
9	Buchanan, Patrick	11	2	1938		Rep. Author, TV	t	B	–	B	B	–		Cons		ProLib	Cons	RE	Elitist	e
10	Buckley, Wm. F. Jr	11	24	1925	2008	Rep. Author, TV	t	–	B	B	B	–	Prog			ProLib		LM	Humanist	c
11	Carlson, Tucker	5	16	1969		W.Times/TV	a	R	+	R	B	–		Lib			LibCon	RE	Otherist	ec
12	Cavett, Dick	11	19	1936		TV Host	t	–	–	–	–	R		Cons			ConLib	RM	Otherist	ec
13	Cockburn, Alexander	6	6	1941		Columnist/Editor	a	–	B	–	+	B	Rad			RadLibCon		RE	Selfist	e
14	Cooper, Marc	12	18	1950		Author/Radio	t	+	B	R	+	B	Prog					LM	Selfist	·
15	Cosby, Bill	7	12	1937		TV Comic		B	–	B	–	–		Lib			Lib	RM	Otherist	ec
16	Coughlin, Fr. Charles	10	25	1891	1979	Hate Radio		R	–	R	–	R		Lib			Lib	RM	Elitist	·
17	Coulter, Ann	12	8	1961		Rep. Author, TV		R	B	R	B	+	Rad		ProRad	RadConPro		LE	Humanist	ec
18	Cronkite, Walter	11	14	1916		TV News		B	R	+	B	R		Cons		ConPro		LE	Otherist	c
19	Cusack, John	6	28	1966		Actor/Activist		–	B	–	B	–		Lib		LibPro		LE	Otherist	ec
20	Disney, Walt	12	5	1901	1966	Movies/Comics	t	R	R	B	R	B	Prog			ProCon		RE	Selfist	e
21	Dobbs, Lou	9	24	1945		TV/Radio News		–	B	–	–	+	Rad			RadCon		RE	Selfist	·
22	Donahue, Phil	12	21	1935		TV Host		–	–	–	B	+	Rad			RadLib		RM	Humanist	ec
23	Dowd, Maureen	1	14	1952		NYT/Author	t	+	+	+	+	R		Cons		ConRad		LE	Elitist	·
24	Eastwood, Clint	5	31	1930		Actor/Producer	t	B	R	B	B	+	Rad			RadCon		RE	Humanist	ec
25	Flynt, Larry	11	1	1942		Porn Publisher	t	+	+	B	B	–		Lib		LibRad		RE	Elitist	·
26	Fonda, Henry	5	16	1905	1982	Actor	t	R	–	R	–	R					LibCon	LE	Elitist	ec
27	Fonda, Jane	12	21	1937		Actor/Activist	t	B	B	B	–	+	Rad			RadConLib		RE	Humanist	ec
28	Forbes, Steve	7	18	1947		Mag. Publisher	t	R	R	R	+	B		Cons		LibPro		LM	Elitist	ec
29	Franken, Al	5	21	1951		Radio/SNL/Actor	t	R	–	–	B	+	Rad		Rad			LE	Elitist	e
30	Friedman, Tom	7	20	1953		NYT/Author	t	B	+	+	R	R					LibCon	LE	Elitist	·
31	Godkin, Edwin L.	10	2	1831	1902	Fdr. The Nation	a	–	R	R	+	B	Rad			ConPro		RE	Humanist	ec
32	Goodman, Amy	4	13	1957		Author/Radio		+	R	R	+	B	Rad			RadCon		LE	Elitist	e
33	Gregory, Dick	10	12	1932		Comed./Activist		R	+	–	B	B	Prog		Prog	ProRadCon		LM	Humanist	ec
34	Griffin, Merv	7	6	1925	2007	TV/Movies		B	+	–	B	–	Prog					LM	Otherist	c
35	Hearst, William R.	4	29	1863	1951	Newspapers	t	–	–	B	–	+		Cons		LibPro		RE	Humanist	c
36	Hefner, Hugh	4	9	1926		Media		–	B	–	B	+	Rad		RadPro		ConLib	LM	Otherist	c
37	Heston, Charlton	10	4	1923	2008	Actor/Rep/NRA	t	B	B	B	+	B	Prog			ProLib		RE	Humanist	c
38	Hitchens, Christopher	4	26	1949		Columnist/Author		+	R	R	+	R		Cons		ConRad		LM	Elitist	c
39	Huffington, Arianna	7	7	1950		TV/Books	t	R	R	–	B	–		Lib		LibRad		RE	Elitist	·
40	Hume, Brit	6	22	1943		W.Times	a	B	+	+	+	–		Lib		LibRad		LE	Elitist	e

B-35 Human Nature

Table 6. US Media Figures

#	Name			Year	Year2	Role													
41	Ifill, Gwen	9	29	1955		TV News/Host		−	+	+	+	Rad			RadLib		LE	Selfist	•
42	Jennings, Peter	7	29	1938		TV News		B	−	−	+	Rad					LM	Selfist	e
43	King, Larry	11	19	1933		TV Host		+	R	−	R					ConLib	RE	Otherist	ec
44	Kristol, William	12	23	1952		Neocon/Rep	p	+	B	−	−		Cons		LibRad		LE	Elitist	•
45	Leno, Jay	4	28	1950		TV Host	a	+	−	−	−		Lib			Lib	RM	Elitist	•
46	Letterman, David	4	12	1947		TV Host	t	B	−	B	B		Lib				LM	Selfist	•
47	Limbaugh, Rush	1	12	1951		Rep. Radio Host	t	R	+	+	−	Prog			LibRad		LM	Elitist	•
48	Maddow, Rachel	4	1	1973		TV/Radio News	t	−	+	+	+	Rad					LE	Selfist	•
49	Maher, Bill	1	20	1956		TV Host/Comic		B	+	+	+	Rad					LE	Selfist	•
50	Matthews, Chris	12	17	1945		TV News/Host	p	+	+	+	+	Rad					LE	Selfist	•
51	Miller, Dennis	11	3	1953		Rep. TV guest	a	R	+	+	R				ConRad		LE	Elitist	•
52	Moon, Sun Myung	1	6	1920		Fdr.Wash.Times		−	+	B	R				ConRad		LE	Otherist	c
53	Moore, Michael	4	23	1954		Film Producer		−	+	B	R				ConPro		RM	Elitist	•
54	Moyers, Bill	6	5	1934		Journ/Author/TV	a	R	+	+	+	Rad			RadLib		LM	Humanist	ec
55	Murdoch, Rupert	3	11	1931		Fox Network	t	+	B	−	−		Lib			LibCon	RE	Otherist	ec
56	Murrow, Edward R.	4	25	1908	1965	TV Host/News		+	R	B	R		Cons		ConRad		LE	Elitist	•
57	Newman, Paul	1	26	1925		Actor/Philan.		−	B	B	B	Prog			ProLib		LM	Humanist	e
58	Novak, Robert	2	26	1831		Columnist/TV		R	+	−	−		Lib			Lib	RE	Otherist	c
59	O'Donnell, Rosie	3	21	1962		TV Host		−	R	−	−	Rad			RadCon		RE	Humanist	ec
60	Olbermann, Keith	1	27	1959		TV News/Host		R	R	+	+	Prog			ProLibCon		RM	Humanist	ec
61	O'Reilly, Bill	9	10	1949		Fox TV Host		R	B	+	+		Lib		LibPro		LM	Otherist	c
62	Pearson, Drew	12	13	1897	1969	Columnist/Radio		+	+	+	+	Rad					LE	Selfist	•
63	Podhoretz, John	4	18	1961		Neocon/Rep	t	+	R	B	R	Rad					LE	Humanist	ec
64	Rather, Dan	10	31	1931		TV News		−	+	B	+		Cons			ConLib	RM	Otherist	ec
65	Rich, Frank	6	2	1949		NY Times	t	R	−	+	+	Rad			RadCon		LE	Selfist	•
66	Rose, Charlie	1	5	1942		TV News/Host		B	+	R	+		Cons		ConRad		RE	Elitist	•
67	Russert, Tim	5	7	1950	2008	TV News/Host	a	R	−	+	−		Lib				RE	Selfist	•
68	Safire, William	12	17	1929		NY Times/TV		−	+	R	B	Rad			RadCon		RE	Elitist	•
69	Sawyer, Diane	12	22	1945		TV News/Host	t	R	R	B	+		Cons		ConRad		RE	Humanist	ec
70	Shields, Mark	5	25	1937		Columnist/TV	t	+	+	+	R	Prog			ProCon		RM	Humanist	ec
71	Stephanopoulos, Geo.	2	10	1961		Dem./TV News	t	R	+	B	B	Prog			ProCon		RE	Elitist	•
72	Stone, Oliver	9	15	1946		Film Producer	t	B	R	B	R		Cons		ConPro		LE	Elitist	•
73	Turner, Ted	11	19	1938		CNN/Time Warn.	t	+	+	+	+		Cons		ConRad		LE	Humanist	ec
74	vanden Heuvel, Katrina	10	7	1959		Ed. The Nation	p	R	−	+	+	Rad					LE	Humanist	ec
75	Walters, Barbara	9	25	1929		TV Interviewer	t	+	B	−	−	Rad				LibCon	LE	Humanist	ec
76	Williams, Brian	5	5	1959		TV News		R	R	B	R		Lib				RE	Otherist	ec
77	Winfrey, Oprah	1	29	1954		TV Host	t	B	+	R	+	Rad					LE	Selfist	•
78	Woodward, Bob	3	26	1943		Journ/Author/TV	t	+	B	+	B	Prog	ProRad		RadCon		LE	Selfist	•

Table 6. US Media Figures

Table 6. Totals & Analysis

											Type Summary		
B	12	19	18	19	14	41	37	18	45	15	LM	14	18%
+	21	15	22	29	27		78			78	LE	31	40%
−	20	21	16	18	18	L	R	Leftist	Conflicted	Rightist	RM	13	17%
R	25	23	22	12	19	53%	47%	23%	58%	19%	RE	20	26%
	°	°	°	°	°							78	100%

Total Names= **78**
Total Impulses= 390

Impulse Deviations from Norm   **Projection High, Balanced Low**

Maximum Value   25 23 22 29 27
Typical Pattern   R   R   +   +   +
(Tied Count)   R

	E/C Summary	
E&C	26	33%
E Only	12	15%
C Only	11	14%
Neither	29	37%
	78	100%

J-P Summary		
Humanists	21	27%
Otherists	16	21%
Selfists	20	26%
Elitists	21	27%
	78	100%

t=timed birth; p or a= Will system differs if pm or am birthtime

APPENDIX B: TABLES OF INDIVIDUALS   B-38

Table 7. World Political Figures

No.	Name	Birthdate Mo	Birthdate Day	Birthdate Year	Died	Data		W	T	F	J	P	Attitude	Perspective Leftist	Perspective Conflicted	Perspective Rightist	Type	J-P	E/C
1	Adenauer, Konrad	1	5	1876	1967	Germany	t	+	R	R	–	–	Lib			LibCon	RE	Otherist	ec
2	Agustus Caesar	9	23	-63	14	Italy	a	+	R	R	R	R	Cons			Cons	RE	Elitist	e
3	Aitkin, Jonathan	8	30	1942		Ireland	t	+	R	R	R	–	Lib			LibCon	RE	Elitist	e
4	Alexander III, Czar	3	10	1845n	1894	Russia	t	+	R	B	R	R	Cons			Cons	RE	Elitist	·
5	Andreotti, Giulio	1	14	1919		Italy	t	+	R	+	R	–	Lib		LibRad		LE	Otherist	c
6	Annan, Kofi	4	8	1938		Ghana	a	+	–	–	–	–	Rad		RadLib		RM	Humanist	ec
7	Aquino, Corazon	1	25	1933		Philippines	t	B	R	–	B	B	Prog		ProLib		RM	Otherist	ec
8	Arafat, Yassar	8	27	1929	2004	Egypt	t	R	R	–	–	R			ConPro		RM	Humanist	ec
9	Assad, Heliz al-	10	6	1930	2000	Syria	p	–	–	–	B	R	Prog		ProLib		RM	Otherist	ec
10	Attlee, Clement	1	3	1883	1967	England	t	–	–	–	–	B	Cons			ConLib	RM	Humanist	ec
11	Bandaranaike, Sirimavo	4	17	1916	2000	Ceylon	t	R	R	+	B	+	Rad		RadCon		LE	Humanist	c
12	Barak, Ehud	2	12	1942		Israel	t	–	B	B	R	+	Rad		RadCon		RE	Selfist	e
13	Batista, Fulgencio	1	16	1901	1973	Cuba	t	R	R	R	R	+	Cons			Cons	RE	Elitist	·
14	Benes, Eduard	5	28	1884	1948	Bohemia	t	B	–	+	B	B	Rad		RadLib		LM	Selfist	e
15	Ben-Gurion, David	10	16	1886	1973	Poland	t	R	R	B	R	R	Rad		RadCon		RE	Selfist	·
16	Beria, Levrenti	3	29	1899n	1953	Abkhasia	a	B	+	+	–	B	Prog	ProRad			LE	Selfist	e
17	Bertusconi, Silvio	9	29	1936		Italy	t	R	+	R	B	–	Rad		RadLib		RM	Humanist	·
18	bin Laden, Osama	3	10	1957		Saudi	t	–	–	–	R	–					LM	Elitist	ec
19	Bismarck, Otto von	4	1	1815	1898	Germany	t	B	R	B	+	+	Lib			LibCon	LE	Humanist	e
20	Blair, Tony	5	6	1953		Scotland	t	+	B	B	–	+	Lib	RadPro	LibRad		LE	Elitist	c
21	Bolivar, Simon	7	24	1783	1830	Venezuela	t	R	–	B	–	B		Prog			LM	Selfist	·
22	Bonaparte, Louis Nap. III	4	20	1808	1873	France	t	B	–	B	+	B	Prog	Prog			LM	Humanist	·
23	Bonaparte, Napoleon	8	15	1769	1821	Corsica	p	+	+	+	+	B	Prog		ProLib		RM	Humanist	c
24	Brandt, Willy	12	18	1913	1992	Germany	p	+	R	–	–	B	Prog	ProRad			LE	Humanist	ec
25	Briand, Aristide	3	28	1862	1932	France	t	–	B	B	–	B	Prog		ProLib		RM	Humanist	c
26	Brown, Gordon	2	20	1951		Scotland	t	+	B	B	–	–			LibPro		LM	Elitist	ec
27	Brundtland, Gro Harlem	4	20	1939		Norway	t	+	–	–	+	B	Prog		ProLib		LM	Humanist	e
28	Cassin, Rene	10	5	1887	1976	France	t	B	B	B	–	–	Prog	ProRad			LM	Selfist	c
29	Castro, Fidel	8	13	1926		Cuba	t	R	B	R	–	+	Rad	RadPro			LM	Humanist	·
30	Catherine the Great	5	2	1729n	1796	Poland	t	R	B	+	–	R				LibCon	RE	Elitist	c
31	Ceausescu, Nicholae	1	26	1918	1989	Romania	a	B	B	B	+	B	Rad	RadPro			LE	Humanist	c
32	Chamberlain, Neville	3	18	1869	1940	England	t	–	–	–	+	R					LM	Otherist	c
33	Chavez, Hugo	7	28	1954		Venezuela	t	B	B	R	B	B	Prog		ConPro		LM	Selfist	c
34	Chiang Kai-Shek	10	31	1887	1975	China	t	–	–	–	R	B			ProLib		RM	Elitist	·
35	Chirac, Jacques	11	29	1932		France	t	+	+	+	–	B	Prog		ProRadLib		LM	Humanist	ec
36	Churchill, Winston	11	30	1874	1965	England	t	B	B	R	B	+	Rad	RadPro		Lib	LE	Humanist	c
37	Clemenceau, Georges	9	28	1841	1929	France	t	B	B	B	–	B	Rad	RadPro			LE	Selfist	·
38	Cohn-Bendit, Daniel	4	4	1945		France	t	–	+	+	R	+	Prog	Prog			LE	Selfist	·
39	Collins, Michael	10	16	1890	1922	Ireland	t	B	R	R	B	+	Rad	Rad			LE	Selfist	·
40	Cromwell, Oliver	5	5	1599	1658	England	t	B	R	B	B	–	Lib		LibPro		LM	Elitist	·

Table 7. World Political Figures

#	Name																
41	Dayan, Moishe	5	4	1915	1981	Palestine	t	B +	R -	R -	B -	Rad	Lib		LibProCon	RM	Otherist	ec
42	De Gasperi, Alcide	4	3	1881	1954	Italy	t	+	-	-	+	Rad			RadLib	RM	Humanist	ec
43	De Valera, Eamon	10	14	1882	1975	NYC	t	-	R	R	B	Prog			ProLibCon	RM	Selfist	e
44	Deng Xiaoping	8	22	1904	1997	China	t	B	B	B	B	Prog				LM	Selfist	e
45	Devereaux, Robert	11	10	1566	1601	England	t	-	R	R	R		Cons	Prog	ConLib	RM	Otherist	c
46	Disraeli, Benjamin	12	21	1804	1881	England	t	+	R	R	B	Prog				LM	Humanist	ec
47	Duvalier, Francois	4	14	1907	1971	Haiti	t	-	B	B	B	Prog				RM	Selfist	e
48	Elizabeth I	9	7	1533	1603	England	t	-	-	-	R		Cons		ProLib	RE	Elitist	e
49	Farouk, King	2	11	1920	1965	Egypt	t	B	B	B	B	Rad				LM	Humanist	c
50	Fox, Vicente	7	2	1942		Mexico	t	+	+	+	+		Lib		RadLibPro	LE	Elitist	e
51	Franco, Francisco	12	4	1892	1975	Spain	t	B	R	R	R	Rad		RadPro	LibRad	LE	Selfist	e
52	Frederick the Wise	1	17	1463	1525	Saxony	t	+	B	B	B	Prog		Prog		LM	Selfist	c
53	Gandhi, Indira	11	19	1917	1984	India	t	B	B	B	B		Cons		ConPro	LM	Otherist	e
54	Gandhi, Mohandas	10	2	1869	1948	India	t	+	-	-	-	Prog			ProLib	LM	Humanist	e
55	Garabaldi, Guisseppe M.	7	4	1807	1882	France	t	R	R	R	R		Cons		ConRad	LE	Otherist	c
56	Gaulle, Charles de	11	22	1890	1970	France	t	+	+	+	+	Rad		Rad		LE	Selfist	c
57	Geismar, Alain	7	17	1939		France	t	R	B	B	B		Cons		Cons	LE	Elitist	•
58	George III	6	4	1738n	1820	England	t	R	B	B	B	Rad		RadPro		RE	Humanist	•
59	Giolitti, Giovanni	10	27	1842	1928	Italy		R	-	-	+		Lib		LibCon	LM	Elitist	ec
60	Gladstone, William	12	29	1809	1898	England	t	+	-	-	-		Cons		ConRad	RE	Elitist	•
61	Gorbachev, Mikhail	3	2	1931		Russia	t	+	B	B	R		Lib		LibCon	LE	Otherist	c
62	Guevarra, Che	5	14	1928	1967	Argentina	t	B	+	+	+		Cons		ConPro	LM	Otherist	ec
63	Gusmao, Xanana	6	21	1946		E.Timor	t	+	R	R	R	Rad			RadCon	RE	Selfist	c
64	Haider, Joerg	11	22	1950		Austria	t	R	+	+	+		Cons		ConRad	LE	Elitist	•
65	Hari, Mata	1	26	1878	1917	Neth		R	B	B	B		Cons			LM	Humanist	ec
66	Henry VIII	8	7	1491	1547	England	t	+	+	+	R	Prog		Prog	ConCon	LE	Elitist	•
67	Hideki, Tojo	6	28	1884	1948	Japan	t	+	+	+	R		Lib		LibPro	RE	Elitist	•
68	Hitler, Adolf	12	30	1889	1945	Austria	t	+	B	B	B		Lib		LibPro	RE	Elitist	•
69	Ho Chi Minh	4	20	1890	1969	Vietnam	t	+	R	R	R		Cons		ConRad	LE	Elitist	•
70	Hussein, Saddam	5	19	1937	2006	Iraq	t	+	+	+	-		Lib		Lib	RM	Otherist	ec
71	John the Steadfast	6	30	1468	1532	Germany	t	B	B	B	B		Lib		LibPro	LM	Otherist	ec
72	Kell, Vernon	11	21	1873	1942	England		R	R	R	R		Lib		Lib	RM	Otherist	c
73	Kim Jong-il	2	16	1941		Russia	p	-	+	+	+	Prog			ProCon	RE	Selfist	e
74	Kim Sung Ju	4	15	1912	1994	N. Korea	t	+	R	R	R	Rad			RadCon	RE	Elitist	e
75	Kohl, Helmut	4	3	1930		Germany		-	+	+	+	Rad			RadCon	RE	Humanist	ec
76	Koizumi, Junichiro	1	8	1942		Japan		B	B	B	R		Cons		ConLib	RE	Elitist	e
77	Krushchev, Nikita	4	17	1894n	1971	Russia		+	B	B	R	Rad		RadPro		LM	Selfist	•
78	Lafayette, Marquis de	9	6	1757	1834	France	p	+	B	B	B		Lib		LibRad	LE	Otherist	c
79	Lenin, Vladimir	4	22	1870n	1924	Russia	t	+	B	B	-		Lib		LibPro	LM	Elitist	•
80	Louis XII	6	27	1462	1516	France	t	B	B	B	R		Cons		ConPro	LE	Elitist	

APPENDIX B: TABLES OF INDIVIDUALS

Table 7. World Political Figures

#	Name			Born	Died	Country													
81	Louis XIII	9	27	1601	1643	France	t	R	–	R	+						RE	Selfist	e
82	Louis XIV	9	5	1638	1715	France	t	+	R	R	+				RadCon		RE	Elitist	e
83	Louis XV	2	15	1710	1774	France	t	–	B	+	–				LibRadCon		LE	Selfist	.
84	Louis XVI	8	23	1754	1793	France	t	–	R	+	+	Rad					RE	Elitist	.
85	Makhno, Nestor	10	27	1889*	1934	Ukraine					R					Cons	RE	Elitist	.
86	Mandela, Nelson	7	18	1918		South Africa	t	B	+	+	–			Lib	LibConRad		LM	Otherist	o
87	Mao Tse-Tung	12	26	1893	1976	China	t	+	+	+	R			Lib	LibProRad		LE	Elitist	.
88	Marcos, Ferdinand	9	11	1917	1989	Philippines	t	B	B	R	B			Lib	LibRad		LE	Otherist	o
89	Medici, Lorenzo de	1	10	1449	1492	Italy		B	R	+	–			Cons	ConRad		RE	Elitist	.
90	Milosevic, Slobodan	8	20	1941	2006	Yugoslavia	t	R	+	R	R	Rad		Lib		LibCon	LE	Selfist	o
91	Mitterand, Francois	10	26	1916	1996	France	p	+	+	–	+			Cons	RadCon		LE	Otherist	o
92	Mubarak, Hosni	5	4	1928		Egypt		B	R	+	R			Cons	ConRadPro		RE	Otherist	e
93	Mussolini, Benito	7	29	1883	1945	Italy		+	B	–	B	Prog	ProRad			Cons	LM	Selfist	.
94	Naidu, Sarojini	2	13	1879	1949	India	t	B	R	+	+	Rad	RadProLib				LM	Humanist	ec
95	Nassar, Adbal Gamal	1	15	1918	1970	Egypt	t	+	B	–	R		ConRad				LE	Otherist	.
96	Nehru, Jawaharlal	11	14	1889	1964	India	t	+	R	B	R			Cons	LibCon		LE	Elitist	.
97	Netanyahu, Benjamin	10	21	1949		Israel	t	B	+	+	B	Prog	ProRad	Lib			RE	Selfist	.
98	North, Frederick	4	13	1732	1792	England	p	B	+	+	+	Rad	Rad				LE	Selfist	.
99	Papandreou, Andreas	2	5	1919	1996	Greece	t	+	+	B	B	Prog	ProRad				LM	Humanist	.
100	Peres, Shimon	8	16	1923		Russia	t	+	–	B	–	Prog	ProRad				LM	Humanist	.
101	Petain, Henri	4	24	1856	1951	France	t	+	B	–	R			Lib		Lib	RM	Otherist	o
102	Pol Pot	5	19	1925	1998	Cambodia	t	+	R	+	R			Lib		Lib	RM	Otherist	.
103	Putin, Vladimir	10	7	1952		Russia	t	+	B	B	B	Prog	ProRad	Cons	ConPro		LM	Selfist	.
104	Rabin, Yitzhak	3	1	1922	1995	Israel	t	+	B	B	+		RadPro				LE	Otherist	o
105	Richard III	10	2	1452	1485	England	t	R	B	B	R	Rad		Cons	ConRad		LE	Selfist	.
106	Robespierre, Maximilian	5	6	1758	1794	France	t	+	+	+	+			Cons	ConRad		LE	Elitist	.
107	Röhm, Ernst	11	28	1887	1934	Germany	t	R	R	+	R				ProCon		RE	Elitist	.
108	Salazar, Antonio	4	28	1889	1970	Portugal		B	+	+	B	Prog		Lib		LibCon	RE	Elitist	.
109	San Martin, Jose de	2	25	1778	1850	Argentina		R	+	+	–		ProRad	Cons	ConRad		LE	Selfist	.
110	Sarkozy, Nicolas	1	28	1955		France	a	R	B	+	R	Prog					LE	Selfist	.
111	Schicklgruber, Alois	6	7	1837	1903	Austria	t	R	R	+	R	Rad			RadCon		LE	Selfist	.
112	Schindler, Oskar	4	28	1908	1974	Moravia		+	B	R	B		ProRad		ConRad		LE	Elitist	e
113	Schröder, Gerhard	4	7	1944		Germany	a	+	R	B	R	Rad		Cons	RadCon		LE	Selfist	.
114	Sharon, Ariel	2	27	1928		Israel	t	B	+	–	+			Cons		Cons	RE	Otherist	e
115	Stael, Germaine de	4	22	1766	1817	France	t	B	R	–	R			Cons		ConLib	RM	Otherist	o
116	Stalin, Joseph	1	2	1880n	1953	Russia	t	+	+	+	R			Lib	LibPro		LE	Elitist	o
117	Sugimara, Chiune	1	2	1900	1985	Japan	a	B	+	B	+			Cons	ConRad		LE	Elitist	.
118	Sukarno, Achmed	6	6	1901	1970	Indonesia	t	–	+	+	R	Prog			ProCon		RE	Selfist	.
119	Sun Yat-Sen	11	12	1866	1925	China	t	+	B	+	B					Lib	RM	Otherist	o
120	Thatcher, Margaret	10	13	1925		England	t	R	+	R	–	Prog	Prog	Lib			LM	Humanist	o

B-40

Table 7. World Political Figures

						t	R	–	B	+	R			Cons		RE	Elitist	•
121	Tito, Josep Broz	5	19	1892	1980	Yugoslavia												
122	Trotsky, Leon	11	7	1879n	1940	Ukraine	t	+	B	R	+	–			Lib	RM	Otherist	ec
123	Trujillo, Rafael	10	24	1891	1961	Dom.Rep.	t	–	B	B	+	–		LibPro	Lib	LM	Elitist	•
124	Wellington, Duke of	5	1	1769	1852	Ireland	t	–	B	R	–	–	Rad		Lib	RM	Otherist	ec
125	Wilhelm II	1	27	1859		Germany	t	B	R	R	–	+		RadCon		RE	Humanist	ec
126	Yeltsin, Boris	2	1	1931	1941	Russia		–	R	R	B	B	Prog	ProCon		RM	Humanist	ec

Table 7. Totals & Analysis

	B	36	38	32	24	31	61	30	65	31	
	+	37	27	40	34	30				126	
	–	23	22	25	34	34	L	Leftist	Conflicted	Rightist	
	R	30	39	29	34	31	48%	24%	52%	25%	

Total Names= **126**
Total Impulses= 630

Impulse Deviations from Norm **Slight**

Maximum Value   37 39 40 34 34
Typical Pattern   + R + + –
(Tied Count)   – R
(Tied Count)

Type Summary
LM	35	28%
LE	34	27%
RM	25	20%
RE	32	25%
	126	100%

E/C Summary
E&C	28	22%
E Only	26	21%
C Only	30	24%
Neither	42	**33%**
	126	100%

J-P Summary
Humanists	28	22%
Otherists	30	24%
Selfists	33	26%
Elitists	35	28%
	126	100%

n=NS date   t=timed birth; p or a= Will system differs if pm or am birthtime

APPENDIX B: TABLES OF INDIVIDUALS   B-42

Table 8. Philosophic Intellectuals

No.	Name	Birthdate Mo	Birthdate Day	Birthdate Year	Died	Data	W	T	F	J	P	Attitude	Perspective Leftist	Perspective Conflicted	Perspective Rightist	Type	J-P	E/C
1	Bacon, Francis	1	22	1561	1626	England	t	B	B	–	B	–	Rad	RadPro			LM	Humanist	ec
2	Berkeley, George	3	12	1685*	1753	Ireland		R	B	R	B	R	Cons		ConPro		RE	Otherist	ec
3	Comte, Auguste	1	17	1798	1857	France	a	R	B	–	+	R	Cons			Cons	RE	Elitist	e
4	Descartes, René	3	31	1596	1650	France	t	–	R	B	B	+		Rad			LE	Selfist	•
5	Feuerbach, Ludwig	7	28	1804	1872	Germany	t	+	+	R	+	+	Rad	Rad			LE	Humanist	ec
6	Fichte, Johann Gottlieb	5	19	1762	1814	Germany		+	R	+	B	R	Cons		ConRad		LE	Otherist	c
7	Hegel, George W.F.	8	27	1770	1831	Germany	p	B	–	R	B	R	Cons		ConPro		RM	Otherist	ec
8	Heidegger, Martin	9	26	1889	1976	England	t	+	+	+	R	B	Prog	ProRad			LE	Selfist	•
9	Hobbes, Thomas	4	15	1588n	1679	England	t	R	–	–	R	+	Rad		RadConLib		RE	Elitist	ec
10	Hume, David	5	7	1711n	1776	Scotland		–	R	R	–	–	Lib			LibCon	LE	Selfist	e
11	Hutcheson, Francis	8	8	1694	1746	N. Ireland	p	B	R	–	–	+	Rad	Rad			RE	Otherist	e
12	Kant, Immanuel	4	22	1724n	1804	Germany	t	B	B	R	–	R	Cons		ConPro	Cons	LE	Otherist	ec
13	Keyserling, Hermann	7	20	1880	1946	Germany	t	B	B	B	B	R	Cons		LibConPro		RM	Elitist	ec
14	Leibniz, Gottfried	7	1	1646n	1716	Germany	t	R	R	R	–	–	Lib			Lib	RM	Otherist	ec
15	Locke, John	9	9	1632n	1704	England		–	B	–	–	–	Lib			LibCon	RE	Otherist	ec
16	Mill, John Stuart	5	20	1806	1873	USA	p	+	R	R	–	B	Lib	ProRad			LE	Humanist	ec
17	Minnerly, Dick	5	31	1933		England		–	+	+	–	–	Prog		LibRad		RM	Otherist	c
18	Moore, G. E.	11	4	1873	1958	England	t	+	+	+	–	B	Prog	ProRad			LE	Selfist	•
19	Nietzsche, Friedrich	10	15	1844	1900	Germany	t	+	+	B	R	B	Cons		ConPro		LM	Otherist	ec
20	Rousseau, Jean J.	6	28	1712n	1778	Switzerland	t	B	B	B	R	B	Lib			LibCon	RM	Elitist	e
21	Sartre, Jean Paul	6	21	1905	1980	France	t	R	B	–	R	–					LE	Elitist	e
22	Schelling, Friedrich	1	27	1775	1854	Germany	t	+	–	R	–	B	Prog		ProLib		RM	Humanist	ec
23	Schopenhauer, Arthur	2	22	1788	1860	Germany	t	–	–	+	R	R				ConLib	RE	Elitist	•
24	Spencer, Herbert	4	27	1820	1903	England	t	+	R	+	B	–	Cons		LibPro		LM	Otherist	•
25	Spinoza, Baruch	12	4	1632n	1677	Netherlands	t	B	B	B	–	B	Lib		ProLib		LM	Humanist	ec
26	Wittgenstein, Ludwig	4	26	1889	1951	Austria	t	B	R	B	R	–	Prog		LibProCon		RM	Elitist	•

Table 8. Philosophic Intellectuals

Table 8. Totals & Analysis

Total Names= **26**
Total Impulses= **130**

Impulse Deviations from Norm: **Projection Low, Reversals High**

Maximum Value
Typical Pattern
(Tied Count)

B	8	10	4	7	5	10	16	7	12	7
+	7	6	4	4	5		26			
–	5	4	7	8	8	L	R	Leftist	Conflicted	Rightist
R	6	6	11	7	8	38%	62%	27%	46%	27%

8	10	11	8	8
B	B	R	–	R

Type Summary
LM 4   15%
LE 7   27%
RM 8   **31%**
RE 7   27%
    26 100%

J-P Summary
Humanists 5   19%
Otherists 10 **38%**
Selfists   5   19%
Elitists   6   23%
           26 100%

E/C Summary
E&C   13 **50%**
E Only   5   19%
C Only   2   8%
Neither   6   23%
          26 100%

n=NS date   t=timed birth; p or a= Will system differs if pm or am birthtime
*=Date given by all references, with no OS/NS designation

Table 9. Political Intellectuals

No.	Name	Birthdate Mo	Birthdate Day	Birthdate Year	Died	Politics	W	T	F	J	P		Attitude		Perspective Leftist	Perspective Conflicted	Perspective Rightist	Type	J-P	ocw
1	Ali, Tariq	10	21	1943		Leftist Author	B	+	B	+	+	p	Rad		RadPro			LE	Selfist	•
2	Bakunin, Mikhail A.	5	30	1814n	1876	Anarchist	R	B	+	–	B	p	Prog		Prog			LM	Humanist	c
3	Bentham, Jeremy	2	15	1748*	1832	Reformer	–	+	–	B	+		Rad			RadLib		LM	Humanist	ec
4	Bookchin, Murray	1	14	1921	2006	Anarch/Socialist	–	+	B	–	–			Lib			Lib	RM	Otherist	c
5	Burke, Edmund	1	12	1729n	1797	Cons. Whig	–	+	–	B	+					RadLib		LM	Humanist	ec
6	Carlyle, Thomas	12	4	1795	1881	Transcendentalist	B	–	R	B	+	t	Rad		Rad			LE	Selfist	e
7	Chernyshevsky, Nikolay	7	24	1828n	1889	Egoist/Reformer	R	B	R	R	B	p	Rad			ProCon		RE	Selfist	c
8	Croce, Benedetto	2	25	1866	1952	Liberal	B	B	B	B	–		Prog			LibPro		RM	Otherist	e
9	Diderot, Denis	10	5	1713	1784	Reformer	a	+	+	B	B	a		Lib		LibRad		RE	Otherist	c
10	Engels, Friedrich	11	28	1820	1895	Socialist	+	+	R	B	B	t		Lib				LM	Humanist	ec
11	Ferrer, Francisco	1	10	1859	1909	Anarch.Educator	B	B	R	–	R	p	Prog		Prog			RE	Otherist	ec
12	Fourier, F. M. Charles	4	7	1772	1837	Socialist	B	+	–	–	+	a	Rad	Cons		RadLib	Cons	LM	Humanist	ec
13	Godwin, William	3	2	1756	1836	Anarchist/Social.	+	–	+	R	R			Cons		ConRad		RE	Eliitist	•
14	Goldman, Emma	6	27	1869	1940	Anarch/Socialist	+	B	–	B	+	t		Lib			Lib	RM	Otherist	c
15	Hamilton, Alexander	1	11	1755	1804	Federalist	–	–	–	–	–			Lib			Lib	RM	Eliitist	•
16	Helvetius, Claude Adrien	2	26	1715	1771	Reformer	R	–	R	–	R			Cons			ConLib	RE	Otherist	ec
17	Jefferson, Thomas	4	13	1743	1826	Decentralist		B	B	B	B	t	Prog			ProLib		LM	Humanist	ec
18	Kropotkin, Peter	12	9	1842*	1921	Anarchist	B	B	+	B	B		Prog		Prog			LM	Selfist	•
19	Lenin, Vladimir	4	22	1870n	1924	Communist	+	B	–	B	–	t		Lib		LibPro		LM	Otherist	c
20	Machiavelli, Niccolò	5	2	1469	1527	Opportunist	+	+	B	R	+	t	Prog			ProCon	LibCon	RE	Otherist	ec
21	Maletesta, Errico	12	14	1853	1932	Anarchist	R	B	B	B	–			Cons				RM	Humanist	ec
22	Marx, Karl	5	5	1818	1883	Socialist	B	+	B	–	B		Prog		Prog		Lib	RM	Otherist	c
23	Mason, George	12	11	1725	1792	Decentralist	–	+	B	+	+	t	Prog		ProRad			LM	Selfist	•
24	Molinari, Gustave de	3	3	1819	1912	Anti-State Libtn.	R	–	B	B	R			Cons		ConPro		RE	Otherist	c
25	Montesquieu, Charles	1	18	1689	1755	Const.Monarchist	R	B	R	B	R			Cons			ConLib	RM	Otherist	ec
26	More, Thomas	2	6	1478	1535	RC Communist	R	B	R	B	+	t	Rad			RadConPro		LE	Humanist	ec
27	Owen, Robert	5	14	1771	1858	Socialist	B	B	B	R	–			Lib		LibPro		RM	Otherist	ec
28	Paine, Thomas	1	29	1737	1809	Reformer/AntiFed	B	–	–	–	+		Rad		RadPro			LM	Humanist	c
29	Proudhon, Pierre	1	15	1809	1865	Anarch/Socialist	B	–	B	B	B	t		Lib		LibPro		LM	Otherist	c
30	Saint-Simon, Henri de	10	17	1760	1825	Socialist	–	+	B	B	+	p	Rad		Rad			LE	Selfist	•
31	Sorel, Georges	11	2	1847	1922	Anarch/Socialist	+	+	+	R	+		Rad			LibRad		RE	Eliitist	•
32	Spooner, Lysander	1	19	1808	1887	Indl.Anarchist	R	B	+	B	B			Cons			Cons	RE	Otherist	ec
33	Stirner, Max	10	25	1806	1856	Egoist/Anarchist	R	R	R	B	R			Lib			LibCon	RE	Otherist	ec
34	Tucker, Benjamin	4	17	1854	1939	Indl.Anarchist	+	B	–	B	B		Prog		Prog			LM	Humanist	ec
35	Voltaire	11	21	1694	1778	Reformer	R	+	–	+	+		Rad		Rad			LE	Selfist	e
36	Wollstonecraft, Mary	4	27	1759	1797	Femin/Anarch	–	–	+	B	–			Lib		LibRad		RM	Eliitist	•

Table 9. Political Intellectuals

Table 9. Totals & Analysis

Total Names= **36**
Total Impulses= **180**

Assimilation High, Reversals Low

Impulse Deviations from Norm

B	7	10	12	13	8	17	19
+	7	10	6	8	9		36
–	11	12	7	12	13	L	R
R	11	4	11	3	6	47%	53%

					10	16	10
							36
					Leftist	Conflicted	Rightist
					28%	44%	28%

Maximum Value / Typical Pattern / (Tied Count)

	11	12	12	13	13
	–	–	B	B	–
	R				

E/C Summary

E&C	15	42%
E Only	3	8%
C Only	10	28%
Neither	8	22%
	36	100%

Type Summary

LM	12	**33%**
LE	5	14%
RM	9	25%
RE	10	28%
	36	100%

J-P Summary

Humanists	10	28%
Otherists	15	**42%**
Selfists	7	19%
Elitists	4	11%
	36	100%

n=NS date   t=timed birth; p or a= Will system differs if pm or am birthtime
*=Date given by all references, with no OS/NS designation   Italized names also on a previous table(s)

APPENDIX B: TABLES OF INDIVIDUALS   B-46

Table 10. Political Literary Figures

No.	Name	Birthdate Mo	Birthdate Day	Birthdate Year	Died	Birth Place		W	T	F	J	P	Attitude	Perspective Leftist	Perspective Conflicted	Perspective Rightist	Type	J-P	E/C
1	Beauvoir, Simone de	1	9	1908	1965	France	t	R	–	–	R	R					RE	Elitist	e
2	Blake, William	11	28	1757	1827	England	t	B	–	R	B	+		RadPro		Cons	LM	Selfist	·
3	Brecht, Bertold	2	10	1898	1956	Germany	t	+	R	B	+	+		Rad			LE	Selfist	·
4	Camus, Albert	11	7	1913	1960	Algeria	t	+	+	R	–	–			LibRad		RE	Otherist	ec
5	Cervantes, Miguel de	9	29	1547	1616	Spain	t	B	B	–	–	B	Lib				LM	Selfist	e
6	Coleridge, Samuel Taylor	10	21	1772	1834	England	t	R	B	–	–	+	Prog		RadLib		RM	Humanist	ec
7	Conrad, Joseph	12	3	1857*	1924	Ukraine		–	B	–	B	B	Rad		ProLib		LM	Humanist	ec
8	Dickens, Charles	2	7	1812	1870	England	t	R	B	–	B	+	Prog				LM	Humanist	c
9	Dostoyevsky, Fyodor	11	11	1821n	1881	Russia		+	–	B	–	B	Rad	RadPro			LM	Humanist	ec
10	Emerson, Ralph Waldo	5	25	1803	1882	USA	t	R	+	B	B	B			ConPro		LE	Otherist	ec
11	Goethe, Johann W.	8	28	1749	1832	Germany		–	+	–	–	–	Prog		ProCon		RM	Humanist	ec
12	Hecht, Ben	2	28	1894	1964	USA		+	–	–	+	–			LibRad	Lib	RE	Otherist	·
13	Hoffer, Eric	7	25	1902	1983	USA	a	R	R	+	R	+	Rad		LibRad		RE	Elitist	e
14	Holcroft, Thomas	12	10	1746*	1809	England		B	+	–	B	+	Rad		RadCon		LM	Selfist	e
15	Kafka, Franz	7	3	1883	1924	Czech.		+	B	R	R	–			RadLib		LM	Humanist	ec
16	Mailer, Norman	1	31	1923	2007	USA	t	B	+	B	B	B	Lib			LibCon	RE	Elitist	e
17	Montaigne, Michel de	2	28	1533	1592	France		+	+	–	+	–	Prog				LM	Humanist	e
18	Orwell, George	6	25	1903	1950	India	t	B	+	R	R	R				ConLib	RE	Elitist	e
19	Pound, Ezra	10	30	1885	1972	USA		B	+	R	R	+	Prog		LibRad		LE	Elitist	e
20	Rand, Ayn	2	15	1905n	1982	Russia		R	R	R	R	R				LibCon	RE	Elitist	e
21	Shelley, Mary W.	8	30	1797	1851	England	t	+	B	R	R	+	Rad		RadCon		LE	Selfist	e
22	Shelley, Percy Bysshe	8	4	1792	1822	England		–	R	+	+	+		Rad		Cons	RE	Elitist	e
23	Sinclair, Upton	9	20	1878	1968	USA	t	–	–	–	–	–	Rad			Lib	RM	Otherist	ec
24	Thoreau, Henry David	7	12	1817	1862	USA	t	–	+	R	–	R				ConLib	RE	Otherist	c
25	Tolstoy, Leo	9	9	1828n	1910	Russia	t	B	–	B	R	–				LibCon	RM	Elitist	e
26	Turganev, Ivan S.	11	9	1818n	1883	Russia	a	R	R	R	R	B				LibCon	RM	Otherist	e
27	Vidal, Gore	10	3	1925		USA	t	R	B	B	B	B					LM	Humanist	c
28	Whitman, Walt	5	31	1819	1892	USA	t	R	R	B	B	+	Prog	Prog	RadConPro		LE	Humanist	c
29	Wordsworth, William	4	7	1770	1850	England	t	–	–	R	–	B	Rad		RadLib		RM	Humanist	c
30	Zola, Emile	4	2	1840	1902	France	t	+	B	B	+	B	Prog	ProRad			LM	Selfist	·

Table 10. Political Literary Figures

Table 10. Totals & Analysis

B	5	9	6	8	6	16	14	8	12	10
+	7	5	5	8	10					30
−	7	9	8	7	9	L	R	Leftist	Conflicted	Rightist
R	11	7	11	7	5	53%	47%	27%	40%	33%

Total Names= **30**
Total Impulses= 150

Impulse Deviations from Norm **Slight**

Maximum Value
Typical Pattern

	11	9	11	8	10
	R	B	R	B	+
					+
					−

(Tied Count)

E/C Summary

E&C	9	30%
E Only	10	33%
C Only	6	20%
Neither	5	17%
	30	100%

Type Summary

LM	9	30%
LE	6	20%
RM	6	20%
RE	9	30%
	30	100%

J-P Summary

Humanists	9	30%
Otherists	6	20%
Selfists	7	23%
Elitists	8	27%
	30	100%

n=NS date   t=timed birth; p or a= Will system differs if pm or am birthtime
*=Date given by all references, with no OS/NS designation

Appendix B: Tables of Individuals B-48

Table 11. Academics and Scientists

No.	Name	Birthdate Mo	Birthdate Day	Birthdate Year	Died	Subject	W	T	F	J	P	Attitude Leftist	Attitude	Perspective Conflicted	Perspective Rightist	Type	J-P	E/C
1	Adler, Alfred E.	2	7	1870	1937	Psychology	t	B	B	B	B	Prog		ProLibCon		LM	Humanist	c
2	Arendt, Hannah	10	14	1906	1975	Phil/Pol.Sci.	a	–	R	R	B	Prog		ConRad		RM	Selfist	e
3	Austin, John	3	3	1790	1859	Jurisprudence		R	+	+	B		Cons			LE	Elitist	•
4	Ayer, A.J.	10	29	1910	1989	Philosophy/Logic	p	–	R	+	R		Cons	ConRad		RE	Elitist	e
5	Bergson, Henri	10	18	1859	1941	Phil/Biol/Soc.		B	+	B	B	Prog				LM	Humanist	ec
6	Berlin, Isaiah	6	6	1909	1997	Phil/Pol.Sci/ethics		B	B	R	B	Prog		ProCon		LM	Selfist	e
7	Blackstone, William	6	21	1723n	1780	Jurisprudence		+	+	+	R		Cons		ConLib	RM	Otherist	ec
8	Bloom, Allan	9	14	1930	1992	Jurisprudence		+	+	–	B		Lib	LibRad		RM	Otherist	ec
9	Bohr, Neils	10	7	1885	1962	Polit. Science		R	–	–	R	Prog				LE	Selfist	e
10	Brahe, Tycho	12	14	1546	1601	Astron./Astrol.	t	B	–	+	B		Cons	ConRad		LE	Elitist	•
11	Campbell, Joseph	3	26	1904	1987	Mythologist	t	B	+	+	R	Rad				LE	Selfist	e
12	Carnap, Rudolf	5	18	1891	1970	Lang/Phil/Logic	t	R	R	+	B		Lib	LibConRad		RE	Elitist	•
13	Cassirer, Ernst	7	28	1874	1945	History/Phil	p	B	+	–	B	Prog		ProLib		LM	Humanist	ec
14	Chomsky, Noam	12	7	1928		Activist	p	+	+	–	B	Prog		ProRadLib		LM	Humanist	ec
15	Condorcet, Marquis de	9	17	1743	1794	Phil/Science	t	B	–	+	B		Lib		Lib	RM	Otherist	ec
16	Darwin, Charles	2	12	1809	1882	Naturalist		–	R	B	B	Prog				LM	Humanist	c
17	Derrida, Jacques	7	15	1930	2004	Phil/Language	t	+	+	B	B		Lib		Lib	LE	Otherist	ec
18	Dershowitz, Alan	9	1	1938		Jurisprudence		+	–	+	–		Cons	ConRad		RM	Elitist	e
19	Dewey, John	10	20	1859	1952	Psyc/Educ/Phil	t	–	–	–	R	Prog		ProLib		LM	Humanist	ec
20	Dworkin, Ronald	12	11	1931		Jurisprudence	t	–	R	–	+	Rad		RadLib		RM	Otherist	ec
21	Einstein, Albert	3	14	1879	1955	Physics	t	+	B	R	R		Cons		Cons	RE	Humanist	ec
22	Ellis, Havelock	2	2	1859	1939	Psychology		R	–	B	+	Rad				LE	Otherist	c
23	Fisher, Irving	2	27	1867	1947	Economics	t	+	B	–	R		Cons		ConLib	RM	Otherist	ec
24	Freud, Anna	12	3	1895	1982	Child Psychology	t	R	B	+	R	Rad		RadCon		LE	Selfist	e
25	Freud, Sigmund	5	6	1856	1939	Psychology		+	–	B	+		Cons		Cons	RE	Otherist	ec
26	Friedman, Milton	7	31	1912	2006	Economics	a	B	R	R	+	Rad		RadCon		LM	Selfist	e
27	Fukuyama, Frances	10	27	1952	2006	Economics	p	+	–	+	–		Lib	LibRad		RE	Elitist	•
28	Galbraith, John Kenneth	10	15	1908	2006	Economics		B	–	–	–	Prog		ProLib		LM	Selfist	e
29	Galileo, Galilei	2	15	1564	1642	Physics	t	R	B	B	–		Lib		LibCon	RM	Otherist	c
30	Gauquelin, Françoise	6	19	1929		Psyc/Stat/Astrol	t	+	R	B	+	Rad		RadPro		LM	Humanist	c
31	Gauquelin, Michel	11	13	1928	1991	Psyc/Stat/Astrol	t	+	R	–	–	Rad			LibCon	RE	Otherist	ec
32	Gentile, Giovanni	5	29	1875	1944	Phil/Pol.Sci.	t	B	–	B	B	Rad		RadLib		LM	Humanist	ec
33	Gibbon, Edward	5	8	1737n	1794	History	p	–	+	R	+		Lib	LibRad		RE	Elitist	•
34	Grotius, Hugo	4	10	1583	1645	Intern'tl. Law	p	R	R	+	R	Prog		ProCon		RE	Selfist	e
35	Guicciardini, Francesco	3	6	1483	1540	History		R	+	R	B		Cons		Cons	RM	Elitist	•
36	Hart, H. L. A.	7	18	1907	1992	Jurisprudence	p	B	–	R	–		Lib		LibCon	LM	Elitist	e
37	Hawking, Stephen	1	8	1942		Physics	p	B	–	+	B		Cons		ConLib	RE	Elitist	•
38	Hayek, Friedrich v.	5	8	1899	1992	Economics	a	+	R	R	B	Prog		LibRad		LE	Selfist	e
39	Heisenberg, Werner	12	5	1901	1976	Physics		R	R	R	B	Prog		ProCon		RE	Elitist	•
40	Husserl, Edmund	4	8	1859	1938	Math/Log/Phil	t	+	R	R	–	Rad		RadLib		RE	Humanist	ec

Table 11. Academics and Scientists

#	Name				Field													
41	James, William	1	11	1842	1910	Psychology	t	–	–	B	R	–			Lib		RM	Elitist	•
42	Jaspers, Karl	2	23	1883	1969	Psych/Phil	t	–	B	–	R	B		Cons			RM	Otherist	ec
43	Jung, Carl	7	26	1875	1961	Psychology	t	B	B	+	B	+	Rad		ConLibPro		LM	Humanist	ec
44	Kaku, Michio	1	24	1947		Physics	t	R	+	+	–	B	Prog				LE	Selfist	•
45	Kelsen, Hans	10	11	1881	1973	Jurisprudence		–	+	–	B	–	Prog		ProLib		RM	Humanist	ec
46	Kepler, Johannes	12	27	1571	1630	Astron./Astrol.	t	B	–	B	B	B		Lib	LibPro		RM	Otherist	c
47	Keynes, John Maynard	6	5	1883	1946	Economics	t	+	B	+	R	–	Prog			Lib	LM	Selfist	e
48	Kurtz, Paul W.	12	21	1925		Philosophy		R	–	+	B	–		Lib			RM	Otherist	c
49	Lemarck, Jean-Batiste	8	1	1744	1829	Naturalist		–	B	–	B	+	Rad		RadLib		RE	Humanist	ec
50	Lorentz, Hendrik	7	18	1853	1928	Physics	t	R	B	B	B	B		Cons	ConPro		LE	Otherist	ec
51	Malthus, Thomas R.	2	14	1766	1834	Economics		–	R	B	R	+	Rad				RM	Humanist	ec
52	McLuhan, Marshall	7	21	1911	1980	Media	a	R	B	R	B	B		Lib	LibCon		RE	Elitist	e
53	Mead, Margaret	12	16	1901	1978	Anthropology	t	R	+	R	+	R	Prog				RM	Selfist	c
54	Menger, Carl	2	28	1840	1921	Economics		B	–	+	B	–		Lib	ProCon	Lib	RM	Elitist	e
55	Mills, C. Wright	8	28	1916	1962	Sociology	a	–	R	B	R	–		Lib	LibPro		RM	Otherist	c
56	Mises, Ludwig v.	9	29	1881*	1973	Economics		R	B	–	B	–	Prog		ProLib		RE	Humanist	e
57	Morison, Samuel Eliot	7	9	1887	1976	History		–	+	–	+	–		Cons	ConLibRad	Lib	RE	Elitist	ec
58	Newton, Isaac	1	4	1643n	1727	Physics		R	–	+	B	–		Lib			RM	Elitist	e
59	Nostradamus, Michel de	12	14	1503	1566	Astrol./Prophet		+	+	+	B	+		Lib	LibCon		LM	Elitist	ec
60	Nozick, Robert	11	16	1938	2002	Philosophy	a	B	B	B	R	–		Cons	ConPro		LM	Humanist	c
61	Pascal, Blaise	6	19	1623	1662	Science/Math	t	R	+	+	R	B	Rad		ConRad		RE	Elitist	e
62	Peirce, Charles S.	9	10	1839	1914	Science/Phil		+	+	+	R	–		Cons	ProCon	ConLib	LE	Selfist	c
63	Petrarch, Francesco	7	20	1304	1374	History/Poetry	t	B	R	B	R	B	Prog		RadCon	Lib	LE	Selfist	c
64	Piaget, Jean	8	9	1896	1980	Child Psychology	t	R	B	R	+	+	Rad		RadLibCon		RE	Selfist	e
65	Popper, Karl	7	28	1902	1994	Phil/Pol.Sci/ethics	t	–	–	B	+	+	Rad				RE	Selfist	e
66	Quine, Willard	6	25	1908	2000	Logic/Phil		+	+	+	B	–		Cons		ConLib	RE	Elitist	c
67	Rawls, John	2	21	1921	2002	Soc./Pol.Science	a	+	–	–	R	–	Prog		ProCon	Lib	RM	Otherist	c
68	Reich, Wilhelm	3	24	1897	1957	Psychology		R	B	B	B	–	Rad		RadLib		RM	Selfist	•
69	Ricardo, David	4	18	1772	1823	Economics		B	–	–	R	–		Cons		ConLib	RE	Humanist	ec
70	Rothbard, Murray N.	3	2	1926	1995	Economics		R	+	+	–	R		Lib		Lib	RM	Otherist	c
71	Russell, Bertrand	5	18	1872	1970	Math/Log/Phil		–	B	–	B	B	Prog				LM	Humanist	c
72	Santayana, George	12	16	1863	1952	Phil/Literature	t	B	R	B	B	+	Rad		RadLibPro		LE	Humanist	e
73	Schumpeter, Joseph	2	8	1883	1950	Economics	a	B	–	B	B	+	Rad				LM	Humanist	ec
74	Skinner, B. F.	3	20	1904	1990	Psychology		+	R	+	B	R	Prog			Cons	RE	Humanist	•
75	Smith, Adam	6	5	1723^	1790	Economics		B	R	B	+	B		Cons			LM	Humanist	ec
76	Spengler, Oswald	5	29	1880	1936	History/Phil		+	B	R	B	+	Prog		RadLib		RE	Elitist	ec
77	Strauss, Leo	9	20	1899	1973	Polit. Science	t	B	+	+	B	–	Rad			LibCon	LM	Humanist	ec
78	Tocqueville, Alexis de	7	20	1805	1859	Polit. Science	t	B	B	B	R	B	Prog				RE	Elitist	•
79	Toynbee, Arnold	4	14	1889	1975	History	t	+	+	B	R	B	ProRad				LE	Selfist	ec
80	Velikovsky, Immanuel	6	10	1895	1979	Psych/History	a	–	–	B	B	B	Prog		ProLibRad		LM	Selfist	•

Table 11. Academics and Scientists

							t						p					
81	Vygotsky, Lev S.	11	17	1896	1934	Child Psychology	R	–	–	+	+	–	R	–	–	+	Lib	RE
82	Wallace, Alfred R.	1	8	1823	1913	Naturalist	R	–	–	B	–	–	R	–	B	–	Lib	RM
83	Weber, Max	4	21	1864	1920	Sociol/Economics	+	R	+	–	–	Rad	R	+	–	–	Lib	RE
84	Whitehead, Alfred N.	2	15	1861	1947	Math/Phil/Theol	R	R	R	B	+		R	R	R	B	+	LibRad RadCon	RE

Table 11. Totals & Analysis

B	23	20	13	18	24	42	16	43	25
+	19	17	20	16	18		Leftist	Conflicted	Rightist
–	19	26	25	24		L	19%	51%	30%
R	23	21	22	25	18	50%			

Total Names= **84**
Total Impulses= 420

Assimilation High

Impulse Deviations from Norm

Maximum Value   23 26 29 25 24
Typical Pattern   B   –   –   –   B   –
(Tied Count)   R   –   R   –

	E/C Summary		J-P Summary	
E&C	29	**35%**	Humanists	24	29%
E Only	22	26%	Otherists	19	23%
C Only	14	17%	Selfists	18	21%
Neither	19	23%	Elitists	23	27%
	84	100%		84	100%

Type Summary		
LM	19	23%
LE	13	15%
RM	27	**32%**
RE	25	**30%**
	84	100%

n=NS date   t=timed birth; p or a= Will system differs if pm or am birthtime
^=Birthdate unknown; Baptism was 6/16 NS; 6/5 is a guess to show the general time, but his will system might be projective.

Table 12. Business Leaders

No.	Name	Birthdate Mo	Birthdate Day	Birthdate Year	Died	Major Activity	W	T	F	J	P	Attitude			Perspective			Type	J-P	E/C
															Leftist	Conflicted	Rightist			
1	Agnelli, Giovanni, Sr	8	13	1866	1945	Auto, FIAT	R	–	+	B	B	Prog			Prog			LM	Humanist	c
2	Anderson, Robert O.	4	13	1917	2007	Oil/Cattle/Land	I	–	R	B	B	Prog			Prog			LM	Humanist	c
3	Annenberg, Moses	2	11	1877	1942	Publishing	R	R	R	B	+	Rad				RadCon		RE	Humanist	ec
4	Astor, John Jacob	7	17	1763	1848	Furs/Finance	R	+	R	+	R		Cons				Cons	RE	Otherist	c
5	Avis, Warren	4	8	1915	2007	Car Rent/Travel	+	R	–	–	B	Prog				ProLib		RM	Humanist	ec
6	Barnato, Barney	6	12	1852	1897	Diamonds/Bnkg	R	B	R	–	B	Prog				ProCon		RM	Humanist	ec
7	Barnum, Phineas T.	7	5	1810	1881	Promoter	p	+	–	+	–		Lib			LibRad		LM	Otherist	c
8	Baťa, Tomáš	4	3	1876	1932	Shoes, etc	R	R	–	–	+		Lib			RadConLib		RE	Humanist	ec
9	Bernardin, Alin	1	9	1916	1994	Restaurants, &c	B	+	+	B	I	Rad				LibRad		LM	Otherist	c
10	Bogart, Neil	2	3	1943	1982	Records	R	B	B	R	B	Prog				ProCon		LM	Selfist	•
11	Botton, Pierre	5	30	1955		Investor/Deals	R	B	R	R	B	Prog				ProCon		LM	Selfist	•
12	Buffett, Warren E.	8	30	1930		Investm/Textiles	a	R	+	R	–		Lib				LibCon	RE	Otherist	ec
13	Busch, Adolphus	7	19	1839	1913	Brewing	+	B	B	+	B		Cons			ConPro		LM	Elitist	•
14	Cardin, Pierre	7	2	1922		Fashion	R	+	B	R	B		Cons			ConRadPro		LE	Otherist	c
15	Carnegie, Andrew	11	25	1835	1919	Steel	R	R	R	R	B	Prog				ProConRad		LE	Selfist	•
16	Chigi, Agostino	12	1	1466	1520	Banking	R	R	R	–	B	Prog				ProCon		RE	Humanist	ec
17	Chrysler, Walter P.	4	4	1875	1940	Automotive	+	R	–	+	B	Rad			Rad			LE	Humanist	ec
18	Citroen, Andre-Gustave	2	5	1878	1935	Automotive	–	–	R	–	B	Prog				ProLib		RM	Humanist	ec
19	Disney, Walt	12	5	1901	1966	Media	R	+	+	R	B	Prog				ProCon		RE	Selfist	•
20	Douglas, Donald	4	6	1892	1981	Aircraft	R	B	–	+	+	Rad			Rad			RE	Selfist	•
21	Erhard, Werner	9	5	1935		Therapy (EST)	R	–	B	–	I		Lib			RadCon	Lib	RM	Otherist	ec
22	Ferrari, Enzo	2	18	1898	1988	Automotive	B	+	B	+	R		Cons		Rad			LE	Elitist	•
23	Field, Marshall	8	18	1834	1906	Retail/R.E.	+	+	R	+	+	Rad				ConProRad		LE	Selfist	•
24	Flick, Frederick	7	10	1883	1972	Industrialist	+	B	B	+	+		Lib			LibRad		RE	Elitist	•
25	Forbes, Steve	7	18	1947		Media	B	B	B	R	B		Lib			LibPro		LM	Elitist	•
26	Ford, Henry	7	30	1863	1947	Automotive	+	+	R	B	+	Rad			RadPro			LE	Humanist	c
27	Gallup, George	11	18	1901	1984	Pollster	R	R	–	+	B		Lib			ProCon	LibCon	RE	Elitist	e
28	Gates, Bill	10	28	1955		Software	t	R	B	R	R		Cons			ConRad		LE	Elitist	•
29	Gould, Jay	5	27	1836	1892	RR/Brok/AT&T	+	B	B	R	B	Prog			Prog			LM	Selfist	•
30	Griffin, Merv	7	6	1925	2007	Media/Hotels	I	+	B	–	I		Lib			LibPro	ConLib	LM	Otherist	c
31	Hearst, William R.	4	29	1863	1951	Media	–	+	–	+	R	Prog				LibPro		RE	Otherist	c
32	Hefner, Hugh	4	9	1926		Media	I	–	B	–	+		Lib					LM	Humanist	c
33	Hughes, Howard	12	24	1905	1976	Aircraft/Media	+	B	R	B	+	Rad			RadPro			LE	Elitist	e
34	Jobs, Steve	2	24	1955		Computer/Media	R	R	R	B	R		Lib			LibRad		LM	Elitist	•
35	Kaiser, Henry	5	9	1882	1967	Ships/Metals	B	R	+	B	–		Lib			LibPro		RE	Otherist	c
36	Kennedy, Joseph Sr	9	6	1888	1969	Finance/Deals	B	B	B	R	B		Cons			ConPro	Cons	RE	Elitist	c
37	Kreugar, Ivar	3	2	1880	1932	Finance/Deals	B	R	R	B	R		Cons			LibPro		RM	Otherist	ec
38	Krupp, Gusta v. Bohlen	8	7	1870	1950	War/Industry	–	–	R	–	+	Rad						LM	Humanist	c
39	Lay, Kenneth	4	15	1942	2006	Energy	R	+	+	+	–	Rad				RadLib		LM	Selfist	e
40	Lowenstein, Alfred	3	11	1877	1928	Finance/Deals	R	R	–	–	–		Lib				LibCon	RM	Otherist	ec

APPENDIX B: TABLES OF INDIVIDUALS B-52

Table 12. Business Leaders

#	Name				Industry													
41	Mattei, Enrico	4	29	1906	1962	Oil	t	–	B	–	–	R				Cons	Rad	RM	Elitist	e
42	Mellon, Andrew W.	3	24	1855	1937	Banking	p	+	–	+	+	+			ConLib			LE	Humanist	ec
43	Messerschmitt, Willy	6	26	1898	1978	Aircraft	t	B	+	R	B	R		Cons		ConRad		LE	Elitist	ec
44	Michelin, Edouard	6	23	1859	1940	Tires	t	+	R	+	R	R		Lib				RE	Otherist	•
45	Morgan, J. P.	4	17	1837	1913	Banking	t	R	–	+	+	–	Rad			RadLib		LE	Selfist	ec
46	Murdoch, Rupert	3	11	1931		Media	t	R	R	+	–	–		Lib			LibCon	RE	Otherist	ec
47	Niarchos, Stavros S.	7	3	1909	1996	Shipping	t	B	B	R	R	B		Lib				RM	Elitist	e
48	Onassis, Aristotle	1	20	1906	1975	Ship/Tobacco	t	R	–	–	–	–	Prog			LibPro		RM	Selfist	e
49	Perot, Ross	6	27	1930		Data Proc.										ProConLib	Lib	RM	Otherist	ec
50	Rockefeller, John D.	7	8	1838	1937	Oil	t	R	–	R	+	–		Lib		LibRad		RE	Elitist	•
51	Rose, Billy	9	6	1899	1966	Entertainment	t	+	+	+	B	–		Lib		LibRad		LE	Elitist	•
52	Rothschild, Mayer A.	2	23	1743	1812	Banking	t	+	+	–	–	–	Rad	Lib			Lib	RM	Otherist	ec
53	Rubenstein, Serge	5	31	1908	1955	Finance/Deals	t	+	R	–	R	+				RadLib		RE	Selfist	e
54	Rubinstein, Helena	12	25	1870	1965	Cosmetics	t	R	–	B	–	R		Cons			ConLib	RM	Otherist	c
55	Sage, Russell	8	4	1816	1906	RR/Tele/AT&T	t	B	R	+	–	B						LM	Humanist	c
56	Soros, George	8	12	1930		Finance/Deals		R	R	+	B	B	Prog		Prog	ProCon		RM	Humanist	ec
57	Stewart, Martha	8	3	1941		Home Products	t	R	R	–	+	+				RadCon		RE	Selfist	e
58	Trump, Donald	6	14	1946		Real Estate	t	R	R	B	+	+				RadCon		LE	Selfist	•
59	Turner, Ted	11	19	1938		Media	a	+	B	–	+	R				ConRad		LE	Elitist	e
60	Walton, Sam	3	29	1918	1992	Retail		–	+	+	–	+	Rad	Cons				RM	Humanist	c
61	Wanamaker, John	7	11	1838	1922	Retail	t	–	–	–	–	–		Lib	Rad	LibRad		RM	Elitist	•
62	Welch, Jack	11	19	1935		G.E., War	t	–	–	R	–	R		Cons			ConLib	RM	Otherist	ec
63	Westinghouse, George	10	6	1846	1914	Inventions/Mfg.	t	B	+	B	B	+	Rad		RadPro			LE	Selfist	•
64	Wilson, Charles E.	7	18	1890	1961	GM, Secy Def.		+	B	B	R	R		Cons			Cons	RE	Elitist	•
65	Winfrey, Oprah	1	29	1954		Media	t	R	R	R	B	+	Rad			RadCon		LE	Selfist	•
66	Wozniak, Steve	8	11	1950		Computers	t	–	–	B	R	B	Prog			ProLib		RM	Selfist	•

Table 12. Business Leaders

Table 12. Totals & Analysis

B	11	17	18	14	15	32	34	12	39	15
+	15	11	18	20	17		66			66
–	14	15	15	19	20	L	R	Leftist	Conflicted	Rightist
R	26	23	15	13	14	48%	52%	18%	59%	23%

	26	23	18	20	20
	R	R	B	+	–
			+		

Total Names= **66**
Total Impulses= 330

Impulse Deviations from Norm   **Slight**

Maximum Value
Typical Pattern
(Tied Count)

Italicized names also on a previous table(s)   *t=timed birth; p or a= Will system differs if pm or am birthtime*

Type Summary

LM	15	23%
LE	17	26%
RM	16	24%
RE	18	27%
	66	100%

E/C Summary

E&C	19	29%
E Only	11	17%
C Only	14	21%
Neither	22	33%
	66	100%

J-P Summary

Humanists	16	24%
Otherists	17	26%
Selfists	16	24%
Elitists	17	26%
	66	100%

Appendix B: Tables of Individuals   B-54

Table 13. Religionists and Other Mystics

No.	Name	Birthdate Mo	Birthdate Day	Birthdate Year	Died	Activity	W	T	F	J	P	Attitude	Perspective Leftist	Perspective Conflicted	Perspective Rightist	Type	J-P	E/C
1	*Abernathy, Ralph*	3	11	1926	1990	Baptist Activist	R	B	–	–	R				Cons	RE	Otherist	c
2	*Alger, Horatio*	1	13	1832	1899	Unitarian Minister	–	R	R	+	R				Cons	RE	Elitist	e
3	*Appelwhite, Marshall*	5	17	1931	1997	Cultist/Mass Suicide	–	R	R	B	R				Lib	LibCon	RM	Otherist	ec
4	*Bakker, Jim*	1	2	1940		Media Evangelist	+	B	R	R	R				Cons	RE	Elitist	e
5	*Bakker, Tammy Faye*	3	7	1942	2007	Media Evangelist	–	B	R	+	R				Cons	RE	Elitist	e
6	*Besant, Annie*	10	1	1847	1933	Theosophist	–	–	+	+	R	Prog				LE	Selfist	•
7	*Bishop Fulton J. Sheen*	5	8	1895	1979	Media Catholic	–	–	+	R	B			Lib		RM	Selfist	•
8	*Blavatsky, Helena P.*	8	12	1831	1891	Theosophic Soc Fdr	R	R	R	R	+	Rad	RadCon			RE	Selfist	e
9	*Booth, William*	4	10	1829	1912	Salvation Army Fdr	–	R	R	+	+	Rad	RadCon			RE	Selfist	e
10	*Bourdin, Gilbert*	6	25	1923	1998	Fr.Guru/'Messiah'	B	B	–	–	R		LibPro			LM	Otherist	c
11	*Buchman, Frank*	6	4	1878	1961	Peace Evangelist	B	R	–	–	+	Rad	RadLib			RE	Humanist	ec
12	*Cardinal Richelieu*	9	9	1585	1642	Minister, Louis XIII	B	–	R	R	R				Cons	RE	Elitist	e
13	*Chopra, Deepak*	10	22	1946		Holistic Health	B	B	+	+	B	Prog	ProCon			LE	Selfist	•
14	*Day, Dorothy*	11	8	1897	1980	RC Activist	B	–	+	R	R	Prog			Cons	RE	Elitist	e
15	*Dederick, Charles E.*	3	22	1913	1997	Synanon Fdr	+	+	–	+	B	Prog			Cons	LE	Selfist	•
16	*Dobson, James C.*	4	21	1936		Evangel. Activist	–	B	R	R	R		ProRad		Cons	RM	Otherist	ec
17	*Eddy, Mary Baker*	7	16	1821	1910	Christ.Science Fdr	+	R	R	+	R		ConRad			LE	Elitist	e
18	*Escriva De Balaguer, Jos.*	1	9	1902	1975	St./Opus Dei Cult	–	R	–	+	R		LibRad			RE	Elitist	e
19	*Falwell, Jerry*	8	11	1933	2007	Baptist Activist	B	+	+	B	B	Prog			Lib	LM	Humanist	•
20	*Farrakhan, Louis*	5	11	1933		Nation of Islam	+	–	+	R	R			Lib		RM	Otherist	ec
21	*Ford, Arthur*	1	8	1896	1971	Clairvoyant/Medium	B	B	+	+	B		ConRad			LE	Elitist	•
22	*Fr. Bruce Ritter*	2	25	1927	1999	Covenant Hse Fdr	+	+	+	B	–	Rad	LibPro			LM	Otherist	c
23	*Fr. Daniel Berrigan*	5	9	1921		Anti-War Activist	R	–	+	B	–	Rad			Lib	LM	Otherist	c
24	*Graham, Billy*	11	7	1918		Media Evangelist	+	+	R	R	–		LibPro			RM	Otherist	c
25	*Gurdjieff, Georges*	1	13	1872	1949	Mystic	B	–	+	B	–			Lib		LM	Otherist	c
26	*Hagee, John*	4	12	1940		Evangel. Activist	R	R	R	R	B	Rad	RadCon			RE	Otherist	c
27	*Heindel, Max*	7	23	1865	1919	Rosicrucian Fdr	+	B	+	B	+	Rad			Lib	LE	Humanist	e
28	*Hubberd, L. Ron*	3	13	1911	1986s	Scientology Fdr	R	–	R	B	–			Lib		RM	Elitist	e
29	*Jackson, Jesse L.*	10	8	1941		Baptist Activist	R	–	+	R	–	Rad	RadLib			RE	Selfist	e
30	*Jones, James*	5	13	1931	1978s	Cultist/Murderer	R	R	R	B	–	Prog			LibCon	RE	Otherist	ec
31	*Jouret, Luc*	10	18	1947	1994	Cultist/Murderer	+	R	R	B	+				LibCon	LE	Selfist	•
32	*Kerri, Johannes*	1	11	1887	1941	Reich Min.Relig.	R	R	B	R	R				Cons	RE	Elitist	e
33	*Khomeini, Ruhollah*	5	17	1900	1989	Ayatollah, Iran	R	R	B	R	R			LibCon		RE	Elitist	e
34	*King, Martin L. Jr.*	1	15	1929	1968	Baptist Activist	B	+	–	B	–		LibPro			LM	Otherist	c
35	*Koresh, David*	8	17	1959	1993	Cultist	R	+	+	–	B	Prog	ProLib			RM	Humanist	ec
36	*Krishnamurti, Jeddu*	5	12	1895	1986	Buddhist/Brahm.	R	–	R	–	–					RE	Elitist	e
37	*Lavey, Anton Szandor*	4	11	1930	1997	Satan Cultist	–	+	+	R	+	Rad	RadLib			RM	Humanist	ec
38	*Leadbeater, Charles*	2	16	1854	1934	Angl.,Theosophist	R	–	–	–	B	Prog	ProLib			RE	Humanist	ec
39	*Manson, Charles*	11	12	1934		Cultist/Murderer	–	+	–	R	R			Lib		RM	Otherist	ec
40	*Mararishi, Mahesh Yogi*	1	12	1917	2008	Trans. Meditation	–	+	+	B	R		ConRad			LE	Otherist	c

Table 13. Religionists and Other Mystics

#	Name																				
41	McPherson, Aimee S.	10	9	1890	1944	Evangel. Activist	t	−	+	+	+	R	R	+	Rad		Rad		LE	Selfist	•
42	Melancthon, Philipp	2	15	1497	1560	Lutheran Organizer	t	+	+	+	R	B	B	R		ConRad			LE	Otherist	ec
43	Moon, Sun Myung	1	6	1920		Unification Church		−	−	+	R	R	R	R		ConRad			LE	Otherist	c
44	Mother Teresa	8	26	1910	1997	Missionary		−	−	−	B	+	B	B			ConLib		RE	Elitist	e
45	Muhammad, Elijah	10	7	1897	1975	Nation of Islam		+	−	B	R	R	R	−	Prog	ProLib			LM	Selfist	•
46	Muller, Ludwig	6	23	1883	1946	Ger.Faith Mvmt.		+	B	R	R	R	R	B			LibCon		RE	Elitist	e
47	Olcott, Henry Steele	8	2	1832	1907	Theosophic Soc Fdr	t	−	+	−	R	−	R	−	Prog	ProCon			RE	Selfist	e
48	Padre Pio	5	25	1887	1968	Cath.St./Stigmatic	t	−	R	−	+	+	B	+	Rad	RadLib			RE	Selfist	e
49	Peale, Norman Vincent	5	31	1898	1993	Media Pastor	t	+	R	R	B	+	+	+	Rad			Rad	LE	Selfist	•
50	Pope Alexander VI	12	31	1430	1502	Borgia Pope	t	R	+	+	−	B	−	−			LibCon		RE	Otherist	c
51	Pope Leo X	12	11	1475	1521	Medici Pope	t	+	−	+	R	−	+	+		RadLib			RE	Humanist	ec
52	Pope Pius XII	3	2	1876	1958	WW II Pope	t	R	R	−	R	−	−	R	Rad		Cons		RE	Otherist	ec
53	Prophet, Elizabeth Clare	4	8	1939		CUT cultist	t	+	B	−	+	+	−	B	Prog	ProLib			LM	Humanist	•
54	Ramakrishna	2	18	1836	1886	Hindu Mystic	t	−	+	−	+	−	+	B	Prog	ProLibRad			LM	Selfist	•
55	Reed, Ralph	6	24	1961		Prot./Rep.Organizer		−	R	+	R	+	B	+			ConLib		RM	Otherist	ec
56	Roberts, Oral	1	24	1918		Evangelist	t	B	R	+	R	R	B	+	Rad		Cons		LE	Otherist	c
57	Robertson, Pat	3	22	1930		Media Evangelist		−	R	+	R	−	+	+	Rad	RadLibCon			RE	Humanist	ec
58	Robespierre, Maximilian	5	6	1758	1794	Cult of Supr.Being		R	B	+	+	+	+	R		ConRad		RadPro	LE	Elitist	•
59	Savonarola, Girolamo	9	21	1452	1498	Fransiccan Friar		B	+	B	+	+	−	B	Rad		Cons		LE	Selfist	•
60	Schweitzer, Albert	1	14	1875	1965	Missionary/Dr.		+	R	+	−	+	−	−		LibRad			RE	Otherist	e
61	Sharpton, Al	10	3	1954		Protest. Activist		R	−	B	R	−	R	B	Prog	ProCon		RadPro	RM	Selfist	•
62	Smith, Joseph	12	23	1805	1844	Mormon Fdr.	t	+	R	+	+	R	−	R			Cons		RE	Otherist	ec
63	Ste. Bernadette	1	7	1844	1879	RC Hallucinator	t	R	B	−	B	+	−	R			Cons		RE	Elitist	•
64	St. Frances Cabrini	7	15	1850	1917	Missionary	t	+	−	+	R	−	+	+			Lib		RM	Otherist	ec
65	Ste. Joan of Arc	1	6	1413	1431	RC Militarist	t	+	−	+	+	+	B	−			Lib		LE	Elitist	e
66	St. John Bosco	8	16	1815	1888	Missionary	t	B	−	+	R	+	B	+	Rad		LibCon		LE	Humanist	c
67	Sunday, Billy	11	19	1863	1935	Presb. Revivalist	t	B	+	+	R	R	B	−			Lib		RM	Otherist	c
68	Swaggart, Jimmy	3	15	1935		Media Evangelist	t	R	+	R	R	B	R	−		LibPro	LibCon		RE	Otherist	c
69	Williamson, Marianne	7	8	1952		LA Celebrity Guru	t	B	B	B	B	R	−	−		ConRad			LM	Elitist	ec
70	Wright, Jeremiah	9	22	1941		Unification Church		R	+	−	R	−	+	R			Cons		RE	Otherist	•
71	X, Malcolm	5	19	1925	1965	Islamic Activist	t	−	+	−	−	−	−	−			Lib		RM	Otherist	c
72	Young, Andrew	3	12	1932		Protest. Activist	t	B	+	−	−	+	−	R			ConLib		RM	Otherist	ec
73	Young, Brigham	6	1	1801	1877	Mormon Pres.	t	+	B	R	+	R	−	+	Rad		Cons		LE	Humanist	ec

Table 13. Religionists and Other Mystics

Table 13. Totals & Analysis

B	14	13	9	16	12	28	45	11	31	31
+	18	16	24	19	16		73			73
−	24	18	15	21	24	L	R	Leftist	Conflicted	Rightist
R	17	26	25	17	21	38%	62%	15%	42%	42%

24	26	21	24
−	R	R	−	−

Total Names= **73**
Total Impulses= 365

Impulse Deviations from Norm: **Balanced Very Low, Reversals High**

Maximum Value
Typical Pattern

E/C Summary
E&C	22	30%
E Only	18	25%
C Only	15	21%
Neither	18	25%
	73	100%

Type Summary
LM	9	12%
LE	17	23%
RM	18	25%
RE	29	**40%**
	73	100%

J-P Summary
Humanists	12	16%
Otherists	25	**34%**
Selfists	16	22%
Elitists	20	27%
	73	100%

t=timed birth; p or a= Will system differs if pm or am birthtime

Table 14. Theologians

No.	Name	Birthdate Mo	Birthdate Day	Birthdate Year	Died	Data	W	T	F	J	P		Attitude	Perspective Leftist	Perspective Conflicted	Perspective Rightist	Type	J-P	E/C
1	Aquinas, Thomas	5	1	1224	1274	RC Aristotelian	t	–	–	R	–	R	Cons			ConLib	RM	Otherist	ec
2	Augustine	11	13	354	430	RC Neoplatonist	a	+	R	B	R	R	Cons			Cons	RE	Otherist	ec
3	Barth, Karl	5	10	1886	1968	Prot. Reformist	t	R	+	R	R	–	Lib			LibCon	RE	Elitist	e
4	Bauer, Bruno	9	6	1809	1882	Prot./Polit/Phil	a	R	–	+	–	R	Cons			ConLib	RE	Otherist	c
5	Calvin, John	7	10	1509	1564	Prot. Reformist	t	–	+	B	R	R	Cons			Cons	RE	Elitist	•
6	Erasmus, Desiderius	10	27	1469	1536	RC 'Humanist'		R	R	B	–	R	Lib			LibCon	LM	Otherist	ec
7	Francis of Assisi	9	26	1182	1226	RC 'Realist'		B	B	B	–	+	Rad				LM	Humanist	c
8	Kierkegaard, Soeren	5	5	1813	1855	Prot. Existentialist		–	B	–	–	R		RadPro			RM	Otherist	c
9	Luther, Martin	11	10	1483	1546	Prot. Reformist	t	+	+	R	B	R	Cons		ConLibPro		RE	Elitist	•
10	Melancthon, Philipp	2	15	1497	1560	Lutheran		–	+	R	B	R	Cons			Cons	LE	Otherist	ec
11	More, Thomas	2	6	1478	1535	RC Humanist	t	R	B	R	B	+	Rad		ConRad		LE	Humanist	ec
12	Niebuhr, Rienhold	6	21	1892	1971	Evangelical		–	B	+	+	R			RadConPro		LE	Elitist	•
13	Scotus, John Duns	4	1	1265	1308	RC 'Realist'		–	B	B	+	B	Cons			ConLib	RM	Otherist	ec
14	Teilhard de Chardin, P.	5	1	1881	1955	Jesuit/Scientist	t	R	B	B	–	–	Prog	Prog			LM	Selfist	•
15	Tillich, Paul	8	20	1886	1965	Lutheran	t	R	+	R	+	+	Rad		RadCon	Lib	LE	Otherist	ec
16	Whitehead, Alfred N.	2	15	1861	1947	Math/Phil/Theol	p	R	R	R	R	+	Rad		RadCon		RE	Humanist	ec

	B	+	–	R
W	1	2	4	9
	5	5	3	3
	6	1	1	8
	4	3	6	3
	1	4	3	8

	L	R
	5	11
		16
	31%	69%

	Leftist	Conflicted	Rightist
	2	5	9
			16
	13%	31%	56%

	9	5	8	6	8
	R	B	R	–	R
			+		

Table 14. Totals & Analysis

Total Names = 16
Total Impulses = 80

Reversals Very High, All Others Low

Impulse Deviations from Norm

Maximum Value
Typical Pattern
(Tied Count)
(Tied Count)

Type Summary

LM	2	13%
LE	3	19%
RM	4	25%
RE	7	44%
	16	100%

J-P Summary

Humanists	3	19%
Otherists	7	44%
Selfists	2	13%
Elitists	4	25%
	16	100%

E/C Summary

E&C	7	44%
E Only	2	13%
C Only	3	19%
Neither	4	25%
	16	100%

Italicized names also on a previous table(s)   *t=timed birth; p or a = Will system differs if pm or am birthtime*

Table 15. Non-Governmental Assassins or Murderers

No.	Name	Birthdate Mo	Day	Year	Died	Data	W	T	F	J	P	Attitude	Perspective Leftist	Conflicted	Rightist	Type	J-P	E/C
1	Baader, Berndt A.	5	6	1943	1977	Germany	t	+	+	R	–	Lib		LibRadCon		RE	Elitist	e
2	Berkowitz, David	6	1	1953		USA	t	+	B	+	+	Rad	Rad			LE	Selfist	.
3	Booth, John Wilkes	5	10	1838	1865	USA	t	R	+	+	R	Lib			LibCon	RE	Elitist	.
4	Bundy, Ted	11	24	1946	1989	USA	t	+	R	B	B	Prog	ProRad			LE	Selfist	.
5	Carlos the Jackal	10	12	1949		Venezuela	t	R	B	+	B	Prog	ProRad			LE	Selfist	.
6	Dider, Christian	2	11	1944		France	t	B	R	B	–	Rad	RadPro			LE	Selfist	.
7	Gallinari, Prospero	1	1	1951		Italy	t	+	–	B	–	Lib				LM	Elitist	.
8	Godse, Nathuram	5	19	1910	1949	India		R	B	R	R	Cons		LibRad		RE	Elitist	e
9	Guiteau, Charles J.	9	8	1841	1882	USA		+	–	B	–	Cons		ConRad	Cons	LE	Elitist	.
10	Jones, James	5	13	1931	1978	USA		R	R	R	R	Lib			LibCon	RE	Otherist	ec
11	Jouret, Luc	10	18	1947	1994	Zaire/France	t	+	R	B	–	Prog	ProRad			LE	Selfist	.
12	Manson, Charles	11	12	1934		USA	t	B	–	–	–	Lib			Lib	RM	Otherist	ec
13	McVeigh, Timothy	4	23	1968	2001	USA	t	R	R	–	R	Cons			ConLib	LE	Otherist	ec
14	Muhammed, John Allen	12	31	1960		USA	p	R	R	–	–	Lib			LibCon	RE	Otherist	ec
15	Oswald, Lee Harvey	10	18	1939	1963	USA		B	–	B	+	Rad		RadLib		LM	Selfist	e
16	Princip, Gavrillo	7	25	1894n	1918	Bosnia		+	–	+	+	Rad	Rad			LE	Selfist	.
17	Ray, James Earl	3	10	1928	1998	USA	t	+	+	B	R	Cons		ConProRad		LE	Otherist	c
18	Ruby, Jack	4	25	1911	1967	USA		–	+	R	–	Lib			LibCon	RM	Elitist	e
19	Sirhan, Sirhan	3	19	1944		USA	t	B	+	B	R	Cons		ConProRad		LE	Elitist	.
20	White, Dan	9	2	1946	1985	USA	t	+	+	+	R	Cons		ConRad		LE	Elitist	.

Table 15. Totals & Analysis

Total Names= 20
Total Impulses= 100

Projection Very High, Balance & Assimilation Low

Impulse Deviations from 25%

	W	T	F	J	P
B	5	3	6	2	3
+	9	4	6	11	4
–	1	7	2	3	7
R	5	6	6	4	6

Maximum Value

	W	T	F	J	P
Typical Pattern	9	7	6	11	7
(Tied Count)	+	–	B	+	–
(Tied Count)				B	R
				+	R

Attitude		
	7	13
	L	R
	35%	65%

Perspective		
6	7	7
		20
Leftist	Conflicted	Rightist
30%	35%	35%

E/C Summary
E&C	4	20%
E Only	4	20%
C Only	1	5%
Neither	11	55%
	20	100%

Type Summary
LM	2	10%
LE	10	50%
RM	3	15%
RE	5	25%
	20	100%

J-P Summary
Humanists	0	0%
Otherists	5	25%
Selfists	7	35%
Elitists	8	40%
	20	100%

Italicized names also on a previous table(s)   *t=timed birth; p or a= Will system differs if pm or am birthtime*

Table 16. Nazis of WWII Era

No.	Name	Birthdate Mo	Birthdate Day	Birthdate Year	Died	Data	t	W	T	F	J	P	Attitude Leftist	Attitude	Perspective Leftist	Perspective Conflicted	Perspective Rightist	Type	J-P	E/C
1	Abetz, Otto Freidrich	3	26	1903	1958	Germany	t	B	R	–	+	B	Prog		Prog			LM	Selfist	e
2	Amann, Max	11	24	1891	1957	Germany	t	–	B	–	+	B	Prog		ProRad			LM	Selfist	•
3	Berger, Gottlob	7	16	1896	1975	Germany	t	R	B	B	+	B		Cons			Cons	RE	Elitist	•
4	Blumentritt, Gunther	2	10	1892	1967	Germany	t	R	B	B	+	B	Prog		Prog			LM	Selfist	•
5	Bormann, Martin	6	17	1900	1945?	Germany	t	R	R	R	B	+	Rad			RadCon		RE	Elitist	•
6	Bouhler, Phillip	9	11	1899	1945	Germany	t	B	R	B	R	–		Lib		LibPro		LM	Selfist	e
7	Bousquet, Rene	5	11	1909	1993	France	t	+	B	–	+	+		Lib		LibRad		LM	Elitist	•
8	Braun, Wernher von	3	23	1912	1977	Germany	t	–	+	–	+	+	Rad			RadLib		LE	Selfist	•
9	Bruckner, Wilhelm	12	11	1884	1954	Germany	t	+	B	–	R	B	Prog			ProCon		RE	Elitist	•
10	Buch, Walter	10	24	1883	1959	Germany	t	+	+	B	+	+		Cons		ConRad		LE	Elitist	e
11	Canaris, Wilhelm	1	1	1887	1945	Germany	t	R	–	–	+	–		Lib		LibRad		LE	Elitist	e
12	Conti, Leonardo	8	24	1900	1945	Switzerland	t	+	+	B	R	R		Cons		ConRad		RE	Elitist	e
13	Cruwell, Ludwig	3	20	1892	1958	Germany	t	+	+	B	R	+				RadConPro	Lib	LE	Selfist	•
14	Darre, Richard W.	7	14	1895	1953	Argentina	t	R	–	B	R	+	Rad					RM	Elitist	•
15	Diels, Rudolg	12	16	1900	1957	Germany	t	R	+	B	R	+		Lib		RadCon		LE	Selfist	•
16	Dietl, Eduard	7	21	1890	1944	Germany	t	–	R	B	+	R	Rad				Cons	RE	Elitist	•
17	Dietrich, Josef	5	28	1892	1966	Germany	t	R	B	B	+	+	Rad			RadLib		LM	Elitist	•
18	Dietrich, Otto	8	31	1897	1952	Germany	t	R	B	B	+	+		Lib		LibPro		LM	Elitist	•
19	Doenitz, Karl	9	16	1891	1980	Germany	t	–	–	B	+	–		Lib			Lib	RM	Elitist	•
20	Eiche, Theodor	10	17	1892	1943	Germany	t	B	+	B	+	+	RadPro					LM	Selfist	•
21	Eichmann, Adolf	3	19	1906	1962	Germany	t	–	B	B	R	+		Cons		RadCon	Cons	RE	Elitist	e
22	Esser, Hermann	7	29	1900	1981	Germany	t	B	+	B	+	+	RadPro					LE	Selfist	•
23	Fegelein, Hermann	10	30	1906	1945	Germany	t	R	–	R	R	+	Rad				Lib	LE	Elitist	e
24	Frank, Hans	5	23	1900	1946	Germany	t	–	R	B	R	+	Rad			RadCon		RE	Elitist	•
25	Frank, Walter	2	12	1905	1945	Germany	t	B	B	B	+	+	Rad			RadProCon		LE	Selfist	•
26	Freisler, Roland	10	30	1893	1945	Germany	t	B	B	+	+	+		Lib		LibProRad		LM	Elitist	•
27	Frick, *Wilhelm*	3	12	1877	1946	Prussia	t	R	R	–	–	–		Lib			LibCon	RM	Otherist	ec
28	Friedeburg, Georg	7	15	1895	1945	France	t	–	B	–	–	–		Lib			Lib	RM	Elitist	•
29	Friedrichs, Helmuth	9	22	1899	?	Germany	t	B	R	B	+	R		Lib			LibCon	RE	Elitist	•
30	Galland, Adolf	3	19	1912	1996	Germany	t	R	–	B	+	R		Cons		ConRad	Cons	RE	Elitist	•
31	Goebbels, Paul Joseph	1	12	1897	1945	Germany	t	B	–	–	R	R		Cons		ConRad		LE	Elitist	•
32	Goering, Hermann	2	16	1893	1946	Germany	t	B	+	B	+	R		Cons				LE	Elitist	•
33	Gunther, Hans	5	6	1891	1968	Germany	t	R	B	B	R	R						LE	Selfist	•
34	Henlein, Konrad	4	26	1898	1945	Germany	t	B	B	B	+	R	Rad	Cons		ConRad		LE	Elitist	•
35	Hess, Rudolph	3	7	1894	1987	Egypt	t	+	–	–	R	R		Cons		ConPro		LM	Elitist	•
36	Heydrich, Reinhard	3	7	1904	1942	Germany	t	+	B	–	R	R		Cons		ConRad		RE	Elitist	•
37	Himmler, Heinrich	10	7	1900	1945	Germany	t	+	R	R	R	+	Rad		Rad			LE	Selfist	•
38	*Hitler, Adolf*	4	20	1889	1945	Austria	t	B	+	B	–	–		Lib		LibPro	Lib	LM	Elitist	•
39	Hossbach, Friedrich	11	21	1894	1980	Germany	t	+	+	R	+	+		Lib				RM	Elitist	•
40	Jodl, Alfred	5	10	1890	1946	Germany	t	+	+	+	+	R		Cons		ConRad		LE	Elitist	•

APPENDIX B: TABLES OF INDIVIDUALS   B-60

Table 16. Nazis of WWII Era

#	Name						Country													
41	Karajan, Herbert von	4	5	1908	1989	Austria	t	+	–	R	+	Rad	Lib		RadCon	Lib	RE	Selfist	e
42	Keitel, Wilhelm	9	22	1882	1946	Germany	t	–	B	R	–						RM	Elitist	e
43	Keppler, Wilhelm Carl	12	14	1882	1960	Germany	t	R	R	+	B	Rad	Lib		RadConPro	LibCon	LE	Humanist	ec
44	Kerrl, Johannes	1	11	1887	1941	Germany	t	R	R	R	+		Cons			ConLib	RE	Elitist	e
45	Kesserling, Albert	11	20	1885	1960	Germany	t	+	+	+	–	Rad			RadLib		LE	Elitist	e
46	Kirdoff, Emil	4	8	1847	1938	Germany	t	–	–	R	R		Cons			Cons	LE	Selfist	e
47	Knochen, Helmut	3	14	1910	2003	Germany	t	B	R	+	+	Rad					RE	Elitist	e
48	Koch, Erich	6	19	1896	1959	Germany	t	R	+	+	R		Cons		ConRad		LE	Selfist	•
49	Kraft, Karl Ernst von	5	10	1900	1945	Switzerland	t	+	B	B	+			Rad			LM	Humanist	c
50	Krupp, Gusta von Bohlen	8	7	1870	1950	Netherlands	t	+	B	–	+	Rad	Cons	RadPro			LM	Elitist	•
51	Lutze, Victor	12	28	1890	1943	Germany	t	R	–	+	R		Lib			LibCon	RE	Elitist	e
52	Mengele, Josef	3	16	1911	1985	Germany	t	R	+	R	R		Cons		ConRad		RE	Elitist	e
53	Messerschmitt, Willy	6	26	1898	1978	Germany	t	B	+	+	R	Rad		RadPro			LM	Selfist	•
54	Milch, Erhard	3	30	1892	1975	Germany	t	–	B	R	+	Rad			RadCon		LM	Elitist	•
55	Model, Walther	1	11	1891	1945	Germany	t	R	–	+	R		Lib			LibCon	RE	Elitist	e
56	Muller, Ludwig	6	23	1883	1946	Germany	t	+	B	R	+		Lib			Lib	RM	Selfist	•
57	Naujocks, Alfred	9	20	1911	1960	Germany	t	R	B	R	–	Prog	Cons		ProCon	Cons	RE	Elitist	e
58	Ohlendorf, Otto	2	4	1907	1951	Germany	t	R	R	R	B		Cons			ConLib	RE	Selfist	•
59	Papon, Maurice	9	3	1910	2007	France	t	B	+	R	R		Lib			Lib	RE	Elitist	e
60	Pohl, Oswald	6	30	1892	1951	Germany	t	–	–	–	+		Lib		LibPro		RM	Elitist	•
61	Rademacher, Franz	2	20	1906	1973	Germany	t	B	B	+	–	Prog	Lib		ProCon		LM	Elitist	e
62	Ribbentrop, Joachim von	4	30	1893	1946	Germany	t	B	R	+	B				LibRad		LE	Elitist	e
63	Röhm, Ernst	11	28	1887	1934	Germany	t	R	R	R	–		Lib		ConRad		RE	Selfist	•
64	Rommel, Erwin	11	15	1891	1944	Germany	t	B	+	+	R	Rad	Lib		LibRad		LE	Elitist	e
65	Rosenberg, Alfred	1	12	1893	1946	Estonia	t	–	–	+	–	Rad	Lib		RadCon		LE	Elitist	e
66	Saukel, Fritz	10	27	1894	1946	Germany	t	+	+	B	R			RadPro	RadCon		RE	Selfist	•
67	Schmundt, Rudolf	8	13	1896	1944	France	t	R	B	+	+						LM	Selfist	•
68	Schoemer, Ferdinand	6	12	1892	1973	Germany	t	+	B	R	B		Cons		ConRad	Cons	LE	Elitist	e
69	Shellenberg, Walter	1	16	1910	?	Germany	t	B	–	–	–	Prog		ProRad	LibPro		LM	Elitist	e
70	Speer, Albert	3	19	1905	1981	Germany	t	B	–	R	B		Lib			Lib	RM	Elitist	•
71	Streicher, Julius	2	12	1885	1946	Germany	t	–	R	+	–	Prog		Prog			LE	Selfist	•
72	Todt, Fritz	9	4	1891	1942	Germany	t	–	B	R	B						RM	Elitist	•
73	Warlimont, Walther	10	3	1894	1976	Germany	t	+	+	B	B						LM	Selfist	•

Table 16. Nazis of WWII Era

Table 16. Totals & Analysis

Total Names= **73**
Total Impulses= 365

Impulse Deviations from Norm **Slight**

	19	24	29	1	8	28	45	13	37	23
B	13	13	15	43	20		73			73
+	19	24	15	2	24	L	R	Leftist	Conflicted	Rightist
−	22	12	14	27	21	38%	62%	18%	51%	32%
R										

° ° ° ° °

Maximum Value

Typical Pattern
(Tied Count)

22	24	29	43	24
R	B	B	+	−
			−	

° ° ° ° °

E/C Summary

E&C	2	3%
E Only	27	37%
C Only	1	1%
Neither	43	59%
	73	100%

Type Summary

LM	17	23%
LE	21	29%
RM	11	15%
RE	24	33%
	73	100%

J-P Summary

Humanists	2	3%
Otherists	1	1%
Selfists	26	36%
Elitists	44	60%
	73	100%

Italized names also on a previous table(s)   *t=timed birth; p or a= Will system differs if pm or am birthtime*

Appendix C: The Psychologic Eras

Table B below lists the psychologic eras and their quadrants for those who wish to do historical research along the lines suggested in the text. I explained there why the twelve periods of Pluto's cycle are not of equal length and why, due to retrograde motion, its change of signs cannot be given with only one date of transition. The date shown in this table is for the first ingress of Pluto into the sign indicated, but invariably it retrogrades back to the prior sign and then reenters the sign shown, sometimes more than once. So, for borderline birth dates falling within months or even a year of the date shown, it is best to confirm Pluto's longitude with an ephemeris or astrological software and apply the anticipation rules discussed in *Appendix A*. The temporary names that I use in the text for six of these eras are also indicated here.

Table B. The Psychologic Eras

Era 1	Sign	Generation	♇ 1st Ingress
I-1	♑	- H&O	-696?
I-2	♒	+ S&E	
I-3	♓	- H&O	
II-4	♈	+ S&E	
II-5	♉	- H&O	May 30 -587
II-6	♊	+ S&E	Jul 22 -558
III-7	♋	- H&O	Aug 22 -534
III-8	♌	+ S&E	Sep 26 -516
III-9	♍	- H&O	Oct 18 -502
IV-10	♎	+ S&E	Nov 6 -490
IV-11	♏	- H&O	Nov 11 -478
IV-12	♐	+ S&E	Dec 11 -465

The Sophist Era

Era 2	Sign	Generation	♀ 1st Ingress
I-1	♑	- H&O	Mar 11 -449
I-2	♒	+ S&E	Mar 25 -429
I-3	♓	- H&O	Mar 28 -404
II-4	♈	+ S&E	Apr 27 -375
II-5	♉	- H&O	Jun 16 -344
II-6	♊	+ S&E	Jul 11 -314
III-7	♋	- H&O	Jul 24 -289
III-8	♌	+ S&E	Oct 11 -271
III-9	♍	- H&O	Sep 11 -256
IV-10	♎	+ S&E	Oct 9 -244
IV-11	♏	- H&O	Dec 21 -233
IV-12	♐	+ S&E	Dec 30 -220

Era 3	Sign	Generation	♀ 1st Ingress
I-1	♑	- H&O	Mar 3 -204
I-2	♒	+ S&E	Feb 17 -184
I-3	♓	- H&O	Mar 22 -160
II-4	♈	+ S&E	May 22 -132
II-5	♉	- H&O	May 17 -100
II-6	♊	+ S&E	Jun 30 -70
III-7	♋	- H&O	Aug 25 -45
III-8	♌	+ S&E	Aug 10 -25
III-9	♍	- H&O	Oct 20 -11
IV-10	♎	+ S&E	Dec 8 -1
IV-11	♏	- H&O	Nov 25 13
IV-12	♐	+ S&E	Feb 21 26

The Christian Era

Era 4	Sign	Generation	♀ 1st Ingress
I-1	♑	- H&O	Jan 2 42
I-2	♒	+ S&E	Mar 30 60
I-3	♓	- H&O	Mar 26 84
II-4	♈	+ S&E	May 2 112
II-5	♉	- H&O	Jun 12 143
II-6	♊	+ S&E	Jun 25 174
III-7	♋	- H&O	Jul 29 200
III-8	♌	+ S&E	Aug 23 220
III-9	♍	- H&O	Sep 26 235
IV-10	♎	+ S&E	Nov 21 247
IV-11	♏	- H&O	Nov 15 259
IV-12	♐	+ S&E	Jan 9 272

Era 5	Sign	Generation	♀ 1st Ingress
I-1	♑	- H&O	Jan 18 287
I-2	♒	+ S&E	Mar 13 305
I-3	♓	- H&O	Apr 8 328
II-4	♈	+ S&E	Apr 19 356
II-5	♉	- H&O	May 21 387
II-6	♊	+ S&E	Jun 19 418
III-7	♋	- H&O	Sep 20 444
III-8	♌	+ S&E	Sep 10 465
III-9	♍	- H&O	Sep 7 481
IV-10	♎	+ S&E	Nov 14 493
IV-11	♏	- H&O	Nov 10 505
IV-12	♐	+ S&E	Dec 22 517

Era 6	Sign	Generation	♀ 1st Ingress
I-1	♑	- H&O	Feb 19 532
I-2	♒	+ S&E	Mar 11 550
I-3	♓	- H&O	Mar 9 573
II-4	♈	+ S&E	Apr 17 600
II-5	♉	- H&O	Jul 8 630
II-6	♊	+ S&E	Jun 18 662
III-7	♋	- H&O	Aug 10 689
III-8	♌	+ S&E	Aug 1 711
III-9	♍	- H&O	Aug 27 727
IV-10	♎	+ S&E	Nov 19 739
IV-11	♏	- H&O	Nov 14 751
IV-12	♐	+ S&E	Dec 16 763

Era 7	Sign	Generation	♀ 1st Ingress
I-1	♑	- H&O	Jan 18 778
I-2	♒	+ S&E	Mar 22 794
I-3	♓	- H&O	Apr 9 817
II-4	♈	+ S&E	Apr 19 844
II-5	♉	- H&O	Jun 18 874
II-6	♊	+ S&E	Jun 17 906
III-7	♋	- H&O	Jul 19 934
III-8	♌	+ S&E	Aug 18 956
III-9	♍	- H&O	Oct 26 972
IV-10	♎	+ S&E	Dec 2 985
IV-11	♏	- H&O	Nov 24 997
IV-12	♐	+ S&E	Dec 18 1009

Era 8	Sign	Generation	♇ 1st Ingress
I-1	♑	- H&O	Jan 2 1024
I-2	♒	+ S&E	Feb 3 1041
I-3	♓	- H&O	Mar 25 1062
II-4	♈	+ S&E	May 2 1088
II-5	♉	- H&O	Jun 13 1118
II-6	♊	+ S&E	Jun 18 1150
III-7	♋	- H&O	Sep 5 1178
III-8	♌	+ S&E	Sep 11 1201
III-9	♍	- H&O	Oct 16 1218
IV-10	♎	+ S&E	Sep 26 1232
IV-11	♏	- H&O	Dec 17 1243
IV-12	♐	+ S&E	Dec 28 1255

The Scholastic Era

Era 9	Sign	Generation	♇ 1st Ingress
I-1	♑	- H&O	Dec 24 1269
I-2	♒	+ S&E	Feb 26 1286
I-3	♓	- H&O	Mar 18 1307
II-4	♈	+ S&E	May 31 1332
II-5	♉	- H&O	Jun 11 1362
II-6	♊	+ S&E	Jun 20 1394
III-7	♋	- H&O	Aug 2 1423
III-8	♌	+ S&E	Aug 2 1447
III-9	♍	- H&O	Oct 8 1464
IV-10	♎	+ S&E	Oct 11 1478
IV-11	♏	- H&O	Oct 26 1490
IV-12	♐	+ S&E	Jan 21 1502

The Classic Era

Era 10	Sign	Generation	♀ 1st Ingress
I-1	♑	- H&O	Dec 23 1515
I-2	♒	+ S&E	Feb 1 1532
I-3	♓	- H&O	Mar 20 1552
II-4	♈	+ S&E	Apr 24 1577
II-5	♉	- H&O	Jul 7 1606
II-6	♊	+ S&E	Jul 8 1638
III-7	♋	- H&O	Jul 23 1668
III-8	♌	+ S&E	Sep 2 1692
III-9	♍	- H&O	Oct 17 1710
IV-10	♎	+ S&E	Nov 13 1724
IV-11	♏	- H&O	Dec 5 1736
IV-12	♐	+ S&E	Dec 9 1748

The Modern Era

Era 11	Sign	Generation	♀ 1st Ingress
I-1	♑	- H&O	Jan 7 1762
I-2	♒	+ S&E	Apr 3 1777
I-3	♓	- H&O	Apr 10 1797
II-4	♈	+ S&E	Apr 16 1822
II-5	♉	- H&O	May 19 1851
II-6	♊	+ S&E	Jul 21 1882
III-7	♋	- H&O	Sep 10 1912
III-8	♌	+ S&E	Oct 7 1937
III-9	♍	- H&O	Oct 19 1956
IV-10	♎	+ S&E	Oct 4 1971
IV-11	♏	- H&O	Nov 5 1983
IV-12	♐	+ S&E	Jan 17 1995

The New Era

Era 12	Sign	Generation	♇ 1st Ingress
I-1	♑	- H&O	Jan 25 2008
I-2	♒	+ S&E	Mar 23 2023
I-3	♓	- H&O	Mar 8 2043
II-4	♈	+ S&E	Jun 18 2066
II-5	♉	- H&O	Jun 9 2095
II-6	♊	+ S&E	Jun 15 2127
III-7	♋	- H&O	Aug 14 2157
III-8	♌	+ S&E	Aug 25 2183
III-9	♍	- H&O	Oct 30 2202
IV-10	♎	+ S&E	Nov 5 2217
IV-11	♏	- H&O	Dec 24 2229
IV-12	♐	+ S&E	Dec 18 2241

Era 13	Sign	Generation	♇ 1st Ingress
I-1	♑	- H&O	Feb 2254